Journey through the Text of *A Course in Miracles*

Volume Four

Chapter 25 through Chapter 31

Journey through the Text of
A Course in Miracles

Volume Four
Chapter 25 through Chapter 31

KENNETH WAPNICK, Ph.D.

Foundation for A COURSE IN MIRACLES®

Foundation for A Course in Miracles®
41397 Buecking Drive
Temecula, CA 92590
www.facim.org

1st printing, 2014

Printed in the United States of America

Portions of *A Course in Miracles* copyright 1992,
Psychotherapy: Purpose, Process and Practice copyright 1976, 1992,
The Song of Prayer copyright 1978, 1992,
The Gifts of God copyright 1982,
by the Foundation for Inner Peace
used by permission.

Catalog-in-Publication data available from the Library of Congress

ISBN 978-1-59142-907-4

CONTENTS

CONTENTS

Chapter 25

THE JUSTICE OF GOD

Introduction

My introduction to Chapter 24 quoted from the end of Chapter 23: "Who with the Love of God upholding him could find the choice of miracles or murder hard to make?" (T-23.IV.9:8). While Chapter 24 dealt largely with murder, the current chapter focuses on the miracle, referred to as *justice* in this and the following chapter. These are, in fact, the only places in the text in which this theme appears, though its content is apparent throughout. Justice is the principle that *no one loses and everyone gains*, correcting the ego's principle of murder in which we win at someone's expense: others die as punishment for the sins we have projected, leading us magically to believe we are free of them. By so doing we gain the sinlessness that ensures that another's sin deserves punishment. This perverted version of justice exemplifies the ego's *one or the other*, its purpose for the world. Indeed, *purpose* is another prominent theme here, the shift from the ego's desire to attack and kill to the Holy Spirit's forgiveness and healing.

We begin by looking at the ego's thought system, specifically its need to imprison us in a body without our realizing it is a prison. This removes us from the mind, the locus of the ego's fear that our decision-making self would choose miracles instead of murder, Atonement instead of separation. Our focus will then be on the theme of purpose, which will take us finally into a discussion of forgiveness and justice.

Mind and Body: The Home of Sin

Our starting-off point is the Introduction to the chapter, its opening line continuing the motif of "the Christ in you" with which we ended the 24th movement of our symphony:

(In.1:1-4) The Christ in you inhabits not a body. Yet He is in you. And thus it must be that you are not within a body. What is within you cannot be outside.

The Christ in us is in the mind, not the body. More specifically, He is present through the memory of Who we are as God's one Son. "What is within you cannot be outside" as *ideas leave not their source*: we forever remain minds—in truth as Christ, in illusion as ego—despite the convincing nature of our body's dreams of specialness.

(In.1:5-9) And it is certain that you cannot be apart from what is at the very center of your life. What gives you life cannot be housed in death. No more can you. Christ is within a frame of Holiness whose only purpose is that He may be made manifest to those who know Him not, that He may call to them to come to Him and see Him where they thought their bodies were. Then will their bodies melt away, that they may frame His Holiness in them.

This, as we know, is the ego's great fear. The memory of our Identity as Christ is in the mind, held in place by the Holy Spirit's Atonement. To defend against this thought that literally means the end of its existence, the ego counters with its thought system of sin, punishment, and death. This is ultimately projected as a moribund body, its demise being the frame that houses the ego's picture of mortality. When we learn to forgive, however, the miracle is able to lead us from the bodily frame to the wrong-minded picture, behind which is the picture of life that Jesus holds out to us: Christ's frame of Holiness that is our Self.

(In.2:1-2) No one who carries Christ in him can fail to recognize Him everywhere. *Except* **in bodies.**

Christ is everywhere because He is in our mind, which is everywhere since the world is nowhere. As a defense, the ego develops its strategy of proving to us there is a problem in the mind (guilt) from which we have to flee. Enter the mindless body that camouflages the real problem: the mind's having chosen against the Atonement principle and for the special self the ego made as substitute for the Christ that is our Self. Though the body is the last place we would ever find salvation and remember Who we are, our attention has been focused exclusively on the physical/psychological person we think is our self.

(In.2:3-4) And as long as he believes he is in a body, where he thinks he is He cannot be. And so he carries Him unknowingly, and does not make Him manifest.

Christ is made manifest through our choosing to remember Him through forgiveness. This corrects the ego's purpose of specialness for the body, not to mention its engendering amnesia of the mind's power of decision. Becoming mindful restores awareness of our Identity as Christ, undoing the ego's strategy of a world of mindless bodies.

(In.2:6-7) The son of man is not the risen Christ. Yet does the Son of God abide exactly where he is, and walks with him within his holiness, as plain to see as is his specialness set forth within his body.

Our holiness is not in the body but the right mind, as our specialness is not experienced in the mind but the body, held apart from the mind's decision maker that would easily dissolve it. Note the contrast we saw at the end of Chapter 24 between the Son of God (the undifferentiated Christ) and the son of man (the separated ego).

(In.3:1-2) The body needs no healing. But the mind that thinks it is a body is sick indeed!

Sickness is never of the body, as we have seen many times, but is the mind's decision for guilt.

This theme becomes increasingly prominent as our symphony moves to its consummation, the final vision of the mind's healing in which we accept the Atonement for ourselves and return home, where God "would have us be" (T-31.VIII.12:8).

(In.3:3-5) And it is here that Christ sets forth the remedy. His purpose folds the body in His light, and fills it with the Holiness that shines from Him. And nothing that the body says or does but makes Him manifest.

The fact that both problem and answer are in the mind continually motivates our egos to keep attention rooted in the body. However, when Jesus helps us penetrate the veils of denial and projection, we are able to choose Christ's Holiness as our own, the decision that leads away from the body and enables the mind to reflect its healing love in the body and the world. While this does not necessarily mean that bodily symptoms or world problems disappear, it does mean that everything we think, feel, and do (the *form*) will manifest the mind's *content* of forgiveness and light. The theme of picture and frame (T-17.IV and T-24.VI.6) is reflected here, and will return specifically below with the body seen as the frame that enfolds the mind's newly found purpose of remembering Christ.

(V.2:1-4) Attack makes Christ your enemy, and God along with Him. Must you not be afraid with "enemies" like these? And must you not be fearful of yourself? For you have hurt yourself, and made your Self your "enemy."

This explains why we attack, a theme repeated continually throughout our symphony. Attack keeps Christ away for it says that sin is real, not in ourselves but in other bodies. Nonetheless, attacking another merely reinforces the mind's belief in its own sinfulness, wherein we attacked Christ by substituting our self for His. Because we believe our attack was real, we expect His justified counter-attack, which is the reason the battleground is such an important image (shown in the wrong-minded box in the chart [see Appendix]). We truly think we are at war with God or Christ, and projecting this thought, we perceive the world to be at war with us, the innocent victims of the unfair assaults of others.

(V.2:5) And now you must believe you are not you, but something alien to yourself and "something else," a "something" to be feared instead of loved.

This important theme highlights that we have become what we are not. The ego tells us we are a separated and sinful self, a "something else" that is filled with guilt and deserving of punishment. Highly vulnerable now, we cower in terror in a world of bodies, all the while our identity in the dream remains hidden: a decision-making mind that can correct the mistake of having preferred specialness to holiness, choose again, and remember its Self.

(V.2:6-7) Who would attack whatever he perceives as wholly innocent? And who, *because* he wishes to attack, can fail to think he must be guilty to maintain the wish, while wanting innocence?

The need to attack reinforces our guilt, a reference to the line we read earlier: "…defenses *do* what they would defend" (T-17.IV.7:1). The fact that we need defenses such as attack tells us there is something in us that needs defense: our guilt. This means that the more we attack, the more we support our unconscious belief in guilt—the ego's perennial guilt-attack cycle. Nevertheless, we maintain that we want innocence above all else, and are willing to kill anyone, anytime, anywhere in order to acquire it. Because of this need to preserve guilt and maintain our separated self, the cycle seemingly has no end: guilt, attack, and still more guilt and attack. This helps us understand why it is so difficult to let go of judgment: it keeps the mind's intolerable guilt out of awareness and safe from all correction.

(V.2:8) For who could see the Son of God as innocent and wish him dead?

If we believe our innocence is purchased at another's expense, we cannot know God's Son as He created him, for creation is whole. If we see ourselves as sinful and guilty, we must see others that

way too—*projection makes perception.* Believing that *one or the other* works is a lie; and yet our whole world is built upon this thought that prevents us from seeing the innocence in another, which heralds our return to the Innocence that created us as Itself.

(V.2:9-11) Christ stands before you, each time you look upon your brother. He has not gone because your eyes are closed. But what is there to see by searching for your Savior, seeing Him through sightless eyes?

Jesus is not speaking of our physical eyes, but the wrong mind that has been closed to holiness and Atonement. As a result, it sees only sin and guilt. Looking through the lens of the ego's purpose, our eyes cannot see beyond the separation and specialness that justifies judgment and attack. These misperceptions become easily corrected through the mind's vision of Christ, the happy outcome of choosing the Holy Spirit's forgiveness as our teacher.

(V.3:1-4) It is not Christ you see by looking thus. It is the "enemy," confused with Christ, you look upon. And hate because there is no sin in him for you to see. Nor do you hear his plaintive call, unchanged in content in whatever form the call is made, that you unite with him, and join with him in innocence and peace.

We call out for love every time we attack, saying, in effect: "Please show me I am wrong. Demonstrate there is another thought system I can choose in my mind." This heals, for another's example—the best teacher—shows us the right-minded alternative, allowing the one we perceived as enemy to become our Friend (W-pI.161.12:6). Still, we must hear our resistance to this perception, for it is the beginning of salvation and the end of all specialness.

(V.3:5) And yet, beneath the ego's senseless shrieks, such is the call that God has given him, that you might hear in him His Call to you, and answer by returning unto God what is His Own.

This is the call our egos wish to silence. We have seen how the voice of specialness drowns out the Holy Spirit's Voice (T-24.II.4-5), for we do not want to hear the call of Christ to Christ that returns us to our Self. We choose instead to hear the senseless, raucous shrieks of the ego calling us to hell. Incidentally, the above sentence is one more foreshadowing of "For They Have Come" (see T-26.IX.1:1).

We turn to a paragraph that owes its presence to Plato, containing a veiled reference to the Greek master's "Allegory of the Cave." Plato tells the tale of prisoners chained in a cave so that they look only toward the interior wall on which they perceive shadows cast by figures walking along a road outside the cave's mouth, illuminated by the sun. One of the prisoners, representing Socrates, is freed and makes his way out of the cave, gradually adjusting his eyes to the light. Returning, he attempts to remove the chains of the remaining prisoners, who then kill him as they do not wish to be free. This incisive allegory reflects our being so accustomed to guilt's shadows of hate that we cannot tolerate the bright vision of forgiveness, for specialness makes its home in the light-less world of illusion, a home for which we would kill to preserve its existence.

(VI.2:1-3) Eyes become used to darkness, and the light of brilliant day seems painful to the eyes grown long accustomed to the dim effects perceived at twilight. And they turn away from sunlight and the clarity it brings to what they look upon. Dimness seems better; easier to see, and better recognized.

The dimness is the ego's sight, through which we see only guilt's projections onto others and cannot see the light of Christ shining brilliantly in everyone, including ourselves. We do not see it for the reason that the mind chooses not to; the differences of individual existence, which disappear in the vision of forgiveness, are far preferable to the truth of the sameness of God's Son.

(VI.2:4-5) Somehow the vague and more obscure seems easier to look upon; less painful to the eyes than what is wholly clear and unambiguous. Yet

this is not what eyes are for, and who can say that he prefers the darkness and maintain he wants to see?

Part of us wants to learn this course, telling Jesus we wish to take his hand, learn to forgive, and return home. At the same time we do not want to give up our special self, which means we wish to remain in darkness, protesting that we want the light. Jesus helps us see that this ambivalence is within the mind, and wants us to be gentle with ourselves when we do not forgive, are not kind to others, and clearly prefer the joys of specialness to the peace of God. We need to recognize how we have adjusted to lives enshrouded by guilt, fear, and hate, making it almost impossible to conceive of existence without these dark "friends" that protect us from the light of forgiveness and truth.

Jesus now considers sin, another of the ego's "friends." We have seen how it is one of the cornerstones of the ego's defense against choosing Atonement. It says that separation is real, but is so egregious an act that we have to flee the mind's inevitable punishment and hide in the body.

(VII.1:2-3) Sin is the only thing in all the world that cannot change. It is immutable.

Everything in the world changes. This is considered life, and even inanimate objects change over time. To the ego, sin does not change because it paradoxically represents the original change when we left God. Everything that comes from sin mimics that change, except sin itself—the belief that change is possible and is the reality.

(VII.1:4-5) And on its changelessness the world depends. The magic of the world can seem to hide the pain of sin from sinners, and deceive with glitter and with guile.

The "glitter" is the special relationship frame we saw in "The Two Pictures" (T-17.IV), and its "guile" is that it purports to be love and happiness, while it is truly guilt, hate, and murder. Recall that the frame's sparkling jewels are really tears and drops of blood, the palpable consequence of sin's immutability.

(VII.1:6-9) Yet each one knows the cost of sin is death. And so it is. For sin is a request for death, a wish to make this world's foundation sure as love, dependable as Heaven, and as strong as God Himself. The world is safe from love to everyone who thinks sin possible.

Sin means we must die because we first killed, and therefore deserve to be killed in return. In the magical, insane attempt to forestall our certain death at the hands of God, we project the sin and proceed to kill everyone else—if not in deed, certainly in thought. If we think sin is possible, we will be driven out of our minds, literally and figuratively, believing in madness that we are bodies. And as long as we identify with the body, we remain mindless and can never choose love. Indeed, the ego has become forever safe from the threat of truth by our belief in sin, which we project in maladaptive attempts to get rid of it by seeing it in bodies we think are separate from us.

(VII.1:10-11) Nor will it change. Yet is it possible what God created not should share the attributes of His creation, when it opposes it in every way?

God's creation is changeless, and the seeming changelessness of sin mocks the reality of Heaven, as the ego boasts that it has also made something that does not change. In this delusional thought system we remain sinners for all time, and the world is needed as a defense to hide our sin so it can be seen everywhere but in the mind.

(VII.2:1-8) It cannot be the "sinner's" wish for death is just as strong as is God's Will for life. Nor can the basis of a world He did not make be firm and sure as Heaven. How could it be that hell and Heaven are the same? And is it possible that what He did not will cannot be changed? What is immutable besides His Will? And what can share its attributes except itself? What wish can rise against His Will, and be immutable? If you could realize nothing is changeless but the Will of God, this course would not be difficult for you.

This explains why *A Course in Miracles* is so hard to learn. We do not believe God's Will is changeless. To the contrary, we believe we have changed it into the will of the ego. As specialness teaches, we were not created by God but are self-created. The ego resists Jesus' attempts to have us recognize that the original change is the world's cause, for if we looked within to the Atonement, we would realize there was no change at all; hence no sin and no us. This fear of losing our special self is what makes the Course seem difficult. Heaven and hell are not the same, and the changeable ego cannot survive in the presence of the changeless Will we share with God. Thus sin—in the mind and body—is our armor and shield, protecting us from the unchanging truth Jesus continuously holds out to us.

(VII.2:9-10) For it is this that you do not believe. Yet there is nothing else you could believe, if you but looked at what it really is.

Our orchestra intones this theme: "if you but looked." If we looked at the ego's thought system built on sin, we would see there was nothing there. Forestalling what will ultimately be, the ego quickly removes the separated self from the mind and places it in the body, dropping a veil to protect us from ever returning within. Stuck in a mindless world, we are not able to let go of the ego through the mind's acceptance of the changeless Atonement.

(VIII.3:1-2) There is a kind of justice in salvation of which the world knows nothing. To the world, justice and vengeance are the same, for sinners see justice only as their punishment, perhaps sustained by someone else, but not escaped.

Jesus speaks now of the ego's notion of *one or the other*, its version of justice in which sin is punished. *We* deserve punitive action because of our sinfulness; yet projecting our sin causes another to be the one deserving of vengeance. This punishment of perceived evil is how the world defines what is just, and we hope against hope that we can escape God's wrath by having Him believe these wicked ones are the sinners. Throughout this charade, however, our mind's sin remains, silently generating the need to blame others in a defiant show of justice.

(VIII.3:3-7) The laws of sin demand a victim. Who it may be makes little difference. But death must be the cost and must be paid. This is not justice, but insanity. Yet how could justice be defined without insanity where love means hate, and death is seen as victory and triumph over eternity and timelessness and life?

The world's version of justice is our own, coming from the thought we triumphed over God and Christ. Because we survived as an original ego self by attacking love and eternal life, triumphing over others becomes our ongoing means of survival. It matters not whom we attack, as long as we attack someone. The projections of guilt are indiscriminate for they serve the same goal of mindlessly demanding sacrifice of one seen as different from ourselves.

(VIII.4:5-10) Justice demands no sacrifice, for any sacrifice is made that sin may be preserved and kept. It is a payment offered for the cost of sin, but not the total cost. The rest is taken from another, to be laid beside your little payment, to "atone" for all that you would keep, and not give up. So is the victim seen as partly you, with someone else by far the greater part. And in the total cost, the greater his the less is yours. And justice, being blind, is satisfied by being paid, it matters not by whom.

If we are to exist, someone has to lose, as in the original moment when God was sacrificed so our separated self would gain. Consequently, the world functions by our feverishly trying to get rid of sin by blaming others. We actually retain sin, though, since *ideas leave not their source*, despite the ego's insane thought that other people can be punished instead of us. Impelled to continually blame others, we seek to make them pay for our projected sin. This explains our tremendous need to find evil outside the mind by striving to find fault through judgment of another.

(VIII.5) Can this be justice? God knows not of this. But justice does He know, and knows it well.

For He is wholly fair to everyone. Vengeance is alien to God's Mind *because* He knows of justice. To be just is to be fair, and not be vengeful. Fairness and vengeance are impossible, for each one contradicts the other and denies that it is real. It is impossible for you to share the Holy Spirit's justice with a mind that can conceive of specialness at all. Yet how could He be just if He condemns a sinner for the crimes he did not do, but thinks he did? And where would justice be if He demanded of the ones obsessed with the idea of punishment that they lay it aside, unaided, and perceive it is not true?

This is the God the ego knows not of, but it does know that if the decision-making mind chooses justice over vengeance, forgiveness over attack, it loses the foundation of its existence and must perish. Specialness comes to its rescue as the ego fragments God's one Son into special parts, some to be cannibalized (special love) and others to be killed (special hate). God's fairness, which embraces all creation equally, is banished from the mind, its place taken by the "justice" of the "innocent" triumphing over the guilty sinner who is to be punished. In this way, vengeance reigns supreme in the ego's kingdom, and God and His justice are dead.

We turn to the heart of the chart's wrong-minded box, where the Creator is transformed from a God of justice, Whose Holy Spirit sees everyone as the same, to an insane God demanding punishment for the sin of separation:

(VIII.6:1-5) It is extremely hard for those who still believe sin meaningful to understand the Holy Spirit's justice. They must believe He shares their own confusion, and cannot avoid the vengeance that their own belief in justice must entail. And so they fear the Holy Spirit, and perceive the "wrath" of God in Him. Nor can they trust Him not to strike them dead with lightning bolts torn from the "fires" of Heaven by God's Own angry Hand. They *do* believe that Heaven is hell, and *are* afraid of love.

The reality of sin is predicated on our perceived attack on Heaven's love and Oneness. The ego DNA, as it were, is the thought of *one or the other* (one lives, another dies), which gives meaning to its existence and promotes its form of justice. Taken one step further, this means that someone must pay for what we did, justice being that we find the evildoers who will be punished. By so doing, we emerge innocent and sinless: *one or the other*.

Since this is how we think, it must be the way God and the Holy Spirit think too—*projection makes perception*. We need recall that our very existence is built on the idea that we gained and God lost. As He is now (mis)created in our likeness, He believes in this madness, a slight which He is eager to correct at our expense. Rampaging through our defensive walls, He will hurl one vengeful thunderbolt after another until He succeeds in taking back the life we stole from Him. Incredible though it seems, this patent insanity remains our choice and is the source of the world we see. Yet the true God waits patiently beyond our shabby, sin-laden self for us to return to sanity and His Love.

(VIII.6:6-8) And deep suspicion and the chill of fear comes over them when they are told that they have never sinned. Their world depends on sin's stability. And they perceive the "threat" of what God knows as justice to be more destructive to themselves and to their world than vengeance, which they understand and love.

This is why we are so comfortable with hate, vengeance, and murder—as both individuals and collective members of society—calling them justice. Since our individual selves cannot exist within a thought system of innocence, Christ's sinless reality can never be forgiven for it is the greatest threat to our specialness.

(VIII.7:1) So do they think the loss of sin a curse.

Without sin we cannot live, which is why we curse sinlessness as blasphemous to the ego's thought system, the reason that "to the ego, *the guiltless* [or *sinless*] *are guilty*" (T-13.II.4:2).

(VIII.7:2-4) And flee the Holy Spirit as if He were a messenger from hell, sent from above, in treachery and guile, to work God's vengeance on them in the guise of a deliverer and friend.

What could He be to them except a devil, dressed to deceive within an angel's cloak? And what escape has He for them except a door to hell that seems to look like Heaven's gate.

This is the gate that organized religion, especially in the West, holds out to us. We pass through it to hell by following God's system of justice: someone wins, another loses. For example, the innocent sheep pass through, while the guilty goats are left to be destroyed. The love of the biblical Jesus does not embrace all people, only those who embrace him and his true followers. Interestingly, each gospel has its own definition of the "good people," as did St. Paul. None of the evangelists, or St. Paul, embraced *all* God's Sons. They, like each of us, were terrified of God's justice that is the all-inclusive Love of Christ's Oneness. We have already seen how the ego works its perverted sense of justice through the body, which perpetuates the perception of differences by proving that some are sinful while others are innocent.

(IX.1) What can it be but arrogance to think your little errors cannot be undone by Heaven's justice? And what could this mean except that they are sins and not mistakes, forever uncorrectable, and to be met with vengeance, not with justice? Are you willing to be released from all effects of sin? You cannot answer this until you see all that the answer must entail. For if you answer "yes" it means you will forego all values of this world in favor of the peace of Heaven. Not one sin would you retain. And not one doubt that this is possible will you hold dear that sin be kept in place. You mean that truth has greater value now than all illusions. And you recognize that truth must be revealed to you, because you know not what it is.

Our happiness rests with the decision-making mind, and nowhere else. Taking Jesus' hand, we are gently led from our fragmenting misperceptions of God's Son to their source in the wrong mind. Looking at the horrific decision for the ego, we choose again, saying in effect: "I have ceased to value a thought system of separation, attack, and punishment. Instead, I choose the Oneness of

Heaven as my Self, seeing in every seemingly separated fragment of the Sonship a picture of the Holiness of Christ we share as one." Glad and grateful we were wrong, we have recognized at last that the *tiny, mad idea* of separation had no effect on God's perfect and all-loving justice. The illusion of sin could not change the changeless reality of His innocent Son, and we *are* this Son.

Purpose – *Projection Makes Perception*

(I.2:2) Perception tells you *you* are manifest in what you see.

We discussed the principle *projection makes perception* in the previous chapter, earlier as well, and look at it again here. Perception is the means to serve the ego's end of proving that the separated and external world is real, which means that the separated and internal world is real as well. Therefore, we are *not* as God created us.

(I.2:3-4) Behold the body, and you will believe that you are there. And every body that you look upon reminds you of yourself; your sinfulness, your evil and, above all, your death.

This is because "defenses *do* what they would defend" (T-17.IV.7:1). We see evil in others and know on some level this is the mind's projection of the perceived evil in ourselves in order to escape certain death. As we have already observed, the need for a defense tells us there is something real in us (sin) that needs defending; otherwise why would we be defending it?

(I.2:5) And would you not despise the one who tells you this, and seek his death instead?

We continually seek to hurl others over the precipice (T-24.V.4:2), and no chasm is too deep to hold all those we condemn to death. While the more people we throw over, the freer we think we have become, this only serves to reinforce our guilt. Once again, "defenses *do* what they would defend." To serve our need for guilt-preservation, it is impossible not to be compelled to seek and find villainously evil people to attack in the name of our specialness. And each time we do, we hate them all the more as they remind us of the sinner we secretly believe ourselves to be.

(I.2:6-8) The message and the messenger are one. And you must see your brother as yourself. Framed in his body you will see your sinfulness, wherein you stand condemned.

Ideas leave not their source. The message of sin and the sinful messenger are the same; we cannot be separate from what we project. The condemnation of another's body is a hidden attack on our sinful mind.

(II.1:1) Is it not evident that what the body's eyes perceive fills you with fear?

The body's eyes must engender fear, for they were made to see outside threat impinging on us, threatening our innocent existence. This misperception justifies the need to defend ourselves through attack, perpetuating our "secret sins and hidden hates" (T-31.VIII.9:2) that are the source of fear.

(II.1:2-6) Perhaps you think you find a hope of satisfaction there. Perhaps you fancy to attain some peace and satisfaction in the world as you perceive it. Yet it must be evident the outcome does not change. Despite your hopes and fancies, always does despair result. And there is no exception, nor will there ever be.

So much for finding happiness and peace here. The truly honest realize that nothing works here, and even when it seems to, it does not last. In addition, even when the world appears to give us what we want, we believe in the dark recesses of our minds it will be taken from us because God would never leave us happy. How could He tolerate happiness in those who sinned against Him? Given the hopelessness of the world's situation, Jesus poses this question:

(II.2:1-2) Is it not strange that you should cherish still some hope of satisfaction from the world you see? In no respect, at any time or place, has anything but fear and guilt been your reward.

Since this is not our usual experience, Jesus educates us as to how truly painful it is to be living here. Again, notwithstanding moments of respite where we seem to get our needs satisfied, bodily satisfactions evanesce and we are ultimately left with the bitter taste of despair that defines our worldly existence.

(II.2:3-6) How long is needed for you to realize the chance of change in this respect is hardly worth delaying change that might result in better outcome? For one thing is sure; the way you see, and long have seen, gives no support to base your future hopes, and no suggestions of success at all. To place your hopes where no hope lies must make you hopeless. Yet is this hopelessness your choice, while you would seek for hope where none is ever found.

Why do we persist in waiting and waiting when Jesus offers us the opportunity to alleviate our pain *now*? Enter the theme of *seeking and finding*: the ego has us seek for hope in the world, knowing full well we will never find it there. Looking externally for hope reinforces the mind's belief in guilt, re-enacting the original instant when we looked beyond Heaven for love, telling God that His was not enough. Such futility paradoxically impels us to look outside for the remedy, which reflects the ego's despairing circle of hopelessness. Real hope lies only in returning to the mind where the mistaken choice was made, is still being made, and then change it. Jesus continues:

(II.3) Is it not also true that you have found some hope apart from this; some glimmering,—inconstant, wavering, yet dimly seen,—that hopefulness is warranted on grounds that are not in this world? And yet your hope that they may still be here prevents you still from giving up the hopeless and unrewarding task you set yourself. Can it make sense to hold the fixed belief that there is reason to uphold pursuit of

what has always failed, on grounds that it will suddenly succeed and bring what it has never brought before?**

This is the function of specialness, that we seek and never find what we truly want. Directing attention onto the body—ours and others—for hope of pleasure, the ego never allows us to look to the mind's decision-making self, the true source of hope. Echoing the psalmist, Jesus plaintively asks us in the workbook: "How long, O holy Son of God, how long?" (W-pII.4.5:8). How long do we need to put ourselves through such pain until we admit—happily!—that we were wrong and he was right? There *is* no hope here.

The theme of *form* (frame) *and content* (picture), returns:

(II.4:1-3) Its past *has* failed. Be glad that it is gone within your mind, to darken what is there. Take not the form for content, for the form is but a means for content.

Specialness, rooted in the illusory past, has failed because its purpose is to fail: *seek and do not find* is the ego's reigning mantra. When we finally recognize the pain intrinsic to the special relationship (the price of guilt), we will be glad indeed we were wrong, having shifted attention from the ego's form to its content. The special body, with its seeming pleasures and pain, is how the ego achieves its goal of guilt, pain, and death. Real pleasure comes only from the mind's choosing Atonement, God's Will on earth (T-1.VII.1:4), as pain is deciding against it. Again, "form is but a means for content," being nothing more than the way we express the ego's or the Holy Spirit's purpose.

(II.4:4-6) And the frame is but a means to hold the picture up, so that it can be seen. A frame that hides the picture has no purpose. It cannot be a frame if it is what you see.

The purpose of a frame is to hold the picture to be seen. The ego's purpose for the frame of specialness, in contrast, is to call attention to it by hiding its picture of guilt, concealing our identity as decision-making minds. The body, and specifically the special relationship, is the frame that hides not only the mind's guilt but its picture of forgiveness, our pathway home. When we bring our relationships to the Holy Spirit, however, He uses them to return us to His content of innocence. The body becomes a vehicle solely to understand that the outer world is a projection of the inner, with the Holy Spirit's frame highlighting the mind's right-minded picture instead of it being concealed.

(II.4:7-8) Without the picture is the frame without its meaning. Its purpose is to set the picture off, and not itself.

The purpose of a frame is to augment the picture's appeal. We do not usually choose a picture to augment the frame. We have seen how the ego focuses only on the frame (the body's form) at the expense of the picture (the mind's content).

(II.5:1-2) Who hangs an empty frame upon a wall and stands before it, deep in reverence, as if a masterpiece were there to see? Yet if you see your brother as a body, it is but this you do.

Jesus encourages us to look at the body from the point of view of the ego's purpose of separation and attack, designed to prove that sin is real. Opening our eyes to the truth, we see that the ego's content is nothingness pretending to be something (i.e., the body). This is why guilt needs no defense, only our quiet recognition of what it is and why we have chosen it. We return now to perception's purpose:

(I.3:1-3) Perception is a choice of what you want yourself to be; the world you want to live in, and the state in which you think your mind will be content and satisfied. It chooses where you think your safety lies, at your decision. It reveals yourself to you as you would have you be.

We look inside and decide whether to believe the ego or Jesus. If we choose the ego, we want the world to house the thought of separation for the purpose of preserving our special selves, keeping sin away at another's expense. If, on the other hand, we want Atonement, we will perceive the world as an opportunity to reveal what is in our minds; indeed, that we in fact have a mind. This reversal of projection is Jesus' purpose for the body, which corrects the ego's purpose of maintaining its separated, hateful state through perceptions of specialness.

(I.3:4-6) And always is it faithful to your purpose, from which it never separates, nor gives the slightest witness unto anything the purpose in your mind upholdeth not. Perception is a part of what it is your purpose to behold, for means and end are never separate. And thus you learn what seems to have a life apart has none.

The body is not separate from the mind (*ideas leave not their source*): the purpose the mind ascribes to the world remains in the mind, perception's lies to the contrary. If the purpose is to make guilt real, the body's perception will reaffirm this purpose by proving that separation is a fact, justifying the guilt that deserves punishment. Employing the ego's magic, we will believe that others are to be punished instead of ourselves. But if our purpose is to accept Atonement and awaken from the dream, the world will be seen as a classroom in which our minds are healed.

Next is the section "Perception and Choice," as Jesus expands on the principles we have been discussing:

(III.1:1-2) To the extent to which you value guilt, to that extent will you perceive a world in which attack is justified. To the extent to which you recognize that guilt is meaningless, to that extent you will perceive attack cannot *be* justified.

Attack is justified when we believe someone else is the miserable sinner and deserves the punishment demanded by our sin. We know that our bodily attack thoughts—in thought, word, and deed—are generated by the mind's guilt, the ultimate proof that the sinful separation has occurred. Yet when our decision makers choose the guiltlessness of God's Son as reality, attack will have no meaning since there will be no guilt to be defended.

(III.1:3-6) This is in accord with perception's fundamental law: You see what you believe is there, and you believe it there because you want it there. Perception has no other law than this.

The rest but stems from this, to hold it up and offer it support. This is perception's form, adapted to this world, of God's more basic law; that love creates itself, and nothing but itself.

We see the world because we put it there, out of the desire to prove that the miscreating thought of a separated self is real. This is a variation of *projection makes perception*: we look within the mind, decide what we want and project it, thereby perceiving it. In Heaven's world of knowledge, the same dynamic is the law of extension. What is in God's Mind is the Son He creates (or extends), as the workbook states: "Love created me like itself" (W-pI.67).

(III.2) God's laws do not obtain directly to a world perception rules, for such a world could not have been created by the Mind to which perception has no meaning. Yet are His laws reflected everywhere. Not that the world where this reflection is, is real at all. Only because His Son believes it is, and from His Son's belief He could not let Himself be separate entirely. He could not enter His Son's insanity with him, but He could be sure His sanity went there with him, so he could not be lost forever in the madness of his wish.

The God of non-dualistic oneness (knowledge) cannot have created a dualistic world of subject and object (perception). Nonetheless, God's laws of love, unity, and eternal life are reflected here through the recognition of our common need and purpose. When we fell asleep and began to dream, we took with us the memory of Who we are as Christ. This is the Holy Spirit and His principle of Atonement, which is why we are never totally insane. There remains a place of sanity in the mind the world was made to hide, in which we learn from our Teacher that illusion can serve the purpose of truth. We are taught that perception's world is a classroom that reflects Heaven's Oneness, even midst the ego's chaotic world of separation and fragmentation.

(III.3:1-4) Perception rests on choosing; knowledge does not. Knowledge has but one law

because it has but one Creator. But this world has two who made it, and they do not see it as the same. To each it has a different purpose, and to each it is a perfect means to serve the goal for which it is perceived.

This is the reason the Creator God has nothing to do with the perceptual world, the phenomenal universe of division and death. Our world, however, has two makers—the ego and Holy Spirit—that reflect their different purpose. The ego's goal for its world of specialness is separation, while the Holy Spirit's is to awaken us from the dream of guilt, hate, and death through forgiveness.

(III.3:5-6) For specialness, it is the perfect frame to set it off; the perfect battleground to wage its wars, the perfect shelter for illusions which it would make real. Not one but it upholds in its perception; not one but can be fully justified.

The world of specialness begins as a thought in the mind and seems to emerge as the world we experience as real: the projected battleground in which truth and illusion appear to be vying for our special attention.

(III.4:1-3) There is another Maker of the world, the simultaneous Corrector of the mad belief that anything could be established and maintained without some link that kept it still within the laws of God; not as the law itself upholds the universe as God created it, but in some form adapted to the need the Son of God believes he has. Corrected error is the error's end. And thus has God protected still His Son, even in error.

The word "Maker" is capitalized because it refers to the Holy Spirit. He is not the Creator, for the forgiven world He offers us, ultimately the real world, is illusory. His world contains the correction of Atonement that awaits our choice to undo the mind's belief in separation that made the universe of bodies. This correction is the miracle, which returns us to the decision-making mind where the mistake was made, allowing Jesus to correct the ego's misuse of the world. Whereas the world was made to kill, it must first become a place in which the Sonship is healed through happy dreams, later to awaken from the dream entirely, a theme that will soon return in our symphony.

(III.5:1) There is another purpose in the world that error made, because it has another Maker Who can reconcile its goal with His Creator's purpose.

God's purpose is to create or extend, reflected here by the Holy Spirit's forgiveness (right-minded extension).

(III.5:2-4) In His perception of the world, nothing is seen but justifies forgiveness and the sight of perfect sinlessness. Nothing arises but is met with instant and complete forgiveness. Nothing remains an instant, to obscure the sinlessness that shines unchanged, beyond the pitiful attempts of specialness to put it out of mind, where it must be, and light the body up instead of it.

We see here one more statement of the ego's strategy of displacing specialness from the mind onto the body, where its remedy—love's distortion (the special relationship)—is found and cherished. The ego tells us that the problem lies in the world of another's sinful darkness, and the solution is our attaining light-filled specialness. This is of course only the illusion of light, for guilt's darkness remains, shrouded in the shadows of mind and body. Recall that the ego's goal is to make guilt real, but have it be perceived outside the mind. As correction, Jesus uses the world of sin to bring our attention to the thought system of sin, and then beyond that to the sinlessness of God's Son. When we are returned to right-minded innocence, the law of *projection makes perception* has us see only expressions of this innocence in others, or calls for it. No other perception is justified in the illusory world of existence.

(III.5:5-6) The lamps of Heaven are not for mind to choose to see them where it will. If it elects to see them elsewhere from their home, as if they lit a place where they could never be, then must the Maker of the world correct your

error, lest you remain in darkness where the lamps are not.

We have illusions of the light of sinlessness in our bodily self, bought at the price of someone else's sin: the ego's perverted version of justice (*one or the other*). Responding to this madness, the Holy Spirit begins His healing work with our perceptions of the world, where we believe we are, and shifts our attention to the mind where the belief in sinfulness is understood as nothing but a flimsy defense against the innocence of God's Son.

(III.6:1-3) Everyone here has entered darkness, yet no one has entered it alone. Nor need he stay more than an instant. For he has come with Heaven's Help within him, ready to lead him out of darkness into light at any time.

The idea that "he has come with Heaven's Help within him" prefigures "For They Have Come" in Chapter 26. We are the ones who choose when we will be led out of darkness, a choice born of the realization that the ego never works and no hope or happiness can ever be found in the world of specialness. Throwing up our hands in despair we say there must be another way, and so we choose again: the Holy Spirit's light of shared interests in place of the shadowy world of the ego's separate and competing interests.

(III.6:4-8) The time he chooses can be any time, for help is there, awaiting but his choice. And when he chooses to avail himself of what is given him, then will he see each situation that he thought before was means to justify his anger turned to an event which justifies his love. He will hear plainly that the calls to war he heard before are really calls to peace. He will perceive that where he gave attack is but another altar where he can, with equal ease and far more happiness, bestow forgiveness. And he will reinterpret all temptation as just another chance to bring him joy.

Jesus has told us his patience is infinite (T-5.VI.11:6), which is why there is no need to feel guilty when our fear of love is too great to accept his teachings of forgiveness. In addition, the opportunities for learning remain with us despite this fear, as do our teacher's kind reminders that at any instant we may choose to see a situation or relationship differently. What the ego made to attack is transformed through his vision into a classroom in which we learn that God's Son cannot be at war, for he remains as he was created, at one with the Oneness of Heaven. Thus does a world of pain and death give way to one of joy, as our eyes slowly open to the truth that we journey home together. Eternity, like love, waits on decision, not time. It waits at the mind's altar for us to choose again, for ourselves and for all God's Sons.

(III.7:1-7) How can a misperception be a sin? Let all your brother's errors be to you nothing except a chance for you to see the workings of the Helper given you to see the world He made instead of yours. What, then, *is* justified? What do you want? For these two questions are the same. And when you see them as the same, your choice is made. For it is seeing them as one that brings release from the belief there are two ways to see.

This is how the illusory world becomes an instrument that leads us beyond illusions to the truth, a classroom of forgiveness that transforms guilt to love. No other perception of the world can be justified, since all we truly want is to take Jesus' hand and walk home. *Projection makes perception*: we decide which teacher will guide our journey, and this choice determines how we perceive the world. Choosing Jesus leads to the vision that sins demanding punishment are mistakes calling for correction, and as we see each other we see ourselves. Heaven's Oneness is joyously returned to awareness in this unity of our inner and outer perceptions of forgiveness.

(III.7:8-9) This world has much to offer to your peace, and many chances to extend your own forgiveness. Such its purpose is, to those who want to see peace and forgiveness descend on them, and offer them the light.

All that happens in the world, each situation and relationship, has the potential to transform our mind's purpose. We need but want to have it changed from guilt to guiltlessness; from the ego's version of justice in which one wins and another loses, to the Holy Spirit's justice where everyone wins and no one loses—the essence of forgiveness.

(III.8:1-3) The Maker of the world of gentleness has perfect power to offset the world of violence and hate that seems to stand between you and His gentleness. It is not there in His forgiving eyes. And therefore it need not be there in yours.

Through the world's eyes we see violence and hate, pain and death—the ego's attempts to have the illusory world serve its hidden purpose of proving sin and separation real, which follows the principle of one gaining at another's expense. How different from the Holy Spirit's vision that does not see through guilt-riddled eyes of specialness! His is a gentle and forgiving perception that looks past illusory darkness to the unifying light of truth.

(III.8:4-7) Sin is the fixed belief perception cannot change. What has been damned is damned and damned forever, being forever unforgivable. If, then, it is forgiven, sin's perception must have been wrong. And thus is change made possible.

The "fixed belief" is that what our eyes see is real, a sinful world in which some suffer and others get away with murder, sometimes even literally. We fear forgiveness because we do not want "sin's perception" to be wrong: we killed God and therefore we exist. If this original change is wrong, we have been wrong about ourselves, which is why we tenaciously fight against the notion that sin is unreal. Guilt is a powerful ally here for it witnesses to the changelessness of sin. Our horrific feelings of self-loathing and the pain they engender clearly demonstrate the sin that deserves punishment, the sin that proves the truth of the change from oneness and that our separated reality is permanent, making return to the Changeless impossible as sin is forever unchangeable.

(III.8:8-13) The Holy Spirit, too, sees what He sees as far beyond the chance of change. But on His vision sin cannot encroach, for sin has been corrected by His sight. And thus it must have been an error, not a sin. For what it claimed could never be, has been. Sin is attacked by punishment, and so preserved. But to forgive it is to change its state from error into truth.

The theme of sin and error, punishment and correction, is more than familiar at this point, and is a major focus of this chapter. Choosing vision means we are willing to re-examine the belief in unredeemable sin and admit the errors of our thinking and perceptions. God's Son *is* innocent, and in his innocence we are healed together. Truth has never ceased to be itself, and dreams of sin do not escape their illusory origin, which means they never existed.

(III.9:1-5) The Son of God could never sin, but he can wish for what would hurt him. And he has the power to think he can be hurt. What could this be except a misperception of himself? Is this a sin or a mistake, forgivable or not? Does he need help or condemnation?

Recall the earlier theme that we are free to believe in illusions (sin), but not free to establish their reality (e.g., T-3.VI.10:2). As it is only in dreams that truth can be changed, it is only in dreams that the sin that never happened can be punished. The Holy Spirit's forgiving judgment enables us to look at our mistaken belief about ourselves and choose to see differently. In this way we are helped to forgive the "sin" that made us what we are not, releasing the innocent memory of our Self that replaces the sinful face we had put upon God's holy Son.

(III.9:6-10) Is it your purpose that he be saved or damned? Forgetting not that what he is to you will make this choice your future? For you make it *now*, the instant when all time becomes a means to reach a goal. Make, then, your choice. But recognize that in this choice the purpose of the world you see is chosen, and will be justified.

Jesus is asking us to choose our goal. Do we wish that our brothers be damned or saved, remembering that what we condemn in them we do to ourselves, the same with forgiveness. If we choose separation as our purpose, we will see the world as real, justifying our specialness. Inevitably, then, we will seek to defend this specialness by attacking others, wherein they become specially guilty and we specially innocent. Yet in the holy instant we are perceived as we truly are: God's innocent Son, at one with himself and with his Creator.

(IV.2:1) Perception's basic law could thus be said, "You will rejoice at what you see because you see it to rejoice."

This is the same principle articulated in the preceding section (III.1:3). The melody and harmonics of the theme differ, but its content of the purposive nature of perception remains the same: we see what we wish to see.

(IV.2:2) And while you think that suffering and sin will bring you joy, so long will they be there for you to see.

Suffering and sin bring joy, as that ensures God will punish others instead of ourselves. We give someone else the sin we rightfully believe is our own, and gladly suffer at that person's hands so we can say: "'Behold me, brother, at your hand I die'" (T-27.I.4:6). We made bodies to feel pain—"Thus were specifics made" (W-pI.161.3:1)—because behind every form of suffering is the accusing and damning finger that says: "Because you did this to me, you deserve to die at the hands of God's justice." The distortions of our perceived world mirror the ego's thought system of guilt, attack, and punishment our minds chose in place of the Holy Spirit's Atonement.

(IV.2:3-5) Nothing is harmful or beneficent apart from what you wish. It is your wish that makes it what it is in its effects on you. Because you chose it as a means to gain these same effects, believing them to be the bringers of rejoicing and of joy.

We gladly suffer the effects of our brothers' sins so that God will recognize the sin is theirs and not our own. This wish makes our thoughts real in the perception, even if they are unknown to us. We need Jesus' course to lift the veil that fell across our minds, that we may recognize what we have chosen. Only then can the motivation be there to change. To suffer so that someone else is punished is insane in light of the Holy Spirit's principle that *no one suffers and everyone gains.* The problem is resistance, as our very existence is predicated on the ego's opposing principle that *someone loses and another wins,* the source of its triumphant joy. Despite this patent madness, salvation asks only a "little willingness" to look at error, the subject of our next section.

"The Little Willingness"

We turn now to the beginning of the section "Justice Returned to Love." What makes this seemingly impossible course possible is that we are not asked to change our minds about who we are, but simply to let in a little light of reason. This is sufficient to allow our Teacher to begin the process of motivating us to change our perceived identity, when we are ready. This is the meaning of "the little willingness."

(VIII.1:1) The Holy Spirit can use all that you give to Him for your salvation.

What we give to the Holy Spirit are our special relationships. We ask His help to look at them as He does, not seeking to prove that the ego is right and guilt is real, but to accept His happy vision that shows the ego to be wrong: forgiveness, not guilt, is salvation.

(VIII.1:2-4) But He cannot use what you withhold, for He cannot take it from you without your willingness. For if He did, you would believe He wrested it from you against your will. And so you would not learn it *is* your will to be without it.

Jesus expresses what we have seen many times already, most clearly at the beginning of the text when he told us not to ask him to take away our fear. If he did, he would be tampering with the law of cause (mind) and effect (body), thereby depreciating the mind's power to choose (T-2.VII.1:4-5). Instead, he implores us to ask his help to remove the conditions that led to the fear: our willingness (or decision) to be separate (T-2.VI.4:3-4).

The point here is that we must choose forgiveness on our own. Jesus cannot overpower our minds by choosing for us. He does, however, remind us that we need his help to choose again. Jesus cannot choose for us, and we cannot choose rightly without him. Without doing our part in this "collaborative venture" (T-8.IV.4:8) we would feel he is dominating us, wresting from our feeble grasp the self to which we cling. As long as we wish to luxuriate in specialness he stands back, his kind presence reminding us that this will not make us happy. When we recognize that he is right, or at least that we are wrong ("the little willingness"), we will be willing to ask for and receive his help.

(VIII.1:5) You need not give it to Him wholly willingly, for if you could you had no need of Him.

We would not need Jesus and his course if we could change our minds completely. This is the reason we should be cautious of those who say they have done so, and that we should do likewise. We would not be in the world as bodies if we truly believed we were not here. The fact is that all students believe they are individuals who are reading and studying *A Course in Miracles.* This emphasizes their need for help to learn they are minds, not bodies; a help that is gently patient, not imposing its will as it awaits the mind's decision to change teachers.

(VIII.1:6-8) But this He needs; that you prefer He take it than that you keep it for yourself alone, and recognize that what brings loss to no one you would not know. This much is necessary

to add to the idea no one can lose for you to gain. And nothing more.

We may still hold on to what we should be giving to the Holy Spirit, but there is at least a part of us now that is sane, realizing we would be happier without the special images of defense we draw upon ourselves. We need only understand that we do not know how to live whereby everyone wins and no one loses, for this goes against the thought system the ego made the world to reflect, and which we still value. Jesus asks nothing but that we be aware that the principle of *no one loses and everyone gains* is the one thing that will make us happy and give us peace.

(VIII.2:1-2) Here is the only principle salvation needs. Nor is it necessary that your faith in it be strong, unswerving, and without attack from all beliefs opposed to it.

Thankfully, we do not have to be consistent in our learning. Our need, again, is only to have the "little willingness" that asks Jesus for help because our way has led us ever more deeply into the throes of madness and pain.

(VIII.2:3-9) You have no fixed allegiance. But remember salvation is not needed by the saved. You are not called upon to do what one divided still against himself would find impossible. Have little faith that wisdom could be found in such a state of mind. But be you thankful that only little faith is asked of you. What but a little faith remains to those who still believe in sin? What could they know of Heaven and the justice of the saved?

Here is another example of our teacher's gentleness, not only as he guides us in our personal lives, but in *A Course in Miracles* as well. Jesus does not confront us with the truth, but merely presents the fact that we cannot achieve salvation without him, which in our insanity we still choose against. He tells us we need not pretend that we want Heaven, and thus can honestly say that while we no longer desire the pain of the split mind, we still cling to it even as we know that suffering comes from the belief that someone must pay for sin. Secretly, we believe that we must pay the price through sacrifice, yet projection enables us to believe that another can do it for us. A "little willingness" makes us aware of the madness that is the source of all pain, and our sane minds no longer find this tolerable. This "nod to God" (T-24.VI.12:4) enables Jesus to shift the purpose of our relationships from murder to miracles.

The Holy Relationship – Forgiveness

Our theme for this next part of this symphonic movement is the holy relationship, the reflection of Heaven's Oneness. We shall see how this specifically interfaces with the principle of justice: *no one loses and everyone gains*. We begin with the first section, "The Link to Truth," of which the last three paragraphs are unique insofar as Jesus provides the clearest explication of why his course is written as it is. Even though truth is non-dualistic, meaning reality is perfect oneness, *A Course in Miracles* is couched in dualistic terms, especially evident in the treatment of forgiveness. The fact is that we forgive only ourselves as there is no one out there to forgive, the world being a mere projection. Moreover, the sin we forgive needs no forgiveness because it never happened. While this may make intellectual sense, it certainly is not our experience. This is the reason behind Jesus speaking to us about forgiving someone else, *as if there were a "someone else."* In addition, we are told that forgiveness is impossible without the Holy Spirit's help, *as if He were separate from us.*

Jesus' explanation is important to understand, otherwise we will be caught in the dualistic trap of believing there is actually a Teacher outside our individual mind Who helps us in the world and, even more to the point, helps us forgive someone outside us. This language is used since the dualistic body is our experience, even though we are only minds. Caught in the ego snare of projected illusion, we are precluded from making our way up the ladder and beyond, to the recognition there is God and nothing else: perfect oneness remains perfectly undivided and whole.

(I.5:1-2) Since you believe that you are separate, Heaven presents itself to you as separate, too. Not that it is in truth, but that the link that has been given you to join the truth may reach to you through what you understand.

"Heaven presents itself to you as separate" refers to the Father, Son, and Holy Spirit—the three Members of the Trinity—apart from Each Other and from our special selves. While the words *non-duality* and *duality* do not appear in the Course, *oneness* and *separation, sameness* and *differences* do. A non-dualistic statement, for example, is: "We say 'God is,' and then we cease to speak…" (W-pI.169.5:4). On the other hand, talking about God the Father, Christ the Son, and the Holy Spirit's Voice, and then us as separated Sons who need divine help, is the language of the dualistic condition in which we think we exist. This means that the words should not be taken literally but as symbols we can understand, pointing beyond themselves to the truth of God's Oneness and Love.

(I.5:3) Father and Son and Holy Spirit are as One, as all your brothers join as one in truth.

If They are truly One, we cannot really speak of three Persons. Recall that earlier in the text Jesus says God is first in the Trinity, but there is no second or third (T-14.IV.1:7-8), another not-so-veiled correction for the mystery of the Christian triune God of Father, Son, and Holy Spirit.

(I.5:4-6) Christ and His Father never have been separate, and Christ abides within your understanding, in the part of you that shares His Father's Will. The Holy Spirit links the other part—the tiny, mad desire to be separate, different and special—to the Christ, to make the oneness clear to what is really one. In this world this is not understood, but can be taught.

It is impossible for dualistic minds to understand the statement that Christ and His Father are One, forever unseparated. Yet the separated Son can be taught to remember this Oneness within his dream of duality, sharing with all people the common purpose of choosing the right mind's memory of Christ over the wrong mind's specialness. This shared interest reflects Heaven's unity that can never be understood, but known.

(I.6:1-4) The Holy Spirit serves Christ's purpose in your mind, so that the aim of specialness can be corrected where the error lies. Because His purpose still is one with both the Father and the Son, He knows the Will of God and what you really will. But this is understood by mind perceived as one, aware that it is one, and so experienced. It is the Holy Spirit's function to teach you how this oneness is experienced, what you must do that it can be experienced, and where you should go to do it.

Within the illusion, the Holy Spirit teaches us the *how* (the holy instant), *what* (forgiveness), and *where* (special relationships) of awakening from the mind's dualistic dream to our non-dualistic reality of Christ's Oneness, at one with Its Source. His gentle teaching leads us through the dualistic world of attack and forgiveness—body to mind—to the unified Mind and Will of God.

(I.7:1) All this takes note of time and place as if they were discrete, for while you think that part of you is separate, the concept of a Oneness joined as One is meaningless.

Jesus refers to our experience in the dualistic world of linear time (past, present, and future) in which separate bodies appear to relate to us. As our experience as temporal/spatial creatures prevents us from understanding "the concept of a Oneness joined as One," Jesus asks us to focus only on the purpose we share with each other: walking a common pathway (*together, or not at all*) that corrects the ego's thought system of separation (*one or the other*).

(I.7:2-4) It is apparent that a mind so split could never be the Teacher of a Oneness which unites

all things within Itself. And so What is within this mind, and does unite all things together, must be its Teacher. Yet must It use the language that this mind can understand, in the condition in which it thinks it is.

Since true correction, abstract and non-specific, must be adapted to the dualistic forms of our dualistic condition, the split mind automatically translates its decision for the Holy Spirit into bodily forms we can recognize. And so *A Course in Miracles* comes to us in words (*holy relationship, holy instant, forgiveness*) we can relate to. These symbols are the means for awakening from the dream of duality to our reality as spirit: God's one Son.

(I.7:5-7) **And It must use all learning to transfer illusions to the truth, taking all false ideas of what you are, and leading you beyond them to the truth that *is* beyond them. All this can very simply be reduced to this:**

> *What is the same can not be different, and*
> *what is one can not have separate parts.*

We reflect simple, non-dualistic truth by recognizing that we and our brothers share both a dualistic insanity and the need to awaken from the ego's dream to the Christ Who greets us as our Self. To summarize, the Course is written in dualistic language, for that is the condition we think we are in. Understanding this helps us move beyond the belief that Jesus speaks of bodies, helping us to avoid the snares of taking literally what is meant symbolically; i.e., forgiveness occurs between two separated people. It is the *mind* that attacks and forgives, and in his kind and gentle teaching Jesus does not demand we come to where he is. Rather, he takes our hands as we move from his reflected presence in the body to its source in the healed mind that is outside the dream.

We turn now to expressions of the holy relationship and forgiveness, continuing where we left off in our previous discussion that compared the ego's use of the body in special relationships to hanging an empty frame on a wall:

(II.5:3-8) **The masterpiece that God has set within this frame is all there is to see. The body**

holds it for a while, without obscuring it in any way. Yet what God has created needs no frame, for what He has created He supports and frames within Himself. His masterpiece He offers you to see. And would you rather see the frame instead of this? And see the picture not at all?

God has set the picture of our Identity as Christ—perfect Oneness—within this frame, which symbolizes the holy or forgiven relationship. We may say that Jesus recasts his question "Why would you choose to pursue the special relationship when it is a frame that holds the ego's nothingness?" to read: "I offer you the frame of forgiveness that allows you to see that everyone shares your purpose. This frame will lead you beyond all pictures to Christ, *a Oneness joined as One*. Come, take my hand and I shall lead you there, along with all your brothers."

(II.6:1-3) **The Holy Spirit is the frame God set around the part of Him that you would see as separate. Yet its frame is joined to its Creator, one with Him and with His masterpiece. This is its purpose, and you do not make the frame into the picture when you choose to see it in its place.**

Jesus urges us not to make bodily relationships into anything important. A holy relationship is not with another, any more than a special one is. Relationships exist only in the mind, with the ego or the Holy Spirit. Believing we are mindless, however, we experience the mind's projections as real, perceiving the special relationship as between ourselves and others. We do not realize that their purpose is to attack our projected guilt over joining the ego. The unholy purpose shifts when we perceive that we and our brothers share the same need to forgive. This new perception returns us to the mind, for seeing common purpose reflects the "little willingness" that comes from joining with Jesus. He asks of us only that we look at the world differently, seeing it as a frame to reflect the picture of holiness the decision-making mind has chosen instead of sin. Our changed purpose takes us from the body's form to the mind's content, undoing the ego's purpose that bound us to the mindless form as a means of avoiding the mind's healing.

(II.6:4-5) The frame that God has given it but serves His purpose, not yours apart from His. It is your separate purpose that obscures the picture, and cherishes the frame instead of it.

The point of the special relationship is to have us not know the mind's guilt, but to keep it hidden by the projection that liberates us from self-hate. Our guilt becomes expressed in special relationships here (the frame), in which others will be punished instead of us. This guilt and specialness obscure the light-filled picture of the Self that is lightly framed by forgiveness, ready to disappear when we choose shared over separated interests, God being our only goal.

(II.6:6-8) Yet God has set His masterpiece within a frame that will endure forever, when yours has crumbled into dust. But think you not the picture is destroyed in any way. What God creates is safe from all corruption, unchanged and perfect in eternity.

God's frame "will endure forever" since His frame is His Love. Our true Self, too, is forever "unchanged and perfect," beyond anything the ego attempts to make of It in its dreams of sin and hate.

(II.7:1) Accept God's frame instead of yours, and you will see the masterpiece.

To accept God's frame is to accept the Holy Spirit's purpose for relationships here. The ego had us come into the world to avoid the mind's choosing God, and we then blamed others for our misery. The Holy Spirit changes this purpose, helping us see the world as the means of returning to the mind's mistaken choice, so we may acknowledge that the ways of specialness brought us nothing and that we want the Everything: Self instead of self.

(II.7:2-3) Look at its loveliness, and understand the Mind that thought it, not in flesh and bones, but in a frame as lovely as itself. Its holiness lights up the sinlessness the frame of darkness hides, and casts a veil of light across the picture's face which but reflects the light that shines from it to its Creator.

Jesus speaks of the glorious Self we are, of which the body is simply a "travesty," a description we saw before (T-24.VII.10:9). We cannot know true holiness in this world, but we can be its reflection by giving up the veils of darkness—guilt, specialness, hate—that conceal its light. The gentleness of forgiveness will give way to the Masterpiece that is the Light of Christ into which we ultimately disappear, "not to be seen but known" (T-19.IV-D.19:1).

(II.7:4-5) Think not this face was ever darkened because you saw it in a frame of death. God kept it safe that you might look on it, and see the holiness that He has given it.

Despite what we believe we have done, the Love of Christ that is our Self waits patiently in the mind for our return. Although we buried its shining face beneath our guilt, seeking to destroy it, the soft light of forgiveness gently dissolves the thin veils of specialness that keep us from remembering our holiness, shared with all the Sonship.

(II.8:1-5) Within the darkness see the savior *from* the dark, and understand your brother as his Father's Mind shows him to you. He will step forth from darkness as you look on him, and you will see the dark no more. The darkness touched him not, nor you who brought him forth for you to look upon. His sinlessness but pictures yours. His gentleness becomes your strength, and both will gladly look within, and see the holiness that must be there because of what you looked upon in him.

We made others our saviors so they would hide us from guilt's darkness, which still enshrouds us in its shadow. But when we look through vision's eyes and see the purpose of forgiveness in our projections, the darkness in the mind is revealed so we may choose against it. As the light of innocence shines out, heretofore hidden by guilt, it flows through the mind of God's one Son who remembers the holiness that teaches him that he *is* God's Son.

(II.8:6-8) He is the frame in which your holiness is set, and what God gave him must be given you. However much he overlooks the masterpiece in him and sees only a frame of darkness, it is still your only function to behold in him what he sees not. And in this seeing is the vision shared that looks on Christ instead of seeing death.

Regardless of what we do to each other, the truth of our shared Identity is unassailed, for the mind is affected only by our decision that can be changed in an instant. This is the reason we need to choose the miracle, which returns us to the decision-making mind that wishes to keep the ego's secret: our existence is based on the insane premise we killed God. We are fearful of recognizing this insanity for what it is, for we would instantly know that the special self is illusory. To perpetuate the ego's madness, we resist looking at God's masterpiece in another, as we would surely see it in ourselves. Judgment, then, is the ego's ally in its war against God, and vision its mortal enemy.

(II.9:1-2) How could the Lord of Heaven not be glad if you appreciate His masterpiece? What could He do but offer thanks to you who love His Son as He does?

Our purpose is to forgive, moving from the ego's frame of specialness to its picture of death. Jesus is helping us see all this as a flimsy defense that can barely cover the glorious picture of our Self, which we love as God does.

(II.9:3-13) Would He not make known to you His Love, if you but share His praise of what He loves? God cherishes creation as the perfect Father that He is. And so His joy is made complete when any part of Him joins in His praise, to share His joy. This brother is His perfect gift to you. And He is glad and thankful when you thank His perfect Son for being what he is. And all His thanks and gladness shine on you who would complete His joy, along with Him. And thus is yours completed. Not one ray of darkness can be seen by those who will to make their Father's happiness complete, and theirs along

with His. The gratitude of God Himself is freely offered to everyone who shares His purpose. It is not His Will to be alone. And neither is it yours.

As always, a passage such as this makes no sense without our recognizing the inherent unity of the Sonship, forever one with its Source. "One brother is all brothers" (W-pI.161.4:1), which means that to forgive one is to forgive all, and this includes ourselves. God's "gratitude" is simply the symbol of His Oneness, which cannot be compromised by illusory ideas of specialness. In the Presence of His Love, no thoughts of sin or death can ever darken our light-filled minds, shared joyously with all our brothers, without exception.

(II.10:1) Forgive your brother, and you cannot separate yourself from him nor from his Father.

What we hold against God we hold against others; what we hold against them we hold against Him. Guilt is one, as is forgiveness, and in the presence of one the other disappears, for darkness and light cannot coexist.

(II.10:2-3) You need no forgiveness, for the wholly pure have never sinned. Give, then, what He has given you, that you may see His Son as one, and thank his Father as He thanks you.

Gratitude, again, symbolizes the love that unites Father and Son. To experience this gratitude we must be willing to see the common purpose that joins us with each other: a central theme of our symphony. This shared interest is the world's reflection of Heaven's Oneness, demonstrated by our being the same in illusion as we are united in truth. Guilt or peace cannot be in one without being in all: the Son of God remains one—as he was made, as he was created.

(II.11:1-2) You and your brother are the same, as God Himself is One and not divided in His Will. And you must have one purpose, since He gave the same to both of you.

We repeatedly return to this point: as our brains were made not to understand what is beyond duality, we cannot comprehend non-dualistic truth.

However, within a dualistic world we can be taught what it means to share one need and a single purpose, that we reach Heaven *together, or not at all*, for the "ark of peace is entered two by two" (T-20.IV.6:5). This means that salvation cannot come at another's expense, as peace is impossible when we judge, condemn, or seek to harm another. All this we *can* learn, and Jesus assures us that we will.

(II.11:3-4) His Will is brought together as you join in will, that you be made complete by offering completion to your brother. See not in him the sinfulness he sees, but give him honor that you may esteem yourself and him.

We need each other as reminders that there is another self, purpose, and teacher we can choose. This is accomplished by reflecting the peace and kindness that comes from choosing the thought system of sinlessness. As form is nothing and content everything, we are not concerned with behavior but only with the innocence our minds share.

(II.11:5) To you and your brother is given the power of salvation, that escape from darkness into light be yours to share; that you may see as one what never has been separate, nor apart from all God's Love as given equally.

This recurring theme of the equality of God's Love corrects the Bible's unequivocal teaching of the opposite. We saw this correction, for example, at the very beginning of the text where Jesus tells us he is different from us only in time, which does not exist (T-1.II.3-4). Our elder brother asks only our "little willingness" to understand that we share one purpose and one need. Even more to the point, he shows how much we do not want to recognize our common interest, clinging to the mentality of *one or the other*: you have something I want, without which I will not be happy or peaceful, satisfied or whole. Further, Jesus helps us understand how our attempts to secure this special something through love or attack interferes with our learning and makes forgiveness seem so difficult.

(V.4) The Son of God asks only this of you; that you return to him what is his due, that you may

share in it with him. Alone does neither have it. So must it remain useless to both. Together, it will give to each an equal strength to save the other, and save himself along with him. Forgiven by you, your savior offers you salvation. Condemned by you, he offers death to you. In everyone you see but the reflection of what you choose to have him be to you. If you decide against his proper function, the only one he has in truth, you are depriving him of all the joy he would have found if he fulfilled the role God gave to him. But think not Heaven is lost to him alone. Nor can it be regained unless the way is shown to him through you, that you may find it, walking by his side.

Projection makes perception. Over and over Jesus returns to this theme, in an almost endless number of variations. In the above passage we are taught that we see in everyone the reflection of what we have first chosen in our minds: separation or oneness, condemnation or salvation, injustice or justice. Our perception is made not only for ourselves, but for the entire world of separate bodies. The mind's decision for Jesus joins us with his true perception of *one for all, and all for one*, to borrow from Dumas' Musketeers. When justice is returned to love, forgiveness reigns supreme in the Son's kingdom, heralding the oneness that ends the ego's tyrannical rule of guilt and attack.

(V.6) Against the hatred that the Son of God may cherish toward himself, is God believed to be without the power to save what He created from the pain of hell. But in the love he shows himself is God made free to let His Will be done. In your brother you see the picture of your own belief in what the Will of God must be for you. In your forgiveness will you understand His Love for you; through your attack believe He hates you, thinking Heaven must be hell. Look once again upon your brother, not without the understanding that he is the way to Heaven or to hell, as you perceive him. But forget not this; the role you give to him is given you, and you will walk the way you pointed out to him because it is your judgment on yourself.

What we choose for ourselves and our brothers we choose for God. The prisons of hate in which we seek to hold God's Son, hold our Father as well. Since oneness exists both in reality and illusion, if we seek to know our minds' decision we need only look at our perceptions. If they fragment the Sonship in specialness, we know it is the ego's eyes we have looked through. If we recognize the presence of the same split mind in everyone, without judgment, we can only have been guided by Christ's vision. We either walk separately the road to hell, or return unto our God with our brothers, the journey that reflects Heaven's Will of perfect unity.

OUR SPECIAL FUNCTION: LEARNING THE MEANING OF JUSTICE

We begin this subsection with "The Special Function," in which we find clearly articulated the idea that the ego speaks first, is wrong, and the Holy Spirit is the Answer. The ego spoke first by establishing its special self, independent of God. It protected its existence by projecting the sin associated with specialness, seeing sin in all relationships. When tolerance for pain becomes too high and we exclaim "There *must* be a better way" (T-2.III.3:5-6), we mean there must be another way of perceiving relationships, a purpose in them we do not as yet understand. This "little willingness" to consider alternatives to our perception is enough to invite Jesus to begin teaching us our "special function." This is where the special relationship's purpose of guilt is shifted to forgiveness, providing us with the specific (i.e., special) classrooms in which we learn to forgive ourselves. We begin in the middle of the section.

(VI.4:1) Such is the Holy Spirit's kind perception of specialness; His use of what you made, to heal instead of harm.

We use the special relationship to hurt, reflecting the murderous principle of *kill or be killed.* Our willingness allows Jesus to teach us that the same relationship in form can serve a different purpose: "to heal instead of harm."

(VI.4:2) To each He gives a special function in salvation he alone can fill; a part for only him.

It can be tempting to misconstrue Jesus' meaning. He is not referring to behavior, that he has some *special* work we are to do for him. Rather, the "special function" is the special relationship *we* chose, so when we now choose a different teacher it becomes a classroom that will lead us beyond the mind's guilt, fear, and pain. In point of fact, Jesus never really speaks of behavior, but the change of mind that alone is salvation in the world of illusion.

(VI.4:3) Nor is the plan complete until he finds his special function, and fulfills the part assigned to him, to make himself complete within a world where incompletion rules.

Once more, Jesus speaks of the need to have our *minds* be healed, accepting the Atonement for ourselves so that it extends throughout the mind of God's one Son, reminding him that he is complete, healed, and whole.

(VI.5:1) Here, where the laws of God do not prevail in perfect form, can he yet do *one* perfect thing and make *one* perfect choice.

Nothing here is perfect because the world was made not to be perfect, having come from an imperfect thought. When we decide for Jesus as our teacher, however, we change the world's purpose and learn to do the one perfect thing of forgiveness. We grow to realize that the problem is not in another but in ourselves, and as specialness is our dream in which others are the victimizers (our special love and hate partners), we can choose a different dream.

(VI.5:2-4) And by this act of special faithfulness to one perceived as other than himself, he learns the gift was given to himself, and so they must be one. Forgiveness is the only function meaningful in time. It is the means the Holy Spirit uses to translate specialness from sin into salvation.

When we perceive others as different from us, we are involved in the ego's hateful principle of *one or the other*, for this perception of differences justifies our attacking them. Yet when we change teachers we see all people as one in purpose. To state this once again, Jesus is not speaking of doing great works in the world, writing brilliant books, or giving wonderful workshops. He speaks only of the one meaningful function he knows: changing our minds. Instead of special relationships being battlegrounds where one sacrifices so another wins, one dies for another to live, they become classrooms in which our new Teacher helps us learn His justice: *no one loses and everyone gains*. We need not understand how salvation works, but need only realize that since the ways of sin and judgment do not work, we no longer want them.

(VI.5:5-8) Forgiveness is for all. But when it rests on all it is complete, and every function of this world completed with it. Then is time no more. Yet while in time, there is still much to do.

Time was made by guilt, and when guilt is undone through forgiveness, time disappears. Nonetheless, while we remain guilty there is work to do. This does not entail understanding "a Oneness joined as One," but learning how to reflect non-dualistic truth within a dualistic world: shifting perception of erstwhile enemies so they become our friends, *along with everyone else*. In this way the Sonship is made complete in our healed perception.

(VI.5:9-11) And each must do what is allotted him, for on his part does all the plan depend. He *has* a special part in time for so he chose, and choosing it, he made it for himself. His wish was not denied but changed in form, to let it serve his brother and himself, and thus become a means to save instead of lose.

We all must do our part in releasing the ego's belief in guilt and specialness, for such is the Course's purpose. Jesus does a clever thing here by appealing to our wish to be special, born of the need to have our bodies be instruments of the specialness that attests to our separation from God, including the "fact" that our sin makes its home in another who will be justly punished. We crave this specialness, regardless of its form, so no one will realize

that we are the guilty sinners our minds believe is the truth. Jesus therefore retains this wish for specialness, but changes its purpose, the meaning of "changed in form." The special relationship is now transformed into a classroom that teaches that no one is special, being the means by which we undo the belief in specialness itself. The special function of forgiveness is what makes us special, and so our wish is not denied. We are special, not by proving separation is real, but by learning to forgive in the specific form established by our relationships.

(VI.6:6-8) The specialness he chose to hurt himself did God appoint to be the means for his salvation, from the very instant that the choice was made. His special sin was made his special grace. His special hate became his special love.

In the same instant the separation seemed to happen, spinning out a world of specialness, the correction appeared in our minds which we took into the dream as the memory of Who we are as Christ. Not taking the Course's words literally, we understand that our Source does not really do anything. Jesus uses a dualistic symbol that originally reflected an anthropomorphic deity reacting to sin, to express the Presence of Love that corrects the ego's tale of divine hatred. Incidentally, *special love* is meant here in the positive sense of the term, correcting the ego's guilt-laden purpose of exclusion.

(VI.7:1-5) The Holy Spirit needs your special function, that His may be fulfilled. Think not you lack a special value here. You wanted it, and it is given you. All that you made can serve salvation easily and well. The Son of God can make no choice the Holy Spirit cannot employ on his behalf, and not against himself.

Again, Jesus turns the tables on the ego's value of specialness. "You want to be special," he says to us. "Well, then, you are." Armed with the gift to him of our "little willingness," he changes the source of our special value from the ego's need to exclude, its use for the special relationship, to the Holy Spirit's all-inclusive function of forgiveness: "His use of what you made, to heal instead of harm."

(VI.7:6-8) Only in darkness does your special-ness appear to be attack. In light, you see it as your special function in the plan to save the Son of God from all attack, and let him understand that he is safe, as he has always been, and will remain in time and in eternity alike. This is the function given you for your brother.

This statement is another example of the loving gentleness of Jesus' teaching. He does not take our special relationships away from us (e.g., T-17.IV.2:3), but simply changes their purpose from guilt to forgiveness. The fact that we believe we are here says we believe in specialness, and if we give it a prominence through judging our sin, or journaling about it ad infinitum, our self-indulgence shrouds us still further in guilt's darkness. This is inevitable, for special relationships are shadows of guilt, no matter how veiled the true nature of their frame or attractive their gifts.

Gratefully we hear Jesus say to us: "Do not wallow in pain and guilt, because this merely holds them in darkness, apart from truth's correction. Instead, look at your ego with me, which will shift the special relationship from a prison of guilt to a classroom of forgiveness." Relationships that only an instant earlier were cloaked in the darkness of hate become bathed in a light that embraces all God's Sons. Who could not, then, feel gratitude for the special relationship, as its new purpose has made it the means of healing the mind? To repeat, we are asked not to dwell on our specialness with guilt, indulgence, or spiritualization, but rather to invite Jesus' help to look at it differently, as an outward picture of the mind's wish to be separate. This returns us to the decision maker that can right-mindedly choose safety and peace, letting danger and conflict go forever.

(VI.7:9-10) Take it gently, then, from your brother's hand, and let salvation be perfectly fulfilled in you. Do this *one* thing, that everything be given you.

This is the reason Jesus says his is a simple course. It asks nothing of us. We are not asked to change the world or our minds, but only to want to shift the purpose of our relationships from special

love to the all-inclusive love our teacher reflects for us. The "little willingness" to forgive—our special function—brings salvation to all of us as one.

(VII.5:1-2) The Holy Spirit has the power to change the whole foundation of the world you see to something else; a basis not insane, on which a sane perception can be based, another world perceived. And one in which nothing is contradicted that would lead the Son of God to sanity and joy.

This is the same shift we saw earlier, which culminates in the world's transformation into the real world. The Holy Spirit's "power" is simply our choosing His purpose, for He has no power in the dream, nor does Jesus or God. Only we have that power, inasmuch as it is our decision maker's dream. Choosing the Holy Spirit as our Teacher helps us change from nightmares of sin, hate, and specialness to happy dreams of forgiveness, healing, and peace. From these it is a small step to the forgiven or real world, which becomes the reflection of Heaven's perfect love and Oneness. While this world is not real, when we look through Jesus' eyes we see nothing that contradicts Heaven's perfection, for illusion cannot alter God's Love. Consequently, non-dualistic truth is expressed in a dualistic world of illusion, the only joy possible while appearing to live in a world of guilt and death.

(VII.5:3–6:3) Nothing attests to death and cruelty; to separation and to differences. For here is everything perceived as one, and no one loses that each one may gain.

Test everything that you believe against this one requirement, and understand that everything that meets this one demand is worthy of your faith. But nothing else. What is not love is sin, and either one perceives the other as insane and meaningless.

The world is perceived as one, for all separated things share a single purpose. Christ's vision leads us beyond appearances (the separation of form) to the Holy Spirit's reality (the content of justice). Recall the uncompromising statement: "What is not love is murder" (T-23.IV.1:10). Love and sin cannot understand each other for they are mutually exclusive states. Jesus wants us to use the above as a guideline for daily living, seeing how quickly we fall into the mentality of *one or the other*: someone has to lose so we get what we want; another must be seen as different so we can be happy. Looking clearly at this madness allows us to choose again, placing faith in truth and not illusion.

(VII.6:4-7) Love is the basis for a world perceived as wholly mad to sinners, who believe theirs is the way to sanity. But sin is equally insane within the sight of love, whose gentle eyes would look beyond the madness and rest peacefully on truth. Each sees a world immutable, as each defines the changeless and eternal truth of what you are. And each reflects a view of what the Father and the Son must be, to make that viewpoint meaningful and sane.

Remember that this is an all-or-nothing course, one or the other in the right-minded sense. What is not love is sin, and love returns to the place that sin has left (T-26.IV). *A Course in Miracles* is asking us to recognize the inherent insanity in a world ruled by perception, which is the shadow of the sinful relationship between Father and Son. Sanity, on the other hand, is found only in Christ's vision. In His eyes, the changeless Identity of God's Son is reflected in the sane perception of interests shared equally among the seemingly separated fragments of the Sonship, uniting them in their common search for the one Father.

(VII.7) Your special function is the special form in which the fact that God is not insane appears most sensible and meaningful to you. The content is the same. The form is suited to your special needs, and to the special time and place in which you think you find yourself, and where you can be free of place and time, and all that you believe must limit you. The Son of God cannot be bound by time nor place nor anything God did not will. Yet if His Will is seen as madness, then the form of sanity which makes it most acceptable to those who are insane requires special choice. Nor can this choice be

made by the insane, whose problem is their choices are not free, and made with reason in the light of sense.

As long as we believe we live in an insane world of form, our experience of truth—God's living content of love—must be mediated through its reflection. We practice learning of God's sanity and perfect Oneness by seeing each of us walking the same pathway home: the wrong mind being gently corrected by the right-minded Teacher, Whose loving sanity we happily choose over the ego's hate-filled madness. Through our special relationships that are rooted in time and space, the Holy Spirit teaches how our non-spatial and atemporal minds have chosen wrongly, and can now choose truth over illusion. Thus specialness becomes a special classroom of forgiveness, and the fear of God's loving Oneness is gradually replaced by the miracle that restores us first to sanity, and then to Sanity Itself.

(VII.8:1-2) It *would* be madness to entrust salvation to the insane. Because He is not mad has God appointed One as sane as He to raise a saner world to meet the sight of everyone who chose insanity as his salvation.

The dualistic language is of course symbolic. God did not "appoint" the Holy Spirit in response to an insane thought system that does not exist. Jesus' purpose is to counter the thought system, *in their own language*, of those who believe that God will punish them as a consequence of their sin. The meaning beyond the symbols is that God's Love is changeless, unaffected by the *tiny, mad idea* of separation. He did not send the Holy Spirit with thunderbolts in His hand to destroy us. Rather, the symbolic story of correction continues, God sent His Voice into the dream because He cares for us. As Jesus is addressing guilty children, he uses their myth of hateful revenge to convey his message of forgiveness for a sin that never happened. Recalling his prior caution, "neither sign nor symbol should be confused with source" (T-19.IV-C.11:2), we need go beyond symbols to their source, words to their meaning.

(VII.8:3-4) To this One is given the choice of form most suitable to him; one which will not attack the world he sees, but enter into it in quietness and show him he is mad. This One but points to an alternative, another way of looking at what he has seen before, and recognizes as the world in which he lives, and thought he understood before.

Just as the Holy Spirit is the Alternative, Jesus wants us to be his alternative in form, demonstrating the peace that comes when we no longer think our needs have to be met at the expense of others. The form in which we learn is determined by us, our special relationships, for the ego speaks first. Once we become truly sickened by the joys and pains of specialness, we turn to the Word of Atonement that says there is another way of looking. The same bodily forms that were mistakes, *not sins*, are changed in purpose by a kind and loving shift of the mind's content, and we look with joy upon the forgiven world through Christ's holy and unified vision.

(VII.9:1) Now must he question this, because the form of the alternative is one which he cannot deny, nor overlook, nor fail completely to perceive at all.

Having come this far in our symphony, we realize there is a wisdom and love in *A Course in Miracles* that is the clear alternative to the hate-driven insanity of our perceptions. But it is helpful to be aware that even though we cannot deny the truth of Jesus' message, a part of us does not want to let the ego go. Our non-judgmental awareness reflects the "little willingness" to be shown the truth, that we may question the illusion.

(VII.9:2) To each his special function is designed to be perceived as possible, and more and more desired, as it proves to him that it is an alternative he really wants.

We have seen that the journey of forgiveness is not something we can complete right away; it is a process that needs to be "more and more desired." As Jesus told us that he knows of our fear, we can proceed at our own pace, without pressuring

ourselves or others to move ahead. I often tell people that Jesus' favorite tempo is *molto adagio e pianissimo e dolcissimo* (very slowly, softly, and sweetly). Since Jesus does not compel us, we should not compel anyone either. As our fear gradually abates over time, we will increasingly want his alternative of love.

(VII.9:3-4) From this position does his sinfulness, and all the sin he sees within the world, offer him less and less. Until he comes to understand it cost him his sanity, and stands between him and whatever hope he has of being sane.

Our motivation to change comes with the realization of the insanity in believing we could benefit from someone else's misfortune, or that we need something from others to complete us and make us happy. We realize, too, that our needs will never be satisfied totally, meaning that whatever fulfillment we experience will need to be continually replenished. How, then, could we ever be at peace, for there will always be the constant tension of needing more love and attention. However, standing beside this insane thinking, based on sin, is the Holy Spirit's loving sanity that offers us a way of living more peacefully and kindly in the dualistic world. He teaches that nothing outside can hurt or help us, for the source of our suffering *and* salvation is within: the decision maker's power to choose.

(VII.9:5-6) Nor is he left without escape from madness, for he has a special part in everyone's escape. He can no more be left outside, without a special function in the hope of peace, than could the Father overlook His Son, and pass him by in careless thoughtlessness.

Whereas the Son's true Self is part of God's living and loving Oneness, his mad dreams of separation and specialness remain but dreams and not reality. And this, the Atonement principle, is his release from all of them, as it is for each of God's fragmented Sons. The right mind contains the reflected truth of Heaven's love, and patiently awaits our corrected decision—sanity over madness—to fulfill its special part in salvation's plan.

(VII.11:1-3) The whole belief that someone loses but reflects the underlying tenet God must be insane. For in this world it seems that one must gain *because* another lost. If this were true, then God is mad indeed!

Jesus is speaking of the biblical God, Whose insane justice promotes the principle of *one or the other* (someone wins, another loses) as the divine punishment for sin. We also find a restatement of the striking line about the world that guilt had wrought: "If this were the real world, God *would* be cruel" (T-13.in.3:1). The good news is that He is not, for the simple reason that the ego's world of separation does not exist because God and His Love cannot change.

(VII.11:4-6) But what is this belief except a form of the more basic tenet, "Sin is real, and rules the world"? For every little gain must someone lose, and pay exact amount in blood and suffering. For otherwise would evil triumph, and destruction be the total cost of any gain at all.

Jesus exposes the underlying justification for the world's insanely vicious rules. People must be killed to prevent them from harming others: "For every little gain must someone lose, and pay exact amount in blood and suffering. For otherwise would evil triumph...." The evil ones are out there, for the world was made that we would see them there and never know the evils of sin we made real within ourselves.

(VII.11:7) You who believe that God is mad, look carefully at this, and understand that it must be either God or this must be insane, but hardly both.

It is the ego's maxim that for one to be sane, another must be insane. If we believe the world's justice of punishment makes sense, then must God be mad and the ego's triumph secure throughout eternity.

(VII.12:1-3) Salvation is rebirth of the idea no one can lose for anyone to gain. And everyone *must* gain, if anyone would be a gainer. Here is sanity restored.

The major theme of this movement is clearly enunciated: *no one loses and everyone gains*. The only sane response for living in this world is to reflect the Oneness of Heaven: we all win as one or we all lose as one. Insanity alone would have us believe that some can actually win when others lose.

(VII.12:4-6) And on this single rock of truth can faith in God's eternal saneness rest in perfect confidence and perfect peace. Reason is satisfied, for all insane beliefs can be corrected here. And sin must be impossible, if this is true.

The insane thought that someone wins and another loses can be corrected only by right-minded reason, not the world's. When that correction takes place, sin becomes impossible as it is based on the idea that the Son wins and the Father loses. This is the origin of the mad belief in sin and the ego's distorted notion of justice, leading to the equally distorted thought of vengeance: we killed God so we could be Him, and now He will return the compliment and wreak His maniacal retribution on us. The terrifying thought of *kill or be killed* is blotted from awareness and then projected, making a world of differences where we act out this battleground with each other, to the death.

(VII.12:7) This is the rock on which salvation rests...

In the New Testament, Jesus told Peter he was the rock on which his (Jesus') church would be built (Matthew 16:18a). In Greek, *Peter* is *cephas*, which means "rock"; hence the word play. In this passage, Jesus says the rock on which salvation and his true church rest is the principle that *no one loses and everyone gains*; we are one and sin does not exist.

(VII.12:7-8) This is the rock on which salvation rests, the vantage point from which the Holy Spirit gives meaning and direction to the plan in which your special function has a part. For here your special function is made whole, because it shares the function of the whole.

The vantage point is above the battleground (T-23.IV). With Jesus' love beside us, we rise above the ego thought system of guilt and attack, and look down on its shadows in the world of bodies. From this, the observing mind, we recognize how insane everything here is, understanding as well that this insanity is the projection of the delusional thought system we share. There can be no hierarchy of madness for we are equally mad, having as one Son participated in the thought that we exist separately from our Source. This required a world to protect this existence, a world in which others are punished instead of us. Despite our identification with the ego, we can recall our special function that while not truly whole—after all, wholeness exists only in Heaven—nevertheless reflects wholeness, for vision in no way contradicts God's Oneness. By seeing only the sameness in God's Sons and not their bodily differences, true perception heals the mind and allows the truth of God's one Son to be remembered.

(VIII.11) As specialness cares not who pays the cost of sin, so it be paid, the Holy Spirit heeds not who looks on innocence at last, provided it is seen and recognized. For just *one* witness is enough, if he sees truly. Simple justice asks no more. Of each one does the Holy Spirit ask if he will be that one, so justice may return to love and there be satisfied. Each special function He allots is but for this; that each one learn that love and justice are not separate. And both are strengthened by their union with each other. Without love is justice prejudiced and weak. And love without justice is impossible. For love is fair, and cannot chasten without cause. What cause can be to warrant an attack upon the innocent? In justice, then, does love correct mistakes, but not in vengeance. For that would be unjust to innocence.

This is the key to all our responses: we come from love, not guilt; justice, not vengeance. Since we are all the same, when we see one person as wholly innocent, we have extended the Love of our Teacher Who loves us all the same. Our special function of forgiveness undoes the special relationship that would exclude, and in that vision we are freed together, for justice, the right-minded response to perceived sin, is returned to love. Our cleansed perception sees sin solely as a call for love, answered by the justice that love gave rise to. No one who embraces Jesus can fail to embrace the world in innocence, as he does, for his all-loving justice can only bless and heal, condemning no one for his innocence.

(VIII.12) You can be perfect witness to the power of love and justice, if you understand it is impossible the Son of God could merit vengeance. You need not perceive, in every circumstance, that this is true. Nor need you look to your experience within the world, which is but shadows of all that is really happening within yourself. The understanding that you need comes not of you, but from a larger Self, so great and holy that He could not doubt His innocence. Your special function is a call to Him, that He may smile on you whose sinlessness He shares. His understanding will be yours. And so the Holy Spirit's special function has been fulfilled. God's Son has found a witness unto his sinlessness and not his sins. How little need you give the Holy Spirit that simple justice may be given you.

We again return to the theme of a "little willingness." The gentleness of Jesus as our teacher is exhibited in his patience in not expecting us to learn his lessons quickly or totally. Fear cannot be undone all at once, for the terror of perfect love looms ever so high in our minds. We are asked only to want to see our brother sinless (T-20.VII.9:2); to choose the principle of *together, or not at all* instead of *one or the other*. This invites divine justice to be reflected in a world where injustice always has the final word. The special function calls forth the wisdom of Christ to lend His innocence to our perception, leading us to bring all God's Sons into its forgiving and healing circle. There, Heaven's sinlessness shines away our sin in the gentle smile that ends the nightmare of guilt, vengeance, and death.

(VIII.14) You have the right to all the universe; to perfect peace, complete deliverance from all effects of sin, and to the life eternal, joyous and complete in every way, as God appointed for His holy Son. This is the only justice Heaven knows, and all the Holy Spirit brings to earth. Your special function shows you nothing else but perfect justice can prevail for you. And you are safe from vengeance in all forms. The world deceives, but it cannot replace God's justice with a version of its own. For only love is just, and can perceive what justice must accord the Son of God. Let love decide, and never fear that you, in your unfairness, will deprive yourself of what God's justice has allotted you.

The last three sentences are our Atonement principle: no matter how unjust we are to God's Son, ourselves or others, we cannot remove the thought of Heaven's justice from our minds. We and all the Sonship deserve the love that is truly ours, even when guilt over nonexistent sin tells us otherwise. Its lies have no effect upon the truth, and God's Love for His Son forever prevails over the vengeance that is the world's demented version of justice.

Our final discussion in this subsection is based on "The Justice of Heaven."

(IX.3) Be certain any answer to a problem the Holy Spirit solves will always be one in which no one loses. And this must be true, because He asks no sacrifice of anyone. An answer which demands the slightest loss to anyone has not resolved the problem, but has added to it and made it greater, harder to resolve and more unfair. It is impossible the Holy Spirit could see unfairness as a resolution. To Him, what is unfair must be corrected *because* it is unfair. And every error is a perception in which one, at least, is seen unfairly. Thus is justice not accorded to the Son of God. When anyone is seen as losing, he has been condemned. And punishment becomes his due instead of justice.

This reiterates the crucial theme of the all-inclusive nature of justice. Central to the Course's correction for the ego, the principle of *together, or*

not at all cannot be stated often enough. Justice as vengeance remains the core of the ego's thought system of specialness, whereby one must be sacrificed to support another's innocence: another's guilt witnesses to our guiltlessness. Such misperception must be brought to the Holy Spirit's right-minded correction, allowing our decision makers to choose again by recognizing the inevitability of perceiving separation in the world once the mind has chosen the teacher of separation: *projection makes perception.* Only when our forgiveness rests on everyone, without exception, can Heaven's justice be truly accepted for ourselves.

(IX.5:1-3) The Holy Spirit's problem solving is the way in which the problem ends. It has been solved because it has been met with justice. Until it has it will recur, because it has not yet been solved.

True justice undoes separation and fear of punishment. The ego's justice, on the other hand, means that in order for one to gain, someone must be sacrificed. The Holy Spirit's justice, reflecting Heaven's Oneness, corrects the ego's injustice through His principle of *no one loses and everyone wins.* Nothing can change here unless we first change our minds. The underlying guilt, born of the belief that we exist through another's suffering, permeates every aspect of our lives, being the mind's thought of sacrifice that is projected into the world as hate and vengeance.

(IX.5:4-6) The principle that justice means no one can lose is crucial to this course. For miracles depend on justice. Not as it is seen through this world's eyes, but as God knows it and as knowledge is reflected in the sight the Holy Spirit gives.

This is the answer to the ego's response to the idea of choosing miracles or murder (T-23.IV.9:8). Mindless murder means someone must forfeit happiness for another to have it, while the mindful miracle teaches that no one suffers and no one loses. We all win and return home together for the just God knows only Oneness, and the Holy Spirit's perception of shared interests reflects Heaven's justice in the world of illusion.

(IX.6:1-3) No one deserves to lose. And what would be unjust to him cannot occur. Healing must be for everyone, because he does not merit an attack of any kind.

No matter what others have done, however heinous their crime or egregious their sin, they deserve forgiveness and not attack. We all equally deserve love, but need to be reminded that whatever viciousness may have been perpetrated resulted from fear, itself a defense against the love we sought to bury. In other words, we are no different from each other except in form. While some may perform their murderous deeds more discretely than others, the differing form does not change the sameness of the mind's underlying content, nor the need for correction. This new understanding reflects the humility that no one is better or worse than another. Choosing to see through Jesus' non-judgmental eyes, we look the same way at villains and saints—historically and personally—which is how we learn we are forgiven, forever loved by our one Father. When we condemn another we affirm that *we* deserve to be condemned as a result of our sin, the self-hate that transforms God's justice into vengeful punishment.

(IX.6:4-9) What order can there be in miracles, unless someone deserves to suffer more and others less? And is this justice to the wholly innocent? A miracle *is* justice. It is not a special gift to some, to be withheld from others as less worthy, more condemned, and thus apart from healing. Who is there who can be separate from salvation, if its purpose is the end of specialness? Where is salvation's justice if some errors are unforgivable, and warrant vengeance in place of healing and return of peace?

No one's sin is beyond forgiveness, for everyone's sin is *everyone's* sin, found in the mind that is shared by the separated Sonship as one. This is why *there is no order of difficulty in miracles*: every problem is the same, each undone by bringing the ego's justice to God's. Our decision for the miracle undoes the error of separate interests, corrected by the Holy Spirit's vision of shared interests and the healing that is shared equally by all.

(IX.7:1-4) Salvation cannot seek to help God's Son be more unfair than he has sought to be. If miracles, the Holy Spirit's gift, were given specially to an elect and special group, and kept apart from others as less deserving, then is He ally to specialness. What He cannot perceive He bears no witness to. And everyone is equally entitled to His gift of healing and deliverance and peace.

"Everyone is equally entitled." This simple phrase undoes the twenty-five hundred years of spiritual specialness that has held such an important place in Western religions. God's Love cannot be divided—the elect and non-elect, special and non-special—and still be His Love; any more than can the Holy Spirit's Atonement—present in equal measure in every Son's split mind—be bestowed on some Sons or groups and not all.

(IX.7:7-8) No one can be unjust to you; unless you have decided first to *be* unjust. And then must problems rise to block your way, and peace be scattered by the winds of hate.

These sentences have great practical import. Whenever we are tempted to be upset by anyone or anything, we need to re-read the above lines. No one can treat us unfairly, hurt or rob us of our peace, *unless we first decided that we were unfair*, that we were better off being separated from God's Love for which another now is to blame. To perpetuate this lie, we embrace the problems that we perceive as destroying our peace, seeing them as the fault of those who cut us off on the highway, push in front of us in line, or outright abuse us. Despite what appear to be the facts that justify our hateful responses, if we think of another as un-Christ-like, it is only because we were unkind in our thoughts. Recall: "If he speaks not of Christ to you, you spoke not of Christ to him" (T-11.V.18:6). We continually strive to have others be villains so our mind's decision to be unjust to God and the Sonship will be hidden, protected by projection from our ever choosing the Holy Spirit's correction.

(IX.8:1) Unless you think that all your brothers have an equal right to miracles with you, you will not claim your right to them because you were unjust to one with equal rights.

The one to whom we are unjust has equal rights, as do all people—God's Son is one. Depriving one member of the Sonship his rights to the Holy Spirit's gift of healing and peace deprives all of them, including ourselves.

(IX.8:2-6) Seek to deny and you will feel denied. Seek to deprive, and you have been deprived. A miracle can never be received because another could receive it not. Only forgiveness offers miracles. And pardon must be just to everyone.

If we choose to push Jesus' love away, we will perforce project our guilt, reminiscent of the original decision to exclude God and His Son. We claim that the reason we lack peace is that others deprived us of it. "Seek to deny and you will feel denied"—the experience of lack or scarcity inevitably leads to the belief in deprivation, which in turn justifies our attacking others to get what we believe is ours. Yet "a miracle can never be received because another could receive it not"; we cannot live at someone else's expense and hope to find peace.

(IX.9:1-4) The little problems that you keep and hide become your secret sins, because you did not choose to let them be removed for you. And so they gather dust and grow, until they cover everything that you perceive and leave you fair to no one. Not one right do you believe you have. And bitterness, with vengeance justified and mercy lost, condemns you as unworthy of forgiveness.

Guilt, retained through repression, is inevitably projected. This double shield (W-pI.136.5:2) of guilt and projection protects our secret sins so that they "gather dust and grow." As what we project we see all around us (*projection makes perception*), we cannot but attack and condemn the world outside, as we have attacked and condemned the world inside (*ideas leave not their source*). To undo this insanity, Jesus asks us to look with him at what our projections have kept hidden. He does not ask that

we be without our madness, but simply that we not withhold it from him. Recall his earlier words: "The necessary condition for the holy instant does not require that you have no thoughts that are not pure. But it does require that you have none that you would keep" (T-15.IV.9:1-2). Opening our eyes to the ego's lies, with Jesus' love beside us, expresses the miracle that returns justice to God's separated Son and blesses him with the forgiveness that is his right as Heaven's creation.

(IX.9:5-6) The unforgiven have no mercy to bestow upon another. That is why your sole responsibility must be to take forgiveness for yourself.

This familiar theme is stated over and over. We need only accept forgiveness (or Atonement) for ourselves, which means accepting Jesus' way of looking at the world: no one loses and everyone wins, correcting the ego's principle that one must be sacrificed in order for another to gain. Once accepted, forgiveness is free to extend throughout the Sonship, embracing all people in the mercy that reflects Heaven's blessings of love.

(IX.10) The miracle that you receive, you give. Each one becomes an illustration of the law on which salvation rests; that justice must be done to all, if anyone is to be healed. No one can lose, and everyone must benefit. Each miracle is an example of what justice can accomplish when it is offered to everyone alike. It is received and given equally. It is awareness that giving and receiving are the same. Because it does not make the same unlike, it sees no differences where none exists. And thus it is the same for everyone, because it sees no differences in them. Its offering is universal, and it teaches but one message:

> *What is God's belongs to everyone, and is his due.*

What belongs to everyone is not Heaven's "justice" of punishment or death, but the eternal Love of our Creator. This movement's theme reverberates throughout the Course's symphonic pages, even when we forget it in our fear. It is vital that we think of it when tempted to see people as different, recognizing that behind all perceptions of differences—meaning that the superficial differences that keep us separate from each other are deserving of judgment—is *the* difference that is the core of specialness: one is sinful, the other sinless. As our awareness becomes total, these perceptions shift and change until we joyfully find ourselves in the real world, *with everyone*. We are brought there by the miracle's healing love that reflects the innocence of God's Son, his unity preserved by Heaven's justice: What is God's belongs to *everyone*, and is his due.

Closing

We conclude our discussion with a lovely excerpt from "The Light You Bring."

(IV.3:1) You maker of a world that is not so, take rest and comfort in another world where peace abides.

Jesus is referring to the real world, where everyone wins and no one loses, where nothing happened to disturb the perfect love and peace of Heaven. This happily corrects the ego's world of specialness and pain.

(IV.3:2-4) This world you bring with you to all the weary eyes and tired hearts that look on sin and beat its sad refrain. From you can come their rest. From you can rise a world they will rejoice to look upon, and where their hearts are glad.

Jesus speaks of our being the same loving presence in the dream that he is, the gentle harbinger of the real world. Thus do we bring rest to the world's weariness that permeates the mind of God's guilt-laden Son and caused him pain. Our defenselessness is the means whereby he learns that nothing happened except in dreams of sin, and these had no effect on the reality of God's sinless creation: "… not one note in Heaven's song was missed" (T-26.V.5:4).

(IV.3:5-7) In you there is a vision that extends to all of them, and covers them in gentleness and light. And in this widening world of light the darkness that they thought was there is pushed away, until it is but distant shadows, far away, not long to be remembered as the sun shines them to nothingness. And all their "evil" thoughts and "sinful" hopes, their dreams of guilt and merciless revenge, and every wish to hurt and kill and die, will disappear before the sun you bring.

The world of cherished sin still needs to accept "the sun [we] bring," but having accepted its light for ourselves we offer the world this alternate way of living: Horrific things will literally disappear from perception as we accept our function of Atonement, in the sense that they will no longer affect our peace. Our eyes may see suffering and death, our ears hear stories of hurt and pain, but the vengeful burden of projected guilt will have been lifted, leaving only the soft light of forgiveness to bless the world that is newly born in love, joy, and hope.

(IV.4) Would you not do this for the Love of God? And for *yourself?* For think what it would do for you. Your "evil" thoughts that haunt you now will seem increasingly remote and far away from you. And they go farther and farther off, because the sun in you has risen that they may be pushed away before the light. They linger for a while, a little while, in twisted forms too far away for recognition, and are gone forever. And in the sunlight you will stand in quiet, in innocence and wholly unafraid. And from you will the rest you found extend, so that your peace can never fall away and leave you homeless. Those who offer peace to everyone have found a home in Heaven the world cannot destroy. For it is large enough to hold the world within its peace.

There is our answer. If we truly want peace, we must offer it to everyone, withholding it from no one. This is not a positive offering, but the simple removal of the negative interferences—guilt and specialness—that impeded the flow of peace throughout the Sonship. By accepting the function of forgiveness for ourselves, we do so for all. And true justice can come in peace to claim its own: God's Son as He created him. We should note that Jesus again describes this as a process ("they go farther and farther off," etc.), indicating that we are not expected to let go of the ego completely, all at once. Fear dictates that forgiveness be merciful and slow, keeping gentle pace with our gradually diminishing resistance. Of such kindness is born the Kingdom of Heaven on earth.

Now this beautiful closing:

(IV.5) In you is all of Heaven. Every leaf that falls is given life in you. Each bird that ever sang will sing again in you. And every flower that ever bloomed has saved its perfume and its loveliness for you. What aim can supersede the Will of God and of His Son, that Heaven be restored to him for whom it was created as his only home? Nothing before and nothing after it. No other place; no other state nor time. Nothing beyond nor nearer. Nothing else. In any form. This can you bring to all the world, and all the thoughts that entered it and were mistaken for a little while. How better could your own mistakes be brought to truth than by your willingness to bring the light of Heaven with you, as you walk beyond the world of darkness into light?

To make this loveliness possible, all we need is the "little willingness" that says to Jesus: "Please help me see that I am wrong, that my looking at this person as my enemy is illusion." His loving response is our and the world's comfort: "Do not worry about saving the world. Do not concern yourself with being its light. Simply allow my gentle love to shine into your mind by relinquishing your hold on guilt, and then God's justice will illuminate His one Son who thought he walked in darkness, alone. Now is he redeemed. Now has the light dawned on his perturbed mind. Now does he return at last to his home in Heaven's love."

Chapter 26

THE TRANSITION

Introduction

There are several noteworthy aspects of Chapter 26 to mention before we begin. First, it contains two very beautiful sections, "Where Sin has Left" and "For They Have Come," whose beauty is manifest not only in the language but in their message. We have already observed that as we continue toward the magnificent close of our symphony, the writing becomes increasingly more poetic. Indeed, much of what we read now is Shakespearean in its use of iambic pentameter and blank verse, leaving us with an inspiring blend of form and content where the loveliness of the language mirrors the power of the teaching. Another section, "The Laws of Healing," uniquely summarizes the theory of *A Course in Miracles* with Jesus saying to us, in effect: "Before we go any further, let me summarize everything I have taught you so far."

We also find clear enunciation of the Course's formula for salvation: seeing the face of Christ in our brothers and remembering God. Seeing Christ's face, as we have seen, is looking upon the innocence in others instead of the guilt we have projected onto them. This undoes the ego thought system entirely, allowing the memory of God to surface in awareness. The formula is sublimely articulated in "For They Have Come."

Finally, what is unusual in this chapter is that in five separate passages the Course speaks about itself, what it teaches and what it does not. We begin by looking at these statements that summarize the purpose of *A Course in Miracles* in its own words.

A Course in Miracles Speaking about Itself

We begin with the Oneness of Heaven:

(III.1:13-14) Yet is this magnitude [the oneness of our reality] **beyond the scope of this curriculum. Nor is it necessary we dwell on anything that cannot be immediately grasped.**

Jesus is letting us know still once again that his course is not about love. As he states in the introduction to the text, *A Course in Miracles* does not aim at teaching the meaning of love (reality and oneness) because that is beyond what can be taught (T-in.1:6-7). Nonetheless, we can be taught how to remove the interferences to remembering the love that we both *have* and *are*. This, then, becomes the Course's purpose, which it achieves through our learning to forgive the special relationships that constitute these blocks.

(III.5) Salvation stops just short of Heaven, for only perception needs salvation. Heaven was never lost, and so cannot be saved. Yet who can make a choice between the wish for Heaven and the wish for hell unless he recognizes they are not the same? This difference is the learning goal this course has set. It will not go beyond this aim. Its only purpose is to teach what is the same and what is different, leaving room to make the only choice that can be made.

The above is another statement of the Atonement. Nothing has happened except we think something has. Heaven has not been lost, for we have merely gone to sleep, with a veil of amnesia having fallen across our minds to conceal the truth of the Holy Spirit's healing Thought. Salvation is certainly not needed for Christ, Who remains outside the ego's dreams of separation, but only for the split mind to change its decision to be different from its Creator.

We have often seen the theme of discernment, which will be articulated throughout this chapter as well as those to come. We may characterize the Course's purpose as helping us discern the difference between the thought system of God, reflected in the right-minded Atonement, and that of the ego. The latter, needless to say, has us confuse the two. When the ego speaks of God, as formal religions do, it is really speaking of hell because it refers to a dualistic deity that is outside perfect Oneness. In other words, this God is the projected state of the split mind: the condition of separation where the Creator is merely an image of the ego thought system. This is why *A Course in Miracles* teaches us how to differentiate between Heaven and the ego. We learn that we, God's separated Sons, are the same—as Christ *and* in the dream, there being only one One Mind and one split mind. The seeming differences within the dream are nothing more than the single illusion of separation. Our recognizing the clear distinction between truth and illusion, oneness and separation, sameness and differences, *is* salvation.

(V.1:1-4) A little hindrance [the title of this section] **can seem large indeed to those who do not understand that miracles are all the same. Yet teaching that is what this course is for. This is its only purpose, for only that is all there is to learn. And you can learn it in many different ways.**

This is our very familiar first principle of miracles: *there is no order of difficulty among them.* Miracles are the same, because the correction—the nature of the miracle—is the same: one problem (the belief the ego's lies are true) and one solution (the Holy Spirit's truth of Atonement). *A Course in Miracles* teaches us what is the same and what is different. While illusions appear to be distinct from each other, they are identical in content and thus different from the truth. Consequently, correction is always the same. When the miracle undoes our illusions by exposing their lies, we remember the oneness of God's Son in Heaven, inherently different from the ego's son in hell.

We see again how the first miracle principle runs through our symphony as a leitmotif, permeating every movement. If we had truly understood this principle at the beginning we would not have needed the Course at all, which tells us that the Atonement is true, and the special forms taken by the ego's nothingness remain nothing. Our insane belief to the contrary (nothing is really something) requires a single correction: the miracle's teaching that all special relationships are the same, only seeming to manifest the differences that are the ego's foundation. We learn the lesson through each relationship and situation until we are able to generalize to all of them, recognizing that everything here is equally illusory, as form symbolizes the one error of the mind's choosing the ego over the Holy Spirit.

(VII.1:1-2) This is a course in miracles. As such, the laws of healing must be understood before the purpose of the course can be accomplished.

Given the Course's purpose of teaching that all problems and miracles are the same, it follows that all healing must be the same as well. Not only is there *no order of difficulty in miracles*, but none in healing because every perceived problem or symptom comes from the mind's belief in separation, corrected by the one miracle. This must be accepted before the ego's thought system of specialness and differences can be healed and undone.

(V.10:1-3) Would God allow His Son to lose his way along a road long since a memory of time gone by? This course will teach you only what is now. A dreadful instant in a distant past, now perfectly corrected, is of no concern nor value.

This refers to the holy instant, a central theme in the Holy Spirit's thought system. It recognizes there is no past: sin never existed and does not exist now. How then could there be a *fearful future*, which would simply be the projection of a *sinful past* that we believe in the *guilty present* deserves punishment? Jesus is instructing us that the ego is an illusion, which is why, again, *there is no order of difficulty in miracles*. Nothing exists to correct except the mind's one mistaken choice, so easily undone. Healing is the happy acceptance of that happy fact.

The Atonement Principle

We continue our symphonic movement with the Atonement principle's simple statement that the ego and its thought system of separation is illusory. This is the basis for there being *no order of difficulty in miracles*. The only problem that needs correction is the belief there is a problem that needs correction. It does not matter what form problems seem to take, or however varied our experience of differing upsets, they are all the same. Each expresses the need to prove that the ego's thought system of an individual self (the person with whom we identify) is real, and Christ (our true Identity as spirit) is an illusion. It is our need to defend this special self that gave rise to the physical universe, along with the bodily pleasures and pains that define our physical existence.

(I.6:1-2) You can lose sight of oneness, but can not make sacrifice of its reality. Nor can you lose what you would sacrifice, nor keep the Holy Spirit from His task of showing you that it has not been lost.

The ego tells us that because of the *tiny, mad idea* that we could be separate from our Source, we have lost Heaven's love and shattered the unity of Father and Son. The Atonement says that although we can lose sight of this Oneness and forget it ever existed, it is not gone. Its reality is always with us through the Holy Spirit's Presence, and it is this thought the ego attacks and defends against through its special relationships, trying to prove that the Wholeness of Christ is forever irretrievable.

(III.1:1-2) Complexity is not of God. How could it be, when all He knows is one?

We can see in this paragraph how often the words *one* or *oneness* appear, Heaven's principal characteristic. The ego fears our choosing the Teacher of oneness, as that is a choice against its fragmentation—our separated and special identity—and for the remembering of Christ that marks the ego's end. It desperately tries to show how different we are from each other, and makes a complicated world to witness to this "fact." Yet the true fact remains that there are no differences in Heaven's perfect Oneness, a state totally unaffected by our insane dreams of guilt and hate.

(III.1:3) He knows of one creation, one reality, one truth and but one Son.

The clear implication is that God does not know anything other than *one*, such as separation and differences. Could Perfection Itself know about an imperfect world of individuals, let alone the insane thought system that made it? He knows only His Self of perfect Oneness—"one creation, one reality, one truth, and but one Son."

(III.1:4) Nothing conflicts with oneness.

This is what drives the ego into terror, and us who believe in it. The ego itself is a thought of conflict with oneness; a battleground that is the birthplace of sin and death. In point of fact, specialness *is* in mortal combat with God, in ongoing conflict with His Oneness. It goes without saying, this is purely one-sided because God knows nothing of this madness, a truth that is the origin of all fear: if God cannot recognize the ego, He cannot acknowledge the separated self that is the hero of our dreams of specialness. After all, what is not reality does not exist, and the ego meets this fact with nothing other than a thought system of such complexity that the simple truth of *being* is concealed:

(III.1:5-6) How, then, could there be complexity in Him? What is there to decide?

Jesus has told us that "complexity is of the ego" (T-15.IV.6:2). We live in a complex world that is the projection of a complex thought system, and it is essential we recognize how complicated we have made our lives by making up problems designed to cloud awareness of the simple truth of Who we are. Indeed, the thought system of God is simplicity itself: He is One, and there is nothing else but Him and His creation; hence nothing to choose between.

(III.1:7) For it is conflict that makes choice possible.

Do we choose the ego or God, crucifixion or resurrection, attack or forgiveness? These are meaningful choices only within the dream of conflict, for they have nothing to do with reality in which conflict and choice do not exist.

(III.1:8-9) The truth is simple; it is one, without an opposite. And how could strife enter in its simple presence, and bring complexity where oneness is?

This is the Atonement, whereby the Holy Spirit says to us: "Why are you upset? Nothing happened. You are not in battle with God and He is not at war with you." In this statement, salvation's simplicity (T-31.I), our Self is preserved, unchanged by the war against oneness in which complexity seeks to triumph over the simple truth of God.

(III.1:10-12) The truth makes no decisions, for there is nothing to decide *between*. And only if there were could choosing be a necessary step in the advance toward oneness. What is everything leaves room for nothing else.

This is what ultimately makes living in the world so easy. When we realize there is nothing here, then we also realize there is nothing to choose between. When we make the final decision to choose the Holy Spirit over the ego, life becomes incredibly simple. Our having become the reflection of God's Love, there is nothing to choose between. We recognize that no choice here is meaningful, except the one that is not in the world at all: the *mind's* decision for Atonement that is reflected in the statement that God is everything—wholeness and totality. As nothing can be outside His Oneness, the world witnesses to a state of mind that does not exist.

(VII.11:1-5) What is the Will of God? He wills His Son have everything. And this He guaranteed when He created him *as* everything. It is impossible that anything be lost, if what you *have* is what you *are*. This is the miracle by which creation became your function, sharing it with God.

Think back to "The Lessons of the Holy Spirit" in Chapter 6 that equated *having* and *being* (T-6.V-B): we *have* the Love of God because we *are* the Love of God. Our earthly function of forgiveness, equated with the miracle, recalls to us our function in Heaven, which is to create as does our Creator.

(VII.11:6) It is not understood apart from Him, and therefore has no meaning in this world.

Creation is the act of spirit extending itself, without leaving its Source. It is a way of expressing love's non-dualistic nature. Because creation does not occur over time or space, it cannot be known in a world in which there is no referent or context for non-duality.

(VII.11:7-9) Here does the Son of God ask not too much, but far too little. He would sacrifice his own identity with everything, to find a little treasure of his own. And this he cannot do without a sense of isolation, loss and loneliness.

Asking for the little crumbs of specialness we need to satisfy ourselves, cannibalizing others to sustain the ego's constant cravings, we ask for far too little. Specialness, along with everything in the world, is nothing. From the beginning, and continuing throughout time, God's Voice has told us we are sacrificing the everything we are to embrace a self of literal nothingness. This is the special self we defend by making a body and world in which to hide, and our sense of alienation and depression has its origin in sacrificing our Identity, in its place embracing the false self that we literally defend to the death. Insanely, we steadfastly choose not to heed the Holy Spirit's warning because we adore the special gifts that are our personal treasure.

(VII.11:10-14) This is the treasure he has sought to find. And he could only be afraid of it. Is fear a treasure? Can uncertainty be what you want? Or is it a mistake about your will, and what you really are?

Jesus helps us understand how seeking and finding the treasure of a special self is the birthplace of fear. The ego told us we acquired this self by sinfully destroying God and crucifying His

Son, placing ourselves on creation's throne. Fear is the inevitable consequence of believing in sin, for it demands our punishment. However, despite the belief in the seeming power of this thought system, it remains a simple mistake about who we are, *a tiny, mad idea* that is easily corrected by a simple change of mind.

The following cites our oft-discussed theme of *ideas leave not their source*. We are an Idea in the Mind of God, our Source; as Effect of His Cause, we have never left His holy Will:

(VII.13:1-2) Cause and effect are one, not separate. God wills you learn what always has been true: that He created you as part of Him, and this must still be true because ideas leave not their source.

This is the Atonement, the response to our choice for the ego, saying: "What is all this about separation? *Ideas leave not their source.* You have not left your Source; the *tiny, mad idea* of separation never occurred." Nevertheless, we are hellbent (literally!) on proving it did, and the separated self that is housed in a body seems to be the proof that ideas have in fact left their source, turning the Holy Spirit into a deceiver and the ego into God.

(VII.13:3-6) Such is creation's law; that each idea the mind conceives but adds to its abundance, never takes away. This is as true of what is idly wished as what is truly willed, because the mind can wish to be deceived, but cannot make it be what it is not. And to believe ideas can leave their source is to invite illusions to be true, without success. For never will success be possible in trying to deceive the Son of God.

In the original moment when we chose illusion over truth, the Holy Spirit told us that while we can believe what we wish, and deceive ourselves into believing we accomplished the impossible, we cannot make deception real or truly go against God's Will. This "simple statement of a simple fact" (see below T-26.III.4:5) is the source of our rejecting Jesus, not to mention hating his course. Its truth denies our special identity, a truth we refuse to accept for it means the end of our individual self.

We also see here the return of the theme of the ego's *wishing* and spirit's *willing*. But one is true, and what we choose to identify with, *wish* or *will*, becomes reality in the mind as well as in the world we perceive: *projection makes perception*. Still, what we think is outside never leaves the mind (*ideas leave not their source*), for separation and Atonement remain within, awaiting our decision.

(VII.15:6) If you believe what is the same is different you but deceive yourself.

We are the same as God—one Self, one Love, one Will—yet we insist we are different by claiming that effects *do* leave their cause. The universe of bodies is a paean to the seeming reality of differences. We praise the world's complexity and worship its differentiations: "How wonderful to be unique!" This reflects the ego's original cry of triumph: "I exist at last, different from God and outside His Heaven!" But in all this madness the Holy Spirit gently shakes His head, saying simply to our deluded minds: "My brothers, what you believe is not the truth."

(VII.15:7-8) What God calls one will be forever one, not separate. His Kingdom is united; thus it was created, and thus will it ever be.

As we will soon see, "not one note in Heaven's song was missed" (T-26.V.5:4), reality has not changed. The ego, though, would have us believe that Heaven's unity has been disrupted by the change in God's now-separated Son.

(V.6:6-10) And who can stand upon a distant shore, and dream himself across an ocean, to a place and time that have long since gone by? How real a hindrance can this dream be to where he really is? For this is fact, and does not change whatever dreams he has. Yet can he still imagine he is elsewhere, and in another time. In the extreme, he can delude himself that this is true, and pass from mere imagining into belief and into madness, quite convinced that where he would prefer to be, he *is*.

We have fallen asleep, dreaming we are in the ego's hell and not God's Heaven. Penetrating our defenses, however, Jesus softly speaks to us: "My child, you are free to believe whatever you choose, but that freedom cannot make illusion real. You dream you are on a distant shore in the world of bodies, but that does not mean you are there. Your feverish thoughts and frantic wishes have no effect upon Where you truly are. Take my hand and come home." And to his loving and comforting voice, we gratefully answer "I will."

What follows is our symphonic movement's final statement of the Atonement principle. It is Jesus' attempt to warn us against our impending choice for the ego, his ongoing caution not to choose against our Friend for it will have unhappy consequences; not in reality, but in our experiences within the friendless dreams of time and space:

(VI.2) Lead not your little life in solitude, with one illusion as your only friend. This is no friendship worthy of God's Son, nor one with which he could remain content. Yet God has given him a better Friend, in Whom all power in earth and Heaven rests. The one illusion that you think is friend obscures His grace and majesty from you, and keeps His friendship and forgiveness from your welcoming embrace. Without Him you are friendless. Seek not another friend to take His place. There *is* no other friend. What God appointed has no substitute, for what illusion can replace the truth?

When we choose the ego, we obscure the Holy Spirit's grace-filled majesty and prevent ourselves from embracing His forgiving friendship. The choice for the ego is continually reflected in our choosing special friends: the special needs that demand addictions to special persons and objects to be craved, coveted, and cherished. This leaves us truly friendless for specialness excludes our one true Friend.

(VI.3) Who dwells with shadows is alone indeed, and loneliness is not the Will of God. Would you allow one shadow to usurp the throne that God appointed for your Friend, if you but realized its emptiness has left yours empty and unoccupied? Make no illusion friend, for if you do, it can but take the place of Him Whom God has called your Friend. And it is He Who is your only Friend in truth. He brings you gifts that are not of this world, and only He to Whom they have been given can make sure that you receive them. He will place them on your throne, when you make room for Him on His.

The experience of loneliness originates in the belief we are separated from our Source. Loneliness does not exist in Heaven, but there is the utter aloneness of self-creation. *A Course in Miracles* helps us give back to God His place on creation's throne, and restores the Holy Spirit to His rightful place in the mind as our Friend. His is the only Presence we need in the dream, because only He can lead us home by teaching us to choose again. This is the reason Jesus beseeches us to ask the Holy Spirit to be our Teacher, even while we seek to push Him and His gift of forgiveness away by bringing Him into the dream as another worshipped idol of the ego's gift of specialness.

For the purpose of counteracting the mind's ability to choose this Friend and His Atonement, the ego embarks on the strategy we have seen throughout our symphony: fleeing the mind, making up a world and body where we think we can live in secrecy from God, and then using other bodies as scapegoats onto which we place our guilt so that it is seen in them and not us. This is our segue to the ego's fear of Atonement and its strategy of defense.

The Ego's Fear of the Atonement

The ego's principal weapon in its war against our decision-making power is its myth of sin, guilt, and fear, which convinces us that the mind is a terrible place to be, and remaining there means certain destruction. Believing the ego's lies, we voluntarily choose to leave the mind, projecting our sin and guilt onto the world of bodies and forgetting we even have a mind, the goal of the ego's strategy. This prevents us from dropping the ego as our friend and accepting the Holy Spirit, Who would help us leave the dream by changing our minds, deciding against the ego's thought system of specialness. We start with the belief in sin:

(VII.12:2-3) Sin is belief attack can be projected outside the mind where the belief arose. Here is the firm conviction that ideas can leave their source made real and meaningful.

The first attack occurred in our minds, where we believe we attacked God. The ego labels this as sin, which we project and perceive in others and not ourselves. This leads to "the firm conviction that ideas can leave their source," made real by the belief that we, God's Son, have left *our* Source. The ego makes this magical thought witness to the separation, using it to affirm that the idea of sin can leave its source in the mind and rest in someone else.

(VII.12:4-5) And from this error does the world of sin and sacrifice arise. This world is an attempt to prove your innocence, while cherishing attack.

This, then, is the world's purpose: we retain our separate, sinful identity, but give the sin to others. Predicated on the ego's idea of *one or the other*, they have the sin and we are sin-less. The world therefore affirms our innocence by causing others to sacrifice theirs, the attack that re-enacts the original attack when we believed we could deprive God of his Innocence and make it our own.

(VII.12:6-8) Its failure lies in that you still feel guilty, though without understanding why. Effects are seen as separate from their source, and seem to be beyond you to control or to prevent. What is thus kept apart can never join.

In truth, the ego's strategy does not work, but we do not know why. Guilt remains in the mind and continually generates sadness and pain, but our mindless state prevents recognizing their source. Referring to the chart (see Appendix), the bottom portion is the world of bodies, the state of mindlessness, which is where the ego wants our attention directed. We experience the effects of the mind's decision for guilt, but unknowing of their cause we can never undo it.

(VII.8:7-8) Sins are beliefs that you impose between your brother and yourself. They limit you to time and place, and give a little space to you, another little space to him.

Once we project guilt from our minds, others become different from us: they have the sin and we are without it. By making us different bodies, the ego puts a gap between ourselves and our brothers. This space of sin, secretly believed to be our own, solidifies the mind's belief in the original gap between an angry God and His guilty Son.

(VII.8:9-10) This separating off is symbolized, in your perception, by a body which is clearly separate and a thing apart. Yet what this symbol represents is but your wish to *be* apart and separate.

By seeing others as separate, we also insist we are different. This reflects the mind's secret wish that we be separate and different from God, which is the source of our belief in sin. The ego tells us we can detach the sin from our individual identity and give it to others—ideas *do* leave their source—paralleling the *tiny, mad idea* that God's Son has left his Heavenly Source. The world, our birth as bodies, and our very existence are all attempts to prove the separation is real, the special sin for which someone else is responsible and will be punished in our stead.

We turn now to the last section of this chapter, "The End of Injustice." This is a continuation of what we read in Chapter 25 about *injustice*, the Course's term that describes the ego's view of the world as unjust, a world in which evil and sinful people are vicious and cruel to others. This injustice must then be brought to the ego's justice, which we insist on so we may avoid the just and punitive deserts of our sinfulness.

(X.1:2-4) ...you have a differential view of when attack is justified, and when you think it is

unfair and not to be allowed. When you perceive it as unfair, you think that a response of anger now is just. And thus you see what is the same as different.

To have a differential view of attack means I can be justified in attacking you, because I do so in self-defense. Your attack on me, however, is unjustified, because of my nascent innocence. All this, of course, has only to do with my perceptions, not necessarily your behavior. It is my *need* to perceive you as the aggressor—that my guilt may rest on you—that is the real issue. Every government that launches an attack does so under the guise of self-defense, which sanctions its aggression but no one else's. This is another way of delineating the clear differences between sin and innocence the ego establishes to cloak our inherent sameness as minds.

As we saw previously, the purpose of *A Course in Miracles* is to help us distinguish what is the same from what is different. Juxtaposed with the Holy Spirit's, the ego's thought system is demonstrably different. But all things within the system itself (the chart's wrong-minded box), and the world of bodies that arose from it, are the same because they serve the same purpose. We differ on the level of form, but the content is one for we share the common goal of preserving our separate identities at the expense of another, continually seeking to blame this person for our wrong-minded sin. Our right minds are the same as well, for they share the single purpose of forgiveness.

(X.1:5-11) Confusion is not limited. If it occurs at all it will be total. And its presence, in whatever form, will hide Their Presence. They are known with clarity or not at all. Confused perception will block knowledge. It is not a question of the size of the confusion, or how much it interferes. Its simple presence shuts the door to Theirs, and keeps Them there unknown.

The confusion of truth and illusion leads to our not recognizing that there are no hierarchies within illusions. Being nothing, illusions are all the same; they either exist or they do not. This is an all-or-nothing course. To believe in one illusion denies the absolute nature of truth. Separation and oneness are mutually exclusive states, as are the ego and God. To accept the truth of one denies the reality of the other. This important point continues:

(X.2:1-5) What does it mean if you perceive attack in certain forms to be unfair to you? It means that there must be some forms in which you think it fair. For otherwise, how could some be evaluated as unfair? Some, then, are given meaning and perceived as sensible. And only some are seen as meaningless.

What is truly fair reflects Heaven's all-inclusive love in there being no exceptions to our forgiveness. No one can ever treat us unfairly, nor can we ever be treated fairly. How could we be, since no one is outside our minds to do so? All we ever judge is a projection of the judgment of ourselves: are we Sons of Love or sons of guilt? This means that only we can be unfair to ourselves (choosing the ego) or fair to ourselves (choosing the Holy Spirit). That thought alone has meaning within the ego's meaningless world. Jesus continues with the ego's "differential view of when attack is justified"—my attack is justified but not yours:

(X.2:6-7) And this denies the fact that *all* are senseless, equally without a cause or consequence, and cannot have effects of any kind. Their Presence is obscured by any veil that stands between Their shining innocence, and your awareness that it is your own and equally belongs to every living thing along with you.

The veils of the ego thought system and its world obscure the Presence of God and Christ in our right minds. The ego's attacks may have manifest effects within the dream, but they cannot affect our shared reality as spirit. In the end, these attacks will not be able to obscure the mind's power to choose Their Presence by releasing the ego and choosing Jesus as our friend. In this way we remember for all God's Sons that our Identity is Christ, Who never left His Creator and Source.

(X.2:8-10) God limits not. And what is limited cannot be Heaven. So it must be hell.

We know this world is hell because everything here is limited, in contrast to Heaven's limitlessness.

(X.3:1) Unfairness and attack are one mistake, so firmly joined that where one is perceived the other must be seen.

I must see you as behaving unjustly because I want to see you as the sinner. This makes my counterattack in self-defense fair, behind which is God's rightful attack on you so I will escape His punishment. In order for this insane plan of fooling God to work, I need sinful bodies. This is why we made a world that provides an abundance of evildoers, at whose guilty heads we point an accusing finger that focuses God's vengeance in the right place: *them.* How else to explain the plethora of wrath-of-God passages in Old and New Testaments alike? We need enemies, heretics, and sinners—a multitudinous number of individuals and groups—whom the Creator can destroy. Clearly, then, others being unfair to us and our seeming justification to attack in return are one and the same mistake.

(X.3:2) You cannot be unfairly treated. The belief you are is but another form of the idea you are deprived by someone not yourself.

What is omitted here is that we *can* be unfairly treated, but only by ourselves when we choose the injustice of believing we are separate from our Source. That is the ultimate unfairness, not what others have done to us. If we lack the peace of God, if we do not feel His Love within us, it is not because of the world's depriving us of love by abuse, attack, or betrayal, but because of our self-accusations (guilt) over betraying the Father's Love.

(X.3:4-5) Projection of the cause of sacrifice is at the root of everything perceived to be unfair and not your just deserts. Yet it is you who ask this of yourself, in deep injustice to the Son of God.

The cause of sacrifice—losing our awareness of the Oneness of Christ—is our own decision-making, not anyone else's. Despite our magical projections, only we can be unjust to ourselves for mind is

everything. This is elaborated on in one of *A Course in Miracles'* more well-known statements:

(X.4:1-3) Beware of the temptation to perceive yourself unfairly treated. In this view, you seek to find an innocence that is not Theirs but yours alone, and at the cost of someone else's guilt. Can innocence be purchased by the giving of your guilt to someone else?

The above provides another statement of our ego's purpose in being here: proving our innocence at another's expense. All we need understand is that the world represents the temptation to perceive ourselves unfairly treated, demonstrating our sinlessness for all to see. Yet this is not the innocence of God or Christ as it does not include everyone. Moreover, we have seen many times before that projection does not work. The idea of guilt can never leave its source in the mind, remaining there to fester in its own putrefaction until its foulness is projected once again.

(X.4:4-8) And *is* it innocence that your attack on him attempts to get? Is it not retribution for your own attack upon the Son of God you seek? Is it not safer to believe that you are innocent of this, and victimized despite your innocence? Whatever way the game of guilt is played, there must be loss. Someone must lose his innocence that someone else can take it from him, making it his own.

The ego disagrees. It is much safer, it says, to believe we are innocent of the sin of murdering God and crucifying Christ, having someone else pay the price of our sin. This leads us to perceive ourselves unfairly treated. Again, the world witnesses to the seeming truth of *one or the other,* innocence or guilt. Needless to say, the ego's innocence that is purchased through attack merely reinforces the mind's belief in its own guilt—the infamous guilt-attack cycle.

(X.5:1-3) You think your brother is unfair to you because you think that one must be unfair to make the other innocent. And in this game do you perceive one purpose for your whole

relationship. And this you seek to add unto the purpose given it.

The purpose given our relationship is forgiveness, provided by the Holy Spirit in our minds. His loving Presence notwithstanding, we have substituted our own purpose for His Atonement, seeing others as guilty by accusing them so we will be innocent: the ego's counsel of someone losing that we may gain.

(X.5:7-8) And each unfairness that the world appears to lay upon you, you have laid on it by rendering it purposeless, without the function that the Holy Spirit sees. And simple justice has been thus denied to every living thing upon the earth.

The Holy Spirit's "simple justice" is based on the inherent sameness (in illusion) and oneness (in truth) of God's Son. This is denied when we choose the teacher of separation, whose guidance is to project our sin and keep us separate from all living things and apart from our Source—*one or the other* instead of *together, or not at all.*

(X.6:1-3) What this injustice does to you who judge unfairly, and who see as you have judged, you cannot calculate. The world grows dim and threatening, not a trace of all the happy sparkle that salvation brings can you perceive to lighten up your way. And so you see yourself deprived of light, abandoned to the dark, unfairly left without a purpose in a futile world.

This describes our world, which we love and never want to leave. Our madness is such that we choose to suffer in the darkened hell of guilt that we may point an accusing finger, saying: "Your sin did this to me, and you will be punished for it." We shall return again and again to the insanity of this belief that salvation is sacrifice, ours and others'.

(VII.2) All sickness comes from separation. When the separation is denied, it goes. For it is gone as soon as the idea that brought it has been healed, and been replaced by sanity. Sickness and sin are seen as consequence and cause, in a

relationship kept hidden from awareness that it may be carefully preserved from reason's light.

When Jesus discusses sickness, he does not refer to external appearances but to the mind's sickness of separation and guilt that manifest bodily. These symptoms are not the problem, despite our experience that illness (mental or physical) is due to virulent microorganisms or noxious people. All this denies the real cause of sickness: the mind's choosing sin over Atonement. This means that it is not the body's *effects* (symptoms) that should be our concern, but the mind's *cause* (belief in sin), cleverly concealed by what the mindless body sees and feels. We will find a more extended discussion of sickness' role in the ego's thought system of guilt and sacrifice in Chapters 27 and 28.

(VII.3:1-3) Guilt asks for punishment, and its request is granted. Not in truth, but in the world of shadows and illusions built on sin. The Son of God perceived what he would see because perception is a wish fulfilled.

We have already looked at this in previous chapters (e.g., T-21.V.1; T-24.VII.8:6-10): we see what we want to see, wishing for a world of separation and differences as that establishes the truth of the ego's thought system. We want to see this world so that others will be perceived as guilty, deserving the punishment we secretly believe should be our own. Health and well-being are a small price to pay for our escape from the sin we have put in another.

(VII.3:4) Perception changes, made to take the place of changeless knowledge.

This is the crucial difference (change versus changelessness) between the ego's separated world of perception and God's unified world of knowledge. Everything here changes, the opposite of the permanence of Heaven's love.

(VII.3:5-9) Yet is truth unchanged. It cannot be perceived, but only known. What is perceived takes many forms, but none has meaning. Brought to truth, its senselessness is quite apparent. Kept apart from truth, it seems to have a meaning and be real.

Recall this lovely statement depicting our overcoming the ego's fourth and final obstacle: "Together we will disappear into the Presence beyond the veil…not to be seen but known" (T-19.IV-D.19:1). When the belief in sin is gone, only truth remains. This cannot be perceived by senses born of illusion, but known only by spirit. With the obvious exception of forgiveness, illusions are all the same, for they share the single purpose of reinforcing belief in the senseless, giving meaning where there is none. This keeps truth separate and apart, protecting the illusion from the power of the mind to choose against it.

(VII.4:7-9) Ideas leave not their source, and their effects but seem to be apart from them. Ideas are of the mind. What is projected out, and seems to be external to the mind, is not outside at all, but an effect of what is in, and has not left its source.

This all-important idea is articulated over and over, not only in the current movement but throughout our symphony. It is essential to understand that there is literally nothing outside the mind: *ideas leave not their source.* What we perceive in the world is nothing more or less than a mirror of what we have first made real within. Such realization is the prerequisite for the mind's healing, as we now read:

(VII.5) God's answer lies where the belief in sin must be, for only there can its effects be utterly undone and without cause. Perception's laws must be reversed, because they *are* reversals of the laws of truth. The laws of truth forever will be true, and cannot be reversed; yet can be seen as upside down. And this must be corrected where the illusion of reversal lies.

This is Jesus' response to the ego's strategy of keeping us mindless. "God's answer"—the Holy Spirit's Atonement—is in the mind, where correction is needed. It is inconceivable that this thought be anywhere else since the world does not exist: *ideas leave not their source.* The only error was the decision maker's choice for the ego, which gave rise to the dualistic world of perception. Its laws

root our attention in the body, and since it is this misplaced focus that needs reversal, our gentle teacher leads us from the mindless to the mindful, the projected illusion of the world to its source in the mind's illusory thought of separation. Through the miracle, the ego's upside-down perception is corrected, allowing truth to be restored to our joyful and mindful awareness.

(VII.6) It is impossible that one illusion be less amenable to truth than are the rest. But it is possible that some are given greater value, and less willingly offered to truth for healing and for help. No illusion has any truth in it. Yet it appears some are more true than others, although this clearly makes no sense at all. All that a hierarchy of illusions can show is preference, not reality. What relevance has preference to the truth? Illusions are illusions and are false. Your preference gives them no reality. Not one is true in any way, and all must yield with equal ease to what God gave as answer to them all. God's Will is One. And any wish that seems to go against His Will has no foundation in the truth.

This is another statement of the Course's refutation of the ego's first law of chaos ("there is a hierarchy of illusions"—T-23.II.2:2-3) by the first principle of miracles ("There is no order of difficulty in miracles"—T-1.I.1). Since every problem on the level of form is a shadowy fragment of the mind's single problem of choosing guilt, the specifics of the projected problem are irrelevant to the undoing. The miracle's return of the Son's attention to the mind's mistaken decision, which can be now corrected, undoes all problems simultaneously; the ego's wishes have no power over God's reflected Will, which is the split mind's healing through forgiveness.

(VII.7:1-2) Sin is not error, for it goes beyond correction to impossibility. Yet the belief that it is real has made some errors seem forever past the hope of healing, and the lasting grounds for hell.

Jesus again refers to the first law of chaos. The belief that there is a hierarchy of illusions, some mistakes are worse than others (T-23.II.2-3), constitutes the faith in a thought system of differences that *is* the belief in sin, beyond forgiveness and beyond healing. What follows now is the heart of the ego's thought system, seen in the chart's wrongminded box—the ego's projection of its sinful self onto a maniacally vengeful God:

(VII.7:3-4) If this were so, would heaven be opposed by its own opposite, as real as it. Then would God's Will be split in two, and all creation be subjected to the laws of two opposing powers, until God becomes impatient, splits the world apart, and relegates attack unto Himself.

This is the biblical "end time," where the world will be split into good and evil; one rewarded, the other punished. Said division is the projected shadow of the mind's battleground, whereon the ego does battle with its own projection—insanity confronting itself. How can there be a true winner in such madness?

(VII.7:5-6) Thus has He lost His Mind, proclaiming sin has taken His reality from Him and brought His Love at last to vengeance's heels. For such an insane picture an insane defense can be expected, but can not establish that the picture must be true.

This chaotic world—the passage reflects the second and third laws of chaos (T-23.II.4-8)—is the ego's insane defense of its own insane self-portrait. As we have seen, the Bible portrays this madness, which defends against the true God Who knows nothing of this. The biblical deity, on the other hand, hates the sin *He* has made real, and punishes it even when He seems to be saving it. All this is but a complicated defense against the simple truth of our changeless and sinless Identity as Christ, God's one Son.

Returning to the beginning of Chapter 26, we revisit the theme of sacrifice (*one or the other*): in order for us to exist, God has to be sacrificed; in order for us to exist after the world was made, others have to be sacrificed. Restated, love must be lost for our special identity to be preserved, and to eliminate our sense of sin we must lose our brothers by punishing them for our projections.

(I.1:1-3) In the "dynamics" of attack is sacrifice a key idea. It is the pivot upon which all compromise, all desperate attempts to strike a bargain, and all conflicts achieve a seeming balance. It is the symbol of the central theme that *somebody must lose.*

Here again is our central theme of *one or the other*: the oneness of love must be sacrificed to make room for the ego's fragmenting special love. Attack has triumphed over peace, and the conflict of specialness reigns supreme in the mind where heretofore there was only unity.

(I.1:4-5) Its focus on the body is apparent, for it is always an attempt to limit loss. The body is itself a sacrifice; a giving up of power in the name of saving just a little for yourself.

We sacrificed our real power as Christ, and now think our separated self has it. The guilt over our perceived misuse of this power, usurping God's position as the Creator, impels us to give it up by projecting it onto the body—ours or another's—claiming it has dominion over us. Since the mind is the grantor, it retains the real power to effect change, either through sacrifice or forgiveness.

(I.1:6-8) To see a brother in another body, separate from yours, is the expression of a wish to see a little part of him and sacrifice the rest. Look at the world, and you will see nothing attached to anything beyond itself. All seeming entities can come a little nearer, or go a little farther off, but cannot join.

The perception of the body reflects the mind's wish to make separation real, sacrificing the Oneness of Christ that is our Self. We know this to be the case because the world we see is in fact a world of separation: separated forms perceived by separated entities, solipsistically reinforcing their separate existence by needing other entities to justify their special hate through seeming love.

(I.2:1-3) The world you see is based on "sacrifice" of oneness. It is a picture of complete disunity and total lack of joining. Around each entity is built a wall so seeming solid that it looks as if what is inside can never reach without, and what is out can never reach and join with what is locked away within the wall.

This same idea is pointedly described in Lesson 184. The world we live in, disunity and separateness, is nothing more than the shadowy fragment of the original disunifying thought that we exist separately from God's Oneness. The world, then, must be illusory, as nothing here can be real because nothing of God is discrete and separate. Yet the dichotomy between mind and body appears permanent, for the wall of nothingness—the veil of forgetfulness—that holds them apart seems forever indissoluble, as do the bodily walls that keep us separate from each other.

(I.2:4) Each part must sacrifice the other part, to keep itself complete.

As we saw before (T-16.V), this is the essence of the special relationship: we steal from each other to complete what we believe is lacking in ourselves. The fourth and fifth laws of chaos well describe this viciously insane dynamic of bargaining for salvation (T-23.II.9-13).

(I.2:5) For if they joined each one would lose its own identity, and by their separation are their selves maintained.

This is the core of the ego's fear. If we truly recognize we are one, sharing wrong-minded insanity, right-minded Atonement, and One-Minded Christ, our separate selves would, to borrow (and alter) Dylan Thomas' evocative phrase, go gently into the goodnight of oblivion. To maintain our ego's "life," it is imperative to see others as different from us. This perception is based on the belief that others possess the specialness we lack, which justifies our killing them—physically or psychologically—to seize the priceless pearl and make it our own, staving off the terror of annihilation. The foundation of the ego's salvation is this principle of differences: separation, attack, and a distorted sense of justice.

(I.3) The little that the body fences off becomes the self, preserved through sacrifice of all the rest. And all the rest must lose this little part, remaining incomplete to keep its own identity intact. In this perception of yourself the body's loss would be a sacrifice indeed. For sight of bodies becomes the sign that sacrifice is limited, and something still remains for you alone. And for this little to belong to you are limits placed on everything outside, just as they are on everything you think is yours. For giving and receiving are the same. And to accept the limits of a body is to impose these limits on each brother whom you see. For you must see him as you see yourself.

The discussion continues, focusing on the body's purpose of protecting, promoting, and preserving the ego's thought of separation. The Sonship is fragmented into separated selves, each walled off from the other by the embodiment in form of the ego's separating thought. In this way the Son sacrifices himself for his self that he loves above all else, never hesitating to kill to ensure its survival. Projecting this wish onto other selves, perpetual war is ensured, for each of us must sacrifice the other in order to live. Beyond even this stands Oneness, the ultimate sacrifice, with limitation its most unworthy substitute.

(I.4:1-4) The body *is* a loss, and *can* be made to sacrifice. And while you see your brother as a body, apart from you and separate in his cell, you are demanding sacrifice of him and you. What greater sacrifice could be demanded than that God's Son perceive himself without his Father? And his Father be without His Son?

The real sacrifice is the one that gave existence to us, sacrificing Father and Son (Mind and spirit) for the ego (mind and body). To preserve that illusory life, we continue to sacrifice others by seeing the sin in them that demands their punishment and not our own, never recognizing the ultimate loss to ourselves—life itself.

(I.4:5-6) Yet every sacrifice demands that They be separate and without the Other. The memory

of God must be denied if any sacrifice is asked of anyone.

As God is Oneness, sacrificing it by seeing others as separate and different from us ensures that we will never awaken to our Source, the second part of the formula of seeing the face of Christ in our brother and remembering God. Christ's innocent face appears in our perception through undoing the belief in sacrifice—*one or the other*—allowing God's loving memory to dawn in our awareness.

(I.4:7-9) What witness to the Wholeness of God's Son is seen within a world of separate bodies, however much he witnesses to truth? He is invisible in such a world. Nor can his song of union and of love be heard at all.

Purpose is everything. The world's purpose is to drown out the "forgotten song" (T-21.I). Indeed, it was made to keep this song of love and unity forever hidden from us so we would never choose to hear its sweet melody. By keeping us in a perpetual state of mindlessness (the body), the ego removes all possibility of the mind's choosing again. In addition, we delude ourselves into believing that by virtue of the illusion that others deserve to be punished instead of us, the purpose of special hate, we can live in the world innocent and free from all punishment.

Our final look at the ego in this movement comes in "The Immediacy of Salvation." In the first two paragraphs, Jesus speaks of time and space as one illusion, opposite sides of the same coin of separation. The projected thought of being separate from our Creator takes the form of space when we see differences among us, the gap between ourselves and others that is the shadowy fragment of what we believe to be the gap between ourselves and God. These differences are accentuated by seeing our brothers as sinners who deserve to be punished in time, their fearful future adding to the perceived gap between us, or when we pretend to be right-minded, the time when we deign to forgive them. This is the meaning of the following passage:

(VIII.1) The one remaining problem that you have is that you see an interval between the time when you forgive, and will receive the benefits of trusting in your brother. This but reflects the little you would keep between you and your brother, that you and he might be a little separate. For time and space are one illusion, which takes different forms. If it has been projected beyond your mind you think of it as time. The nearer it is brought to where it is, the more you think of it in terms of space.

Again, we see the space between ourselves and others that reflects our differences: their separate bodies having sinned against ours, and there being a time between when their sin occurred and when it will be punished in the hellish hereafter. Further, the ego's concept of Heaven, understood within a temporal framework, demands that the beneficent effects of our forgiveness remain in the future when we will be rewarded for our kindness. Hence, the reality of time and space is reinforced, preserving the underlying thought of separation.

(VIII.2) There is a distance you would keep apart from your brother, and this space you perceive as time because you still believe you are external to him. This makes trust impossible. And you cannot believe that trust would settle every problem now. Thus do you think it safer to remain a little careful and a little watchful of interests perceived as separate. From this perception you cannot conceive of gaining what forgiveness offers *now*. The interval you think lies in between the giving and receiving of the gift seems to be one in which you sacrifice and suffer loss. You see eventual salvation, not immediate results.

Because the mind's thought of separation is never undone, the guilt it engenders continues to make its ugly presence felt in the projected dream that is the world. We inevitably believe that a sinful past is real in the present and must be punished in the future. To stave off the inevitability of this punishment, we need to continuously project the *thought* of separation into the *body* of separation, seeing others as separate from us—the effect of their sin. Future punishment is consequently demanded, reflecting in *time* the separation that our separated bodies manifest in *space*. And even when the ego tells us we should forgive ("forgiveness-to-destroy"—S-2.II), we have to await the outcome of our forgiveness in terms of God's recognition that we deserve Heaven for our sacrifice and suffering, while others will be condemned to hell. We place our trust in the ego's salvation of judgment and attack, or separate interests that lead to the immediate results of experiencing freedom from guilt. This prevents us from experiencing the true effects of forgiveness *now*, which placing our trust in the Holy Spirit surely brings.

(VIII.3) Salvation *is* immediate. Unless you so perceive it, you will be afraid of it, believing that the risk of loss is great between the time its purpose is made yours and its effects will come to you. In this form is the error still obscured that is the source of fear. Salvation *would* wipe out the space you see between you still, and let you instantly become as one. And it is here you fear the loss would lie. Do not project this fear to time, for time is not the enemy that you perceive. Time is as neutral as the body is, except in terms of what you see it for. If you would keep a little space between you and your brother still, you then would want a little time in which forgiveness is withheld a little while. And this but makes the interval between the time in which forgiveness is withheld from you and given seem dangerous, with terror justified.

The all-important leitmotif of purpose returns, to be considered again in our next section. Fear originates in the mind and serves the ego's carefully crafted purpose of having us believe that sin is real because it deserves to be punished. It tells us we are guilty, meaning we sinned by separating from God, and this unholy trinity (sin, guilt, and fear) leads us into the world of bodies wherein we believe we are protected by forgetting we are the mind that made the world. We seem to exist forever in a state of mindlessness, with no opportunity to return to the decision-making mind that can choose against the ego. Thus is the ego's purpose of preserving our self fulfilled.

Yet the mind's guilt remains, and we need to defend against it by projecting its ugly face onto another, the ego's warped view of salvation. Under its cruel dictates, even when we believe we are forgiven because we have forgiven, sin can still surface and demand punishment. To forestall our harsh fate, we maintain vigilance for another's sin so ours will be forgotten. Not believing that another's forgiveness is deserved, we reinforce the secret belief that our sin is beyond redemption. By so doing, the ego is able to control us through the terror of a punishment that can never be prevented, leading us again and again to perceive the sin of separation in everyone but ourselves.

Enter the neutrality of time. Though made by the ego to protect itself by convincing us that sin is real in the past, deserves to be punished in the future while we experience guilt in the intervening present, time can serve a different purpose. The Holy Spirit uses the temporal world as a classroom that teaches us to choose the holy instant in which the illusion of time is transcended, judgment dissolved, and the separation healed.

(VIII.4:1-2) Yet space between you and your brother is apparent only in the present, *now*, and cannot be perceived in future time. No more can it be overlooked except within the present.

The ego's assertions to the contrary, our problems remain in the present, in the unholy instant when the mind chooses sin over innocence, fear substituting for love. We need always remember that time is an illusion, with the mind being truly time-less. The instant of decision, unholy or holy, is all there is, for the mind's decision maker is the "seat of destiny," to quote Plotinian scholar Emile Bréhier, in which is found Heaven or hell, by our own election.

(VIII.4:3-4) Future loss is not your fear. But present joining is your dread.

Recall this earlier line, which is reiterated by the above: "You are not really afraid of crucifixion. Your real terror is of redemption" (T-13.III.1:10-11). We do not fear the made-up future but are terrified of "present joining." Of course there can be no real "present joining" since we are already joined. We merely accept the truth of eternity's reflection, the holy instant where we realize there is no sin in the past. How, then, can we be separate from each other now when there is no separation in the past? The ego dreads this recognition of the inherent sameness of all minds, for it undoes the belief in sin, guilt, and fear, awakening us from the nightmare unto the Christ we share as one.

(VIII.4:5) Who can feel desolation except now?

Feelings of desolation do not arise from what the world has done or will do to us, or what the Creator's insane wrath might succeed in accomplishing. They are the inevitable result of the mind's *present* choice to be separate from God. This understanding marks a happy conclusion to a hellish story, a quiet end to an insanely frenetic ego. No wonder our individual self quakes in fear at the remembrance of the mind's power to choose against it.

(VIII.4:6-8) A future cause as yet has no effects. And therefore must it be that if you fear, there is a present cause. And it is *this* that needs correction, not a future state.

The ego's "present cause" is the belief in sin. It does not need correction in the future, as in trying to prevent our becoming afraid, nor in undoing the painful past. It is, again, the mind's *present* decision for the ego that is the cause, and it is there that correction needs to be applied. This is the purpose of the holy instant.

(VIII.5:1-4) The plans you make for safety all are laid within the future, where you cannot plan. No purpose has been given it as yet, and what will happen has as yet no cause. Who can predict effects without a cause? And who could fear effects unless he thought they had been caused, and judged disastrous *now*?

Since sin has never happened, how can it cause a dreaded future? Acceptance of the Atonement, our one responsibility and only function, entails recognizing that the illusory sin of separation cannot be the cause of anything. Choosing to see

another as sharing our split-minded thought systems reflects our present decision to undo the causeless effects of separation and specialness. We are reminded by the miracle that our perceptions of devastation and disaster are not what they seem (cf. W-pII.13.1:1-3). As their cause is nothing, allowing the apparent effects—nothing from nothing—to arouse fear and disrupt our peace makes no sense.

(VIII.5:5) Belief in sin arouses fear, and like its cause, is looking forward, looking back, but overlooking what is here and now.

The phrase *here and now* is associated with Gestalt psychology, a popular psychological movement in the 1960s when the text of *A Course in Miracles* was being scribed. In the Course, it denotes the holy instant in which there is no past or future, no separation, guilt, or world of bodies. There is only the Atonement, reminding us of Who we are as Christ. The ego fears our choosing this principle, which it so desperately seeks to conceal from us. To this end, following a strategy more than familiar to us, it fabricates its nightmare reality of sin, guilt, and fear, culminating in the birth of the material universe. Seeing attack all around us (the projection of our own attack thoughts) justifies our counterattacks, rooting attention even more firmly in the world of sinful bodies. In this way we never return to the mind where, in the *here and now*, we would surely choose against sin.

(VI.1) Anything in this world that you believe is good and valuable and worth striving for can hurt you, and will do so. Not because it has the power to hurt, but just because you have denied it is but an illusion, and made it real. And it is real to you. It is not nothing. And through its perceived reality has entered all the world of sick illusions. All belief in sin, in power of attack, in hurt and harm, in sacrifice and death, has come to you. For no one can make one illusion real, and still escape the rest. For who can choose to keep the ones that he prefers, and find the safety that the truth alone can give? Who can believe illusions are the same, and still maintain that even one is best?

This incisive passage summarizes our discussion to date and will lead to the next section on purpose and decision. We saw earlier that bodily pleasure and pain serve the same goal of reinforcing the ego's thought system of separation (T-19.IV-A.17:10-12; IV-B.12). When we ascribe power to the body to make us happy or sad, bring pleasure or pain, we acknowledge the belief that there is indeed a world outside the mind, over which we have no control but that controls us. This only reinforces our mindless and powerless state.

The pain we experience follows directly from this mistake, for it is unavoidable once we have chosen the ego's guilt as our teacher. While bodies clearly prefer the illusion of pleasure to the illusion of pain, our egos chortle in glee over the successful deception of having made illusions real and present, *regardless of what the body seems to feel.* Making illusions true is the ego's purpose for the world, a purpose that remains intact as long as the mind's wrong-minded decision is unchanged.

Purpose – Decision

We look now at the theme of purpose, which blends in naturally with the theme of decision. Our range of purpose is between remaining in the dream or awakening from it, deciding for the teacher of attack or forgiveness. Both themes are intertwined, for what we want (purpose) determines what we choose and will then experience as real.

(I.5:1-2) Those who would see the witnesses to truth instead of to illusion merely ask that they might see a purpose in the world that gives it sense and makes it meaningful. Without your special function has this world no meaning for you.

We have learned that forgiveness is our special function (T-25.VI), which gives the world its only meaning and purpose: seeing it as a classroom wherein we learn Jesus' lessons of shared interests that awaken us from the ego's dreams of separation, sin, and death. His purpose for the world corrects the ego's, which is to make differences real and justify the attacks it calls justice, punishing others for the sins first perceived within ourselves.

(I.5:3-4) Yet it can become a treasure house as rich and limitless as Heaven itself. No instant passes here in which your brother's holiness cannot be seen, to add a limitless supply to every meager scrap and tiny crumb of happiness that you allot yourself.

The world becomes a "treasure house," not because of anything inherently valuable here, but because of the purpose the mind decides to give it. The "crumbs of happiness" are what we seek in our special relationships, while forgiveness opens up Heaven's limitless supply of love—ours for the choosing. Perhaps today.

(VII.15:1-2) Illusions serve the purpose they were made to serve. And from their purpose they derive whatever meaning that they seem to have.

We have already seen the ego's purpose for illusions: perpetuating our separated and special identity. Anything—pain or pleasure, sickness or health, death or life—that reinforces this individual self is meaningful to the ego, cherished as salvation.

(VII.15:3-5) God gave to all illusions that were made another purpose that would justify a miracle whatever form they took. In every miracle all healing lies, for God gave answer to them all as one. And what is one to Him must be the same.

All healing is the same because all miracles are the same: one problem, one solution. The purpose Jesus refers to is forgiveness, and his words about God giving us another purpose are clearly symbolic since perfect Oneness knows only Itself. Nevertheless, within the dream where symbols reign, it is helpful to perceive God as Friend instead of the enemy the ego made of Him. His Love, therefore, is experienced through the Holy Spirit's employing the specialness we used to harm, for the purpose of forgiveness and healing—our special function (T-25.VI.4).

(III.6:1-2) There is no basis for a choice in this complex and overcomplicated world. For no one understands what is the same, and seems to choose where no choice really is.

Perhaps the clearest expression of this theme comes in the last chapter of the text in "The Real Alternative" (T-31.IV), where Jesus tells us that the myriad number of choices offered by this world are merely different ways of reinforcing the ego's goal of death. An illusion is an illusion is an illusion, regardless of its form. The only meaningful alternative to illusion is the truth, the mind's simple choice for the Holy Spirit and His miracle.

(III.6:3-5) The real world is the area of choice made real, not in the outcome, but in the perception of alternatives for choice. That there is choice is an illusion. Yet within this one lies the undoing of every illusion, not excepting this.

That is the final choice we make between the ego's separation and the Holy Spirit's Atonement, a theme to which we shall return presently. Elsewhere Jesus says that forgiveness is illusory, but unlike the ego's illusions, his do not breed further ones (e.g., W-pI.198.3). Choosing to forgive totally, seeing the face of Christ in every living (and nonliving) thing, undoes all illusions and reawakens in us the memory of God.

(III.7:1-6) Is not this like your special function, where the separation is undone by change of purpose in what once was specialness, and now is union? All illusions are but one. And in the recognition this is so lies the ability to give up all attempts to choose between them, and to make them different. How simple is the choice between two things so clearly unalike. There is no conflict here. No sacrifice is possible in the relinquishment of an illusion recognized as such.

Jesus teaches us how to choose between the ego and the Holy Spirit, the only true difference within the dream. The seeming differences in the ego's world of illusions conceal their shared content of guilt, no matter what they look like. Our special function corrects this illusion of differences by returning us to the mind where we recognize the underlying sameness in all form. The process of undoing illusions seems arduous only because we are resistant to recognizing the unreality of the individual self; giving it up would be a sacrifice too great to pay. But understanding there is no *I* helps us realize we are truly giving up nothing and receiving everything (T-16.VI.11:4).

(III.7:7) Where all reality has been withdrawn from what was never true, can it be hard to give it up, and choose what *must* be true?

Again, the ego's fear is of the decision-making mind that gave reality to the illusion. The ego knows that if we go within we will exercise our choice and choose against it, withdrawing all belief in the unreal. Our false self would disappear, as would our belief in the world's reality and the value of specialness. What *would* remain is the simple truth: we are the Christ Whom God created as Himself.

(V.1:5-12) All learning is a help or hindrance to the gate of Heaven. Nothing in between is possible. There are two teachers only, who point in different ways. And you will go along the way your chosen teacher leads. There are but two directions you can take, while time remains and choice is meaningful. For never will another road be made except the way to Heaven. You but choose whether to go toward Heaven, or away to nowhere. There is nothing else to choose.

All roads on which specialness leads end up nowhere. This, then, is a very simple course, for it merely asks that we choose between illusion and reality. Yet we must first recognize that the ego's offerings are meaningless, for since nothing here lasts, there can be no value to its offerings of specialness. The insane need to defend our special self causes us to resist this simple truth, and so we take the Holy Spirit's simplicity and complicate our path, obscuring the simple choice that would fulfill our life's purpose of forgiveness: the one decision that returns us to Heaven.

Forgiveness

In "The Little Hindrance" we find a particularly important passage that helps us understand time's unreality and will introduce this section on forgiveness. We have previously discussed how linear time is a projection of the thought system of sin, guilt, and fear that occurred (and is still occurring) in the ontological instant when as one Son we decided to believe in the ego's lie of separation. As the mind exists outside the world of time and space, it is non-local and atemporal. Everything that has ever been, or will be, happened within the instant when this mind chose the ego and sought to project it into a world, the so-called Big Bang when the separated self splintered into an almost infinite number of fragments, each containing the entirety of the ego thought system as well as the Holy Spirit's correction of forgiveness. Both coexist in the mind, the subject of the first paragraph to be considered:

(V.3:1-4) God gave His Teacher to replace the one you made, not to conflict with it. And what He would replace has been replaced. Time lasted but an instant in your mind, with no effect upon eternity. And so is all time past, and everything exactly as it was before the way to nothingness was made.

The ego alone believes in conflict, which is why the word *battleground* occurs in the chart. The problem, though, is not the presumed Enemy, but rather our disbelief in the Holy Spirit's Atonement that tells us the war is nothing, and the special self is nothing as well, being an aspect of the nothingness of sin. In self-defense we cling to the illusion of a sinful past that had devastating effects—*us*. Even so, midst the raucous sounds of a battle that never was, truth quietly speaks: Heaven has not been changed, nothing had no effect on Everything, time did not alter eternity.

(V.3:5) The tiny tick of time in which the first mistake was made, and all of them within that one mistake, held also the Correction for that one, and all of them that came within the first.

As *ideas leave not their source*, the world of time and space—specialness and sin, pleasure and pain, birth and death—still exists within the non-linear mind, within the original mistake when we chose the ego's separation over the Holy Spirit's Atonement. This seems inconceivable to us who inhabit the fragmented world of multiplicity (see T-18.I.4-5), but this is only because our physical identities seem so palpably real. However, not only are all mistakes found in the ever-present unholy instant, so too are all forgiveness lessons found in the ever-present holy instant—side by side. Even if the error appears in billions of forms, as does the correction, they remain one. No hierarchy of illusions, *no order of miracles*: one problem, one solution (W-pI.80.1:5).

(V.3:6-7) And in that tiny instant time was gone, for that was all it ever was. What God gave answer to is answered and is gone.

Later in our symphony we read: "This world was over long ago" (T-28.I.1:6). In effect, we are living in an afterimage, as if there were something here to relate to, even though it is no longer here. Indeed, it never was, except in dreams that were dissolved by the Holy Spirit's answer of Atonement the instant we seemed to fall asleep.

(V.4) To you who still believe you live in time and know not it is gone, the Holy Spirit still guides you through the infinitely small and senseless maze you still perceive in time, though it has long since gone. You think you live in what is past. Each thing you look upon you saw but for an instant, long ago, before its unreality gave way to truth. Not one illusion

still remains unanswered in your mind. Uncertainty was brought to certainty so long ago that it is hard indeed to hold it to your heart, as if it were before you still.

We have the illusion of taking a journey through time and space, yet the carpet of time spun out in one instant, and in that same instant rolled back and disappeared (T-13.I.3). Walking on a path that is already over, we learn that it was not even here. Understanding this metaphysical fact provides a perspective within which we can better look at our everyday lives. What we judge as important is truly nothing, and we need not get in touch with the ontological instant of insanity, for that same madness infuses our experience in the here and now. It is our right-minded purpose to recognize the delusion of believing that the ego's nothingness has power to affect the mind's peace. After all, can a ripple affect the ocean, or a sunbeam the sun (T-18.VIII.3)? The Holy Spirit's Atonement has answered for all time, undoing time in its gentle reflection of eternal truth.

(V.5:1-4) The tiny instant you would keep and make eternal, passed away in Heaven too soon for anything to notice it had come. What disappeared too quickly to affect the simple knowledge of the Son of God can hardly still be there, for you to choose to be your teacher. Only in the past,—an ancient past, too short to make a world in answer to creation,—did this world appear to rise. So very long ago, for such a tiny interval of time, that not one note in Heaven's song was missed.

This is a beautiful way of telling us that nothing is here, literally, despite the ancient temptation to make the ego our teacher. We read in the manual: "In time this [the separation] happened long ago. In reality it never happened at all" (M-2.2:7-8). We think our lives are significant, so much so that God Himself notices us as a separate fragment: being caring, punishing, and forgiving, even concocting a plan to save us. Since the world never happened, such a God must be insane, having made error real. Still does this ego-made world have a holy purpose when looked at through the eyes of the Holy Spirit: to have us learn there is nothing to forgive because

the sin of separation is an illusion: "...not one note in Heaven's song was missed."

As we will see here, and many times again before our symphony concludes, Jesus asks us to apply his forgiveness to all we meet, demonstrating that not one note in our love has changed because of their "sinful" behavior. No matter what has been thought, said, or done, the reality of Heaven's love is unaffected. This teaching is invaluable if we call upon it every time we are tempted to give power to an illusion, joyfully remembering that nothing has come between us and love, or between others and our love. Separation has had no effect upon oneness, any more than our differentiating judgments and attacks have changed the inherent sameness of God's separated Sons.

(V.5:5-7) Yet in each unforgiving act or thought, in every judgment and in all belief in sin, is that one instant still called back, as if it could be made again in time. You keep an ancient memory before your eyes. And he who lives in memories alone is unaware of where he is.

Memories are always of the past. Each time we hold a grievance or make a judgment, in fact whenever we are in any way disquieted, we call to mind the ancient time when terror seemed to take the place of love, sin triumphed over innocence, and God's Oneness disappeared into the Son's separated state. We think we exist where we do not, for we think we are who we could never be. Yet memory is only a present decision projected into a nonexistent past, and all this madness is the product of a mistaken choice our minds are making *right now*.

(V.6:1-5) Forgiveness is the great release from time. It is the key to learning that the past is over. Madness speaks no more. There *is* no other teacher and no other way. For what has been undone no longer is.

Since time is the projected home of sin, guilt, and fear, forgiveness releases the mind from its prison by demonstrating that the sin of separation and attack had no effects. Without its effects, sin can no longer be a cause, leaving its guilty past nowhere. Sin being gone, the insanity of the ego thought system goes with it, its place taken by the reason of the Holy Spirit, our only Teacher and only Friend.

(V.8:4) And do you want that fearful instant kept, when Heaven seemed to disappear and God was feared and made a symbol of your hate?

The image of the biblical God—a God impossible to overlook in the Western world, whether we were raised as Jew, Christian, or atheist—is a projection of the mind's secret hate. While the true God knows nothing of us, the ego's deity of distortion knows everything about our sinful selves, believing He must respond to them. We hold on to this ontological insanity of believing the ego's lies each moment we indulge our specialness, valuing something enough that it is worth losing our peace over it, or using it to justify withholding love from an aspect of God's Son.

(V.9) Forget the time of terror that has been so long ago corrected and undone. Can sin withstand the Will of God? Can it be up to you to see the past and put it in the present? You can *not* go back. And everything that points the way in the direction of the past but sets you on a mission whose accomplishment can only be unreal. Such is the justice your All-Loving Father has ensured must come to you. And from your own unfairness to yourself has He protected you. You cannot lose your way because there is no way but His, and nowhere can you go except to Him.

Jesus is helping us realize that the past is already over and that we cannot keep revisiting it, except in dreams. The only true pathway to be walked is with him, through illusions back to truth. As convincing as the ego's lies of separation may be, they cannot escape their source in the unreal. And what is not real has no effect upon reality. This, the Atonement truth, is God's eternal promise to His eternal Son, the justice we deserve as His creation.

(V.11:1-2) The Son whom God created is as free as God created him. He was reborn the instant that he chose to die instead of live.

The above is the Course's version of being born again (John 3:3,7). We are reborn when we choose the Holy Spirit as our Teacher instead of the ego. When we decided for the ego, we were born as a separated self. On the other hand, choosing again, we release that self and are born again in Christ, Whose shining face of innocence is the world's final illusion.

(V.11:3) And will you not forgive him now, because he made an error in the past that God remembers not, and is not there?

We find here another instance of Jesus telling us that God does not know about the separation. The Son's sins are not made real and then forgiven; they are simply forgotten as they disappear back into their own nothingness: the true meaning of forgiveness and the source of our healing.

(V.11:4-9) Now you are shifting back and forth between the past and present. Sometimes the past seems real, as if it *were* the present. Voices from the past are heard and then are doubted. You are like to one who still hallucinates, but lacks conviction in what he perceives. This is the borderland between the worlds, the bridge between the past and present. Here the shadow of the past remains, but still a present light is dimly recognized.

When we are anxious or angry, we have made our sinful past real and experience the consequences of that decision. In Jesus' vision, however, there are no effects of sin since their cause is gone. The movie "A Beautiful Mind" reflects this passage. At the end, the mentally-ill hero was aware he was hallucinating, but no longer paid attention to it. This is our situation. We have reached the point when we are still aware of our hallucinations of a world, but no longer give them power to affect our peace, even as we go back and forth between our wrong and right minds. Despite having chosen the ego's fear, we can be taught to look at our mistake without judgment, an operational definition of right-mindedness.

Note another meaning given to *borderland*. Elsewhere the term refers to the real world (see below), marking the transition between perception and knowledge. Here, however, it is the stage wherein we choose the holy over the unholy instant, love's present reflection of forgiveness instead of guilt's shadows of the past.

(V.11:10-11) Once it is seen, this light can never be forgotten. It must draw you from the past into the present, where you really are.

Our attraction to the light is the ego's fear, the reason it strives to prevent any true experience of light from reaching the mind's eye. To be sure, it happily provides its version of light in special visions, dreams, etc., that only enhance our specialness. Moreover, these dualistic perceptions cannot be of our Source, Who is not of this world at all. Nonetheless, once we have a truly egoless vision, its symbols lead us past perception to the memory of love. The forgotten song begins to resonate in us and, drawn to its gentle melody, we are led from the world to the mind, where real choice is exercised as we decide for the Light that is beyond all light.

(V.12) The shadow voices do not change the laws of time nor of eternity. They come from what is past and gone, and hinder not the true existence of the here and now. The real world is the second part of the hallucination time and death are real, and have existence that can be perceived. This terrible illusion was denied in but the time it took for God to give His Answer to illusion for all time and every circumstance. And then it was no more to be experienced as there.

In other words, we live as if there were a life to be led, no longer aware that the thought of sin that made us was undone in the instant it seemed to arise. Shadows have no substance, merely being the absence of light. Similarly, the ego's thought system of guilt is the absence of the love the Son believes he banished from his mind. Substanceless, the ego's shadow voices have no effect upon our reality, which stands beyond illusion in the light of truth. When we have welcomed this light back into our minds, the shadows disappear, what the Course terms the *real world*. This expression of the Atonement principle is God's "Answer" to the separation,

and when it is accepted by the mind, the dream fades away as eternity reclaims the Self that is its home.

(V.13:1) Each day, and every minute in each day, and every instant that each minute holds, you but relive the single instant when the time of terror took the place of love.

All things are shadowy fragments of the original moment when we chose the ego's terror over the Love of God. We need to recognize this every time we experience dis-ease, discomfort, or loss of peace, and are tempted to blame someone or something else for what we feel. Jesus helps us realize that we are choosing *now* to relive that horrifying ontological instant, yet in this same instant our decision-making minds can choose again.

(V.13:2-4) And so you die each day to live again, until you cross the gap between the past and present, which is not a gap at all. Such is each life; a seeming interval from birth to death and on to life again, a repetition of an instant gone by long ago that cannot be relived. And all of time is but the mad belief that what is over is still here and now.

This is a not-so-subtle reference to reincarnation. We continue to learn our lessons in the body's classroom—choosing to "live," "die," and "live" again as bodily heroes in the ego's dreams of specialness—until the mind's need for learning is done and we recognize the insanity of reliving a dreaded moment that never happened. The ego's *here and now* never was, but Jesus' forgiving present opens the door to our true and eternal life in God.

(V.14) Forgive the past and let it go, for it *is* gone. You stand no longer on the ground that lies between the worlds. You have gone on, and reached the world that lies at Heaven's gate. There is no hindrance to the Will of God, nor any need that you repeat again a journey that was over long ago. Look gently on your brother, and behold the world in which perception of your hate has been transformed into a world of love.

Our purpose now is to go through our daily lives, aware that each time we make a judgment or feel another is needed for our happiness, we "but relive the single instant when the time of terror took the place of love" (V.13:1). Jesus asks us to let that madness go, choose love instead of hate, and accept the real world that places us at Heaven's gate, to be carried through by the last step home. To restate the process, when we prefer grievances to miracles, we have decided against hearing the song of love and unity, the gentle melody of which reminds us of the inherent sameness of God's Sons. Recognizing our mistake, no longer choosing to entertain the ego's raucous shrieks that tell of differences demanding punishment, allows our mind's ears to hear Jesus sing of forgiveness, kindness, and love:

(I.6:3-6) Hear, then, the song your brother sings to you, and let the world recede, and take the rest his witness offers on behalf of peace. But judge him not, for you will hear no song of liberation for yourself, nor see what it is given him to witness to, that you may see it and rejoice with him. Make not his holiness a sacrifice to your belief in sin. You sacrifice your innocence with his, and die each time you see in him a sin deserving death.

This is hardly the first time Jesus has urged us not to judge, for then we claim that someone else is guilty and deserves punishment for what we secretly believe to be our sin. If we truly want to be innocent, we must see others as innocent too, because we are the same. If on the other hand we wish to make them sinful, we reinforce our own sinfulness and deny the holiness of God's Son. Not being able to justify our perceptions of differences denies the ego's mentality of *one-or-the-other*, freeing us to choose everlasting life as God's innocent Son. Our minds quiet at last, we gratefully hear Heaven's song of gratitude for the return of what never ceased to be its own.

(I.7:1-2) Yet every instant can you be reborn, and given life again. His holiness gives life to you, who cannot die because his sinlessness is known to God; and can no more be sacrificed by you than can the light in you be blotted out because he sees it not.

The decision to "sacrifice" our thought system of sacrifice is the choice for life instead of death, sanity in place of madness. This releases our minds from fear and we are reborn into the light of sinlessness, joyously remembering that God's innocent Son is as immortal as his Father.

(I.7:3-8) You who would make a sacrifice of life, and make your eyes and ears bear witness to the death of God and of His holy Son, think not that you have power to make of Them what God willed not They be. In Heaven, God's Son is not imprisoned in a body, nor is sacrificed in solitude to sin. And as he is in Heaven, so must he be eternally and everywhere. He is the same forever. Born again each instant, untouched by time, and far beyond the reach of any sacrifice of life or death. For neither did he make, and only one was given him by One Who knows His gifts can never suffer sacrifice and loss.

The ego made the body to bear witness to separation, meaning God has been destroyed and our life in Him sacrificed—oneness giving way to separation. In the next paragraph, Jesus talks about the body as a "rotting prison" to which the ego has condemned us. Made to conceal the mind's imprisoning thought of murder, the body cannot be the temple of the Holy Spirit. In addition, bodies were made to keep God's Son separate and differentiated, obscuring his intrinsic sameness within the illusion. This unity of mind reflects the One Mind we share as our Self. The fact that our Identity has not been truly lost leads the ego to make our seeming differences significant and deserving of judgment, thereby denying Who we are as Christ. We think the body represents life and death, part of the natural law, yet only in dreams is this natural. God alone is the Author of life, and death has no place in the eternal.

We turn again to the all-important theme of *no order of difficulty in miracles*. This helps us realize that everything here is one illusion, regardless of the multitudinous forms the error appears to take.

Such realization helps us reflect Heaven's justice on earth, that *no one loses and everyone gains.*

(II.1) It is not difficult to understand the reasons why you do not ask the Holy Spirit to solve all problems for you. He has not greater difficulty in resolving some than others. Every problem is the same to Him, because each one is solved in just the same respect and through the same approach. The aspects that need solving do not change, whatever form the problem seems to take. A problem can appear in many forms, and it will do so while the problem lasts. It serves no purpose to attempt to solve it in a special form. It will recur and then recur again and yet again, until it has been answered for all time and will not rise again in any form. And only then are you released from it.

It is senseless to try to solve problems here, although on a practical level this is what we seem to do. The problems of conflict, anxiety, tension, or upset—individual and collective—can never be solved except by the mind's turning toward the Atonement and accepting it. For this reason, Jesus teaches us how to use our relationships and everyday situations as the means of learning that our problems are internal, not external: the only problem is guilt, and until it is undone through forgiveness, problems in form will continue to occur and remain essentially insoluble.

(II.2:1-2) The Holy Spirit offers you release from every problem that you think you have. They are the same to Him because each one, regardless of the form it seems to take, is a demand that someone suffer loss and make a sacrifice that you might gain.

Again we see the ego's central principle of sacrifice: you must lose if I am to gain. The Holy Spirit's correction is that we both lose if one of us does, and if I am to gain, you must gain with me. God's separated Sons are always the same and never different from each other. In that happy fact all our problems are solved, as we read:

(II.2:3-6) And when the situation is worked out so no one loses is the problem gone, because it

was an error in perception that now has been corrected. One mistake is not more difficult for Him to bring to truth than is another. For there *is* but one mistake; the whole idea that loss is possible, and could result in gain for anyone. If this were true, then God would be unfair; sin would be possible, attack be justified and vengeance fair.

This explains why loss is such an important part of our world, being reminiscent of the original loss that resulted from the insane belief in sin. As a result, we cannot live in a body without loss: we lose our abilities as we grow old; our loved ones, wealth, and possessions are taken from us (at least we fear such loss); and inevitably we lose our lives to the "natural" law of life and death. The world must always be about loss because it comes from the idea of loss, and *ideas leave not their source.* The original ego thought is that God suffered loss of His Son so we would gain. Since every mistake is found in the original "tiny tick of time" when we chose the ego, our ongoing judgments in the here and now re-enact that moment of insanity, making it forever present and forever real. And so in the ego thought system we have a God Who believes in vengeance. Indeed, in our perverse insanity we love this God Who punishes evil and rewards good, for His specialness proves that differences among His Sons are real. After all, *He* believes in them.

(II.3) This one mistake, in any form, has one correction. There is no loss; to think there is, is a mistake. You have no problems, though you think you have. And yet you could not think so if you saw them vanish one by one, without regard to size, complexity, or place and time, or any attribute which you perceive that makes each one seem different from the rest. Think not the limits you impose on what you see can limit God in any way.

The key to understanding God's justice is to move beyond form to content, separate to shared interests, the perceived problem to its correction. The one problem is the insane belief that attack leads to happiness, and that one can gain at another's expense. This was the ontological error of believing that the living and loving God could be sacrificed so that the god of specialness would reign supreme. Regardless of the forms our problems appear to take, they are reduced to this single mistake in perception: that the limited love of specialness can replace Heaven's limitless love. Jesus asks us to bring all problems to this one problem so that the right mind's correction can be chosen. When we follow the gentle pathway of his miracle, from the mindless to the mindful, our concerns disappear as easily as does the morning mist in the presence of the sun.

(II.4) The miracle of justice can correct all errors. Every problem is an error. It does injustice to the Son of God, and therefore is not true. The Holy Spirit does not evaluate injustices as great or small, or more or less. They have no properties to Him. They are mistakes from which the Son of God is suffering, but needlessly. And so He takes the thorns and nails away. He does not pause to judge whether the hurt be large or little. He makes but one judgment; that to hurt God's Son must be unfair and therefore is not so.

All problems, regardless of how they look, reflect the single error of choosing the ego's guilt-driven justice of punishment over the all-inclusive justice of God's Love. In this world, the error is manifest in the shadowy fragments of our judgments and attacks, which dictate the justice of sacrifice: one's happiness is purchased at the expense of another's hurt. As such unfairness to God's Son calls only for correction, at our invitation the Holy Spirit removes the tools of crucifixion (thorns and nails) we placed on others, replacing them with lilies of forgiveness, resurrection's loving gift to us all.

(II.5) You who believe it safe to give but some mistakes to be corrected while you keep the others to yourself, remember this: Justice is total. There is no such thing as partial justice. If the Son of God is guilty then is he condemned, and he deserves no mercy from the God of justice. But ask not God to punish him because *you* find him guilty and would have him die. God offers you the means to see his innocence. Would it be fair to punish him because you will not look at what is there to see? Each time you keep a problem for yourself to solve, or judge that it is one that has no resolution, you have made it great, and past the hope of healing. You deny the miracle of justice *can* be fair.

Salvation is simple, being of God. What is hurtful and separating is not His Will, and does not exist. Nevertheless, while God's Son sleeps, he dreams of guilt and punishment, seeking to stupefy himself still further by arguing for the truth of his hallucinatory perceptions, not to mention the immensity of problems that defy solution or healing. However, in the instant he desires a dream in which there is no suffering or sacrifice, he accepts the miracle of justice that embraces all people and heals all problems. Mercy replaces attack as the gentle wings of forgiveness enfold the innocence of God's Son in peace, the thinking of the insanely angry world to the contrary.

(II.6:1-4) If God is just, then can there be no problems that justice cannot solve. But you believe that some injustices are fair and good, and necessary to preserve yourself. It is these problems that you think are great and cannot be resolved. For there are those you want to suffer loss, and no one whom you wish to be preserved from sacrifice entirely.

A helpful exercise would be to see how tenaciously we hold to our misperceptions, believing that certain problems are beyond solution, reflecting the ego's first chaotic law that "there is a hierarchy of illusions." We look upon the need for grievances, which preserves our separated identity by giving away its sin and putting it on the now guilty head of others who will sacrifice their innocence for us, being punished for a sin we believe is rightfully our own.

(II.6:5-6) Consider once again your special function. One is given you to see in him his perfect sinlessness.

That one is whomever we are involved with in a special relationship, one we love to love, or love to hate. This is our golden opportunity to see the guilt we projected from our unconscious mind, return it to its source, and choose again: our special function of forgiveness in place of specialness.

(II.6:7-10) And you will ask no sacrifice of him because you could not will he suffer loss. The miracle of justice you call forth will rest on you as surely as on him. Nor will the Holy Spirit be content until it is received by everyone. For what you give to Him is everyone's, and by your giving it can He ensure that everyone receives it equally.

Note that three times in two sentences Jesus says *everyone*. No one can be exempt from our forgiveness and love; no one can be exempt from our hate. If we hate one, we hate everyone, including ourselves, Jesus, and God; if we truly love, we love the whole Sonship because it is one, and love its one Creator. This is why the concept of oneness is essential to the curriculum. As we saw at its beginning, *A Course in Miracles* cannot teach us about oneness or love, but it can teach us how to reflect that oneness in our forgiven relationships.

(II.7:5-7) What seemed once to be a special problem, a mistake without a remedy, or an affliction without a cure, has been transformed into a universal blessing. Sacrifice is gone. And in its place the Love of God can be remembered, and will shine away all memory of sacrifice and loss.

When we forgive, seeing the true face of innocence in our brothers and freeing them from the prison of our projected sin, the memory of God dawns on our minds. This memory, the thought of Atonement, had been covered over by the wrong mind's insane thought system of guilt, which itself was covered by the world's insane perceptions of separation and loss. Withdrawing our projections through forgiveness heralds the undoing of the ego's two-fold dream of sacrifice. The next chapter will discuss in greater depth the world's dream and the mind's secret dream, underneath which is the Love that ends all pain and is our Source.

(II.8:1-3) God cannot be remembered until justice is loved instead of feared. He cannot be unjust to anyone or anything, because He knows that everything that is belongs to Him, and will forever be as He created it. Nothing He loves but must be sinless and beyond attack.**

God's perfect Love is always present through His Holy Spirit, although it remains inaccessible to us until we choose it. We need to learn that shared interests are preferable to separate ones, and that the sinlessness of all God's Sons is what we truly desire, no longer fearing but welcoming His justice into our hearts.

(II.8:4) Your special function opens wide the door beyond which is the memory of His Love kept perfectly intact and undefiled.

All the while we thought we had destroyed God's Love, it remained in safekeeping in our minds, buried by the belief in sin, guilt, fear, and death. This madness is quietly undone by forgiveness, the special function that is the Holy Spirit's answer to the ego's thought system of specialness and attack.

(II.8:5-6) And all you need to do is but to wish that Heaven be given you instead of hell, and every bolt and barrier that seems to hold the door securely barred and locked will merely fall away and disappear. For it is not your Father's Will that you should offer or receive less than He gave, when He created you in perfect love.

How simple! All we need to do is wish for Heaven instead of hell. The problem is that meaningful wish can be exercised only in the mind where meaningful choice occurs. This is the reason the ego keeps us mindless, rooting our attention in the world of bodies with its concomitant problems and magical solutions. Not only that, we wish for Heaven albeit fearing the loving Will of our Father Who knows only oneness. We think we are choosing Heaven, but specialness dictates another version of hell. Our fearful resistance to love prevents knowing the difference between these two mutually exclusive realms, and it is Jesus' purpose to teach us his right-minded discernment.

(VII.8:5-6) Forgiveness is the only function here, and serves to bring the joy this world denies to every aspect of God's Son where sin was thought to rule. Perhaps you do not see the role forgiveness plays in ending death and all beliefs that rise from mists of guilt.

Forgiveness means asking Jesus to help us return to our minds the problems we projected onto the world. By so doing, our one problem of choosing separation can be healed. The perceived problem, therefore, does not have to be healed in a relationship between two bodies, or in any situation in which we find ourselves. How could that be when there is no body to have a relationship with nor any external situation with which to interact—only the displacement of the mind's relationship with the ego onto bodies? Forgiveness actually does nothing but undo the desire to make others responsible for the unhappiness that was caused by the mind's decision for guilt instead of love.

(VII.9:1) Forgiveness takes away what stands between your brother and yourself.

Forgiveness *undoes*, as does the miracle. They do nothing actively. In other words, we need do nothing with our special relationships but look at them without judgment. By withdrawing the projections we magically used to free us from guilt, we return them to the mind where we are able to choose against them. Liberating ourselves from the self-imposed prison of hate, the barriers of sin are undone in our minds and in our relationships.

(VII.9:2-4) It is the wish that you be joined with him, and not apart. We call it "wish" because it still conceives of other choices, and has not yet reached beyond the world of choice entirely. Yet is this wish in line with Heaven's state, and not in opposition to God's Will.

We are already joined, meaning that the wish is really to accept the sameness that already unites us: our shared interest and purpose of awakening from the dream of sin and guilt. Though this recognition remains within the realm of illusion, it reflects Heaven's Oneness, for it does not oppose the truth

of God's loving Will. It is, in fact, the means of remembering that His Will is our own.

(VII.9:5-7) Although it falls far short of giving you your full inheritance, it does remove the obstacles that you have placed between the Heaven where you are, and recognition of where and what you are. Facts are unchanged. Yet facts can be denied and thus unknown, though they were known before they were denied.

We denied the fact of our *being* because we feared what we knew as the truth. Yet in our right minds we recognize the Atonement, which we seek to split off and pretend does not exist. We place obstacles to our remembering, and removing these obstacles is our special function. This function of forgiveness is not Heaven but leads to its holy gate, after which God welcomes us to the home we never left and the Self we have always been.

(VII.10:1) Salvation, perfect and complete, asks but a little wish that what is true be true; a little willingness to overlook what is not there; a little sigh that speaks for Heaven as a preference to this world that death and desolation seem to rule.

Note the recurrence of the word "little." Jesus assures us that we are not asked to have great willingness, only enough to look non-judgmentally with him at the ego's thought system of death and desolation that seems to rule the world as long as we believe we are here. It only *seems* to rule because its thoughts have never left their source in the mind, and they are in the mind because our decision makers put them there, not because they are real. As the existence of these delusions is predicated on our willingness to have them, as answer to the Holy Spirit's Atonement, they can be removed in the blessed instant in which our desire shifts from hell to Heaven.

(VII.10:2-6) In joyous answer will creation rise within you, to replace the world you see with Heaven, wholly perfect and complete. What is forgiveness but a willingness that truth be true? What can remain unhealed and broken from a unity which holds all things within itself? There

is no sin. And every miracle is possible the instant that the Son of God perceives his wishes and the Will of God are one.

Forgiveness means our accepting what is, by rejecting what is not. To say "yes" to Jesus is to look at the ego and say: "I no longer want you." Having returned to sanity, we accept Jesus' truth that there is no sin, words the ego is terrified to hear for they mean the end of its reign of terror. Our acceptance clears the mind to remember that our will and God's are one, for we have chosen to perceive that our will and our brothers' are one: one need, one purpose, one goal—one Son in illusion, one Son in truth. Creation is freed to claim its own, and Heaven joyfully welcomes our return as the miracle fades into the love it reflected.

(VII.16) The miracle but calls your ancient Name, which you will recognize because the truth is in your memory. And to this Name your brother calls for his release and yours. Heaven is shining on the Son of God. Deny him not, that you may be released. Each instant is the Son of God reborn until he chooses not to die again. In every wish to hurt he chooses death instead of what his Father wills for him. Yet every instant offers life to him because his Father wills that he should live.

In the Bible, death is God's punitive form of justice for the sin of miscreation. But Jesus tells us that our Father wills only eternal life for His Son. The choice is ours: the one that calls upon the name of guilt to bring death to God's Son, or the teacher who reminds us of our eternal Name. We recognize the teacher we have chosen by our perceptions of others. If we see them as condemned, we are condemned to the same fate, but if we free them from the burden of guilt we placed upon them, we are released as well. The choice is ours: to be continually reborn to die, or to awaken with joy from the guilt-driven cycle of birth and death, suffering and pain.

(VII.17:1) In crucifixion is redemption laid, for healing is not needed where there is no pain or suffering.

This teaching corrects the temptation to gloss over the ego, saying: "Since I am already home and everything here is an illusion, I need not pay attention to suffering in myself or others." This attitude accomplishes nothing but to reinforce the mind's decision for pain, preventing its correction. *In crucifixion is redemption laid*—we need to get in touch with our pain so we may understand its source in the decision-making mind. Only then can we choose redemption for having crucified God's Son. If we deny his crucifixion we deny his redemption, and the latter is impossible to attain, at least from the Course's perspective, without acknowledging our wish for the former. Hate can be overcome only when we look at the suffering it causes, motivating us to choose healing instead of pain.

(VII.17:2-3) Forgiveness is the answer to attack of any kind. So is attack deprived of its effects, and hate is answered in the name of love.

We do not deny that attack exists in the world; we simply deny the ego's interpretation of it. This enables us not to take personally the actions of others, demonstrating that another's sin had no effect on our peace. In this way hate is deprived of its effects (our hurt), and what (sin) has no effects is not a cause and cannot exist. This is how Jesus teaches that our sins are forgiven, which allows our separated minds to return to the Love that is our Cause.

(VII.17:4-6) To you to whom it has been given to save the Son of God from crucifixion and from hell and death, all glory be forever. For you have power to save the Son of God because his Father willed that it be so. And in your hands does all salvation lie, to be both offered and received as one.

God's Son is both crucifier and savior, and the gift he chooses to give another—thorns or lilies—he chooses for himself. Our forgiveness reflects the Father's Love for His Son, and will we sacrifice this gift for the ego's meager crumbs of specialness that offer nothing but pain, loss, and death? Salvation asks only that we accept its gift and share it with the world, for thus is the mind of God's Son healed as one.

(VII.18) To use the power God has given you as He would have it used is natural. It is not arrogant to be as He created you, nor to make use of what He gave to answer all His Son's mistakes and set him free. But it is arrogant to lay aside the power that He gave, and choose a little senseless wish instead of what He wills. The gift of God to you is limitless. There is no circumstance it cannot answer, and no problem which is not resolved within its gracious light.

The theme of humility and arrogance returns, as Jesus asks us to look at the ego's arrogance in believing its power is greater than God's. But even if God has no power in the dream, where the ego is all-powerful, His Will is the source of the changed perception that heals the world and all problems with it. This is not as the world would see it, but as the mind's eye humbly perceives it through Christ's vision that sees all problems as mere epiphenomena of a mistaken choice, easily corrected when the mind is brought into alignment with the one Will of God.

(VII.19) Abide in peace, where God would have you be. And be the means whereby your brother finds the peace in which your wishes are fulfilled. Let us unite in bringing blessing to the world of sin and death. For what can save each one of us can save us all. There is no difference among the Sons of God. The unity that specialness denies will save them all, for what is one can have no specialness. And everything belongs to each of them. No wishes lie between a brother and his own. To get from one is to deprive them all. And yet to bless but one gives blessing to them all as one.

The ego never wants us to understand the absence of differences among us. God's Son is one, and the world is an insane attempt to witness to a reality of differences and specialness that is not so. "No wishes lie between a brother and his own"— idle wishes of specialness have no effect on God's Will that His Son be one with Him, as well as united within Himself in *a Oneness joined as One*. If we believe we have needs that only others can meet, we not only deprive them and ourselves of the Love of God, but the Sonship as a whole, including Jesus. God's Son is one—in his wrong mind, right mind, and One Mind. This understanding is the basis on which we join together in blessing, and in the soft radiance of this healing vision the world of sin and death fades into nothingness.

(VII.20) Your ancient Name belongs to everyone, as theirs to you. Call on your brother's name and God will answer, for on Him you call. Could He refuse to answer when He has already answered all who call on Him? A miracle can make no change at all. But it can make what always has been true be recognized by those who know it not; and by this little gift of truth but let to be itself, the Son of God allowed to be himself, and all creation freed to call upon the Name of God as one.

The miracle, once again, does not do anything, for how can nothing be changed into something other than itself? Miracles simply allow us to remember the truth that always was, returning our attention to the mind's decision maker, the choice point when in our madness we chose illusion. Now we are sane, and now we correct our mistake by letting the Name of God be the unchanging Oneness it is, excluding no one as we embrace the Sonship as one. Incidentally, the above sentence, 20:2, is paralleled almost word for word in the *Psychotherapy* pamphlet: "Hear a brother call for help and answer him. It will be God to Whom you answer, for you called on Him" (P-2.V.8:4-5).

The Real World

We look briefly now at the real world. This is the state of mind that comes when we no longer see sin as real, realizing that dreams of separation and specialness have not come between the Sons that God created one with Him.

(III.2) There is a borderland of thought that stands between this world and Heaven. It is not a place, and when you reach it is apart from time. Here is the meeting place where thoughts are brought together; where conflicting values meet and all illusions are laid down beside the truth, where they are judged to be untrue. This borderland is just beyond the gate of Heaven. Here is every thought made pure and wholly simple. Here is sin denied, and everything that *is* received instead.

Jesus is describing the part of our journey that he elsewhere refers to as the *last* or *final judgment* (T-2.VIII; W-pII.10; and see below III.4:1-3): the ego thought system of sin, guilt, and fear is an illusion (the chart's wrong-mind box), and what we had chosen against, the Holy Spirit's Atonement, is the truth (the right-mind box). Acceptance of the Atonement, our one responsibility, means attaining the real world, the state of mind "where sin has left" (T-26.IV) in which giving and receiving are the same, for the love we *have* is the love we *are*. Note that Jesus reverts to the Course's more basic understanding of *borderland*, the holy ground that is just before the gate of Heaven, beyond which Christ waits with His creations that complete our Self.

(III.3) This is the journey's end. We have referred to it as the real world. And yet there is a contradiction here, in that the words imply a limited reality, a partial truth, a segment of the universe made true. This is because knowledge makes no attack upon perception. They are brought together, and only one continues past the gate where Oneness is. Salvation is a borderland where place and time and choice have meaning still, and yet it can be seen that they are temporary, out of place, and every choice has been already made.

The *real world* is an oxymoron as the world is not real. Jesus uses the term because this healed state of mind reflects Heaven's reality. Not being Heaven, it cannot be true; but as its reflection, the real world symbolizes the truth of perfect oneness, the penultimate step toward awakening from the dream of separation. On this holy ground of salvation we recognize the illusory nature of the ego's dream and stand outside it, hearing Heaven's call to itself. Answering the call heralds the end of choice for we disappear into the unity of will that is our reality. Perception has gently given way to knowledge, and even salvation becomes a faded memory in the presence of truth.

(III.4:1-3) Nothing the Son of God believes can be destroyed. But what is truth to him must be brought to the last comparison that he will ever make; the last evaluation that will be possible, the final judgment upon this world. It is the judgment of the truth upon illusion, of knowledge on perception: "It has no meaning, and does not exist."

This final judgment occurs when we bring all illusions to the truth. Looking at them through the eyes of Jesus helps us see that everything except forgiveness is a defense against our reality. Since it is truth alone we want, the defenses of specialness serve no purpose and melt away. This judgment of truth upon illusion is the last step of salvation, leaving nothing to interfere with our entering the Heart of God to rest eternally in His Love.

(III.4:4-6) This is not your decision. It is but a simple statement of a simple fact. But in this world there are no simple facts, because what is the same and what is different remain unclear.

Here again is the theme of our not knowing the difference between Heaven and hell, joy and pain, freedom and imprisonment. The simplicity of their difference is obscured by the heavy "clouds of complexity" (W-pI.39.1:4) with which the ego's specialness cloaks our minds, obscuring the simple statement of the simple fact of Atonement: "God is, and there never was or could be anything else."

(III.4:7-10) The one essential thing to make a choice at all is this distinction. And herein lies the difference between the worlds. In this one, choice is made impossible. In the real world is choosing simplified.

In our world choice seems real, possible, and necessary. In the real world our looking at illusions reveals their nothingness, simplifying choice by recognizing there is nothing to choose between. This undoes the original error when the Son judged between the ego and the Holy Spirit, choosing the ego's illusion as his truth. Terror, then, took the place of love, a decision that is now happily reversed in this, the final judgment that presages love's return.

We come now to one of the two sections mentioned at the beginning of the chapter, "Where Sin Has Left." This beautiful section describes the wonderful effects when we release our belief in sin, the culmination of the process of forgiveness that ushers in the real world.

(IV.1:1-5) Forgiveness is this world's equivalent of Heaven's justice. It translates the world of sin into a simple world, where justice can be reflected from beyond the gate behind which total lack of limits lies. Nothing in boundless love could need forgiveness. And what is charity within the world gives way to simple justice past the gate that opens into Heaven. No one forgives unless he has believed in sin, and still believes that he has much to be forgiven.

This is a course for all who believe they are here and think the world offers something they want. Because they believe in sin, they need a teacher and spiritual practice that helps them look at their beliefs so they can choose again. Although forgiveness remains illusory, forgiving what never happened, it is an illusion that reflects Heaven's justice of perfect Oneness. An attitude of simple charity (a word used earlier in the text for forgiveness), wherein we do not see another's interests as separate from our own, helps open Heaven's gate as we increasingly feel love's reflection, allowing it to infuse our everyday lives. The darkness of separation is gradually shone away by justice's healing light, calling us to the home we never left where we still abide as God's true Son.

(IV.1:6-8) Forgiveness thus becomes the means by which he learns he has done nothing to forgive. Forgiveness always rests upon the one who offers it, until he sees himself as needing it no more. And thus is he returned to his real function of creating, which his forgiveness offers him again.

Forgiveness has nothing to do with others for it rests on the one who offers it, the process of healing *our* minds by withdrawing the projections of guilt we had put on another. By recognizing guilt to be a mistake, not reality, we realize there is nothing to project; nothing to forgive, within or without. Our special function on earth made complete, our function in Heaven of creation is joyfully returned to us.

(IV.2) Forgiveness turns the world of sin into a world of glory, wonderful to see. Each flower shines in light, and every bird sings of the joy of Heaven. There is no sadness and there is no parting here, for everything is totally forgiven. And what has been forgiven must join, for nothing stands between to keep them separate and apart. The sinless must perceive that they are one, for nothing stands between to push the other off. And in the space that sin left vacant do they join as one, in gladness recognizing what is part of them has not been kept apart and separate.

Jesus is not speaking of anything in the world. Flowers and birds are symbols reflecting the mind's peace, joy, and beauty when we release our belief in sin. How, then, could we not feel gladness, knowing we were wrong: the ego's *one or the other* was a lie, and the Holy Spirit's *together, or not at all* was the truth. In the place where sin has left we stand together—the Sonship's seemingly separated fragments—as one mind: forgiven and healed at last.

(IV.3) The holy place on which you stand is but the space that sin has left. And here you see the

face of Christ, arising in its place. Who could behold the face of Christ and not recall His Father as He really is? Who could fear love, and stand upon the ground where sin has left a place for Heaven's altar to rise and tower far above the world, and reach beyond the universe to touch the Heart of all creation? What is Heaven but a song of gratitude and love and praise by everything created to the Source of its creation? The holiest of altars is set where once sin was believed to be. And here does every light of Heaven come, to be rekindled and increased in joy. For here is what was lost restored to them, and all their radiance made whole again.

This holy altar is our decision-making mind, made free of thoughts of sin as the vision of Christ's face cleanses our perception and we see only expressions of love or calls for it. God's Son is healed, and the grateful love of Heaven joyously extends throughout the Sonship. The Father's memory dawns from within His Heart to the heart of His Son, and the resplendence of Heaven extends even unto the real world, the holy place where sin has left.

(IV.4) Forgiveness brings no little miracles to lay before the gate of Heaven. Here the Son of God Himself comes to receive each gift that brings him nearer to his home. Not one is lost, and none is cherished more than any other. Each reminds him of his Father's Love as surely as the rest. And each one teaches him that what he feared he loves the most. What but a miracle could change his mind, so that he understands that love cannot be feared? What other miracle is there but this? And what else need there be to make the space between you disappear?

The workbook asks us to take "little steps" of forgiveness (W-pI.193.13:7), and these constitute the daily opportunities to shift our perceptions from judgment to vision, specialness to love. The mind we feared, having listened to the ego's lies of sin, guilt, and punishment, we now embrace, for we remember that it holds the correction for our mistaken decision. As we grow to love the special partners we had hated as projections of our mind's

insanity, we see in them the outward picture of the right mind's nascent beauty. The miracle has restored sanity to minds "made mad by guilt" (T-13.in.2:2), and the space that sin has left is filled with Heaven's gentle blessing of forgiveness, ushering in the Love that created us as Itself.

(IV.5) Where sin once was perceived will rise a world that will become an altar to the truth, and you will join the lights of Heaven there, and sing their song of gratitude and praise. And as they come to you to be complete, so will you go with them. For no one hears the song of Heaven and remains without a voice that adds its power to the song, and makes it sweeter still. And each one joins the singing at the altar that was raised within the tiny spot that sin proclaimed to be its own. And what was tiny then has soared into a magnitude of song in which the universe has joined with but a single voice.

From the space where sin has left arises the real world, its sweet sounds echoing the song of thanks the Son sings to the Father, Who in turn sings to His Son (S-in.1). Its melody calls compellingly to each fragment to return home, and who except the insane could long withstand its invitation? What madmen could maintain their insanity when Jesus gently calls them to choose again? *When* remains their choice, but "the outcome is as certain as God" (T-2.III.3:10).

(IV.6) This tiny spot of sin that stands between you and your brother still is holding back the happy opening of Heaven's gate. How little is the hindrance that withholds the wealth of Heaven from you. And how great will be the joy in Heaven when you join the mighty chorus to the Love of God!

Jesus sings to us of our rapturous joy and peace when we finally choose against the thought of sin. We still resist that step, but our little hindrance cannot withstand the power of God's Love that calls unceasingly to us to return to it. In time, the promise of joy will overcome the pain of resistance, and we will join the mighty chorus of the re-united Sonship, grateful to its Source and to its Self.

Closing

The beautiful vision of the journey's end is expressed in the next section, "For They Have Come." In the Prelude to our symphony, I discussed how important it is in music to hear, in Isaac Stern's wonderful phrase, the silence between the notes. More than anywhere else in *A Course in Miracles*, this section evokes the silence that is not only between the notes (or words), but extends far beyond them. There is an aura around "For They Have Come" that transcends the written word. *Love, holy, hate, light,* and *ancient* are used throughout the Course, but here they have a different tonality, to borrow a musical term. The word *ancient* is particularly important, because it returns us to a state that transcends the world, the ancient moment when we chose hate instead of love, but now happily choose again. Finally, the beauty of this section is enhanced by its blank verse, the poetry being the perfect frame to embrace the inner picture: the Course's formula of seeing the face of Christ in our brother and remembering God.

(IX.1) Think but how holy you must be from whom the Voice for God calls lovingly unto your brother, that you may awake in him the Voice that answers to your call! And think how holy he must be when in him sleeps your own salvation, with his freedom joined! However much you wish he be condemned, God is in him. And never will you know He is in you as well while you attack His chosen home, and battle with His host. Regard him gently. Look with loving eyes on him who carries Christ within him, that you may behold his glory and rejoice that Heaven is not separate from you.

The section opens with a plea for the holy relationship to replace our special loves and hates. How could we awaken from the dream without taking our brothers with us? And would we, in our right minds, choose not to do so? The call of holiness to holiness is far greater than the attraction of sin, for it is the call to our self to yield to the powerfully enduring attraction of love for love (T-12.VIII), returning to the Heaven we never left except in dreams that are now serenely fading into nothingness.

(IX.2) Is it too much to ask a little trust for him who carries Christ to you, that you may be forgiven all your sins, and left without a single one you cherish still? Forget not that a shadow held between your brother and yourself obscures the face of Christ and memory of God. And would you trade Them for an ancient hate? The ground whereon you stand is holy ground because of Them Who, standing there with you, have blessed it with Their innocence and peace.

We forgive our brother for the sake of God's Son, in whom we all make our home. In recognizing Christ's innocence in each other we remember God, for His memory lies just beyond the veils of guilt and attack that sought to desecrate the sinless mind of God's most holy Son. Their Presence, Christ and God, has re-established our holiness for sin cannot abide in the holy place where They have come.

(IX.3) The blood of hatred fades to let the grass grow green again, and let the flowers be all white and sparkling in the summer sun. What was a place of death has now become a living temple in a world of light. Because of Them. It is Their Presence which has lifted holiness again to take its ancient place upon an ancient throne. Because of Them have miracles sprung up as grass and flowers on the barren ground that hate had scorched and rendered desolate. What hate has wrought have They undone. And now you stand on ground so holy Heaven leans to join with it, and make it like itself. The shadow of an ancient hate has gone, and all the blight and withering have passed forever from the land where They have come.

How easily does hate withdraw when the memory of God and Christ have returned! When They have come unto their home, can love and innocence be far behind? And who among us could possibly wish to remain in the unholiness of sin when the living temple calls? Its light has brightened the landscape of our minds and the withering darkness of guilt has been forever banished from the holy ground on which we stand, along with Them—the sacred spot where sin has left and Their sinlessness has come.

(IX.4) What is a hundred or a thousand years to Them, or tens of thousands? When They come, time's purpose is fulfilled. What never was passes to nothingness when They have come. What hatred claimed is given up to love, and freedom lights up every living thing and lifts it into Heaven, where the lights grow ever brighter as each one comes home. The incomplete is made complete again, and Heaven's joy has been increased because what is its own has been restored to it. The bloodied earth is cleansed, and the insane have shed their garments of insanity to join Them on the ground whereon you stand.

The dream of time has ended now, for its source in sin has been undone. Our cleansed mind holds only the gladness of completion, for God and Christ have come to claim Their Own. As one voice, our joyous song rises in gratitude that the madness of hate no longer has a place within the holy mind that God created Son. Nothingness remains nothing, and we see the radiance of God's Son as he was created and has been throughout eternity.

(IX.5) Heaven is grateful for this gift of what has been withheld so long. For They have come to gather in Their Own. What has been locked is opened; what was held apart from light is given up, that light may shine on it and leave no space nor distance lingering between the light of Heaven and the world.

The mind's locked door has been gently opened by forgiveness, and Heaven's song of thanksgiving resounds around the world, heralding the end of time and the dawning of Christ's light. Eternity has come to shine upon itself, for what is one has remained what it always was—*a Oneness joined as One.*

(IX.6) The holiest of all the spots on earth is where an ancient hatred has become a present love. And They come quickly to the living temple, where a home for Them has been set up. There is no place in Heaven holier. And They have come to dwell within the temple offered Them, to be Their resting place as well as yours. What hatred has released to love becomes the brightest light in Heaven's radiance. And all the lights in Heaven brighter grow, in gratitude for what has been restored.

What can be holier than forgiveness, for what else can lead to our home in Holiness Itself, the temple of the living God? God and Christ have returned to our tortured minds, restored at last to truth in the light of an ancient love that softly shone away an ancient hate, leaving only the holy ground that forgiveness has blessed but an instant, before even that disappears into the everlasting radiance of Heaven's love.

(IX.7) Around you angels hover lovingly, to keep away all darkened thoughts of sin, and keep the light where it has entered in. Your footprints lighten up the world, for where you walk forgiveness gladly goes with you. No one on earth but offers thanks to one who has restored his home, and sheltered him from bitter winter and the freezing cold. And shall the Lord of Heaven and his Son give less in gratitude for so much more?

The Presence of Their innocence ensures that fantasies of sin can come no more. Our sight is healed by the vision of Christ's holy face, and when we look upon the truth of Heaven's Son, can God and Christ be far behind? Their memory dawns upon our newly-awakened minds, and the pathway home is emblazoned with the golden footprints of forgiveness as we are gratefully led to Their home, which is our own as well.

(IX.8) Now is the temple of the living God rebuilt as host again to Him by Whom it was created. Where He dwells, His Son dwells with Him, never separate. And They give thanks that They are welcome made at last. Where stood a

cross stands now the risen Christ, and ancient scars are healed within His sight. An ancient miracle has come to bless and to replace an ancient enmity that came to kill. In gentle gratitude do God the Father and the Son return to what is Theirs, and will forever be. Now is the Holy Spirit's purpose done. For They have come! For They have come at last!

This inspired movement of our symphony ends with a rhapsodic tribute to the truth we are accepting. They have come because we are coming to Them. The cross on which we nailed God's Son quietly evanesces in the disappearing mists of hate, its place taken by the risen temple in our hearts. The gratitude of Heaven rings throughout the world as ancient scars are healed in the presence of the miracle of our return. Our voices gladly cry out to God in unison: "We come, our Father, we come! And with us all Your Sons, for we are one—with You, in You, as You. We have come home! We have come home at last!"

Chapter 27

THE HEALING OF THE DREAM

Introduction

My opening statement about Chapter 27 is one I have made about other chapters, but it is particularly appropriate here where we see our master composer bringing together his symphonic themes, taking us still deeper into his thought system as he does so. At the same time, the language becomes ever more expressive and beautiful. We find here a summary of *A Course in Miracles'* approach to the wrong and right minds, the ego's purpose for the world and body, and the Holy Spirit's forgiveness that leads us beyond them. As shown in the chart (see Appendix), the heart of the wrong mind is the unholy trinity of sin, guilt, and fear, referred to specifically here as the secret dream that the ego establishes as real to make us fearful of the mind. The core of this fear is the ego's dire warning that God will destroy us for sinning against Him. To be safe, we choose to flee the mind, make up a world, and conceal our sinful identity in a body that quickly becomes the victim of other bodies. This, the world's dream, will be discussed later in the chapter as well. It is the second phase of the ego's strategy, shown in the box at the bottom of the chart.

As Jesus explains below, the issue is never the gap that appears to exist between the secret and world dreams, but the gap the ego tells us exists between ourselves and God, represented on the chart by the vertical line—home of the *tiny, mad idea*—that seems to descend from the solid line, above which is Heaven. Thus begins the ego's strategy of having us remain in a perpetual state of mindless bodies so that we never return to the mind's choice point (the dot atop the split mind) where we decided for the separation. Its plan originates with the mind's secret dream that quickly evolves into the world's dream. Yet in that same mind is also found the correction: the decision-making power that chose the ego can now choose the Holy Spirit, depicted in the right mind by the principle of Atonement.

The current chapter, especially its final sections "The Dreamer of the Dream" and "The 'Hero' of the Dream," provides particularly clear descriptions of the ego's purpose for making up its inner and outer dreams, and how the Holy Spirit, once invited in, shifts their purpose so we can awaken from them. We begin with portions from "The Dreamer of the Dream" as we discuss the ego's fear of the mind's power to choose Atonement over separation.

The Ego's Fear of the Atonement

(VII.11:1-5) What choices can be made between two states, but one of which is clearly recognized? Who could be free to choose between effects, when only one is seen as up to him? An honest choice could never be perceived as one in which the choice is split between a tiny you and an enormous world, with different dreams about the truth in you. The gap between reality and dreams lies not between the dreaming of the world and what you dream in secret. They are one.

The above expresses the purpose underlying the ego thought system, from inception (the secret dream of sin, guilt, and fear) to conclusion (the dream of a quasi-infinite, material universe). Both are dreams, equal in their unreality, with no meaningful choice existing between them although the ego would have us think otherwise. In truth, we choose only between dreaming and awakening. The ego seeks to preserve the separated self, counteracting its fear of dissolution through Atonement, by concealing the power of the Son's mind to dream. We are left, then, with the mind's terror that needs to be protected through projection—one insane dream replacing another.

(VII.11:6) The dreaming of the world is but a part of your own dream you gave away, and saw as if it were its start and ending, both.

Our dream is the secret dream, so horrific that we have to flee from it, for if we remained in our minds God would surely strike us dead. We project this dream so it appears to be outside, following the ego's principle that ideas do leave their source. Jesus is teaching us to see through the ego's deceptive lies that the world is both the body's beginning and end, the "start and ending, both." That means there is no mind, the state of mindlessness being the Son's only reality. This final untruth completes the camouflage as the mind is now hidden from all possibility of change.

(VII.11:7-8) Yet was it started by your secret dream, which you do not perceive although it caused the part you see and do not doubt is real. How could you doubt it while you lie asleep, and dream in secret that its cause is real?

The ultimate cause of the world is our belief in sin, the heart of the secret dream that we accomplished the impossible and separated ourselves from our Source. This remains secret because of guilt, held in place by one of the most important components of the chart: the veil of forgetfulness, the horizontal line that divides the split mind from the world and causes our amnesia so we have no memory of the secret dream. If we are not aware of the mind's dream, we are not aware of the world's cause which is the decision to listen to the ego instead of the Holy Spirit. This is the real secret the ego protects, and all our pain and discomfort—the mind's and body's guilt, anxiety, and fear—stem from the original misguided decision wherein we told the Voice of Atonement It did not know the truth of the separation. We tell this "truth" to God, Jesus, and anyone who has an answer we do not wish to hear.

Jesus proceeds now to describe these two dreams. The first is the world's dream, the state we believe we are in as innocent victims of what has been done to us. We scripted this so that "life" would begin with a state of vulnerability and absolute helplessness that puts us at the mercy of people and forces beyond our control:

(VII.12:1) A brother separated from yourself, an ancient enemy, a murderer who stalks you in the night and plots your death, yet plans that it be lingering and slow; of this you dream.

While the world is replete with enemies who plot our unhappiness and death, the ultimate enemy is God, Who the ego tells us made the body so it would die. As Freud observed, the minute we are born we prepare for death—a lingering and inevitable demise. In this sad saga we have no control over events, or our feelings and reactions to them. Next the secret dream:

(VII.12:2) Yet underneath this dream is yet another, in which you become the murderer, the secret enemy, the scavenger and the destroyer of your brother and the world alike.

In the mind *we* are the victimizers, the sinful murderers and betraying deceivers. This is the price of sin, guilt, and fear that the ego tells us we paid for winning the separation from God, having placed ourselves over His slain body and proudly proclaiming ourselves to be Creator and First Cause.

(VII.12:3-4) Here is the cause of suffering, the space between your little dreams and your reality. The little gap you do not even see, the birthplace of illusions and of fear, the time of terror and of ancient hate, the instant of disaster, all are here.

The cause of suffering lies in the secret dream, not the world's bodily dreams. It began in the original instant when we said of the *tiny, mad idea*: "This is truth. The gap between God and His Son is real, and our special self witnesses to this happy fact of separation." The gap of course is not real, but the ego tells us it is, and we project the thought of separation and perceive "real" gaps among the world's bodies. We have no recollection of their true source since the ego never has us look within to see the gap's fundamental unreality. Despite the ego's subterfuge, the true problem remains in the mind's decision to believe in separation, belying the illusory nature of the inner and outer dreams we conceived in madness.

(VII.12:5-6) Here is the cause of unreality. And it is here that it will be undone.

Again, the ego conceals this truth from us. The world is not the problem, but its cause most definitely is: our belief in an insane thought system that gave rise to the world. That cause rests within the mind's decision maker (again, the black dot just above the split mind on the chart), and so it is there it will be undone. To ensure this never happens, the ego quickly moves us from the secret dream to the world's dream that establishes the body as its hero, our segue to the beginning of the next section, "The 'Hero' of the Dream":

(VIII.1:1-2) The body is the central figure in the dreaming of the world. There is no dream without it, nor does it exist without the dream in which it acts as if it were a person to be seen and be believed.

Jesus describes all of us. He is not speaking tongue-in-cheek, even though in one sense he is making fun of our reverence for the body. These paragraphs will depict our experience in the world, arrogantly thinking our lives here are important. We will presently see how trivial and insignificant life really is, being a dream, not to mention our grandiosity in thinking the body is the center of the universe and that the Almighty created it so.

(VIII.1:3-4) It takes the central place in every dream, which tells the story of how it was made by other bodies, born into the world outside the body, lives a little while and dies, to be united in the dust with other bodies dying like itself. In the brief time allotted it to live, it seeks for other bodies as its friends and enemies.

So much for the body and its life that we glorify and hold sacred. We enhance this image by seeking out friends and enemies—our special love and hate partners—to symbolize our guilt. They become symbols of death, the inevitable fate of the guilty. The idea of seeking is important: we *seek* others to be our friends and enemies so we will ultimately *find* our guilt in their bodies. Once the mantle of sin and guilt rests in them, God Himself will seek and find them, and in His vengeful wrath will dispense their just punishment, a familiar point we will soon elaborate on.

(VIII.1:5-8) Its safety is its main concern. Its comfort is its guiding rule. It tries to look for pleasure, and avoid the things that would be hurtful. Above all, it tries to teach itself its pains and joys are different and can be told apart.

In previous chapters, Jesus told us we cannot tell the difference between pain and joy, or imprisonment and freedom (T-7.X; T-8.II). This ongoing symphonic theme points out that we think there is a difference between pleasure and pain—physical or psychological. They are the same because they are part of the single mistake of the mind's decision for separation. The ego needs us to believe in a hierarchy of illusions, its first law of chaos. Yet every illusion is the same, whether we judge it as pleasurable or painful. True pleasure, however, comes only through right-mindedness, while pain is always the effect of having mistakenly chosen the ego as our teacher.

(VIII.2:1) The dreaming of the world takes many forms, because the body seeks in many ways to prove it is autonomous and real.

If the body is autonomous and real, then the underlying ego thought, hidden in the mind, is also real and autonomous; i.e., we have successfully separated from our Creator and Source.

(VIII.2:2-3) It puts things on itself that it has bought with little metal discs or paper strips the world proclaims as valuable and real. It works to get them, doing senseless things, and tosses them away for senseless things it does not need and does not even want.

Jesus is not making fun of anyone. He is making fun of *everyone*, all of us who believe in the reality of the world and body. From his perspective above the battleground of the ego's world, the silliness of everything here is strikingly apparent. Nevertheless, our insanity does not stop us from doing "senseless things" that seem to make us happy. Jesus' point is not that we should stop living as we do, buying things we do not truly want, etc., but that we step back with him and look with bemusement at what happens here. We need to realize that our special needs for special things is what we have chosen as the meaningless alternative to God's Love. We cannot know we have done this until we first look at what the world is really like, which is the purpose of these passages.

(VIII.2:4-7) It hires other bodies, that they may protect it and collect more senseless things that it can call its own. It looks about for special bodies that can share its dream. Sometimes it dreams it is a conqueror of bodies weaker than itself. But in some phases of the dream, it is the slave of bodies that would hurt and torture it.

Jesus refers to our special love and hate partners: those whom in the name of love we believe we can conquer through seduction, manipulation, and cunningly insidious bargaining; and those we love to hate because they victimize us. When we examine the first section in this chapter, "The Picture of Crucifixion," we shall discuss the perverse pleasure inherent in our insane choices to be hurt and even tortured by other bodies.

(VIII.3) The body's serial adventures, from the time of birth to dying are the theme of every dream the world has ever had. The "hero" of this dream will never change, nor will its purpose. Though the dream itself takes many forms, and seems to show a great variety of places and events wherein its "hero" finds itself, the dream has but one purpose, taught in many ways. This single lesson does it try to teach again, and still again, and yet once more; that it is cause and not effect. And you are its effect, and cannot be its cause.

We see again the all-important leitmotif of purpose, present in every movement of our symphony. On the chart, the mind is the locus of *cause*, and the world its disastrous *effect*. Since *ideas leave not their source*, effects do not leave their cause, the world has no existence outside the mind that thought it. The ego, of course, tells us exactly the opposite: effects do leave their cause; ideas do leave their source. Moreover, not only does the effect leave its cause, but the ego also denies the mind by drawing a veil across it so that the world's cause is entirely hidden, leaving effects to be their own cause. In other words, we believe that the world caused us, beginning with our birth.

Yet in truth it is the mind that made the world, and continues to do so. This is conveniently forgotten, making it appear that we, the bodily heroes of the dream, are innocent victims of people, powers, and events beyond our control. In this way we avoid responsibility for our feelings, allowing us to say to God: "I am not the sinner who brought this about. These, our special partners, are the ones You should punish."

(VIII.4:1-3) Thus are you not the dreamer, but the dream. And so you wander idly in and out of places and events that it contrives. That this is all the body does is true, for it is but a figure in a dream.

The purpose of the world is to conceal the fact that we are the dreamer. This point is made even more emphatically in the next chapter when Jesus speaks of the miracle, whose purpose is to establish that we are, in fact, the dreamers of the dream. Again, the ego tells us we are bodies in the world's dream, the effect of an external cause that is not our responsibility. The importance of the idea that the ego strives to convince us we are dream figures (bodies) and not dreamers (minds) is evident from the number of times it is repeated in this chapter.

(VIII.7:2) The world you see depicts exactly what you thought you did.

What we thought we did (our secret dream) was attack God and destroy His Love, and now it seems as if the world were attacking us. We are sure our unhappiness is due to what bodies have done to us, the reason why the ego continually provides us with authority figures to accuse of being responsible for our dis-ease and loss of love.

(VIII.7:3-4) Except that now you think that what you did is being done to you. The guilt for what you thought is being placed outside yourself, and on a guilty world that dreams your dreams and thinks your thoughts instead of you.

The world is nothing more than the projection of the mind's secret dream. Its hiddenness means we are unaware of it, which naturally means we cannot change it. This is hardly the first time we have seen this idea, and it recurs frequently throughout our symphonic journey. Jesus wants us to understand the mind's purpose for the world so we can change our mistaken decision for the ego. Since purpose exists in the mind and not the body, the only right-minded purpose in being here is to remember the ego's goal, learning how it is manifest and how miserable it makes us. With the help of this course we will find the motivation to change the mind's purpose from guilt to forgiveness.

(VIII.7:5) It brings its vengeance, not your own.

We are the ones with the vengeance and hate, who want others punished instead of ourselves. It does not appear this way in the world, where we believe that the unkind behavior of others adversely affects us and those innocents with whom we identify.

(VIII.7:6) It keeps you narrowly confined within a body, which it punishes because of all the sinful things the body does within its dream.

Later on we will read, "Who punishes the body is insane" (T-28.VI.1:1). This statement applies to the madness, because it is nothing, of punishing our body or another's. The mind is the true repository of guilt, having nothing to do with the projected and illusory body that has not left its source.

(VIII.7:7) You have no power to make the body stop its evil deeds because you did not make it, and cannot control its actions nor its purpose nor its fate.

Very often we will say we could not help our behavior: "It was an irresistible impulse"; "I do not know what came over me"; "My hormones caused me to act that way"; etc. It certainly does seem that the body acts independently of us, the sinless ones, and this is the lie the ego perpetuates and defends to the death.

(VIII.8:1) The world but demonstrates an ancient truth; you will believe that others do to you exactly what you think you did to them.

We want people to attack and betray us, be unfaithful, deceitful, and even kill us, because we want to see our sins in them. We love to see wicked evildoers in the world for that protects us from seeing the evil we believe is our true self. Until we recognize the mind's insane belief that we are "the home of evil, darkness and sin" (W-pI.93.1:1), we will never understand that evil does not exist. To preserve the ego's delusional thought system, we first accuse ourselves of sin and betrayal, and then through projection perceive it in others.

(VIII.8:2) But once deluded into blaming them you will not see the cause of what they do, because you *want* the guilt to rest on them.

We could not ask for a clearer statement of the world's purpose. The ego tells us the mind's sin is so palpably real and reprehensible that we should not go near it. Our only recourse to be saved from guilt is to get rid of it. We make up a world of separate bodies that offers us ample opportunity to find sinners we can scapegoat. The more who agree that a particular person or group is guilty, the easier it becomes to facilitate the justification for our projections. By so doing, we never recognize that the evildoer resides in our secret dreams and not in the nonexistent world.

We turn to the opening of "The Picture of Crucifixion," one of the most difficult sections in the text, not so much in terms of understanding its words, but because when we read them with an open mind we realize the grim truth they point to about ourselves. The section brings together our prior discussions about why we have voluntarily, and even eagerly chosen lives of pain and suffering.

(I.1:1) The wish to be unfairly treated is a compromise attempt that would combine attack and innocence.

We are innocent and others attack us, or we are innocent in attacking back because the world attacked us first. We wish to be unfairly treated because that proves our innocence, allowing us to attack with impunity in the insane belief that it is possible to hurt another and retain our sinless self.

(I.1:2) Who can combine the wholly incompatible, and make a unity of what can never join?

The ego believes it can, a delusion exemplified by political and religious leaders who seek to combine democratic and spiritual ideals with judgment, division, and attack. Indeed, in one way or another we all do this, for the world represents the magical attempt to integrate the irreconcilable in the hope of getting away with the original attack on God, wherein we sought to unify separation and oneness, sin and sinlessness.

(I.1:3-9) Walk you the gentle way, and you will fear no evil and no shadows in the night. But place no terror symbols on your path, or you will weave a crown of thorns from which your brother and yourself will not escape. You cannot crucify yourself alone. And if you are unfairly treated, he must suffer the unfairness that you see. You cannot sacrifice yourself alone. For sacrifice is total. If it could occur at all it would entail the whole of God's creation, and the Father with the sacrifice of His beloved Son.

This, again, is why the ego fears the kindness of forgiveness. In its gentle presence fear is abolished, without which the ego cannot survive. It maintains its fear through the unforgiving thought of sacrifice—one must die so another lives—and we never recognize that if another loses, we lose; if one Son suffers, we all suffer. In addition, we live in mortal terror lest the scales of sacrifice fall against us, satisfying God's need for vengeance. The ego's need to perpetuate its insanity explains why Christian religions rest so securely on the salvific myth of suffering and sacrifice, with Jesus' atoning death demonstrating the "divine" truth of the ego's thought system of punishment for sin. Yet it is not God's Son who is glorified by this madness, but the ego's special son who was born in guilt and hate.

(I.2:1-2) In your release from sacrifice is his made manifest, and shown to be his own. But every pain you suffer do you see as proof that he is guilty of attack.

Now we can understand why we made bodies susceptible to disease and death, vulnerable to a constant barrage of problems that can never truly be resolved. Bodies break down, suffer, and die because the mind wants them to, with the cause attributed to outside forces and, more specifically and even happily, to attacking sinners whom God will most assuredly punish. The sacrifice of oneness is herewith made complete and we are forever "saved" from sin.

(I.2:3-5) Thus would you make yourself to be the sign that he has lost his innocence, and need but look on you to realize that he has been condemned. And what to you has been unfair will come to him in righteousness. The unjust vengeance that you suffer now belongs to him, and when it rests on him are you set free.

We want our families, colleagues, and people in general to realize what terrible sinners exist in the world. Our suffering bodies, crucified by the unconscionable attacks of others, prove that evil is in them, not us. It is they, therefore, who should be punished. The world of the clearly articulated difference between sin and sinlessness is cherished and upheld by the ego for it demonstrates the world's guilt and our innocence. We say to our special enemies: "Because you attacked me unfairly, you will be justifiably attacked back as I save the world from your next attack."

(I.2:6-7) Wish not to make yourself a living symbol of his guilt, for you will not escape the death you made for him. But in his innocence you find your own.

There are no differences among the Sons of God because we are not separate from each other. If I make you guilty, I witness to my sinfulness. If I withdraw the guilt I placed on you, I also withdraw it from myself, establishing our shared innocence.

(I.3:1) Whenever you consent to suffer pain, to be deprived, unfairly treated or in need of anything, you but accuse your brother of attack upon God's Son.

In the secret dream we believe we are the ones who attacked God's Son, crucifying Christ by shattering Him into billions of fragments, obliterating His "Oneness joined as One" (T-25.I.7:1). Our guilt is overwhelming, and the terror over inevitable punishment is equally unbearable. The ego tells us that our only hope is to pretend we did not commit the sin, and then get rid of the secret dream by projecting it onto others. We happily embrace every ounce of pain we suffer at another's hands, for our suffering points an accusing finger, saying: "Since you attacked God's Son (i.e., us), you deserve God's punishment." To repeat, the world's purpose is to allow us to make such statements, and *A Course in Miracles* differs from other non-dualistic spiritualities in that it identifies the motivation for the world's existence: proving another guilty of our "secret sins and hidden hates" (T-31.VIII.9:2) that are the core of the wrong-minded dream.

(I.3:2) You hold a picture of your crucifixion before his eyes, that he may see his sins are writ in Heaven in your blood and death, and go before him, closing off the gate and damning him to hell.

We want God to see the sins of others so they are "writ in Heaven." He will damn them instead of us, dragging them to hell. Since the ego's world is *one or the other*, we become free of sin and must then go to Heaven.

The two sentences of the above paragraph nicely summarize the ego's thought system: We feel guilty over the separation, which causes our individual selves to drip with the blood of sin. Instead of realizing this is a dream, we believe our sin to be real, demanding to be projected. This projection made

the world, and with sin put outside us, our suffering and bloodied deaths prove that another sinned against us. That is why the ego's religions have embraced martyrs who proclaim to God: "The unbelieving ones have sinned against us. Punish them." And He, the ego's insane God, cannot help but notice, pursuing the ego's dictates of guilt, punishment, and death.

From the Course's perspective, we can understand how and why the gospel stories about Jesus were made up. His death says to the guilty world: "Your sins did this to me." For this reason he asks us to forgive him (T-19.IV-B.6) for what he did not do. These tales are the ego's secret dream, played out on the world stage and becoming the world's dream. In effect, Jesus tells us: "I had nothing to do with this madness, and I want you to have nothing to do with it also. Do not make yourselves into pictures of crucifixion that damn those you accuse of sin. This insane dream can only remain a dream, with no effect upon the reality of God's Son."

(I.3:3-6) Yet this is writ in hell and not in Heaven, where you are beyond attack and prove his innocence. The picture of yourself you offer him you show yourself, and give it all your faith. The Holy Spirit offers you, to give to him, a picture of yourself in which there is no pain and no reproach at all. And what was martyred to his guilt becomes the perfect witness to his innocence.

Because we contain this right-minded correction, the ego marshals all its forces of projection and attack to deny the truth that martyrdom, ours or another's, helps no one. It continually bombards the body with guilt so that the mind's forgiveness remains buried beneath layers of fear, and beyond any accessibility for change. How can this insanity be Heaven's will? And in case we missed his point, Jesus repeats it in the next paragraph:

(I.4:3-7) A sick and suffering you but represents your brother's guilt; the witness that you send lest he forget the injuries he gave, from which you swear he never will escape. This sick and sorry picture *you* accept, if only it can serve to punish him. The sick are merciless to everyone, and in contagion do they seek to kill. Death

seems an easy price, if they can say, "Behold me, brother, at your hand I die." For sickness is the witness to his guilt, and death would prove his errors must be sins.

This, then, is where the ego thought system leaves us: the bottom of its ladder of madness that causes us to choose suffering in order for another to be punished. As we have seen, an insane premise (sin is real) can only lead to an insane conclusion (voluntary martyrdom). We all walk this earth, murmuring under our breath in response to every perceived insult or attack: "Behold me, brother, at your hand I suffer, become ill, and die." Inevitably, the ego's separation and sin is accorded reality, while God's living and loving Oneness is relegated to the world of illusion.

(I.4:8-11) Sickness is but a "little" death; a form of vengeance not yet total. Yet it speaks with certainty for what it represents. The bleak and bitter picture you have sent your brother *you* have looked upon in grief. And everything that it has shown to him have you believed, because it witnessed to the guilt in him which you perceived and loved.

Guilt's attraction lies in loving it in others because it means it is not in us. Again, another's guilt is demonstrated by the picture of crucifixion we put before the world. It matters not if the *form* is sickness or death, the purposive *content* of justified attack on the guilty one remains the same. Things not of God's unified Love are equally unreal.

(I.6:3-5) It is not will for life but wish for death that is the motivation for this world. Its only purpose is to prove guilt real. No worldly thought or act or feeling has a motivation other than this one.

Another succinct statement of the world's purpose of not giving glory to God but to the guilt that is seen in everyone but ourselves. Since our purpose in being a body is to prove guilt real, how could it be anything but a "rotting prison" (T-26.I.8:3)? It is guilt that causes the body to rot and die, not old age or the "laws" of nature, for the ego wants us to suffer, even unto death, so that

some other agent is perceived as the sinful architect of our painful demise.

(I.6:6-11) These are the witnesses that are called forth to be believed, and lend conviction to the system they speak for and represent. And each has many voices, speaking to your brother and yourself in different tongues. And yet to both the message is the same. Adornment of the body seeks to show how lovely are the witnesses for guilt. Concerns about the body demonstrate how frail and vulnerable is your life; how easily destroyed is what you love. Depression speaks of death, and vanity of real concern with anything at all.

Recall that pleasure and pain are the same for they both make the body real, differences in *form* belying the sameness of their underlying *content*. This theme of *form and content* reverberates throughout our symphony, and is essential for understanding the ego's strategy and the Holy Spirit's correction. We have been taught that pleasure reflects the dynamic of special love, wherein we seek to conceal our underlying hate with an attractive body. The underside reveals the thought of guilt, for the body's frailty shadows the thought of punishment for sin, the source of all suffering. In this the body is central, for it serves either as an object of depression when it does not perform as we demand, culminating in death, or it becomes an object of veneration and vanity for its many pleasurable gifts. Nonetheless, our body's message to the world is clear: *you*, not my mind, are responsible for the sadness or joy I feel.

(I.7) The strongest witness to futility, that bolsters all the rest and helps them paint the picture in which sin is justified, is sickness in whatever form it takes. The sick have reason for each one of their unnatural desires and strange needs. For who could live a life so soon cut short and not esteem the worth of passing joys? What pleasures could there be that will endure? Are not the frail entitled to believe that every stolen scrap of pleasure is their righteous payment for their little lives? Their death will pay the price for all of them, if they enjoy their benefits or not. The end of life must come, whatever way

that life be spent. And so take pleasure in the quickly passing and ephemeral.

That is how we justify our pleasure-seeking. Life is short and filled with sickness and pain, justifying the pursuit of whatever pleasure we can get, whatever crumbs of specialness we can scrounge for or steal. After all, it is not our fault we are ill; can we be blamed for seeking respite from the pain of physical existence? Yet midst this attraction to the ego's delusions and lies, Jesus relieves our guilt over such "sinful" thoughts and actions by saying:

(I.8) These are not sins, but witnesses unto the strange belief that sin and death are real, and innocence and sin will end alike within the termination of the grave. If this were true, there would be reason to remain content to seek for passing joys and cherish little pleasures where you can. Yet in this picture is the body not perceived as neutral and without a goal inherent in itself. For it becomes the symbol of reproach, the sign of guilt whose consequences still are there to see, so that the cause can never be denied.

This expresses, once again, the body's ultimate purpose of reinforcing guilt, the reason we dream its dream. Since we could have made the body any way we chose—it is *our* dream—why did we have it be vulnerable to causes it cannot control? We have learned the answer: we suffer in weakness so that another will suffer more as the sinful victimizer. The picture of crucifixion we present reflects the ego strategy for salvation, based on the belief that separation is a sin, and death its deserved punishment. Following this perverse plan, even bodily pleasures will be the source of guilt, for the body has been made real, witnessing to the solid truth of the mind's underlying thought of sin.

Forgiveness cannot be understood or practiced apart from the context of the ego's strategy, as it is meant to undo the ego thought system. Without seeing the ego's purpose for bodies and relationships, changing our minds about it is impossible. When we feel repulsed by the hatred in our lives, we will finally be motivated to say: "There must be another way, teacher, and purpose for being

here." But first we need to understand the ego. "The Witnesses to Sin" develops the theme of the ego's purpose, highlighting its use of pain to achieve the goal of self-preservation:

(VI.1:1-2) Pain demonstrates the body must be real. It is a loud, obscuring voice whose shrieks would silence what the Holy Spirit says, and keep His words from your awareness.

We will see how often in this first paragraph of the section the idea of *purpose*, or the word itself, appears in connection with pain. The workbook says: "If God is real, there is no pain. If pain is real, there is no God" (W-pI.190.3:3-4). Pain screams of the body's reality, being the witness that the sin of separation truly occurred. This is the body's purpose, the reason we made it with ultra-sensitive pain receptors. As our dream, we could have made the body be devoid of pain entirely. However, suffering well serves the ego's need to prove that God does not exist. Furthermore, physical and emotional pain demonstrates that some cause other than our minds is responsible for it.

This does not mean we should feel guilty because we suffer or are sick. Jesus merely wants us not to be taken in by the ego's cleverness. At the same time we minister to our pain—remaining in pain is simply masochism—we non-judgmentally watch the ego's machinations at work. In this way we learn of pain's ultimate purpose. To make the point again, since the world and body are our dreams, everything they do is intentional. Freud taught us about the purposive nature of dreams over a century ago, and Jesus expands this understanding to embrace the world. Our sleeping *and* waking dreams are not haphazard, but are chosen deliberately by the mind to keep us asleep. It remains for us to realize their purpose; otherwise we cannot choose to change it and awaken from the dream once and for all.

(VI.1:3-6) Pain compels attention, drawing it away from Him and focusing upon itself. Its purpose is the same as pleasure, for they both are means to make the body real. What shares a common purpose is the same. This is the law of

purpose, which unites all those who share in it within itself.

We could not ask for simpler declarative sentences that say it all: *purpose unites*. This is why pleasure and pain are the same, both making the body real in our experience. We are all here for the insane reason of proving, through our suffering, that there is no God. In our madness we magically seek to blame everyone and everything for our pain (or pleasure). Bodies admirably serve this dual purpose and keep us mindless, seemingly forever.

(VI.1:7-9) Pleasure and pain are equally unreal, because their purpose cannot be achieved. Thus are they means for nothing, for they have a goal without a meaning. And they share the lack of meaning which their purpose has.

Pleasure and pain cannot make the body real, because an illusion is an illusion; nor can they make real the illusory thought of guilt, the body's source. While the purpose of these feelings is to make the ego's existence a fact, they cannot do so, even if in our delusional thinking we believe the ego's thought system exists and God does not.

(VI.2) Sin shifts from pain to pleasure, and again to pain. For either witness is the same, and carries but one message: "You are here, within this body, and you can be hurt. You can have pleasure, too, but only at the cost of pain." These witnesses are joined by many more. Each one seems different because it has a different name, and so it seems to answer to a different sound. Except for this, the witnesses of sin are all alike. Call pleasure pain, and it will hurt. Call pain a pleasure, and the pain behind the pleasure will be felt no more. Sin's witnesses but shift from name to name, as one steps forward and another back. Yet which is foremost makes no difference. Sin's witnesses hear but the call of death.

Our ever-present theme of *form and content* is sounded again. The *content* is the mind's belief in sin, punishable by death. Once projected, the *form* becomes irrelevant, pleasure and pain being the same. Each reflects the sin of separation and rein-

forces its reality to our insane minds. Focusing on the form taken by sin distracts from the mind since it fixes our attention on the mindless, which is the goal of the ego's consummate strategy. This not only strengthens identification with the body, but points to another's as its cause. And so it is not only that we can be happy or suffer, but responsibility for our feelings belongs somewhere else—in a person, place, or thing.

(VI.3:1-4) This body, purposeless within itself, holds all your memories and all your hopes. You use its eyes to see, its ears to hear, and let it tell you what it is it feels. *It does not know.* It tells you but the names you gave to it to use, when you call forth the witnesses to its reality.

The body is purposeless because it is only a projection and has not left its source. Its purpose of attack or forgiveness is given by the decision-making mind, the "you" to whom Jesus addresses his teaching. Allied with the ego, the mind says to the body: "I want you to prove that the separation is real. Furthermore, I want its cause not to be seen within, but outside you in the world." Once again, the mind made the body with sensory organs and receptors that tell us there is an external world that treats us unfairly, an integral part of which is a past (memories) and future (hopes) that govern our lives and seem to give them meaning and purpose.

(VI.3:5-6) You cannot choose among them which are real, for any one you choose is like the rest. This name or that, but nothing more, you choose.

We choose between nothing and nothing. Since there is no hierarchy of illusions, all things here are the same, regardless of the names we use or the feelings we ascribe to them. Being nothing, every illusion is like every other, corrected by the one miracle of forgiveness (there being *no order of difficulty among miracles*).

Our discussion of suffering continues with passages from "The Dreamer of the Dream."

(VII.1) Suffering is an emphasis upon all that the world has done to injure you. Here is the world's demented version of salvation clearly

shown. **Like to a dream of punishment, in which the dreamer is unconscious of what brought on the attack against himself, he sees himself attacked unjustly and by something not himself. He is the victim of this "something else," a thing outside himself, for which he has no reason to be held responsible. He must be innocent because he knows not what he does, but what is done to him. Yet is his own attack upon himself apparent still, for it is he who bears the suffering. And he cannot escape because its source is seen outside himself.**

We do not know our mind's dream, but think we know what others are doing. Having no clue about our "secret sins and hidden hates" (T-31.VIII.9:2), we make ourselves aware of their sins and hates. Even though we desperately try to get rid of guilt through projection, its source (the secret dream) remains within us—*ideas leave not their source.* We are miserable and unhappy, suffer and die, yet do not know the cause, which we attribute to "natural" laws or circumstances beyond our ability to influence or affect, leaving us innocent victims of a harsh, cruel world that seeks only our death.

(VII.3:1-4) The "reasoning" by which the world is made, on which it rests, by which it is maintained, is simply this: "*You* are the cause of what I do. Your presence justifies my wrath, and you exist and think apart from me. While you attack I must be innocent. And what I suffer from is your attack."

The master symphonist returns to his theme of the world's purpose of proving our innocence, purchased through pain. Others, too, must suffer, our projected sins justifying their punishment and our (and God's) righteous wrath.

(VII.3:5) No one who looks upon this "reasoning" exactly as it is could fail to see it does not follow and it makes no sense.

The ego never wants us to look on its strategy, for that would lead to our returning to the mind and choosing sanity over madness. The world that was made to keep us mindless bodies that suffer at the hands of others makes no sense because it cannot be

true. God's Son can be hurt only by his own decision and nothing else, there being nothing else.

(VII.3:6-7) Yet it seems sensible, because it looks as if the world were hurting you. And so it seems as if there is no need to go beyond the obvious in terms of cause.

The ego's reasoning certainly seems sensible, on both individual and collective levels. Bodies, weak and vulnerable, were made to suffer so we could affirm that the cause of suffering is outside us. Since our and the world's brains tell us this, we do not attempt to go beyond the obvious: macro- and microorganisms, the government, weather, etc., are the causes of our distress. Nevertheless, we need not look to externals for the source of our pain, for it exists solely within the decision-making mind, a fact the ego conceals behind the mindless world it forged in guilt and hate.

(VII.4:1-5) There is indeed a need. The world's escape from condemnation is a need which those within the world are joined in sharing. Yet they do not recognize their common need. For each one thinks that if he does his part, the condemnation of the world will rest on him. And it is this that he perceives to *be* his part in its deliverance.

The ego would never have us go from the mindless to the mindful, the body to the mind, but true happiness depends on our doing so—our "common need." One form of ensuring that the mindless state is preserved is martyrdom, a favorite ego device that has been perfected by Christians whose religions are based on the crucified savior, martyred for our sin. Taking the biblical Jesus as their model, they wrong-mindedly believe that innocence must be attacked, reinforcing the divinely inspired truth that their sacrifice of happiness delivers the world from sin, with evil being forever punished and martyred innocence rewarded throughout eternity.

(VII.4:6-9) Vengeance must have a focus. Otherwise is the avenger's knife in his own hand, and pointed to himself. And he must see it in another's hand, if he would be a victim of attack he did not choose. And thus he suffers from the

wounds a knife he does not hold has made upon himself.

We do not want to see that the killer, the cause of our pain, is the mind's decision maker. The ego always directs attention outward, so we perceive the guilt in others and not ourselves. We magically believe our projections will save us, even if it means our own suffering and death. In madness we believe that God's wrath will eventually vindicate us from the injustices foisted on our innocent heads by the world's evil sinners.

(VII.5:1-3) This is the purpose of the world he sees. And looked at thus, the world provides the means by which this purpose seems to be fulfilled. The means attest the purpose, but are not themselves a cause.

Note that *purpose* is mentioned in each of these three sentences. It is essential we see that the world's purpose is to prove that the avenger is outside the mind. Yet this is not really the world's purpose at all, but the ego mind's hate-filled attempt to keep the separation it stole, giving away its sin through projection.

(VII.7:1-4) The witnesses to sin all stand within one little space. And it is here you find the cause of your perspective on the world. Once you were unaware of what the cause of everything the world appeared to thrust upon you, uninvited and unasked, must really be. Of one thing you were sure: Of all the many causes you perceived as bringing pain and suffering to you, your guilt was not among them.

As a society we are astutely capable of identifying the various causes of illness, dysfunction, and the myriad number of problems the world presents to us—physical, psychological, economic, religious, social, and geopolitical. We always look without for the cause, but never to the guilt our minds place their faith and belief in. It is the decision-making self that is the "little space" on which sin and its allies stand, and it is in the decision-making self that the cause of suffering will be

undone, with the memory of our true Cause chosen instead.

(VII.7:5-7) Nor did you in any way request them for yourself. This is how all illusions came about. The one who makes them does not see himself as making them, and their reality does not depend on him.

As Helen said one morning upon awakening, "Never underestimate the power of denial."[1] We do not know we are denying, for we are unaware of the ego's hidden dream. As we know only of the world's dream, seemingly independent of us, how could we be held accountable for a mind that is unconscious and beyond awareness?

(VII.7:8-9) Whatever cause they have is something quite apart from him, and what he sees is separate from his mind. He cannot doubt his dreams' reality, because he does not see the part he plays in making them and making them seem real.

Over and over Jesus urges us to pay attention to our dreaming mind and not the world's dreams, which blind us to the mind's *content*. Having us see only the world of *form*, the ego ensures that the secret dream, the source of the world, remains protected from change and dissolution since the Son has identified only with the mindless.

(VII.8:1-3) No one can waken from a dream the world is dreaming for him. He becomes a part of someone else's dream. He cannot choose to waken from a dream he did not make.

This helps us understand why there is no hope in the world. Jesus points out that we cannot change a dream we do not know we are dreaming, and the ego uses the world of dreams to seal off access to the dreaming mind. On the other hand, our elder brother brings our attention back to it via the miracle, the means of returning us to the mind that is the source of the world and body, the locus of the problem and the answer. Hence, Jesus' course in *miracles* is our life's text.

---

1.   See *Absence from Felicity: The Story of Helen Schucman and Her Scribing of A Course in Miracles*, 2nd Edition, p. 149.

(VII.8:4-7) Helpless he stands, a victim to a dream conceived and cherished by a separate mind. Careless indeed of him this mind must be, as thoughtless of his peace and happiness as is the weather or the time of day. It loves him not, but casts him as it will in any role that satisfies its dream. So little is his worth that he is but a dancing shadow, leaping up and down according to a senseless plot conceived within the idle dreaming of the world.

Now we can see our desperation and perceptions of life as meaningless. It is essential to realize why no hope is possible here, for only then will we be motivated to seek within, where Jesus and his miracle wait for us. He is not in the world, and failing to recognize his presence in the mind, *where we are*, ensures that we will continue to see ourselves tossed about mercilessly by the whims of people, circumstances, even God Himself. Through no fault of our own, we are victims of another's cruel and insensitive dream, cherished by a sick mind we do not know is ours.

(II.10:6-9) Identity and function are the same, and by your function do you know yourself. And thus, if you confuse your function with the function of Another, you must be confused about yourself and who you are. What is the separation but a wish to take God's function from Him and deny that it is His? Yet if it is not His it is not yours, for you must lose what you would take away.

Our Identity is Christ and our function is creation. When we believed the lie of separation, we made ourselves into God, confusing our function with His and making ourselves First Cause instead of being Its Effect. The simple mistake of identity confusion becomes to the ego the egregious sin of usurping God's role, a sin punishable by death. This causes the ego's projected God to share our secret dreams of sin and vengeance, all the while our Self and Its Creator wait patiently beyond these feverish dreams for the deluded mind to awaken to the home it never left.

(II.11:1-2) In a split mind, identity must seem to be divided. Nor can anyone perceive a function unified which has conflicting purposes and different ends.

This is the split wherein we see ourselves with a function separate from God's, a split we project, leading to the belief we have a function separate from everyone else's: another's purpose is to kill, ours to correct or punish. These separate functions or goals establish very real differences among God's Sons, denying their fundamental unity.

(II.11:3-6) Correction, to a mind so split, must be a way to punish sins you think are yours in someone else. And thus does he become your victim, not your brother, different from you in that he is more guilty, thus in need of your correction, as the one more innocent than he. This splits his function off from yours, and gives you both a different role. And so you cannot be perceived as one, and with a single function that would mean a shared identity with but one end.

This, again, goes to the heart of the ego's thought system (*one or the other; kill or be killed*), expressed here in the more subtle form described in *The Song of Prayer* as "forgiveness-to-destroy" (S-2.II). While we project the mind's perceived sin onto others, affirming our sinlessness that would demand their punishment, it appears that we are being kind only to correct their errors. Yet we maintain the separation by demonstrating that others are different from us: we who correct, they who need correction. Stated another way, we do not see a shared, but a split purpose or function, with others being victimizers and we the ones who in all innocence "benignly" suffer from their sin.

(II.13:2-6) From an idea of self as two, there comes a necessary view of function split between the two. And what you would correct is only half the error, which you think is all of it. Your brother's sins become the central target for correction, lest your errors and his own be seen as one. Yours are mistakes, but his are sins and not the same as yours. His merit punishment, while yours, in fairness, should be overlooked.

Perhaps we are not perfect and have made mistakes, but that does not make us sinners. Sure we may have cheated on our income tax, or may not have been totally honest in business, but we are different from others who would rape, torture, and kill. This mentality of a hierarchy of sins, which we all subscribe to, means that we in fact love, and not hate evildoers as we might protest. We cherish their "sins" because they enable us to see functions as split—theirs to sin while ours to "forgive"—in a way that conceals the underlying thought of making the sins of others real and deserving of punishment. This establishes God's Sons as different: one innocent, one guilty.

We proceed now to one of two places in the text where Jesus treats the aforementioned "forgiveness-to-destroy" (the other is T-30.VI.1-4; it is also described in the workbook, W-pI.126.1-7; W-pI.134.1-5). Jesus explains how we typically correct other people's sins, sometimes doing so under the guise of forgiveness whereby we forgive others for what they *have* done, masking our murderous thoughts behind a veil of holiness. There are also the times when we simply punish the sinners outright. Either way, we have established our differentiating moral superiority.

(II.1:5-10) Who has been injured by his brother, and could love and trust him still? He has attacked and will attack again. Protect him not, because your damaged body shows that *you* must be protected from him. To forgive may be an act of charity, but not his due. He may be pitied for his guilt, but not exonerated. And if you forgive him his transgressions, you but add to all the guilt that he has really earned.

Jesus refers to what has gone by the name of forgiveness for over two millennia of the Judaeo-Christian tradition, forgiving others for the terrible things they have done. As many Jewish people said after World War II: "We will forgive, but never forget." In other words, despite their spilled blood, through the kindness of their hearts and spiritual maturity, these holy ones forgive. Such forgiveness is based on having first made real the sins of the attackers, and Jesus asks us to consider

how that could be forgiveness when bodies have been martyred to another's sin. In addition, the ego's cleverness reinforces the guilt of the "forgiven" sinners because the victim's ongoing suffering demonstrates that the aggressors do not deserve to be forgiven.

(II.2:1-3) The unhealed cannot pardon. For they are the witnesses that pardon is unfair. They would retain the consequences of the guilt they overlook.

How is forgiveness possible as long as guilt remains? Our repressed guilt must be projected in the maladaptive attempt to make others feel the guilt we have sought to deny. Being unhealed of guilt, we cannot help but use our suffering as damning witness to another's sin, making forgiveness totally unjustified.

(II.2:4-10) Yet no one can forgive a sin that he believes is real. And what has consequences must be real, because what it has done is there to see. Forgiveness is not pity, which but seeks to pardon what it thinks to be the truth. Good cannot *be* returned for evil, for forgiveness does not first establish sin and then forgive it. Who can say and mean, "My brother, you have injured me, and yet, because I am the better of the two, I pardon you my hurt." His pardon and your hurt cannot exist together. One denies the other and must make it false.

Forgiveness is impossible as long as sin is the perception, which must be the case as long we believe we are separated, having destroyed Heaven and crucified God's Son. This hidden belief impels us to overlook what we have already made real in ourselves and others, the latter reinforced by our misery and pain. The Holy Spirit's forgiveness, however, shows that someone's sin against us had no effect, reflecting that the Son's separation from His Source did not occur. He forever remains as God created him—*one*. As we read earlier: "…not one note in Heaven's song was missed" (T-26.V.5:4). Given that happy fact, the ego thought system cannot be real, which we demonstrate by not giving attack the power to change our love. Such kindness in response to seeming sin truly forgives it.

(II.3) To witness sin and yet forgive it is a paradox that reason cannot see. For it maintains what has been done to you deserves no pardon. And by giving it, you grant your brother mercy but retain the proof he is not really innocent. The sick remain accusers. They cannot forgive their brothers and themselves as well. For no one in whom true forgiveness rests can suffer. He holds not the proof of sin before his brother's eyes. And thus he must have overlooked it and removed it from his own. Forgiveness cannot be for one and not the other.

The ego has two ways of dealing with sin. One is to have us punish it directly, feeling justified because we act in self-defense, proving we are innocent and others guilty. The second, more subtle and therefore more insidious, is that we pretend to forgive, maybe even consciously thinking we do so. Yet we merely show others what they have done to us—"The sick remain accusers"—and only then will we graciously bestow our forgiveness on them. We thereby make their sin real and then overlook it. Once again, this is impossible for how can we make something real, and then say we do not see it? We know we have done this because we consistently demonstrate to people what they have done to hurt us or others. In other words, we have forgiven only to destroy them by having *our* sins rest on their guilty shoulders, ensuring that they lose and we win. Indeed, we bring pain to ourselves by attacking another for our sin. God's Son being one, we must be destroyed as well: if attack is for one, it is for all. Likewise, forgiveness is for all, and our defenselessness attests that no sin occurred because there were no effects. God's Son cannot suffer, except in dreams. To conclude, we cannot attack or forgive another without including ourselves and all the Sonship in the thought we first made real in our wrong or right minds: *projection makes perception.*

The next three paragraphs, which open "Beyond All Symbols," reflect the insanity of the ego's dualistic thought system that purports to be a true substitute for the oneness of creation:

(III.1) Power cannot oppose. For opposition would weaken it, and weakened power is a contradiction in ideas. Weak strength is meaningless, and power used to weaken is employed to limit. And therefore it must be limited and weak, because that is its purpose. Power is unopposed, to be itself. No weakness can intrude on it without changing it into something it is not. To weaken is to limit, and impose an opposite that contradicts the concept that it attacks. And by this does it join to the idea a something it is not, and make it unintelligible. Who can understand a double concept, such as "weakened power" or "hateful love"?

The heart of the ego's thought system is opposition, for the separated Son was born in the insane instant he believed he had successfully opposed his Source. From that moment on his self was one of opposition, which gave rise to a world in which every "living thing" survives by successfully opposing the special love and hate objects of its need to be satisfied. Life in the dream means opposition, and the more powerful the individual, the more successful its special relationships of cannibalism and triumph. Indeed, the ego's Orwellian *doublethink* denies the very thing it affirms: hate masquerading as love can never be love, and the dualistic power of domination is not the power of all-inclusive love, reflected here in recognizing the shared interests that unite the Sonship as one. Christ's Oneness alone is truth, which is its strength, while separation is forever the lie, the home of weakness, attack, and loss.

(III.2) You have decided that your brother is a symbol for a "hateful love," a "weakened power," and above all, a "living death." And so he has no meaning to you, for he stands for what is meaningless. He represents a double thought, where half is cancelled out by the remaining half. Yet even this is quickly contradicted by the half it cancelled out, and so they both are gone. And now he stands for nothing. Symbols which but represent ideas that cannot be must stand for empty space and nothingness. Yet nothingness and empty space can not be interference.

What can interfere with the awareness of reality is the belief that there is something there.

Nowhere is the insanity of the ego's dualistic thought system of opposition more clearly seen than in its special relationships. God's Son is not seen as Christ—His Oneness reflected in the Son's inherent sameness within the illusion—but as a body, designed to meet the demanding needs of special hate that he be the object of our projected guilt. Special partners are seen as egos, symbols of hate, weakness, and death, while we pretend that their bodies represent love, strength, and life. Only a madman could believe this, and still we do believe it. Our very self rests on the lie that we have replaced the Everything of God with the ego's nothingness, seeing something where nothing is.

(III.3) The picture of your brother that you see means nothing. There is nothing to attack or to deny; to love or hate, or to endow with power or to see as weak. The picture has been wholly cancelled out, because it symbolized a contradiction that cancelled out the thought it represents. And thus the picture has no cause at all. Who can perceive effect without a cause? What can the causeless be but nothingness? The picture of your brother that you see is wholly absent and has never been. Let, then, the empty space it occupies be recognized as vacant, and the time devoted to its seeing be perceived as idly spent, a time unoccupied.

We return to the motif of *cause and effect*. The ego is simply the insane attempt to establish its nothingness as something, meaning that what arises from it must also be an insane attempt to establish its nothingness as something: the madness of trying to supplant Heaven's Everything. Since the ego's inherent nothingness is the *cause*, its *effects* (the world of special bodies) must also be nothing. Recognizing this intrinsic emptiness allows us not to take the ego's delusions and hallucinations seriously; i.e., they have no power to affect the peace of God's Son. In this blessed recognition all special projections come to naught, and choosing the holy instant allows Jesus to enter and restore sanity to our perturbed minds. Pictures of hateful weakness must perforce give way to pictures of loving strength, as God's Son remembers that he *is* God's Son.

(IV.1:1-6) In quietness are all things answered, and is every problem quietly resolved. In conflict there can be no answer and no resolution, for its purpose is to make no resolution possible, and to ensure no answer will be plain. A problem set in conflict has no answer, for it is seen in different ways. And what would be an answer from one point of view is not an answer in another light. You *are* in conflict. Thus it must be clear you cannot answer anything at all, for conflict has no limited effects.

Since the ego fears the decision maker's choosing the answer of Atonement and the memory of God, which it can do only in the quietness of forgiveness, it protects itself by keeping the Son in a continual state of conflict. Recall: "The memory of God comes to the quiet mind (T-23.I.1:1)." We are continually doing battle with our projected selves, perceived to be external to the mind. Since this guilty self remains unknown to us, it is always being cast out, giving rise to the experience of being in a perpetual war with the world. All this complexity is the ego's very simple plan to keep us seeking multitudinous answers in its world of multiplicity, which is the reason we never seek or find the right mind's single answer (Atonement) to the wrong mind's single problem (separation).

Continuing the teaching in "The Quiet Answer," we learn that the world's questions are not questions at all, being statements that are "propaganda" for themselves (T-27.IV.5:3). Questions are based on the premise that the world is real and not understandable to the questioner, who seeks an explanation. Consequently, the question attests to the reality of the separated world, leading Jesus to say:

(IV.3:8) It [the world] does not ask a question to be answered, but only to restate its point of view.

Thus the child's question: "How did the world happen, Daddy?" Even when the cosmogonic question is asked of our greatest physicists, it remains a statement affirming the material universe. Again, it is not a legitimate question for its words are a declaration in support of the world's (i.e., the ego's) point of view that the separation is a fact, and one that demands an explanation.

(IV.4:1-2) All questions asked within this world are but a way of looking, not a question asked. A question asked in hate cannot be answered, because it is an answer in itself.

Questions reflect looking through the eyes of hate, being born of the hatred for God that says: "I can create better than You. I *want* to and *can* exist outside You." Everything that follows this original thought is a shadow of that hate, which is why the world is such an unkind and cruel place, stemming from the belief that this is how we acted toward God. Our ego questions provide an ego answer, and conceal the meaningful answer of Atonement that would deny the very questions themselves. Truth is one, and cannot be known by questioning but through acceptance, as we read at the end of the workbook: "We are concerned only with giving welcome to the truth" (W-pII.14.3:7).

(IV.4:3-17) A double question asks and answers, both attesting the same thing in different form. The world asks but one question. It is this: "Of these illusions, which of them *is* true? Which ones establish peace and offer joy? And which can bring escape from all the pain of which this world is made?" Whatever form the question takes, its purpose is the same. It asks but to establish sin is real, and answers in the form of preference. "Which sin do you prefer? That is the one that you should choose. The others are not true. What can the body get that you would want the most of all? It is your servant and also your friend. But tell it what you want, and it will serve you lovingly and well." And this is not a question, for it tells you what you want and where to go for it. It leaves no room to question its beliefs, except that what it states takes question's form.

Not only do questions reflect the ego's hate, but also its foundational premise that sin is real.

Regardless of the form of the question—the content being, "Which sin do you prefer?"—the ego's thought system is declared valid, forever protected from having its existence meaningfully questioned. The body is the primary object of its concern because it holds the mind's existence securely in the vaults of forgetfulness. Yet when we examine the ego through reason's right-minded eyes, we recognize that the question is both question *and* answer ("a double question"), and one we no longer wish to ask. This allows room in our minds for the only question that can be truly asked: *"Do I want to see what I denied because it is the truth?"* (T-21.VII.5:14). And happily we at last answer "yes."

(IV.5:1-5) A pseudo-question has no answer. It dictates the answer even as it asks. Thus is all questioning within the world a form of propaganda for itself. Just as the body's witnesses are but the senses from within itself, so are the answers to the questions of the world contained within the questions that are asked. Where answers represent the questions, they add nothing new and nothing has been learned.

This, then, is the world of bodies: "propaganda for itself," for whatever we do here substantiates the thought of separation. Propaganda is always false, being the attempt to convince others of the lies that serve the propagandist's purpose. This is true of nation states as it is of individuals, because it is the ego's strategy to have the Son believe its lies of separation and specialness. All of us, putting on "the face of innocence" (T-31.V.2:6), continue to make the world and seek to establish its reality through questioning it. Nonetheless, these questions cannot escape their source and merely state the ego's point of view that the separation is real and present. Their propaganda demands that the world explain its own cosmogony and cosmology (origin and nature), illusion explaining itself.

Having completed our discussion of the ego's functioning, we turn to the Holy Spirit and His correction of forgiveness. We have seen the horrific portrait of crucifixion we present to each other that establishes another's guilt through our suffering, culminating in punishment. Gently moving through our delusions, Jesus reassures us that he will not take us directly from the ego's hated and fearful picture of nothingness to the Everything. He first substitutes a kinder picture, the forgiveness that is the immediate subject of "Beyond All Symbols," the next section in the text to be considered.

Forgiveness

(III.4:7-8) Yet true undoing must be kind. And so the first replacement for your picture is another picture of another kind.

One cannot miss the word play here on *kind.* Before we reach the state beyond all pictures or symbols, we need a gentler picture, one that shows others we have not been hurt. It is a picture of the body still, but a kind one that contains no accusations of sin.

(III.5:1-2) As nothingness cannot be pictured, so there is no symbol for totality. Reality is ultimately known without a form, unpictured and unseen.

This truth is our fear, for if at the beginning we had chosen to listen to the Holy Spirit's Voice, we would have promptly disappeared into the Heart we never left. We fled from this awareness because we identified with the idea of individual existence. At this point, then, reality became a threat because its perfect Oneness held no place for a special self, the picture of separation. Since our cherished self remains terrified of God's Love, intervening steps are needed. These are the Holy Spirit's gentle symbols or happy dreams of forgiveness.

(III.5:3-5) Forgiveness is not yet a power known as wholly free of limits. Yet it sets no limits you have chosen to impose. Forgiveness is the means by which the truth is represented temporarily.

Despite being within the dream, forgiveness does not reinforce the dream of sin but corrects or undoes it. It is not truth, although its kindness reflects truth's loving reality. Therefore, if truth is oneness, its reflection is the purpose of forgiveness that we all share. The mind's one problem of guilt and its one solution of forgiveness transcend our bodily differences and make us the same.

(III.5:6-9) It lets the Holy Spirit make exchange of pictures possible, until the time when aids are meaningless and learning done. No learning aid has use that can extend beyond the goal of learning. When its aim has been accomplished it is functionless. Yet in the learning interval it has a use that now you fear, but yet will love.

Our learning aim now is the shift in purpose we give the body. Rather than being an instrument of reinforcing guilt, separation, and specialness, the body becomes the vehicle of returning our attention to the mind that made it. It is the means, ultimately, of undoing itself along with the thought system of guilt that is its source. Fearing this shift because we do not want to lose our self, we cling to it, blaming another for our wretched state. Forgiveness undoes this insanity by teaching that our separated self can exist in the world without being at odds with it. We no longer see others as enemies, but as friends who share the common need to return home.

In the passages that follow we gratefully see the Holy Spirit's answer to the ego's sinister theme song: "Behold me, brother, at your hand I die."

(I.5:1-2) Now in the hands made gentle by His touch, the Holy Spirit lays a picture of a different you. It is a picture of a body still, for what you really are cannot be seen nor pictured.

What we really are strikes terror in our hearts, which is why we need gentle steps that allow us to gradually let go of the purpose we have given to the body. We need these little steps because without them we will think we are one step from Heaven, if not in Heaven itself, when all we really have done is deny the mind's guilt-ridden thoughts of separation, sin, and hate. Before we can really know, not intellectually but experientially, that we are not bodies living in a nonexistent dreamworld, we must retain our bodily identification, albeit differently; too much fear still lurks within for us to think we are non-corporeal. Remember that we made the body to protect us from the supposed terror in our minds, but under Jesus' kind tutelage, the body's purpose is shifted from guilt to forgiveness.

(I.5:3) Yet this one [the Holy Spirit's picture of the body] **has not been used for purpose of attack, and therefore never suffered pain at all.**

Pain should not be equated with external symptoms, but with the pain of guilt that comes from the wrong mind's use of bodily dis-ease for attack. As long as we have physical or psychological pain, Jesus would have us use whatever magic would alleviate it (cf. T-2.IV.4); after all, his is a course in miracles, not masochism. Until we truly know we are not bodies, some form of pain is inevitable. Adopting a quasi-spiritual attitude that denies the suffering that is clearly experienced helps no one, being "a particularly unworthy form of denial" (T-2.IV.3:11). Indeed, this denial reinforces the ego thought system instead of undoing it, our having made its guilt real and fearful before denying it. The focus instead should be on releasing the purpose served by our sick and victimized body. This means that we do not ask Jesus to heal the body, but to help us shift the purpose our minds gave to it, which had us point an accusing finger that said: "Behold me, brother, at your hand I die."

(I.5:4-8) It [the Holy Spirit's picture of the body] **witnesses to the eternal truth that you cannot be hurt, and points beyond itself to both your innocence and his. Show this unto your brother, who will see that every scar is healed, and every tear is wiped away in laughter and in love. And he will look on his forgiveness there, and with healed eyes will look beyond it to the innocence that he beholds in you. Here is the proof that he has never sinned; that nothing which his madness bid him do was ever done, or ever had effects of any kind. That no reproach he laid upon his heart was ever justified, and no attack can ever touch him with the poisoned and relentless sting of fear.**

We are asked to show each other that our sins had no effect: the love and peace that existed before the "attack" has not changed. Once again, Jesus does not speak of anything external, but only of the right-minded attitude that sees God's Sons as the same. Forgiveness undoes the cause that was sin by demonstrating that its effects are nonexistent. Without the result of suffering, sin cannot exist, and it is our defenselessness that witnesses to another's innocence. This argument, which hinges on the recognition that we are minds and not bodies, returns below, and again in the next chapter.

(I.6:1-2) Attest his innocence and not his guilt. Your healing is his comfort and his health because it proves illusions are not true.

This refers to our shift in purpose. We do not deny our suffering body or that someone has hurt it, but we do try to see how the ego revels in the pain, using it as means to accuse another of our secret sin. The right mind recognizes and releases the illusory perception that the attack was against *us*, for the truth is that it was a mere projection of the attacker's guilt. Similarly, any accusation we may make reflects the projection of our guilt. This recognition leads to the following understanding: no projection, no guilt; no guilt, only innocence and love. And so it is that our defenseless forgiveness reflects the healing message of Atonement for all to see and accept.

(I.9:1) Your function is to show your brother sin can have no cause.

We have already seen what the ego does with cause and effect: sin is the cause, suffering the effect. We want this effect manifest so we can say to another: "Look what you have done to me!" By this attack, suffering becomes the effect of another's sin, the cause that justifies punishment. To heal this insanity, Jesus asks us to show each other that sin has no effect. If we can demonstrate that we are not hurt, despite our bodily state of pain, we are not making accusations of sin but teaching that the "sins" against us have not changed our love. If sin has no effect it cannot be a cause, and if not a cause, it cannot exist.

Everything must be a cause or an effect of something, and by showing that attacks have not altered us, we teach they are not sins but only mistakes. This is how sins are forgiven.

Forgiveness of sin is the overriding message of *A Course in Miracles*, somewhat similar to the biblical statement of turning the other cheek (Matthew 5:39), which does not mean we masochistically get struck twice, or even once. The reference is not to external behavior, but to an attitude of defenselessness or shift of the mind's purpose. Again, nothing in the Course would tell us *not* to set limits on a person's ability to miscreate—inflicting physical or psychological harm—but that we do so with non-punitive kindness. We need to recognize that the ego's purpose for relationships is reflected in our *wanting* to be attacked and unfairly treated, as this justifies seeing our sins in another. Our suffering, to repeat this essential point, becomes the effect of that person's sin, a cause now proven to be real and deserving of punishment. Forgiveness shifts this purpose of witnessing to the sins of another, making us "sinless," to realizing we can teach and learn that sin has no effect and therefore does not exist: God's Son is always and forever His innocent Son.

(I.9:2-10) How futile must it be to see yourself a picture of the proof that what your function is can never be! The Holy Spirit's picture changes not the body into something it is not. It only takes away from it all signs of accusation and of blamefulness. Pictured without a purpose, it is seen as neither sick nor well, nor bad nor good. No grounds are offered that it may be judged in any way at all. It has no life, but neither is it dead. It stands apart from all experience of love or fear. For now it witnesses to nothing yet, its purpose being open, and the mind made free again to choose what it is for. Now is it not condemned, but waiting for a purpose to be given, that it may fulfill the function that it will receive.

When we withdraw the ego's purpose for the body—accusation through suffering—we wait for the Holy Spirit's purpose to be given it. After the ego made the body to limit love (T-18.VIII.1:1-4) it became neutral, serving either the goal of perpetuating the illusion of limitation or the purpose of undoing it through forgiveness, restoring to us the awareness of the limitlessness of God's Son. Nothing is done to the body at all when we choose a different Teacher; only the illusion of the mind's projections are lifted. The body, then, can be seen for the nothingness it is, as our investment in being unfairly treated has been recognized and chosen against. Freed of the mind's projected burden of guilt, the body is transformed into the picture of innocence. Without sin and guilt to be projected, the mind is made free to choose the reflected sinlessness of Christ as its one identity.

(I.10:1-2) Into this empty space, from which the goal of sin has been removed, is Heaven free to be remembered. Here its peace can come, and perfect healing take the place of death.

Recall the lovely section "Where Sin Has Left" (T-26.IV). Sin is only purpose, and when we remove it from the mind there is an empty space that allows the Holy Spirit's purpose to take its place. As the ego thought system of death is a defense against the thought of Atonement, when we withdraw belief from the wrong mind we make room for the right mind, the Holy Spirit's Presence, to remind us that the separation never happened. This shift in purpose fulfills our function of choosing the healing principle of undoing: peace instead of war, life over death.

(I.10:3-7) The body can become a sign of life, a promise of redemption, and a breath of immortality to those grown sick of breathing in the fetid scent of death. Let it have healing as its purpose. Then will it send forth the message it received, and by its health and loveliness proclaim the truth and value that it represents. Let it receive the power to represent an endless life, forever unattacked. And to your brother let its message be, "Behold me, brother, at your hand I live."

Once again, Jesus is not speaking of behavior, but of our recognizing the ego's hateful purpose for relationships: making others scapegoats for our sin.

If we can prove how we have suffered at another's hand, we have made the ego's case that sin and projection are both real and justified. Jesus asks us to look at this purpose and bring its illusions to his truth. Our relationship with him is not to make us feel good as such, but to help us see that our attack thoughts hurt us. He speaks to "those grown sick of breathing in the fetid scent of death," hoping to supply the motivation to let these dark and hateful thoughts go. Looking through Jesus' eyes, we happily learn to see the other way. Withdrawing the purpose we have given the body, we make room for his loving purpose to be our own. Everything we now do reflects this healing statement, the only joy the world can offer for it is the means of knowing our sins are forgiven: "Behold me, brother, at your hand I live."

(I.11) The simple way to let this be achieved is merely this; to let the body have no purpose from the past, when you were sure you knew its purpose was to foster guilt. For this insists your crippled picture is a lasting sign of what it represents. This leaves no space in which a different view, another purpose, can be given it. You do *not* know its purpose. You but gave illusions of a purpose to a thing you made to hide your function from yourself. This thing without a purpose cannot hide the function that the Holy Spirit gave. Let, then, its purpose and your function both be reconciled at last and seen as one.

Note how many times *purpose* appears in this paragraph, reflecting its thematic importance in our symphony. All we need do is ask Jesus' help to look at the guilt-laden purpose we have given our special relationships, and how unhappy it has made us. This will impel us to let it go and make room for his purpose, which is to return us to our function of forgiveness here, and our function of creation in Heaven. He is asking his students to set aside the special distractions of the world and focus on the decision-making mind: the place of two purposes, one of which is true.

(II.4:1-5) Forgiveness is not real unless it brings a healing to your brother and yourself. You must attest his sins have no effect on you to demonstrate they are not real. How else could he be guiltless? And how could his innocence be justified unless his sins have no effect to warrant guilt? Sins are beyond forgiveness just because they would entail effects that cannot be undone and overlooked entirely.

Jesus again expresses the principle that forgiveness cannot be for one and not the other. This corrects *forgiveness-to-destroy*, which says: "I forgive, but will never forget your terrible sin." The ego's distorted version of forgiveness rests on the belief that differences are real. We are being taught by Jesus to realize that the "terrible sin" came from the fear that mirrors our own, and we know that fear is the result of believing we are bodies. We need to realize that the apparent differences in *form* among God's Sons belie the underlying sameness of the mind's *content* of fear, our "natural" inheritance as children of guilt. Yet since fear is unreal, as are the sin and guilt that caused it, so too is the world that arose from them: illusions breed illusions; unreal causes have only unreal effects.

(II.5) A broken body shows the mind has not been healed. A miracle of healing proves that separation is without effect. What you would prove to him you will believe. The power of witness comes from your belief. And everything you say or do or think but testifies to what you teach to him. Your body can be means to teach that it has never suffered pain because of him. And in its healing can it offer him mute testimony of his innocence. It is this testimony that can speak with power greater than a thousand tongues. For here is his forgiveness proved to him.

The phrase "mute testimony" reflects that we need not do or say anything. The love and peace that is the content of forgiveness speaks through us, and our special partners understand they have done nothing sinful. Our defenselessness in the face of seeming attack teaches that nothing has been done to warrant guilt. God's Love is totally unaffected by fear, meaning there is nothing to forgive. In this way we learn to forgive our own belief in sin, which necessitated presenting a broken body as witness to the reality of our projection. Now we are healed of the ego's purpose for sickness, and our brothers along with us. The darkness of guilt is replaced by the light of forgiveness that is our changed purpose. As one of Helen's poems has us say to Jesus: "The light around Your head must speak for me" (*The Gifts of God*, p. 82). And happily it does, in mute testimony, as his love shines on all God's Sons as one.

(II.6:1) A miracle can offer nothing less to him than it has given unto you.

The theme of the inherent sameness of God's Son returns. If we are healed, others are healed; if they are healed, we are too. It cannot be that we are different, that something happens to one without the other. Conversely, if we attack, we are attacked. The miracle heals because we are one: one guilt, one forgiveness; one problem, one solution.

(II.6:2-3) So does your healing show your mind is healed, and has forgiven what he did not do. And so is he convinced his innocence was never lost, and healed along with you.

As one Son, we suffer from the same horrific nightmare of believing we killed God and crucified His Son. We all need help because we share the same insanity as well as the need to awaken from it, this world's only purpose. Having made the world to attack God's Love by establishing a world of special love, we now go within and ask Jesus for help to shift our mind's purpose for the dreaming Sonship. The world, then, takes on the different meaning that reason has given it: innocence instead of sin, healing in place of attack and death.

(II.6:4-11) Thus does the miracle undo all things the world attests can never be undone. And hopelessness and death must disappear before the ancient clarion call of life. This call has power far beyond the weak and miserable cry of death and guilt. The ancient calling of the Father to His Son, and of the Son unto His Own, will yet be the last trumpet that the world will ever hear. Brother, there is no death. And this you learn when you but wish to show your brother that you had no hurt of him. He thinks

your blood is on his hands, and so he stands condemned. Yet it is given you to show him, by your healing, that his guilt is but the fabric of a senseless dream.

The ego and its horrific world tell us that sin is irremediable, as we read in the manual for teachers, echoing Lady Macbeth's tormented state of mind (*Macbeth* V,i): "...what was done cannot be done without. The stain of blood can never be removed, and anyone who bears this stain on him must meet with death" (M-17.7:12-13). Each of us carries this indelible stain of sin within, convinced that projection is the only escape, wherein we condemn another for our perceived sinfulness. This, happily for the ego, reinforces our sense of sin as our judgments continue to separate us from God's Son. Nevertheless, there is another choice we can make, for our split minds contain another Voice. This Call of Atonement has been present from the beginning, which is *now*. And so we choose again: listening to the Voice for Life, not the call to death. The last trumpet of Atonement, reminiscent of St. Paul's famous reference (1 Co 15:52), is all we hear, and the ego's sirenic call to death is gently left behind. The Holy Spirit's Call that we have accepted rings throughout the Sonship, and by demonstrating its peace-filled effects to our special loves and hates, we reinforce them in ourselves. Our healing is the world's, and the special function of forgiveness is consummated in a blazing light that dissolves the dream, whose senselessness disappears into its own nothingness.

(II.7:1-6) How just are miracles! For they bestow an equal gift of full deliverance from guilt upon your brother and yourself. Your healing saves him pain as well as you, and you are healed because you wished him well. This is the law the miracle obeys; that healing sees no specialness at all. It does not come from pity but from love. And love would prove all suffering is but a vain imagining, a foolish wish with no effects.

It is important to understand that the above is not true within the dream; only when we are above the battleground, outside the ego's dreams of hate, can suffering be perceived as an illusion, the same as all illusions. This is the perspective of the holy instant, the world looked at through vision in which things are not as they appear—different and special. True healing is not specialness, for it does not differentiate one problem or person from another; for example, someone with a healing gift and another who needs it. We *all* have the same healing gift because healing is the change of mind brought about by asking Jesus' help. Similarly, we *all* have the same need to be healed. Seeing differences in form mean nothing, for we share the same content of love or fear. If we think otherwise, we are trapped in the spiritual specialness of making differences real, which means we have made sin real. This misperception reinforces the ego's dream in which someone perceived as different from us needs to suffer because of our sin.

(II.8:1-7) The "cost" of your serenity is his. This is the "price" the Holy Spirit and the world interpret differently. The world perceives it as a statement of the "fact" that your salvation sacrifices his. The Holy Spirit knows your healing is the witness unto his, and cannot be apart from his at all. As long as he consents to suffer, you will be unhealed. Yet you can show him that his suffering is purposeless and wholly without cause. Show him your healing, and he will consent no more to suffer.

The sameness of the Sonship, reflecting the unity of the split mind, means that the ego's principle of *one or the other* is a lie. It is not true that salvation means others are sacrificed instead of us. Rather, if we seek to punish another for our sin, we both suffer. Similarly, if we seek vision instead of judgment, we do not see sins but only mistakes to be corrected. Healing embraces all God's Sons, otherwise it is not healing but *healing-to-separate* (S-3.III.2:1).

The repetition of *consent* in the final sentences is important. Suffering does not happen *to* us, but is a choice the mind makes to preserve its separated self at another's expense. But let one person demonstrate a different thought system, innocence instead of sin, and we can be inspired to choose Jesus' gentle laughter in place of tears:

(II.8:8-9) For his innocence has been established in your sight and his. And laughter will replace your sighs, because God's Son remembered that he *is* God's Son.

To be God's Son means to be God's *one* Son, meaning that the Sonship is perceived as whole. To see differences as real shatters our unity and re-crucifies God's Son on a cross of sin and guilt. Yet remembering to laugh at the *tiny, mad idea* wipes away our hopelessness and despair, and the memory of the Self quietly dawns on our forgiven mind.

(II.10:1-5) Correction is not your function. It belongs to One Who knows of fairness, not of guilt. If you assume correction's role, you lose the function of forgiveness. No one can forgive until he learns correction is but to forgive, and never to accuse. Alone, you cannot see they are the same, and therefore is correction not of you.

Another familiar theme returns: our "little willingness" that allows the Holy Spirit to fulfill His function. Ours is to choose forgiveness; its extension through us—i.e., correction—is not our concern. This means that our decision-making minds must choose *against* the ego and its judgment, not *for* the Holy Spirit. We turn to Him only to share His perception of the silliness of the thought of separation, recognizing it has no power to change God's Son. What needs correction is only the mistaken belief that change is real, not the illusory change itself.

(II.12) Correction *you* would do must separate, because that is the function given it *by* you. When you perceive correction is the same as pardon, then you also know the Holy Spirit's Mind and yours are One. And so your own Identity is found. Yet must He work with what is given Him, and you allow Him only half your mind. And thus He represents the other half, and seems to have a different purpose from the one you cherish, and you think is yours. Thus does your function seem divided, with a half in opposition to a half. And these two halves

appear to represent a split within a self perceived as two.

This difficult paragraph describes our split mind, and the insanity of believing in the wrong-minded half. The Holy Spirit represents our right-minded self that contains the Atonement, the healing principle of correction that re-unites the separated mind of God's unified Son. Forgiveness is the means of healing (or correction), for it pardons what never happened—ontologically and within our daily dreams, for they are one. God's Son remains perfectly whole and united within the Christ Who is Himself, the ego's nightmare of separation and hate notwithstanding.

Revisiting this important passage, we read:

(II.13:2-6) From an idea of self as two, there comes a necessary view of function split between the two. And what you would correct is only half the error, which you think is all of it. Your brother's sins become the central target for correction, lest your errors and his own be seen as one. Yours are mistakes, but his are sins and not the same as yours. His merit punishment, while yours, in fairness, should be overlooked.

Once we believe we are separated and sinful, it becomes essential for the ego's survival that we split the sin off from our separated self, projecting it onto another. In our insanity we believe in the reality of differences—one Son is sinful, deserving of punishment; the other, merely mistaken and sinless—and forget the truth of the inherent sameness of God's beloved Son.

(II.14) In this interpretation of correction, your own mistakes you will not even see. The focus of correction has been placed outside yourself, on one who cannot be a part of you while this perception lasts. What is condemned can never be returned to its accuser, who had hated it, and hates it still as symbol of his fear. This is your brother, focus of your hate, unworthy to be part of you and thus outside yourself; the other half, which is denied. And only what is left without his presence is perceived as all of you. To this remaining half the Holy Spirit must represent

the other half until you recognize it *is* the other half. And this He does by giving you and him a function that is one, not different.

After our belief that we had successfully separated from our Source, we divided our separated minds into wrong- and right-minded selves. Splitting off from the Holy Spirit, we identified only with the ego, maintaining its thought system of sin. Finally, we left the mind itself and made a world of bodies in which we retained the belief in sin, but saw it in others. We continually attack this despised part of our self in our special hate objects, attempting to sustain the illusion of wholeness at the expense of the hated ones perceived to be outside us. To this madness the Holy Spirit brings His sane reminder that God's Sons are the same, not different. He teaches that the belief in sin must be shared equally, as is the corrected belief in Atonement that is our one function within the illusion. His healing Presence undoes the ego's splitting off from truth, and the Wholeness of God's Son is brought back to awareness through his acceptance of the gentle correction of forgiveness.

(II.15) Correction is the function given both, but neither one alone. And when it is fulfilled as shared, it must correct mistakes in you and him. It cannot leave mistakes in one unhealed and set the other free. That is divided purpose, which can not be shared, and so it cannot be the goal in which the Holy Spirit sees His Own. And you can rest assured that He will not fulfill a function that He does not see and recognize as His. For only thus can He keep yours preserved intact, despite Your separate views of what your function is. If He upheld divided function, you were lost indeed. His inability to see His goal divided and distinct for you and him, preserves yourself from the awareness of a function not your own. And thus is healing given you and him.

Again and again Jesus reminds us of the inherent sameness of our common function (forgiveness) that corrects our common problem (the mind's decision for guilt). His reminders are his answer to our calls for help when we are upset, for whatever reason. As he tells us in the workbook, "Certain it is that all distress does not appear to be but unforgiveness" (W-pI.193.4:1), distress coming from upholding the ego's thought system of separation: *one or the other.* In other words, since there is only one problem and one answer, what is perceived in one must be perceived in all—one judgment, one healing—for minds are joined, undivided and undifferentiated from each other.

We turn now to a portion of "The Quiet Answer" that summarizes the holy instant when, outside time and space, we choose the Holy Spirit instead of the ego.

(IV.1:7–2:3) Yet if God gave an answer there must be a way in which your problems are resolved, for what He wills already has been done.

Thus it must be that time is not involved and every problem can be answered *now*. Yet it must also be that, in your state of mind, solution is impossible. Therefore, God must have given you a way of reaching to another state of mind in which the answer is already there.

Despite the apparent enormity of our problems, or their large numbers, they are all solved in the same way: the decision-making mind corrects its prior decision for the ego, choosing now to hear God's Answer of Atonement. Since the separation never happened in reality, its undoing simply awaits the change of purpose from separate to shared interests in the holy instant, "reaching to another state of mind."

(IV.2:4–3:3) Such is the holy instant. It is here that all your problems should be brought and left. Here they belong, for here their answer is. And where its answer is, a problem must be simple and be easily resolved. It must be pointless to attempt to solve a problem where the answer cannot be. Yet just as surely it must be resolved, if it is brought to where the answer is.

Attempt to solve no problems but within the holy instant's surety. For there the problem *will* be answered and resolved. Outside there will be no solution, for there is no answer there that could be found.

The holy instant undoes the ego strategy because within it we realize that our only problem is the mind's decision for the ego, which it has never wanted us to see. Seeking to have us deny there ever was such a choice, the ego made a dream in which we voluntarily chose to leave the mind and believe in a world in which there exists a multitude of "real" problems. When the veil of forgetfulness fell and we forgot we even had a mind, we had no recourse but to seek in the world for answers to these problems, a process the Course calls "magic." This is the ego's maxim of *seek and do not find,* for the world's problems are never seen for the smoke-screen they are because the real problem of the mind's choice to identify with the ego's sinful self is never looked at. Consequently, their source never being recognized, our problems here can never truly be solved. Again, the cause of suffering is nothing but the decision-making mind's belief in guilt, which is preserved by our searching for answers where they cannot be found—*seek and do not find.*

(IV.7:1) Therefore, attempt to solve no problems in a world from which the answer has been barred.

We all attempt to solve problems "in a world from which the answer has been barred." If we truly wanted peace, happiness, and love, we could have them simply by choosing to be right-minded and forgive all people, all the time. It is clear, however, that we do not want this; otherwise, we would not be in our separate and separating bodies. Sadly, we continue to seek for peace, love, and happiness in the world, but will never succeed because only their parody—the ego's world of special relationships—exists here, thwarting the desire of the sane part of our minds to return home.

(IV.7:2-5) But bring the problem to the only place that holds the answer lovingly for you. Here are the answers that will solve your problems because they stand apart from them, and see what can be answered; what the question *is*. Within the world the answers merely raise another question, though they leave the first unanswered. In the holy instant, you can bring

the question to the answer, and receive the answer that was made for you.

Bringing the question to the answer (the illusion to the truth) and receiving what was made for us undoes the ego's strategy. Forgiveness brings the projected problem from the world to the mind that conceived it so it may choose again. On the right-hand side of the chart we find an arc representing the miracle that returns us to the mind, reversing the ego's arc of projection that brought us to the world, preventing our acceptance of the Atonement. This theme of our one function, task, or part in the Holy Spirit's "plan" continues in "The Healing Example":

(V.1:1-2) The only way to heal is to be healed. The miracle extends without your help, but you are needed that it can begin.

Sentence 2 expresses an important principle that we have seen and will see again. We are not asked to save the world or do anything here, but only to ask for help that the mind be healed through forgiveness; what follows is not our concern. As the miracle is allowed to extend from the right mind, our lives naturally reflect the love that has been released. If its worldly reflection becomes our focus, we know that specialness has returned and our lives once more become a battleground of guilt. Our function is to ask Jesus' help to look at the ego thought system, and with his love beside us lift the veil of denial and expose the ego's purpose of attack to the gentle light of truth.

(V.1:3-12) Accept the miracle of healing, and it will go forth because of what it is. It is its nature to extend itself the instant it is born. And it is born the instant it is offered and received. No one can ask another to be healed. But he can let *himself* be healed, and thus offer the other what he has received. Who can bestow upon another what he does not have? And who can share what he denies himself? The Holy Spirit speaks to *you*. He does not speak to someone else. Yet by your listening His Voice extends, because you have accepted what He says.

If I really want to help you, I first have to be healed. The healing love I accept by turning away from the ego's hate will extend to offer you the witness to your right mind. This defenseless love will help you realize the meaningful choice you can make, as I did by choosing the holy instant. Jesus is not asking us to do more, to heal others or the world, for how can we heal a world of separate people that does not exist? Our one focus should be on asking his help to heal the mind by looking at the mistaken choice that sacrificed our happiness and peace. When we are sufficiently sickened by the ego's "fetid scent of death," we will be motivated to choose our elder brother's reason instead of the ego's madness. In words more than familiar to us at this stage of our journey, the one responsibility of each separated Son is to accept the Atonement for himself. There is in truth just one Son, but as long as we have the illusion of many we need specific forgiveness for our misperceptions of others and ourselves. The healing we accept from Jesus will then flow through the mind of God's one Son, for we are not healed alone (W-pI.137).

(V.2:8-14) The only thing that is required for a healing is a lack of fear. The fearful are not healed, and cannot heal. This does not mean the conflict must be gone forever from your mind to heal. For if it were, there were no need for healing then. But it does mean, if only for an instant, you love without attack. An instant is sufficient. Miracles wait not on time.

We are not asked to be perfectly healed, only to want it. This desire occurs when we are able, if only for an instant, to suspend identification with fear. In that holy instant the miracle of healing is complete, and though we may choose to deny it in the next instant—our minds choosing fear instead of love—healing awaits the return that is as certain as God. Remember the line, "Love waits on welcome, not on time…" (T-13.VII.9:7).

(V.3) The holy instant is the miracle's abiding place. From there, each one is born into this world as witness to a state of mind that has transcended conflict, and has reached to peace. It carries comfort from the place of peace into the battleground, and demonstrates that war has no effects. For all the hurt that war has sought to

bring, the broken bodies and the shattered limbs, the screaming dying and the silent dead, are gently lifted up and comforted.

As always, Jesus does not speak of the material world, but of the mind's thought system of sin, hate, and suffering. The ego's delusional system of separation disappears in the holy instant when the mind chooses forgiveness and peace as its purpose instead of conflict and death. Our right-minded decision illuminates the bloodied world of darkness—mind and body ("within without the same" [*The Gifts of God*, p.73])—as love's healing light comes to bless the dead and comfort the dying, reminding them of the truly good news that dreams have no effect upon reality.

(V.4) There is no sadness where a miracle has come to heal. And nothing more than just one instant of your love without attack is necessary that all this occur. In that one instant you are healed, and in that single instant is all healing done. What stands apart from you, when you accept the blessing that the holy instant brings? Be not afraid of blessing, for the One Who blesses you loves all the world, and leaves nothing within the world that could be feared. But if you shrink from blessing, will the world indeed seem fearful, for you have withheld its peace and comfort, leaving it to die.

We are not asked for more than a little willingness to choose love instead of attack, since in that willingness salvation is found. Regardless of the situation or the distress bodies may feel, the miracle of the mind's holy instant washes clean all sadness and pain. The moribund world may itself not change, but in our healed perception what was made to curse now contains the blessing of forgiveness. And where is fear when love has come?

(V.6:1–7:2) Come to the holy instant and be healed, for nothing that is there received is left behind on your returning to the world. And being blessed you will bring blessing. Life is given you to give the dying world. And suffering eyes no longer will accuse, but shine in thanks to you who blessing gave. The holy instant's

radiance will light your eyes, and give them sight to see beyond all suffering and see Christ's face instead. Healing replaces suffering. Who looks on one cannot perceive the other, for they cannot both be there. And what you see the world will witness, and will witness to.

Thus is your healing everything the world requires, that it may be healed. It needs one lesson that has perfectly been learned.

The one lesson is that every problem is the same (the mind's decision for death), and each one has the same healing (the mind's decision for life). Jesus is helping us return to our right minds, "the stately calm within" (T-18.I.8:2) where we regain our sanity. With hope of meaningful change at last, we return our attention to the despairing world while the ego's curse, brought to the holy instant's blessing, softly evanesces as God's Son is born again. In his healing is the world's: mindfulness replacing mindlessness, the miracle chosen instead of magic, and the innocence of Christ's shining face unveiled to undo the guilt of God's sleeping Son, with all suffering wiped from his tired eyes.

(V.7:3-7) And then, when you forget it, will the world remind you gently of what you have taught. No reinforcement will its thanks withhold from you who let yourself be healed that it might live. It will call forth its witnesses to show the face of Christ to you who brought the sight to them, by which they witnessed it. The world of accusation is replaced by one in which all eyes look lovingly upon the Friend who brought them their release. And happily your brother will perceive the many friends he thought were enemies.

Even when thoughts of fear come to substitute for the love that forgiveness brings, there remains the ever-present memory awaiting our right-minded choice. As *projection* (extension) *makes perception*, this memory continues to remind us of a different decision we can make when we look out on the world, tempted to embrace the ego's allies of guilt and judgment. Christ's face is never far behind our sight, however, and its gentle radiance infuses our vision as we look out on a world of friends, not enemies, and see one interest shared not by some or many, but by all.

(V.8:1-8) Problems are not specific but they take specific forms, and these specific shapes make up the world. And no one understands the nature of his problem. If he did, it would be there no more for him to see. Its very nature is that it is *not*. And thus, while he perceives it he cannot perceive it as it is. But healing is apparent in specific instances, and generalizes to include them all. This is because they really are the same, despite their different forms. All learning aims at transfer, which becomes complete within two situations that are seen as one, for only common elements are there.

As we have discussed previously, not seeing the problem of the mind's guilt is what keeps it intact. Blinded, we perceive problems in the world, where they are not, and of such multitudinous force that any meaningful solution is beyond recognition. Only when we recognize that every problem is the same, the mind's one decision for the one ego, do we understand why *there is no order of difficulty in miracles*: one miracle of healing fits all.

The central teaching of *A Course in Miracles* is expressed in these above sentences, similar to Jesus' discussion in the workbook's Introduction. Generalization, or transfer of training, is how we truly learn. It is not possible in the limited world of time and space to forgive each and every situation or relationship, yet through our daily practice of forgiveness, changing the mind's purpose in specific instances, our learning will generalize. This is why if we forgive one person totally we have forgiven everyone, for the world of differentiating specifics generalizes in our vision to become the forgiven world of common purpose.

(V.8:9–11; 10:1) Yet this can only be attained by One Who does not see the differences you see. The total transfer of your learning is not made by you. But that it has been made in spite of all the differences you see, convinces you that they could not be real…. Leave, then, the transfer of your learning to the One Who really understands its

laws, and Who will guarantee that they remain unviolated and unlimited.

Our daily purpose is to ask for help whenever we become aware of our special love and hate needs. How healing extends within the mind to embrace other minds should not be our concern, as this extension is beyond our ability to comprehend. Further, this vision would only frighten us, for love's extension rests on the illusory nature of the body and the mind's supremacy that would dissolve the special self. But asking Jesus' help each time a thought of specialness appears, in any form, would stop our grandiose fantasies of personal or world healing, or our lives of abysmal failure, and center attention only on the mind's correction. The workbook's one-year training program teaches us to look specifically at our thoughts with the Holy Spirit, the prerequisite for learning that the world of perceived differences conceals the underlying sameness of the Son's wrong and right mind.

(V.10:2-7) Your part is merely to apply what He has taught you to yourself, and He will do the rest. And it is thus the power of your learning will be proved to you by all the many different witnesses it finds. Your brother first among them will be seen, but thousands stand behind him, and beyond each one of them there are a thousand more. Each one may seem to have a problem that is different from the rest. Yet they are solved together. And their common answer shows the questions could not have been separate.

Forgiveness is like a game of dominos. When we totally forgive any one special relationship, the others naturally fall and we will experience love all around us, not necessarily because people are more loving, but because we are. The mind's hate will be gone, removed by Jesus when we bring it to his healing love. This teaches us there is only one problem (guilt and hate) and one answer (forgiveness and love). How simple, then, is salvation from sin! By truly forgiving one person we forgive all, and therefore learn our sins are forgiven: the separation from love occurred only in a dream of separation, from which we now happily awaken.

(V.11) Peace be to you to whom is healing offered. And you will learn that peace is given you when you accept the healing for yourself. Its total value need not be appraised by you to let you understand that you have benefited from it. What occurred within the instant that love entered in without attack will stay with you forever. Your healing will be one of its effects, as will your brother's. Everywhere you go, will you behold its multiplied effects. Yet all the witnesses that you behold will be far less than all there really are. Infinity cannot be understood by merely counting up its separate parts. God thanks you for your healing, for He knows it is a gift of love unto His Son, and therefore is it given unto Him.

This is the reason Jesus continually tells us his course is simple. The world of multiplicity need not be healed, only our individual minds. Distress arises from the decision to believe in the guilt of separation; peace from deciding for forgiveness of what never happened. When peace is restored to our mind, it extends to embrace the mind of the one Son, even while he dreams of individual worlds. The error of fragmentation dissolves into the single error of separation, gently giving way to the memory of love's perfect oneness. As our eyes open, the individual parts of the Sonship disappear into its natural wholeness, joyously hearing God give thanks for the Son's return to His Son.

(VI.5:10) Yet a miracle speaks not but for itself, but what it represents.

Earlier in this section Jesus says fear witnesses unto death, and sickness and suffering point to sin. Yet the miracle is also a witness—to Atonement, innocence, and eternal life. The choice is ours.

(VI.6:1-5) Love, too, has symbols in a world of sin. The miracle forgives because it stands for what is past forgiveness and is true. How foolish and insane it is to think a miracle is bound by laws that it came solely to undo! The laws of sin have different witnesses with different strengths. And they attest to different sufferings.

The miracle is an illusion, but by returning the dream to the dreamer it allows us to look past the ego's thought system to the inner light, reflecting the resplendent Love of our Creator. This light of Atonement, which is the correction for the illusory belief in sin, is the source of the miracle that corrects all suffering. Regardless of the myriad forms and seeming causes of pain, the miracle heals by the simple reversal of the mind's one mistaken decision.

(VI.6:6-11) Yet to the One Who sends forth miracles to bless the world, a tiny stab of pain, a little worldly pleasure, and the throes of death itself are but a single sound; a call for healing, and a plaintive cry for help within a world of misery. It is their sameness that the miracle attests. It is their sameness that it proves. The laws that call them different are dissolved, and shown as powerless. The purpose of a miracle is to accomplish this. And God Himself has guaranteed the strength of miracles for what they witness to.

Everything seen through vision is the same. We see how the first principle of miracles runs through our symphony like a leitmotif. It is the key that undoes the ego and the key to the Holy Spirit's healing. As all expressions of guilt are the same, so too are their undoing: *one problem, one solution.* The ego's laws of separation and projection are summarily dismissed by the miracle, Heaven's perfect Oneness expressed on earth.

(VI.7) Be you then witness to the miracle, and not the laws of sin. There is no need to suffer any more. But there *is* need that you be healed, because the suffering and sorrow of the world have made it deaf to its salvation and deliverance.

This is Jesus' perennial appeal to us: Why continue to suffer when you can so easily choose otherwise? The world—the projected image of the Son's guilt—needs the miracle, for if the mind is not healed the tired world of time will continue to wind on wearily (M-1.4:4). Suffering and sorrow will deafen our ears to the Holy Spirit's call that we accept salvation, and the laws of sin will forever seem to witness to the death of God's innocent Son.

(VI.8:1) The resurrection of the world awaits your healing and your happiness, that you may demonstrate the healing of the world.

The world is healed when we are healed because it exists only as an idea in the mind, and *ideas leave not their source.* The world we see must change, then, not necessarily in form but in how we see it. *Projection makes perception,* and when we begin from a place of love in the mind and not hate, we can only perceive love or calls for love. Judgment becomes impossible, and we experience all people as expressing the same fear and pain that call for the universal remedy of resurrection: the mind's awakening from its dream of separation, sin, and death.

(VI.8:2-3) The holy instant will replace all sin if you but carry its effects with you. And no one will elect to suffer more.

As Jesus said above, "there is no need to suffer any more" (VI.7:2). Suffering is the need to blame another for our sin. Yet as we are sinless in the holy instant of forgiveness, suffering no longer serves a purpose and is gone.

(VI.8:4-6) What better function could you serve than this? Be healed that you may heal, and suffer not the laws of sin to be applied to you. And truth will be revealed to you who chose to let love's symbols take the place of sin.

We live in a world of symbols, and our function is to choose whether our world will reflect love or sin, the laws of healing or guilt. The decision is easy once we see the painful consequences of choosing the latter. In these next two sentences from "The Dreamer of the Dream," Jesus succinctly tells us how to escape from suffering:

(VII.2:1-2) Now you are being shown you *can* escape. All that is needed is you look upon the problem as it is, and not the way that you have set it up.

Once again, the ego's strategy is undone. The ego sets up the problem by convincing us to believe in sin, the mind's secret dream, and then has it appear that problems are not in ourselves but in the world, where they are to be resolved through the "justice" of punishment. However, when we ask Jesus for help to see the problem as it is, we understand that it was our choice to believe in the secret dream that is the issue, not the dream itself. Jesus teaches us that we chose the dream to establish the reality of our separate identity, for the dream of sin affirms that the separation truly happened. Our teacher exposes the problem as the mind's decision to believe in the lie, and not the way we set it up through projection of sin's cause onto the bodily world of specialness—lies built upon the lie.

(VII.2:3) How could there be another way to solve a problem that is very simple, but has been obscured by heavy clouds of complication, which were made to keep the problem unresolved?

The secret dream of sin, guilt, and fear is complicated; the world's dream even more so. Our fear of the simple truth complicates things very quickly, the ego's underlying purpose. To keep the simplicity of the problem and solution hidden, the mind chooses to believe the ego thought system and this decision is the problem. When we decide for the Holy Spirit, however, we find His simple answer that cuts through fear to the simple truth of Atonement.

(VII.2:4-5) Without the clouds the problem will emerge in all its primitive simplicity. The choice will not be difficult, because the problem is absurd when clearly seen.

Asking Jesus' help leads us through the clouds of guilt to the decision-making mind, and this, he assures us elsewhere, is no "idle fantasy" (W-pI.70.9:4). It is absurd to believe we could be happier with the ego than with him; it is equally absurd to believe we could be joyful outside of Heaven, or find love outside of Love.

(VII.2:6) No one has difficulty making up his mind to let a simple problem be resolved if it is seen as hurting him, and also very easily removed.

This is Jesus' purpose for his course, and why he says we do not know the difference between joy and pain. What the ego calls joy is really hurtful because it reinforces separation. Painstakingly, Jesus unveils for us the ego thought system so that once we see clearly it is only our choice to be separate and special that makes us unhappy, we can easily correct the mistake by asking help of the right Teacher. The complex problem then disappears into the simplicity of our easily corrected decision: forgiveness instead of guilt, the joy of healing in place of suffering.

(VII.5:6-8) Look, then, beyond effects. It is not here the cause of suffering and sin must lie. And dwell not on the suffering and sin, for they are but reflections of their cause.

We always have to look at the cause: the mind's *belief* in sin. Its inescapable effects are the suffering and sin we perceive all around us in bodies. To reiterate, we have set up the world's problems so that the mind's problem of choosing wrongly could never be looked at and corrected.

(VII.6:1) The part you play in salvaging the world from condemnation is your own escape.

We need not save others; indeed, we cannot. Our only need is to ask Jesus' help in escaping from the mind's mistaken decision for guilt. As we are healed of self-condemnation, the thought of Atonement we have released saves the world, which was nothing more than the mind's projected guilt crystallized into form.

(VII.6:2-8) Forget not that the witness to the world of evil cannot speak except for what has seen a need for evil in the world. And this is where your guilt was first beheld. In separation from your brother was the first attack upon yourself begun. And it is this the world bears witness to. Seek not another cause, nor look among the mighty legions of its witnesses for its undoing. They support its claim on your allegiance. What conceals the truth is not where you should look to *find* the truth.

The wrong mind has a need to see evil in the world, and so we never realize it is within: *ideas leave not their source.* The guilt we behold outside is the ego's primary defense against looking at the mind's original attack upon God's Son. The workbook tells us that "the [unforgiving] thought protects projection" (W-pII.1.2:3), and this seeming attack against Christ, the true Self, is reflected in our projected judgments against others, sealed in denial so they can never be undone. Inevitably we seek for truth in special relationships where it can never be found, for its pristine simplicity remains in the right mind's thought of Atonement that asks only to be accepted. Hence, seeking truth within is where we shall surely find it, and this is our only need. Given this, Jesus has us wonder why we constantly ask ego witnesses—sin, judgment, and pain—that do not know the way, to lead us to the truth of healing they were made to conceal?

(VII.9:1-4) This is the only picture you can see; the one alternative that you can choose, the other possibility of cause, if you be not the dreamer of your dreams. And this is what you choose if you deny the cause of suffering is in your mind. Be glad indeed it is, for thus are you the one decider of your destiny in time. The choice is yours to make between a sleeping death and dreams of evil or a happy wakening and joy of life.

If we want the truth, we go within to see what we *"denied because it is the truth"* (T-21.VII.5:14). The truth in this context is that we are the dreamer, not the dream. The ego, on the other hand, would have us believe we are the dream figure who suffers at the hands of evil sinners. Nonetheless, the true cause of pain is the mind's mistaken choice, which is why the miracle gently moves us from the dream to the dreamer, the body to the mind. Herein lies our only hope, for we will no longer be at the mercy of a world we cannot control. We, the decision-making mind, are the sole determiners of our fate: Do we live in misery with the ego and blame others, making them miserable too, or do we live in joyful peace because we have chosen to learn from the Teacher of peace? While almost always we have no power over the world around us, we most certainly have command of our minds. The nightmare ends with our decision to let the love within extend into the sleeping world, joyously proclaiming the rebirth of God's Son.

(VII.10:1-6) What could you choose between but life or death, waking or sleeping, peace or war, your dreams or your reality? There is a risk of thinking death is peace, because the world equates the body with the Self which God created. Yet a thing can never be its opposite. And death is opposite to peace, because it is the opposite of life. And life is peace. Awaken and forget all thoughts of death, and you will find you have the peace of God.

Recall that this is an all-or-nothing course, wherein there is no compromise between truth and illusion, eternal life and death. This passage is an elaboration of the paragraph beginning "There is no life outside of Heaven" (T-23.II.19) and the workbook lesson "There is one life, and that I share with God" (W-pI.167), where the same point is emphasized. What the world calls death is merely an aspect of the same illusion of what it calls life. The body neither lives nor dies; it simply does not exist. The belief that peace could come when the body's suffering ends reinforces the ego's strategy of mindlessness, which affirms the body's existence at the expense of the "nonexistent" mind. But the mind's guilt, the cause of all suffering, remains as long as the decision for it is unchanged, regardless of what appears to be happening with the body's birth, life, and death. Only awakening from the ego's dream of separation brings the everlasting peace we seek, and that our sane mind desires above all else.

(VII.10:7) Yet if the choice [between life and death] **is really given you, then you must see the causes of the things you choose between exactly as they are and where they are.**

If we truly want to choose eternal life, we must see the problem where and as it is: not in the world of bodies but in the mind's decision for specialness and sin.

(VIII.5:1-2) How willing are you to escape effects of all the dreams the world has ever had? Is it your wish to let no dream appear to be the cause of what it is you do?

The above is a culmination of everything we have discussed in this chapter: we are no longer victims of dream figures, but only our mind's decision to be the dreamer. We *can* change which dream we will have, the ego's nightmare or the Holy Spirit's happy dream, and our one need is to sincerely answer Jesus' question in the affirmative: "Is it your wish to let no dream appear to be the cause of what it is you do?" Perhaps today. Why need we wait an instant longer to let his peace be ours?

(VIII.5:3) Then let us merely look upon the dream's beginning, for the part you see is but the second part, whose cause lies in the first.

Jesus tells us not to look to the effects ("the second part," the world's dream), but to the cause ("the dream's beginning," the mind's secret dream). Taking his hand, we follow salvation's path from mindlessness to mindfulness and choose again.

(VIII.5:4-10) No one asleep and dreaming in the world remembers his attack upon himself. No one believes there really was a time when he knew nothing of a body, and could never have conceived this world as real. He would have seen at once that these ideas are one illusion, too ridiculous for anything but to be laughed away. How serious they now appear to be! And no one can remember when they would have met with laughter and with disbelief. We can remember this, if we but look directly at their cause. And we will see the grounds for laughter, not a cause for fear.

The theme of laughter assumes a prominent place in the closing pages of this chapter. Jesus reminds us to laugh at the ontological instant when the ego convinced us to choose its serious interpretation of the *tiny, mad idea* instead of the Holy Spirit's. In the holy instant, joining with Jesus, we "see grounds for laughter, not a cause for fear." This is directly opposite to the ego's plan, which is why it made its secret dream of sin, guilt, and fear. The purpose was to have us flee the mind and make a world in which we would hide forever. The mindless world became a smokescreen whose purpose was to conceal our sinful choice for the ego and its projected image of the body. Yet laughter, meaning we no longer give the world power over the mind, enables us to choose again. The ego conceals this ability because were we to return to the mind's choice point, we would look clearly at our prior decision for guilt. Rather than seeing it as reason to fear God's punishment, we would laugh at the silliness of such belief. Jesus continues:

(VIII.6:1) Let us return the dream he gave away unto the dreamer, who perceives the dream as separate from himself and done to him.

Projection leads us to believe that we can reverse cause and effect (a major theme of Chapter 28), preventing us from recognizing that the dream is merely an *effect* of the *cause* that resides in the Son's decision-making mind, the dream's dreamer. Because *effects leave not their cause*, dream and dreamer are forever one and unseparated, the ego's lies to the contrary.

(VIII.6:2) Into eternity, where all is one, there crept a tiny, mad idea, at which the Son of God remembered not to laugh.

This makes it clear that the problem was not the *tiny, mad idea* of separation, but turning our backs on the Holy Spirit's laughter that would have enabled us not to take it seriously. By choosing the ego, we gave the separation power over us and called it *sin*. The practical implications of this teaching are crucial. Our problems are never what happens in the world, but only our having chosen the ego's eyes to interpret what happens here. The desire to put an end to the world's hatred, cruelty, and suffering must be met with our wish to perceive them differently. If we perceive evil, we will counteract it with our own, calling it good. This reinforces the sinful dreams we believe are real in us, but now magically exist in others. However, the Holy Spirit teaches us to see sin and evil as expressions of fear and calls for love. Identified with His vision, all that we do or say will be kind and loving,

for we will have remembered to laugh at the ego's silliness, not only denying its power to affect our peace, but denying its very existence.

(VIII.6:3-5) In his forgetting did the thought become a serious idea, and possible of both accomplishment and real effects. Together, we can laugh them both away, and understand that time cannot intrude upon eternity. It is a joke to think that time can come to circumvent eternity, which *means* there is no time.

Taking the thought of separation seriously, rejecting the Atonement's gentle smile, we believed it was accomplished in reality and had actual effects—the physical universe. Joining with Jesus means that we share his happy laughter at the preposterous thought that the impossible could happen, that time really took the place of eternity.

(VIII.8:3) How childish is the petulant device to keep your innocence by pushing guilt outside yourself, but never letting go!

This is the reaction of spoiled brats when they do not get their way. We are all such bratty children who, when we did not get our special needs met with the Father, threw the temper tantrum of separation. This culminated in seeing our guilt in others, blaming them for our unhappiness. Yet all the while we keep ourselves guilty, for projection does not work and our self-hatred remains within—*ideas leave not their source.*

(VIII.8:4) It is not easy to perceive the jest when all around you do your eyes behold its heavy consequences, but without their trifling cause.

When we lift ourselves above the battleground we realize everything here is silly, for how can a world of separation be real? But on the battleground of bodies where we wage the perennial wars of specialness, we have forgotten that the world's cause is the mind's belief in illusion. Seen through the body's eyes, events here seem significant, and often of great and tragic consequence. How else could the world appear to us, given that the ego has deemed its source in the sinful, guilty, and fearful mind to be significant, of great consequence, and tragic indeed?

(VIII.8:5-7) Without the cause do its effects seem serious and sad indeed. Yet they but follow. And it is their cause that follows nothing and is but a jest.

This is not about looking at the world through the ego's eyes and laughing, which would be bizarre, if not hateful. The gentle laughter and smile come only when we have risen to the mind's level and look down. With Jesus by our side, we realize the insanity of having believed in separation, not to mention in a sinful world that arose from it, containing events that seem most serious and sad. It should be clear by now that to practice this course it is essential to recognize that the decision-making mind is the cause of everything, and needs to be healed of its belief in illusions.

(VIII.9:1) In gentle laughter does the Holy Spirit perceive the cause, and looks not to effects.

This is why we should not attempt to bring the Holy Spirit into the world. He cannot come to a place that has never left its source and does not exist. His sane Presence remains in the mind, the cause of the problem and the locus of the solution. The perceived effects in the world are nothing more than the ego's silly attempts to distract us from the mind. Gently, our Teacher reminds us that mistaken choices call for correction, not punishment.

(VIII.9:2-8) How else could He correct your error, who have overlooked the cause entirely? He bids you bring each terrible effect to Him that you may look together on its foolish cause and laugh with Him a while. _You_ judge effects, but _He_ has judged their cause. And by His judgment are effects removed. Perhaps you come in tears. But hear Him say, "My brother, holy Son of God, behold your idle dream, in which this could occur." And you will leave the holy instant with your laughter and your brother's joined with His.

This holy instant occurs when we are above the battleground with Jesus. Looking on the world as he does, we see all people, victims and victimizers alike, calling for the love they believe they denied and do not deserve; their guilt demanding that they will never have that love again. Because Jesus does not share our insanity, he can invite us to share his vision, born of the gentle laughter in which our silly mistake is healed. We bring our sufferings to him, enabling us to shift perception from effects (worldly events) to their cause in the mind that can now be judged correctly. In this way we are returned to the original instant, since time is not linear, when the Holy Spirit looked at the _tiny, mad idea_, smiling as He told us that nothing happened: _the Idea of God's Son never left His Source._

(VIII.10) The secret of salvation is but this: that you are doing this unto yourself. No matter what the form of the attack, this still is true. Whoever takes the role of enemy and of attacker, still is this the truth. Whatever seems to be the cause of any pain and suffering you feel, this is still true. For you would not react at all to figures in a dream you knew that you were dreaming. Let them be as hateful and as vicious as they may, they could have no effect on you unless you failed to recognize it is your dream.

Nothing in the world has power to take God's peace from us, only our decision for conflict. Once this fact is accepted, the world will have no effect on us. We do not deny events here, but no longer justify the purpose we had imposed on them. This was to see the hateful and vicious world as our escape from the mind's prison of guilt, holding others responsible for the sins we secretly harbor within. We finally understand that the problem is never what happens within the dream, but always that we have chosen to remain asleep, dreaming of separation, sin, and death.

(VIII.11:1–12:3) This single lesson learned will set you free from suffering, whatever form it takes. The Holy Spirit will repeat this one inclusive lesson of deliverance until it has been learned, regardless of the form of suffering that brings you pain. Whatever hurt you bring to

Him He will make answer with this very simple truth. For this one answer takes away the cause of every form of sorrow and of pain. The form affects His answer not at all, for He would teach you but the single cause of all of them, no matter what their form. And you will understand that miracles reflect the simple statement, "*I have done this thing, and it is this I would undo.*"

Bring, then, all forms of suffering to Him Who knows that every one is like the rest. He sees no differences where none exists, and He will teach you how each one is caused. None has a different cause from all the rest, and all of them are easily undone by but a single lesson truly learned.

Every problem is the same, as is every solution. That is why *there is no order of difficulty in miracles,* the only lesson Jesus would have us learn. By bringing all concerns to his healing smile, we are taught they are the same: *one problem* (choosing the ego), *one solution* (choosing the Holy Spirit). What could be simpler? We practice with each form of suffering and upset, looking at it through Jesus' loving vision and coming to learn that forms are the same. As this sameness becomes apparent in every relationship and situation, we approach the one generalization that undoes them all: the many effects in form have one cause, the mind's content of guilt.

(VIII.12:4-9) Salvation is a secret you have kept but from yourself. The universe proclaims it so. Yet to its witnesses you pay no heed at all. For they attest the thing you do not want to know. They seem to keep it secret from you. Yet you need but learn you chose but not to listen, not to see.

All pain and suffering stem from the refusal to accept salvation's presence in the mind. The ego, fearful of its disappearance into nothingness, keeps us from choosing the right mind, home of the Holy Spirit and His Atonement. Salvation remains a secret, *by our own decision,* and it is our one responsibility to change the mind and choose again. This shift is reflected in the decision to forgive, wherein we see the world as witnessing to

our common need and interest, shared with the Sonship we had fragmented into separate parts.

(VIII.13:1-2) How differently will you perceive the world when this is recognized! When you forgive the world your guilt, you will be free of it.

When we forgive the world our projected guilt, we will be released from it. This does not mean that people may not act out their egos, but it does mean realizing that this has nothing to do with us; the world may affect the body, but not our decision-making minds. Vision will have cleansed us of judgment, leaving nothing to interfere with the love that flows through our healed mind to bless a world formerly cursed by guilt.

(VIII.13:3-5) Its innocence does not demand your guilt, nor does your guiltlessness rest on its sins. This is the obvious; a secret kept from no one but yourself. And it is this that has maintained you separate from the world, and kept your brother separate from you.

Thus is the ego strategy of projection undone. No longer do we subscribe to the principle of *one or the other* in which we maintain our innocence by blaming others, or see another's guiltlessness as damning witness to our sin. Through our purified minds we see salvation gleaming through the flimsy veils of guilt, and the ego's secret vaults of hate gently vanish into the radiant vision of the guiltlessness of God's Son: one in Atonement, one in spirit.

(VIII.13:6-9) Now need you but to learn that both of you are innocent or guilty. The one thing that is impossible is that you be unlike each other; that they both be true. This is the only secret yet to learn. And it will be no secret you are healed.

This is the Holy Spirit's answer to the ego's secret dream, based upon the imagined difference between God and His creation, projected as the world's dream in which we perceive differences within the Sonship. Now we recognize the truth of *together, or not at all,* and through Christ's vision see that God's Sons are truly the same, sharing one mind and one goal. Now we are healed together, for we have learned the meaning of Atonement, the only thing salvation had to teach. The memory of God quietly rises in awareness as Idea and Source become what they always were: one Life, one Love, one Self.

Closing

We close with the lovely final paragraphs of "The Dreamer of the Dream," which summarize our discussion in this chapter: We are the dreamer, not the dream figure, and before we can awaken we have first to choose the Holy Spirit's gentle dreams of forgiveness. Our perception of others will joyously shift from sinfulness to sinlessness, and behind each person will stand the God we first made into the enemy Who would sin against us, as we believed we had sinned against Him. By practicing forgiveness, therefore, we forgive ourselves, our brothers, and our Creator.

(VII.13) *You* **are the dreamer of the world of dreams. No other cause it has, nor ever will. Nothing more fearful than an idle dream has terrified God's Son, and made him think that he has lost his innocence, denied his Father, and made war upon himself. So fearful is the dream, so seeming real, he could not waken to reality without the sweat of terror and a scream of mortal fear, unless a gentler dream preceded his awaking, and allowed his calmer mind to welcome, not to fear, the Voice that calls with love to waken him; a gentler dream, in which his suffering was healed and where his brother was his friend. God willed he waken gently and with joy, and gave him means to waken without fear.**

The secret dream of sin, guilt, and fear is nothing but an idle dream, since it has done nothing, being itself nothing. Transformed through projection into the world's dream of a similar terror, the ego thought system continues to strike the fear of God into our guilt-ridden minds. Even though the separation is a dream, we have become convinced of its reality, equating awakening with the certain fate of oblivion if we were ever to abandon the ego and its spiteful dreams of sin. Because of this fear of annihilation by truth, we require the correction of the Holy Spirit's happy dreams, which gently correct the mind's mistaken choice. This alleviates the fear sufficiently that we may continue the journey of awakening until we joyfully reach our goal.

(VII.14) Accept the dream He gave instead of yours. It is not difficult to change a dream when once the dreamer has been recognized. Rest in the Holy Spirit, and allow His gentle dreams to take the place of those you dreamed in terror and in fear of death. He brings forgiving dreams, in which the choice is not who is the murderer and who shall be the victim. In the dreams He brings there is no murder and there is no death. The dream of guilt is fading from your sight, although your eyes are closed. A smile has come to lighten up your sleeping face. The sleep is peaceful now, for these are happy dreams.

The Holy Spirit's dreams of forgiveness reflect His principle of *together, or not at all*, correcting the ego's principle of *kill or be killed* in which the only issue is whether we shall be murderers or the murdered, hardly a sane choice. True sanity lies in the decision-making mind, which we must recognize as the dream's dreamer. Returning to this mind is the function of the miracle, and choosing reason over madness is the decision for joy instead of pain, innocence over guilt. The nightmare fades as Jesus' love softly brushes our eyes with his peace, and they happily open to the truth that is beyond all dreams.

(VII.15-16) Dream softly of your sinless brother, who unites with you in holy innocence. And from this dream the Lord of Heaven will Himself awaken His beloved Son. Dream of your brother's kindnesses instead of dwelling in your

dreams on his mistakes. Select his thoughtfulness to dream about instead of counting up the hurts he gave. Forgive him his illusions, and give thanks to him for all the helpfulness he gave. And do not brush aside his many gifts because he is not perfect in your dreams. He represents his Father, Whom you see as offering both life and death to you.

Brother, He gives but life. Yet what you see as gifts your brother offers represent the gifts you dream your Father gives to you. Let all your brother's gifts be seen in light of charity and kindness offered you. And let no pain disturb your dream of deep appreciation for his gifts to you.

Jesus is asking us to look kindly upon our brother, not only because he is coming from fear, if he is being hurtful, but because he is our brother; namely, we are the same. Moreover, the way we see God's Son is how we see our Source, since *projection makes perception*. We look within and see love or hate, innocence or sin, and what we choose is what we see in everyone, including God. Our perceptions of each other reveal the mind's decision, and the gift Jesus continually holds out to us is the opportunity to choose again. Would we, knowing the certain outcome of the mind's decision—peace or pain—fail to make the correct choice? Jesus' purpose in his course is to help us achieve that realization, and we end this movement of our symphony with his earlier statement:

> Who with the Love of God upholding him could find the choice of miracles or murder hard to make? (T-23.IV.9:8)

Chapter 28

THE UNDOING OF FEAR

Introduction: Cause and Effect

In Chapter 28 we see the culmination of the Course's central theme of cause and effect. In musical terms, we might say that this is the theme's resolution, as well as its fullest exposition. In discussing cause and effect, we are really speaking of two principles: one explicit, the other implicit.

The first principle is that cause and effect are inextricably intertwined, meaning that you cannot have one without the other. If there is a cause, there must be an effect; if there is an effect, there must be a cause. A corollary to this is the principle we have seen throughout our symphony: *ideas leave not their source.* Substituting *cause* for *source*, and *effect* for *idea*, we may say that *effects leave not their cause.* In truth, cause and effect are not only mutually dependent and connected, they are one. We place them in discrete categories only because we would not otherwise be able to understand the causal dynamic. Their appearing to be separate from each other is the problem of the world.

The second principle, essential to the theoretical thought system of *A Course in Miracles*, not to mention its purpose in helping us awaken from the dream, is that if something is shown not to be a cause, it does not exist. In both the worlds of Heaven and illusion, nothing can exist if it is not a cause of something else. If we wish to prove that something does not exist, we need only demonstrate it has no effects. This works for the purposes of the Holy Spirit and the ego. Before beginning the chapter proper, we examine these two principles in greater depth.

In the non-dualistic world of reality, God is First Cause, although we are told earlier that there is no second or third (T-14.IV.1:7-8). He is the "All in all" (T-7.IV.7:4) and there is nothing else. His Son is His Effect, and since cause and effect are one, and *Ideas (Effects) leave not their Source (Cause),* Father and Son are forever joined in *a Oneness*

joined as One (T-25.I.7:1). We have seen, and will see again in this chapter, that the principle of Atonement reflects this unity by averring that the separation from God never happened because it *could* never happen. Again, Effect (the Son) leaves not its Cause (the Father).

The ego turns this principle upside down: ideas *do* leave their source, the Son *has* left his Father. Effects become independent of their cause, establishing themselves as their own creator (or cause). In this warped view of reality the Son (ego) becomes his own creator. As Jesus has told us, the ego believes it is self-created (T-3.VII.4), which is how it teaches there is no God. As He has been deprived of His Effects, which denies His being First Cause, God cannot be a Cause and so does not exist. This is the ego's argument to demonstrate that it alone exists as its own cause, with the Son (body) being its effect. Jesus explains that within the ego system the mind's belief in separation is our true cause. On the chart (see Appendix) we see the word *cause* associated with the separated mind, and the dying world of bodies with the *effect*. To say it differently, our secret dream is the mind's causal belief in sin, for which we will inevitably be punished, while the world's dream (the effect) is the suffering of our mortal bodies (T-27.VII.11-12).

To prove that the cause (separation) is real and that it itself is real, the ego demonstrates that the effects are real: if there is an effect, there must be a cause. To repeat, within the ego system the physical effect is the world, which is why the body was made. We have seen how many passages in the text reflect the fundamental ego strategy that the body specifically demonstrate the world's reality. If it is real, being an effect, the underlying cause in the mind (the ego) must be real as well. Further, if the separation is real it means God cannot be, because the true Cause-Effect relationship is the indissoluble Oneness of Father and Son: a unity that can never be divided or fragmented, nor could One ever oppose the Other. Thus, if the divine Cause-Effect relationship is true, the ego cannot be. If, on the other hand, the ego's cause-effect relationship is fact, then Heaven must be an illusion. Cleverly, the ego has "proven" its causal reality by the world of bodies: the wrong-minded thought system of separation being the efficacious cause, and the world its ever-present effect.

A related theme, found in the second section of Chapter 28, is that once the ego establishes its causal relationship, it reverses it. We have seen that the world's cause is the mind's separated self, but once the world is made, a veil of forgetfulness or denial falls across the mind, as indicated on our chart, preventing us from remembering the true cause of the body's "life." As this amnesia sets in, we are aware only of the effect, and it appears as if the world had caused us, our special self. It seems incontrovertible that this self, which in truth is the cause of the world, is the effect, with the world being its cause. This ploy gives its name to the section: "Reversing Effect and Cause."

Recall our discussion in the previous movement of our symphony: we happily choose to suffer and even end our life, so we may point an accusing finger, saying: "Behold me, brothers, at your hands I die. Look at my betrayed, abandoned, and abused body, and you will see the effect of your sin" (see T-27.I.4:6). Choosing to make our bodies vulnerable to disease and attack, we can be perceived by ourselves, others, and God as innocent victims of what the world has done to us. In this way we claim that our physical and psychological pain is the effect of the world's attacks. Suffering, which is the sick and tortured portrait of

crucifixion, condemns all people to hell because it is shown to be the result of their sin, effects proving that the cause is real. The core of this vicious game of specialness is that we condemn each other for the sins we do not want to accept as our own.

In place of this insanity, we are taught by Jesus to say: "Behold me, brothers, at your hands I live" (see T-27.I.10:7). Another's perceived sins have had no effect on God's peace within us, which was present before the seeming attack, during it, and afterwards as well. How can we angrily seek vengeance for what has not occurred? Having no effect, sin cannot be a cause and—one more time—does not exist. This argument is one of the principal themes of this chapter.

While the emphasis of *A Course in Miracles* is always on forgiving our special love and hate partners, we also find here discussion of the underlying metaphysics of forgiveness. If the Holy Spirit is the "present Memory" (T-28.I) of God's Love that we took with us into the dream, we cannot be separate from our Source. This means that the separation has not happened (the principle of Atonement), the ego's cause is an illusion and, being causeless, the effect that is the physical universe must be illusory too.

To summarize our discussion, *A Course in Miracles* changes our perspective of the world by teaching us that our function is to demonstrate to others that their perceived sins against us have not occurred because they had no effect. In other words, since God's Love and peace remain undefiled within our minds, such sins cannot be a cause. If there is no effect, there cannot be a cause, and if something is not a cause, it does not exist: no effect, no cause, no existence. This is the way sins are truly forgiven.

God

We begin with a statement of Heaven's Cause-Effect relationship.

(II.1:1-5) Without a cause there can be no effects, and yet without effects there is no cause. The cause a cause is *made* by its effects; the

Father *is* a Father by His Son. Effects do not create their cause, but they establish its causation. Thus, the Son gives Fatherhood to his Creator, and receives the gift that he has given Him. It is *because* he is God's Son that he must

also be a father, who creates as God created him.

A cause is made a cause by its effects: what establishes something as causal is that it has effects; what establishes God as Creator, our Father and Source, is that we have *being* in Heaven as Christ, His one Son. However, even though we create like God, we did not create Him; He is forever our Cause, and we His eternal Effect.

(II.1:6-8) The circle of creation has no end. Its starting and its ending are the same. But in itself it holds the universe of all creation, without beginning and without an end.

We read in the workbook that "What He [God] creates is not apart from Him, and nowhere does the Father end, the Son begin as something separate from Him" (W-pI.132.12:4), a unity that cannot be understood in our world of multiplicity. In reality there is no God and Christ, Father and Son, Cause and Effect—only perfect, undifferentiated Oneness. As we have seen, it is helpful in our dualistic condition that Jesus speak to us in dualistic terms (T-25.I.5-7) *as if* there were two Beings in Heaven. We need always remember, though, that Source and Idea are indivisibly one for the circle of creation is forever seamless and unbroken.

(II.2:1-4) Fatherhood *is* creation. Love must be extended. Purity is not confined. It is the nature of the innocent to be forever uncontained, without a barrier or limitation.

Heaven's dynamic of extension or creation is incomprehensible because it is non-spatial and atemporal. God's Love simply extends, and we, as Christ, are its extension. Being part of God, we share in this extension of love, known as our creations, which are also beyond the understanding of a separated mind, let alone a brain. Moreover, our inherent oneness as spirit is indissoluble, a natural state of sinlessness that is unaffected by dreams of separation and specialness. Cause and Effect are eternally One, and this is the principle of Atonement to which we now turn.

The Atonement Principle

The ego tells us we have separated from God, having split effect off from cause, leaving effect to stand on its own and become its own cause. This insane thought of God being denied His Effect is gently corrected by the Atonement.

(I.10:1) You who have sought to lay a judgment on your own Creator cannot understand it is not He Who laid a judgment on His Son.

God is not angry, the ego's lies to the contrary. The belief that God's Judgment sought punishment is what motivated us originally to leave the mind, projecting the separated self to make a world. Having done so, we forgot that it was only *our* judgment, the mind deciding for the ego, that established the need for this unreal place of refuge.

(I.10:2-3) You would deny Him His Effects, yet have They never been denied. There was no time in which His Son could be condemned for what was causeless and against His Will.

This is an expression of the Atonement—nothing happened. In no way could we be judged and punished for a sin that not only did we not commit, but was impossible to commit. What could not happen did not happen: Effect has never left its Cause; the Son could never leave his Father.

(I.10:4-7) What your remembering would witness to is but the fear of God. He has not done the thing you fear. No more have you. And so your innocence has not been lost.

Recall this from the *Psychotherapy* pamphlet: "And who could weep but for his innocence?" (P-2.IV.1:7). All sadness and tears originate in the belief that by separating from God we threw away our innocence and will never get it back. Even if we could somehow retrieve it, the ego tells us,

God would never let us return to Him because His vengeful wrath precludes it. Yet all this madness is part of the ego's secret nightmare that lies, saying to us: "God *has* left His Thoughts," these Thoughts being His sinful Sons. See T-31.IV.9:1 for the Atonement's correction, which reflects the truth that Innocence has created us innocent. Hence, "He has not left His Thoughts!"

(I.10:8-9) You need no healing to be healed. In quietness, see in the miracle a lesson in allowing Cause to have Its Own Effects, and doing nothing that would interfere.

We do not have to be healed because we already are. What alone requires healing is the mistaken belief we need it, for healing is necessary only where there is sickness. But if there is no sickness—i.e., the separation never happened—what is there to be healed? The miracle's role, to be discussed below, is to demonstrate to the sleeping mind that the body is merely a figure in a dream. By asking the question "How can an illusion be sick?", the miracle removes the interference to our remembering that we, as God's Effect, have never left the Cause that is our Source.

(VII.1:5) A space where God is not, a gap between the Father and the Son is not the Will of Either, Who have promised to be one.

In this chapter we see a full treatment of the gap, a synonym for the Son's belief that he separated from his Father. On the chart, this gap (the *tiny, mad idea*) is depicted by the vertical line that seems to come from Heaven, yet does not touch the solid line. The repetition of the word *promise* in this paragraph echoes the previous section, "The Secret Vows," where Jesus speaks of our promise to each other to reinforce the separation. This is the ego's answer to the true promise that reflects the song of oneness Father and Son sing to Each Other, undoing the gap that never was.

(VII.1:6-8) God's promise is a promise to Himself, and there is no one who could be untrue to what He wills as part of what He is. The promise that there is no gap between Himself and what He is cannot be false. What will can come between what must be one, and in Whose Wholeness there can be no gap?

The above is the Holy Spirit's message when we are tempted to listen to the ego. His Voice of wisdom and love, by Its very Presence, tells us that the separation never happened. The previous movements of our symphony have shown us how the ego responds to this message of Atonement by mounting an ingenious strategy against it.

The Ego's Strategy

Cause and Effect

As discussed above, a key dimension in the ego's strategy is proving that effect has left its cause, leaving the effect free to become its own cause and establish its own set of causal relationships. While the mind's separation thought is the cause, with the world of sickness and death the effect outside the repressed cause, we still believe that the cause of our suffering is found in the world of bodies, outside the mind. This reversal of the true causal situation is the ego's substitution for the Cause-Effect relationship of God and Christ.

(II.8:1) The separation started with the dream the Father was deprived of His Effects, and powerless to keep them since He was no longer their Creator.

This is the ego's strange notion of self-creation, wherein it became its own creator, the substitute for God.

(II.8:2-3) In the dream, the dreamer made himself. But what he made has turned against him, taking on the role of its creator, as the dreamer had.

Jesus refers to the beginning of the ego's reversal of effect and cause. We are the author or dreamer of the dream, who then forgot the identity of the dreamer. It now appears as if the dream were dreaming us, being our victimizer: the body, ours or another's, being the sole cause of our suffering.

(II.8:4) And as he hated his Creator, so the figures in the dream have hated him.

The core of the secret dream is that we hate God because we think He hates us. We hate Him because He has become our rival for the throne of creation we usurped, and now proudly sit upon. The world's dream is nothing more or less than the mirror image of the mind's secret dream, except what was there has been projected in the form of separate bodies imposing their will on us. This is a defense against the guilt over having first imposed our will on God, a "fact" we believe. Our paranoid experience of the world, then, is the projection of the dream's origin, the belief we attacked our Creator. We do anything and everything to protect the self we stole from Him, striving mightily to protect it from His wrath, never realizing that our Source knows nothing of this madness and simply loves us.

(II.8:5) His body is their slave, which they abuse because the motives he has given it have they adopted as their own.

Because of projection, we believe the world will hurt, abuse, and betray us, perceiving in others the split-off parts of the sinful self we have denied. In the mind's dream we are the attackers, abusers, and betrayers, the unfaithful ones who broke their promise to God. Our guilt is so intolerable, we need to project it as a sinful, fearful world that is the opposite of Heaven's love and innocence. The world's dream, therefore, inevitably parallels the secret one, our bodies believing that others do to us what our silent guilt tells us we have done to them.

(II.8:6-7) And hate it for the vengeance it would offer them. It is their vengeance on the body which appears to prove the dreamer could not be the maker of the dream.

How, then, in the face of such pain and suffering could we be held responsible? How could we be seen as sinners in the face of the patent abuse perpetrated on our innocent selves? This is why we love to be unfairly treated, the core of the ego's carefully crafted script. It is so skillfully done, in fact, that no one, including God Himself, could ever believe we are the cause of our distress. Following this strategy of the ego, we dream of bodies so that we may appear as innocent victims, a theme that continues up to and including our symphony's final movement.

(II.8:8) Effect and cause are first split off, and then reversed, so that effect becomes a cause; the cause, effect.

The mind's separated self (dreamer) is the source of the world (dream), and the veil of denial that falls across the mind splits it off from the dream, keeping cause and effect separated and us mindless. It appears that this separated self, whose locus is now in the body, is caused by other bodies in the dream. As we grow, our personalities seem to be molded by a world that is outside us. For example, if there were not enough food, as in many countries in the world, our emaciated bodies would very likely perish at an early age, the fault clearly lying outside us. Or perhaps we live in a prosperous country, yet without love in the home. This would render us unable to develop intimate relationships as adults, the cause of this wretched psychological state, again, being justifiably attributed to external forces beyond our control. Incidentally, it makes no difference to the ego if the deprivation is physical or emotional. Either way, suffering bodies demonstrate our innocence, the bitter fate of living in a cruel and insensitive universe, "a dry and dusty world, where starved and thirsty creatures come to die" (W-pII.13.5:1).

(II.9:1-2) This is the separation's final step.... an effect of what has gone before, appearing as a cause.

This consummates the ego strategy, the bottom of the ladder that the separation led us down: our firm foundation in the bodily world with no memory of its source in the mind, effect having successfully been split off from cause and then reversed. The world's witnesses support this amnesia, as well as the belief that we are the effect of an outside cause. One of the ways the ego ensures our believing we are the effect of other people's sins is to have us remember all that has happened to us. These are the memories of past abuses that prove we are the innocent victims of causes we cannot change. As long as we see ourselves as creatures of an unjust past, everything we do becomes an understandable defense against the pain we felt as children. Many forms of psychotherapy are based on uncovering such mindless causes, which are seen to be the source of our conscious experiences of guilt and shame. "The Present Memory," the next section to be examined, affords us an in-depth look at this ego dynamic of remembering.

(I.5:3-5) Memory holds the message it receives, and does what it is given it to do. It does not write the message, nor appoint what it is for. Like to the body, it is purposeless within itself.

Memory is a skill that serves the purpose given it by the teacher we have chosen. Like everything else of the body, memory is neutral. Once we believe we are here, it serves either the purpose of the ego, which is that we remain in the dream by remembering past hurts, or of the Holy Spirit, Who helps us remember God and waken to our Self. It is the decision-making mind alone that gives the body the wrong- or right-minded purpose of memory.

(I.5:6) And if it seems to serve to cherish ancient hate, and gives you pictures of injustices and hurts that you were saving, this is what you asked its message be and that it is.

This is how the ego uses the faculty of memory. We remember what people did to us five, ten, or fifty years ago, or even within the last five minutes or seconds. These injustices are carefully preserved in our minds, kept with us against the time they can serve our hateful purpose. Reaching into this grab bag of memories, we pick out a cherished abuse when it can serve the purpose of our saying to our brother: "Behold my pain, you sinner. Because of you I suffer and die, for you are responsible for my unhappy state, not me." We all have this locked

vault in our minds in which—each and every day, each and every moment—we deposit examples of how we have been unfairly treated. These witnesses to sin are ready to be called up in memory whenever we need a scapegoat for our guilt.

(I.5:7-9) Committed to its vaults, the history of all the body's past is hidden there. All of the strange associations made to keep the past alive, the present dead, are stored within it, waiting your command that they be brought to you, and lived again. And thus do their effects appear to be increased by time, which took away their cause.

This important passage describes the beauty of the ego's thought system, which leads us to say: "Of course I am this way. I was made like this, and there is nothing I can do to alter my fate as the cause lies in a past that is over. I cannot, for example, undo what my family was; nor can I undo the economic conditions I grew up in. I am the unfortunate effect of what has befallen me." With the cause in the mind disappearing into an immutable past, there is no hope for meaningful change, the conclusion the ego loves. Having vitiated the true cause of our miserable state by burying it in a past that is no longer there, all seems lost forever. For all his brilliance, Freud attempted to resurrect the past as a cause, not recognizing that it existed only in the present when the mind chose to hold on to it. This choice is the problem, for memory is simply a present decision projected into a nonexistent past; it is a consequence of a cause that is in the timeless mind. There is no past, not because the ego says it is gone, but because it never existed. Nonetheless, we continue to hold it in memory as if it were here, determining our actions now.

THE EGO'S USE OF THE BODY

(V.4:1) You have conceived a little gap between illusions and the truth to be the place where all your safety lies, and where your Self is safely hidden by what you have made.

Again, the gap is shown on the chart by the vertical line that seems to link the circle (the decision maker) to Heaven. The tiny space between Mind and mind symbolizes the unreality of the separation, which we still maintain is true. The ego teaches that our protection lies within that gap because the memory of God is safely hidden there, inaccessible to our remembering. The world, the effect of the gap, gives cover to the ego's belief in separation, yet true safety lies in the principle *ideas leave not their source*: Effects leave not their Cause; the Son has never left his Father.

(V.4:2-9) Here is a world established that is sick, and this the world the body's eyes perceive. Here are the sounds it hears; the voices that its ears were made to hear. Yet sights and sounds the body can perceive are meaningless. It cannot see nor hear. It does not know what seeing *is*; what listening is *for*. It is as little able to perceive as it can judge or understand or know. Its eyes are blind; its ears are deaf. It can not think, and so it cannot have effects.

Nowhere has this theme of the body's illusory nature been more clearly stated than in the current chapter. The ego's purpose for seeing and listening is to have us perceive sights and sounds that are not there. Because the mind has told the body what to see and hear, we think we do, believing that what we perceive is real, an effect of the cause that is separation and sin. Our mindless bodies prove that true Cause and Effect do not exist: the ego's ultimate goal.

There should be no mistaking what Jesus is saying here, and our minds do recognize the underlying implication: *we, the persons we think we are, do not exist*. The eyes with which we read these words, the ears with which we hear them spoken, the brain with which we think about our perceptions are all illusory. Our special identities are not real, and who except the right-minded could love Jesus, for his course denies their very existence?

(V.5:1-4) What is there God created to be sick? And what that He created not can be? Let not your eyes behold a dream; your ears bear witness to illusion. They were made to look upon a world that is not there; to hear the voices that can make no sound.

We see here an implicit reference to purpose. The body was specifically made so we could prove the world is real. This would make it a real effect of a real cause, establishing the separation as the only reality. This purpose is the method behind the ego's madness of trying to prove the Atonement wrong, and is why our minds choose to dream of sickness—the mind's guilt and the body's infirmities—over our reality as unchanging and eternal spirit.

(V.5:6-8) For eyes and ears are senses without sense, and what they see and hear they but report. It is not they that hear and see, but you, who put together every jagged piece, each sense-less scrap and shred of evidence, and make a witness to the world you want. Let not the body's ears and eyes perceive these countless fragments seen within the gap that you imagined, and let them persuade their maker his imaginings are real.

Throughout his course, the *you* Jesus refers to is not the *you* that has eyes, ears, and a brain, but the decision-making mind that chooses between the ego and the Holy Spirit. The mind follows the ego's plan to prove it exists by making a world that shows the separation is real and oneness is not. In this vein, note the clever word play on *sense*: we sense and perceive things that make no sense, as they originate in a senseless and delusional thought system. "The Secret Vows," the next section to be considered, re-presents our important symphonic theme of the body's illusory nature:

(VI.1:1) Who punishes the body is insane.

We all seek to punish the mindless body, hating it as if it were the problem. The ego is ingenious in its punitive ways of distracting us from the mind, three of its favorites being *asceticism*, *sickness*, and *attacks* on others. These distractions make sin and pain real, perceived in bodies and not the mind that insanely dreams of them.

(VI.1:2) For here the little gap is seen, and yet it is not here.

The gap is separation, manifest in the body. Yet the body does not exist outside the mind, nor is the gap real that is its source. This gap, the mind's belief in a separate self, is carefully kept hidden and protected by the body.

(VI.1:3-5) It has not judged itself, nor made itself to be what it is not. It does not seek to make of pain a joy and look for lasting pleasure in the dust. It does not tell you what its purpose is and cannot understand what it is for.

Over and over, Jesus returns to the theme of purpose: to ask of anything and everything *what it is for*. We think the body's purpose is to be happy and prosperous here, taking care of itself and other bodies. However, we do not realize—the purpose having been buried in our minds—that the body was made only to protect the sham that is the ego, a "parody" or "travesty" that is its special substitute for our glorious Self (T-24.VII.1:11; 10:9).

(VI.1:6-10) It does not victimize, because it has no will, no preferences and no doubts. It does not wonder what it is. And so it has no need to be competitive. It can be victimized, but cannot feel itself as victim. It accepts no role, but does what it is told, without attack.

While we all are would-be philosophers, wondering about who we are and why we are here, it is the ego that instructs the brain to wonder, for this affirms the wrong mind's version of cause and effect. This also holds for our experiences of victimization or having a specific function, which the ego establishes for the purpose of making the world of separation real.

(VI.2:1) It is indeed a senseless point of view to hold responsible for sight a thing that cannot see, and blame it for the sounds you do not like, although it cannot hear.

Jesus is poking gentle fun at our attitudes toward a body that, like a puppet, literally does nothing unless directed by the puppeteer that is the decision-making mind. Blaming the body is as insane as parents yelling at a puppet on stage for behavior they feel is inappropriate for their children. It is the unseen person behind the scenes that would be the correct object for their complaint.

Analogously, it is the mind we need go to for correction, not the body.

(VI.2:2-7) It suffers not the punishment you give because it has no feeling. It behaves in ways you want, but never makes the choice. It is not born and does not die. It can but follow aimlessly the path on which it has been set. And if that path is changed, it walks as easily another way. It takes no sides and judges not the road it travels.

Experience belies this statement because our bodies do seem to feel emotional and physical pain, making choices that determine our fate. This illustrates how effective the ego has been in its strategy, convincing us that our identity is localized in a body that is self-motivated, with desires, needs, and intention.

(VI.2:8-9) It perceives no gap, because it does not hate. It can be used for hate, but it cannot be hateful made thereby.

The mind can use the body to attack, but how can we hate what is nothing? It is instructive to note our reactions as we read these lines about the body's unreality, because our bodily identification should engender tremendous fear in us. Though Jesus means his words literally and frequently returns to this theme, our mindless state precludes understanding him, not to mention its being unable to protect us from the terror that would follow such understanding.

(VI.3:1) The thing you hate and fear and loathe and want, the body does not know.

What is despised and still desired is separation. Even more specifically, as we recall, we crave guilt's comfort and want it (e.g., T-13.II; T-19.IV-A.i), even while we hate it. We know nothing of this attraction to guilt because, as we also saw before, the body was made to look without, not within to the decision-making mind (T-18.IX.4).

(VI.3:2-3) You send it forth to seek for separation and be separate. And then you hate it, not for what it is, but for the uses you have made of it.

Again, Jesus speaks of purpose. The body was made to prove we destroyed our Creator. From this sin-laden thought, our projected guilt demanded we hate the body, even though it had nothing to do with the mind's decision. In the end, it is only the purpose of guilt, given to the body by the mind, that we hate.

(VI.3:4-10) You shrink from what it sees and what it hears, and hate its frailty and littleness. And you despise its acts, but not your own. It sees and acts for *you*. It hears your voice. And it is frail and little by your wish. It seems to punish you, and thus deserve your hatred for the limitations that it brings to you. Yet you have made of it a symbol for the limitations that you want your mind to have and see and keep.

As always, Jesus speaks *about* the mind *to* the mind. The limitations we want our mind "to have and see and keep" are born of separation, the substitute for the limitlessness of our reality as Christ. The body is the perfect expression of this substitution, because it distorts what we are and restricts what we do, keeping us unaware how this reflects the inherent limitation of the mind's belief in separation. We buttress this deception through our alliances in specialness, which help us deny our secret dreams of sin by projecting them onto each other as the world's dream.

These dreams are the ego's dance of death, which we continually invite our special brothers to join. It is the promise we make to one another, forged in guilt, to reinforce separation. Our hated enemies and cherished loves are opposite sides of the same coin of specialness, reflecting our secret bargains to be victims and victimizers. Throughout the hologram of time we do this dance—here the victim, there the victimizer. The specific role does not matter for enemies cling to each other as do lovers. All specialness is the same, despite its differing forms.

(VI.4:1-2) The body represents the gap between the little bit of mind you call your own and all the rest of what is really yours. You hate it, yet you think it is your self, and that, without it, would your self be lost.

Recall that the gap is depicted on the chart as the vertical line between Christ and the little self we think of as ourselves. Our ultimate fear is that without this self there would be nothing, which is why we chose the ego in the beginning and still choose it. The ego tells us, and rightly so from its point of view, that if we choose the Atonement we will lose our separated self. As we will do anything not to lose this identity, we fervently embrace our special bargains with each other—the secret vows, oaths, pledges, and promises we make, as we now read:

(VI.4:3-7) This is the secret vow that you have made with every brother who would walk apart. This is the secret oath you take again, whenever you perceive yourself attacked. No one can suffer if he does not see himself attacked, and losing by attack. Unstated and unheard in consciousness is every pledge to sickness. Yet it is a promise to another to be hurt by him, and to attack him in return.

These promises constitute our special relationships, even though the term is not used here. We take an oath to prove to each other that the ego is alive and well, and sin is real. We do not care in whose body it is found, as long as it is a sinful body that is not our own. Cut from the same ego cloth, we all participate in this vicious dance of death, sharing the goal of sustaining our special self, and through our suffering blaming another for our secret sin.

(VI.5) Sickness is anger taken out upon the body, so that it will suffer pain. It is the obvious effect of what was made in secret, in agreement with another's secret wish to be apart from you, as you would be apart from him. Unless you both agree that is your wish, it can have no effects. Whoever says, "There is no gap between my mind and yours" has kept God's promise, not his tiny oath to be forever faithful unto death. And by his healing is his brother healed.

We and our special partners agree to be in bodies, to hate and love each other. Within the ego's world, hating and loving are the same for they reinforce separation and separate interests. So does bodily sickness, the projection of the mind's self-hatred that perpetuates the illusion of separation by making the body real, the effect of an external cause that can be seen and opposed. All this amounts to a denial of the promise God and His Son made to Each Other that They be forever One. This sacred oath is denied by the secret promise we make to each other, forged in anger, to affirm our specialness. Later in this movement we will discuss how this insanity is healed through our agreement to join instead of separate.

SICKNESS

Sickness is a major ploy in the ego's strategy. It makes the body real, another of the ego's weapons in its war against the mind's decision maker. As we know full well by now, physical sickness is the effect of a cause, which the ego would have us believe lies in microorganisms (or macroorganisms) outside us. In truth, however, the symptoms are only the effects of a sick mind that believes guilt is preferable to love.

(II.3:1-2,6-7) Always in sickness does the Son of God attempt to make himself his cause, and not allow himself to be his Father's Son. For this impossible desire, he does not believe that he is Love's Effect, and must be cause because of what he is.... A mind within a body and a world of other bodies, each with separate minds, are your "creations," you the "other" mind, creating with effects unlike yourself. And as their "father," you must be like them.

Sickness is another name for the Son's arrogant assertion that he is now self-created and, to be sure, creator of others in a sinful image that is no longer seen in himself. He has not only denied his true Cause and Its Effect (the Self), but also his oneness with the Sonship, its place taken by the isolating sickness of the mind's specialness.

(III.3:1-2) The miracle does nothing just *because* the minds are joined, and cannot separate. Yet in the dreaming has this been reversed, and separate minds are seen as bodies, which are separated and which cannot join.

What is discussed here is essential to understanding *A Course in Miracles*, but it cannot be grasped unless we detach from the body, lift ourselves above the battleground, and look down upon the dream. From this perspective of Christ's vision, sickness is clearly not of the body but is the mind's decision to be separate. Since it takes two to separate, the principle of Atonement is true because God never recognized the separation, which means it never happened. For this reason the ego needs God to see His *separated* Son and react accordingly. This is why the Bible, the ego's book, rests on the insane thought that God perceived sin's "reality" and responded to it. From Genesis through Revelation, the Creator treats sin as real, a misperception that has remained intact for millennia.

Atonement heals because it affirms the unreality of the separation. As God knows nothing of it, it remains a fact only in our delusional minds. We relive this belief over and over, desperately trying to prove it real by getting others to agree to it, which is why we need them to witness to the reality of separation, sickness, and the pains and joys of specialness. While it takes two to make the separation of sickness, it only takes one for Atonement. If you present yourself to me as sick and I react as if you were, I am aiding and abetting you in the desire to prove that the separation is real. It is important to note that the miracle is not about behavioral reactions, and in no way does this mean we should let someone remain in pain. It is hardly loving, for example, to say to the suffering: "Since you are not a body and nothing is really wrong with you, there is no need to call a doctor, who is yet another body." To the contrary, the Course speaks only of how we react, *in attitude*. As perception is interpretation, the issue is not what the body's eyes see, but the mind's interpretation of what they see. If my right mind does not perceive you as sick, you are not sick. In this holy instant my healed mind tells you that the separation never happened, meaning you cannot be ill. By my peace and love, through which the miracle extends regardless of what my body does in response to your illness, I demonstrate the truth of Atonement: my mind's loving peace is totally unchanged by your symptoms.

(III.3:3) Do not allow your brother to be sick, for if he is, have you abandoned him to his own dream by sharing it with him.

To stubbornly insist to others they are not sick when that is their clear experience makes you part of the same problem. Why would you insist they are not ill if you did not secretly believe they were, and their sickness was making you fearful? We need always remember that sickness is separation, and healing is joining. Very often we join on the level of form because that is the only way our love can communicate to the "sick." Recall the line from Chapter 2: "The value of the Atonement does not lie in the manner in which it is expressed" (T-2.IV.5:1). It is never the form that heals but the miracle's gentle content, healing the mind of its mistaken choice. Our peace in the face of suffering enables the acrimonious madness of separate interests to give way to the love of shared interests.

(III.3:4-6) He has not seen the cause of sickness where it is, and you have overlooked the gap between you, where the sickness has been bred. Thus are you joined in sickness, to preserve the little gap unhealed, where sickness is kept carefully protected, cherished, and upheld by firm belief, lest God should come to bridge the little gap that leads to Him. Fight not His coming with illusions, for it is His coming that you want above all things that seem to glisten in the dream.

To keep God and His Voice away we made up a thought system of separation that says: "Bodies are enemies, not friends." We need such a world so we do not have to recognize that the cause of sickness—the belief in the gap's reality—is in our minds, as is our yearning for the remedy of Atonement.

(III.4:1) The end of dreaming is the end of fear, and love was never in the world of dreams.

We have been told that the core of every dream is fear (e.g., T-18.II.4), the mind's belief that God will punish us for our sin. Similarly, the core of the world's dream is the fear that others will do to us what we secretly believe we did to them (e.g., T-27.VII.11-12). This insane thinking purposefully excludes love, which exists only in reality and not in the illusory world of dreams.

(III.4:2-6) The gap *is* little. Yet it holds the seeds of pestilence and every form of ill, because it is a wish to keep apart and not to join. And thus it seems to give a cause to sickness which is not its cause. The purpose of the gap is all the cause that sickness has. For it was made to keep you separated, in a body which you see as if it were the cause of pain.

The word *joining* in *A Course in Miracles* refers to the mind, not the body. The cause of sickness is only the mind's decision to be separate, as healing is the mind's decision to accept the joining that is already there. This is the message of Lesson 136, "Sickness is a defense against the truth." We choose to be sick when we are threatened by the truth of our shared identity as mind, not to mention our undivided Identity as spirit, and flee to the apparent safety of the body. Still, true safety lies only in the miracle of Atonement that gently reminds us that the body is illusory, being the projection of the illusion that there is a gap between God and His Son.

(III.7:4) What is the world except a little gap perceived to tear eternity apart, and break it into days and months and years?

This little gap of nothingness is the sum and substance of the world. Since *ideas leave not their source*, the idea of a separated world divided into days, months, and years is merely the outpicturing of the inner condition of the mind's little gap: the mad belief that the *tiny, mad idea* did in fact occur, a cause with real and palpable effects.

(III.7:5) And what are you who live within the world except a picture of the Son of God in broken pieces, each concealed within a separate and uncertain bit of clay?

This is Jesus' answer to our investment in the "wondrous" body to which we devote our time and attention. It remains an "uncertain bit of clay," the form that seems to encase the insane thought that God's Son is fragmented and separate from his

Source. We will soon return to this theme of the body's inherent nothingness.

(V.1:1-5) What is a sense of sickness but a sense of limitation? Of a splitting *off* and separating *from*? A gap that is perceived between you and your brother, and what is now seen as health? And so the good is seen to be outside; the evil, in. And thus is sickness separating off the self from good, and keeping evil in.

Once again, sickness is not of form but the content of separation: a limitation in which we split off from our Source and then our brothers, seeking to prove that the separation from love is an actual fact. In this delusional system, love (the good) appears to be external while the mind's sin of separation (the evil) remains within, buried beneath the ego's double shield of oblivion (W-pI.136.5:2): the thought of guilt and the guilt-engendered world.

(V.1:6-11) God is the Alternate to dreams of fear. Who shares in them can never share in Him. But who withdraws his mind from sharing them *is* sharing Him. There is no other choice. Except you share it, nothing can exist. And you exist because God shared His Will with you, that His creation might create.

We are concerned with the dream because we need it to keep the Alternate apart from us. If we devote attention to our special dream, we will never awaken; if we devote attention to awakening, the dream will decrease in importance as we watch it "melt, thaw and resolve itself into a dew," to again quote Hamlet (I,ii). Consequently, it is only the mind's devotion to these wrong- and right-minded thoughts that gives them power within the dream.

(V.2:1) It is the sharing of the evil dreams of hate and malice, bitterness and death, of sin and suffering and pain and loss, that makes them real.

Once more, our agreement with each other is crucial to the ego's plan, the reason we have sensory organs that report to the brain that there is an outside world. Other bodies then agree with us, and whether they do so in anger or love is irrelevant, as long as they reinforce belief in the body's reality, the shadow of the mind's belief in the ego.

(V.2:2-7) Unshared, they are perceived as meaningless. The fear is gone from them because you did not give them your support. Where fear has gone there love must come, because there are but these alternatives. Where one appears, the other disappears. And which you share becomes the only one you have. You have the one that you accept, because it is the only one you wish to have.

Although what the ego has done in the dream is terrible, we can choose not to share another's illusions. When our minds choose Atonement, the thought of separation is released in the right-minded sense of one or the other. Keeping us mindless, as we know, is the basis of the ego's strategy. Fearful that we would recognize our original mistake and choose again, the ego sees to it that the error will never be corrected by having us leave the mind, root ourselves in the body, and believe we are the world's effect. How, then, can we recognize the real cause of our distress, which is the mind's decision to believe in madness over reason? This is the cause the ego seeks to keep hidden from awareness so we will never choose the miracle and return to God's Love, the true Alternate to fear.

The Miracle

Before turning to the passages on the miracle, let us review its healing purpose. The ego establishes its own cause-effect relationship, the *cause* being the mind's thought of separation, the *effect* the world and body. It then has us forget the cause by introducing repression (the veil of forgetfulness) so that once we find ourselves in the bodily state, the world of effect, we have no memory of the mind. Knowing of nothing else, we search externally for the causes of who we are, and how and why we got here. This is the reversal of effect and cause: the world, which is the effect, now becomes the cause; and the cause, which is our self (a thought in the decision-making mind), is the effect, except it is perceived to be in the world as a body.

Earlier we looked at "separation's final step" (T-28.II.9:1) that is the world, which is also where the miracle begins. The arc on the right-hand side of the chart leads from the body to the decision maker, depicting the course of the miracle: returning effect to cause, reminding us that the mind is the cause and its effects are unreal. It is important to note that the miracle does not establish reality or choose it; it merely exposes the illusory nature of the ego's secret dream of sin, guilt, and fear, and the projected dream of world and bodies. Restating this, the miracle does not do anything except reverse the ego's arc (on the left-hand side) that represents the projection of the mind's thoughts into the world. In this way the miracle leads us up the ladder that separation led us down (T-28.III.1:2).

We begin our discussion of the miracle with the chapter's opening section, "The Present Memory":

(I.1:1-4) The miracle does nothing. All it does is to undo. And thus it cancels out the interference to what has been done. It does not add, but merely takes away.

The miracle does not add the right mind or Heaven. It simply removes the veil that separated the body from the mind, enabling our attention to return to the decision-making point where we made the ego's two dreams. Choosing the Holy Spirit's Atonement, our minds finally realize that what we made never happened. We can see how by exposing the ego's purpose in making the world, *A Course in Miracles* does not emphasize the positive, its focus being only on undoing the negative. The miracle heals because it undoes the ego's reversal of effect and cause, allowing the mind to choose another purpose: healing in place of sickness.

(I.1:5) And what it takes away is long since gone, but being kept in memory appears to have immediate effects.

The secret dream (the wrong-minded thought system) is gone because it was never there: "In time this [the separation] happened very long ago. In reality it never happened at all" (M-2.2:7-8). The mind keeps the thought of separation in memory, but we are unaware of doing this for we have become mindless. We believe that memory is a function of the brain, and that as its cells age and deteriorate, the ability to remember declines. Yet all that happens is that the mind has chosen to be governed by the body's "natural" laws, which dictate the diminution of brain activity over time. Without recognizing that the mind actively holds on to the ego by its own decision, we remain imprisoned by its thought system of separation we believe occurred in the past, but has immediate effects in the world.

(I.1:6) This world was over long ago.

This statement is literally stunning because it does not appear to be true. While the world is "too much with us," as Wordsworth wrote, it was over long ago because it is the effect of a cause that was undone the minute it seemed to have occurred. Our ego selves are terrified to read these words, let alone believe them, for we realize that if this world were over long ago, *we* were over long ago; the self we think we are, reading *A Course in Miracles*, would not exist. It is helpful to observe what we do with this thought, how we collectively defend against it macrocosmically by making the world, and microcosmically by living here as individuals under the laws of specialness.

(I.1:7) The thoughts that made it are no longer in the mind that thought of them and loved them for a little while.

We loved them because the thoughts of separation and guilt seemed to give rise to the individual self we think is special and real. Insanely, we defend this specialness to the death—literally—even though it is long since gone.

(I.1:8-9) The miracle but shows the past is gone, and what has truly gone has no effects. Remembering a cause can but produce illusions of its presence, not effects.

If the past is not here, it cannot be a cause; and if not a cause, there can be no effects. Nonetheless, we strive to remember a cause that never happened, but believing it did, we think it real with present effects. But belief cannot establish reality, and illusions have no power to make themselves true, nor turn truth into illusion.

(I.2:1-3) All the effects of guilt are here no more. For guilt is over. In its passing went its consequences, left without a cause.

Guilt is equated with cause, and its effects are the bodily world of pain and suffering. However, if guilt is gone, its effects must be gone as well. This tells us that experience lies because we are not truly here at all.

(I.2:4) Why would you cling to it in memory if you did not desire its effects?

This very important statement highlights our wanting the effects of separation and guilt. We like being bodies, even when living here entails suffering, for this demonstrates that the separation is real. Because we like the effects, we also like their cause—the mind's attraction to guilt—since this gives reality to the effect that is our special self. As we read these passages and seek to apply them in our lives, we need always think of *purpose*, the key that unlocks the Course's seeming secrets. By understanding the ego's strategy of mindlessness, we understand the purpose Jesus gives to forgiveness as the means of undoing the ego and leading us home.

(I.2:5-7) Remembering is as selective as perception, being its past tense. It is perception of the past as if it were occurring now, and still were there to see. Memory, like perception, is a skill made up by you to take the place of what God gave in your creation.

Remembering and perception are the same: we perceive something we believe is occurring in the present and will have future effects, and remember what we think happened in the past. However, the unreality of linear time means that past, present, and future are one. Memory and perception were

designed by the decision-making mind, the *you* to which Jesus refers, that uses separation and time to substitute for the infinite and eternal Self that God created.

(I.2:8-9) And like all the things you made, it can be used to serve another purpose, and to be the means for something else. It can be used to heal and not to hurt, if you so wish it be.

This other purpose is "the present memory." Recall that the Holy Spirit's purpose is to help us remember Who we are as Christ, for He can be defined as the memory of the Self we took into the dream when we fell asleep. He *is* a memory—not of the past but of what is. *Present memory* is obviously a play on the word "memory," which by definition is always of the past. Yet when we remember with the Holy Spirit, we return to what never ceased to be. We can thus say that the ego's use of memory conceals *what is* with *what was*, Christ's innocence with the Son's sinful, albeit illusory past of separation.

(I.4:1-3) The Holy Spirit can indeed make use of memory, for God Himself is there. Yet this is not a memory of past events, but only of a present state. You are so long accustomed to believe that memory holds only what is past, that it is hard for you to realize it is a skill that can remember *now*.

The Holy Spirit takes what we made to hurt, and transforms it for the purpose of healing. Even though we used memory to keep the sinful past alive, accusing others of sin, that same skill of remembering can be used to recall God by forgetting the sin that never was, forgiving what was not done to us.

(I.4:4-7) The limitations on remembering the world imposes on it are as vast as those you let the world impose on you. There is no link of memory to the past. If you would have it there, then there it is. But only your desire made the link, and only you have held it to a part of time where guilt appears to linger still.

Freud, and all who followed him, would never have understood that last sentence, for the past has an effect only when our decision-making minds—*in the present*—allow it to affect us. We do this when we serve the ego's purpose of keeping sin real, maintaining the illusion of a separate identity that is protected by projecting our guilt and blaming the world for our miserable state. The present decision to choose against the Holy Spirit and for the ego gives rise to our identification with the body and its physical and psychological laws. Though Freud well understood the laws of guilt, repression, and projection, he did not recognize that we are not victims of these laws. It is only the mind's ongoing decision that gives them power over us. The problem (and solution) is always in the present, not in a past that is already gone, never having been.

(I.5:1-2) The Holy Spirit's use of memory is quite apart from time. He does not seek to use it as a means to keep the past, but rather as a way to let it go.

The Holy Spirit corrects our sin-laden use for memory, which reinforced the ego's thought system of guilt and punishment, by releasing us from the past in the holy instant and allowing us to remember the Eternal Present.

(I.6) Yet time is but another phase of what does nothing. It works hand in hand with all the other attributes with which you seek to keep concealed the truth about yourself. Time neither takes away nor can restore. And yet you make strange use of it, as if the past had caused the present, which is but a consequence in which no change can be made possible because its cause has gone. Yet change must have a cause that will endure, or else it will not last. No change can be made in the present if its cause is past. Only the past is held in memory as you make use of it, and so it is a way to hold the past against the now.

Here again we see the ego's clever use of time, a primary means of imprisoning us in its thought system of sin and punishment, with no way out. Since purpose is everything, time is no different from any of the other ego defenses (e.g., sickness, attack, pleasure, or pity) in that they are all means to keep

us trapped in mindless bodies, unable to choose the mind's Atonement. In the ego's hands time is a particularly potent defense, establishing that the past is the cause of the present and the legitimate source of our future concerns. Since the past holds the seeds of our problems, but is already over, it is impossible to undo a cause that is no longer present. Within this closed thought system there is no hope of undoing the painful effects except to choose another Cause or Teacher:

(I.7) Remember nothing that you taught yourself, for you were badly taught. And who would keep a senseless lesson in his mind, when he can learn and can preserve a better one? When ancient memories of hate appear, remember that their cause is gone. And so you cannot understand what they are for. Let not the cause that you would give them now be what it was that made them what they were, or seemed to be. Be glad that it is gone, for this is what you would be pardoned from. And see, instead, the new effects of cause accepted *now*, with consequences *here*. They will surprise you with their loveliness. The ancient new ideas they bring will be the happy consequences of a Cause so ancient that It far exceeds the span of memory which your perception sees.

Asking for another Teacher acknowledges that ours has misled us. Because there is no past, there is no sin, and so the effects of sin, a world of suffering and death, do not exist either. Only in the dream-world of separation are they real, being the effects of an illusory cause that is gone. Yet God is our Cause, and as His Effect we can suffer nothing, for illusions have no effect upon reality. Our awakening to this truth is hastened by asking the Holy Spirit's help to forgive a projected past of illusions. By demonstrating to others that their seeming sins have had no effect upon our love, we experience a peace beyond our dreams: the effect of the right-minded decision that is the prerequisite for remembering our true Cause and Its true Effect, the Christ that is our Self.

(I.8) This is the Cause the Holy Spirit has remembered for you, when you would forget. It

is not past because He let It not be unremembered. It has never changed, because there never was a time in which He did not keep It safely in your mind. Its consequences will indeed seem new, because you thought that you remembered not their Cause. Yet was It never absent from your mind, for it was not your Father's Will that He be unremembered by His Son.

We have seen that the Holy Spirit is the memory of our Cause that we took with us into the dream. Despite the ego's attempts to bury It, Its Love has never left the mind, and we are free to recall It at any time and remember Its message: God's Son did not leave his Father and remains forever His Effect, one with Him Who is his Source.

(I.9:1-2) What *you* remember never was. It came from causelessness which you confused with cause.

Instead of remembering God we remember the separation, which "came from causelessness" because the ego is nothing. Coming from nothing, the separation must be nothing as well, and so could not be a cause of anything real. Nevertheless, we persist in confusing it with cause that has real effects, thereby denying the God Who is our true Cause, and ourselves, His true Effect.

(I.9:3) It can deserve but laughter, when you learn you have remembered consequences that were causeless and could never be effects.

This follows the end of Chapter 27, where even though Jesus urged us to laugh at the *tiny, mad idea* of separation, we continue to remember a sinful past where we were mistreated, reinforcing the ego's hate-filled thought system of victimization. However, this is true only in the causeless dream of separation. To repeat an oft-stated point, these words will make no sense unless we rise above the battleground of our everyday experience and learn from Jesus to detach from the ego and look at our lives—past, present, and future—so we may understand how the belief in linear time supports our bodily (i.e., ego) identification. Life here will become easier for we will have undone the ego's

need to pay the painfully heavy price of guilt. Looking without judgment at the thought system of separation allows us to remember the unreality of sin and the dream that is the world. Although the forms may not change for the better, our experiences will be lighter for we will have recognized that dreams have no effect when we respond to the *tiny, mad idea* with the Holy Spirit's gentle laughter, instead of the ego's serious thoughts of sin, guilt, and fear.

(I.9:4-10) The miracle reminds you of a Cause forever present, perfectly untouched by time and interference. Never changed from what It is. And you are Its Effect, as changeless and as perfect as Itself. Its memory does not lie in the past, nor waits the future. It is not revealed in miracles. They but remind you that It has not gone. When you forgive It for your sins, It will no longer be denied.

The miracle does nothing except unveil the ego's strategy so we see it for what it is. Supported by the Atonement, we remember that the ego's thought of change had no effect upon our Changeless Cause. Yet to the extent we do not want the veil lifted, we will find this course threatening and will attack it—directly (special hate) or indirectly (special love)—no different from what the world has done with Jesus and his healing message of forgiveness.

(I.11) The miracle comes quietly into the mind that stops an instant and is still. It reaches gently from that quiet time, and from the mind it healed in quiet then, to other minds to share its quietness. And they will join in doing nothing to prevent its radiant extension back into the Mind which caused all minds to be. Born out of sharing, there can be no pause in time to cause the miracle delay in hastening to all unquiet minds, and bringing them an instant's stillness, when the memory of God returns to them. Their own remembering is quiet now, and what has come to take its place will not be wholly unremembered afterwards.

When, following the mindful path of the miracle, we choose to silence the ego and listen to the Holy

Spirit, we do so for the entire Sonship since it is one. The miracle's extension is only the mind's acceptance of its inherent oneness, and denial of its separate state as a fragmented body. Happily, the Son forgets the sin he had remembered, and remembers the innocence that will soon be beyond memory, being his one Thought. Our forgetting and remembering occur in the holy instant, the locus of the atemporal and non-spatial mind's healing. From there our quiet acceptance of the truth reverberates throughout the Sonship, calling the fragmented Son to his inherent unity.

(I.13:1) How instantly the memory of God arises in the mind that has no fear to keep the memory away!

Just as the memory of God is returned to our sleeping minds by forgiveness, the fear of awakening leads us to retain our grievances. Jesus helps us understand our resistance in choosing to have that memory be brought back into awareness. Yet the willingness to remember is all we need to restore it, for that begins the process of healing whose "outcome is as certain as God" (T-2.III.3:10).

(I.13:2-4) Its own remembering has gone. There is no past to keep its fearful image in the way of glad awakening to present peace. The trumpets of eternity resound throughout the stillness, yet disturb it not.

This is an interesting use of the symbol. Trumpets are loud, but Jesus tells us that the trumpets of eternity "resound throughout the stillness, yet disturb it not." They are loud only in the sense that the Atonement's message is clear and unmistakable, a clarity that undoes the fear that seemed to wall off in sin the memory of God's true Son.

(I.13:5-6) And what is now remembered is not fear, but rather is the Cause that fear was made to render unremembered and undone. The stillness speaks in gentle sounds of love the Son of God remembers from before his own remembering came in between the present and the past, to shut them out.

Here again we see the implicit use of *purpose*. Fear's purpose is to keep God away, which is why we chose to believe in the ego's myth of sin, guilt, and fear, and continue to do so. We decided for the ego to exclude the Atonement, thereby remembering separation instead of union, a memory that safeguards our special self. But in the stillness of Jesus' presence we slowly remember the Cause that always was, and forget the cause that never existed. In the end, our attraction to love's gentle sounds is far more compelling than the harsh dissonances of war and conflict.

(I.14) Now is the Son of God at last aware of present Cause and Its benign Effects. Now does he understand what he has made is causeless, having no effects at all. He has done nothing. And in seeing this, he understands he never had a need for doing anything, and never did. His Cause *is* Its Effects. There never was a cause beside It that could generate a different past or future. Its Effects are changelessly eternal, beyond fear, and past the world of sin entirely.

Having chosen Christ's vision over the ego's judgment, we have dissolved the thought system of separation and sin and allowed the memory of God, our Cause, to rise in awareness. We remember we are His eternal Effect, at one with His Will and Love, and forget a cause and effect that never were, nor ever could be except in dreams.

(I.15) What has been lost, to see the causeless not? And where is sacrifice, when memory of God has come to take the place of loss? What better way to close the little gap between illusions and reality than to allow the memory of God to flow across it, making it a bridge an instant will suffice to reach beyond? For God has closed it with Himself. His memory has not gone by, and left a stranded Son forever on a shore where he can glimpse another shore that he can never reach. His Father wills that he be lifted up and gently carried over. He has built the bridge, and it is He Who will transport His Son across it. Have no fear that He will fail in what He wills. Nor that you be excluded from the Will that is for you.

Never having been, the ego's pseudo-cause and pseudo-effect simply disappear into their nothingness. How, then, could there be a sense of loss or sacrifice? In their place arises the memory of God, brought to awareness through our forgiveness; its gentle healing carrying us back to where our Self softly waits, awakening us from a sleep we did not dream, and helping us remember the Love that created us one with It, as we are one within the Christ. God's Will is done, always being what it forever is: *a Oneness joined as One*.

We return to "Reversing Effect and Cause":

(II.4:1) Nothing at all has happened but that you have put yourself to sleep, and dreamed a dream in which you were an alien to yourself, and but a part of someone else's dream.

In this one sentence Jesus dismisses all of civilization, and our individual lives as well. Because life here is only a dream, it is nothing. Furthering the illusion that life is something, we believe we are an effect of another's dream: parents who gave birth to us, a country that makes laws that govern our behavior, a God Who created our bodies.

(II.4:2-3) The miracle does not awaken you, but merely shows you who the dreamer is. It teaches you there is a choice of dreams while you are still asleep, depending on the purpose of your dreaming.

The arc on the chart shows us that the miracle leads us back to the dreamer/decision maker. It teaches that we have a choice between the ego's nightmares of hate, judgment, and pain, and the Holy Spirit's happy dreams of forgiveness that end the dream of separation. Which ones we experience depend on our purpose: sleep or awakening.

(II.4:4-5) Do you wish for dreams of healing, or for dreams of death? A dream is like a memory in that it pictures what you wanted shown to you.

The world is an "outward picture of a wish" (T-24.VII.8:10); what we perceive, make real, and react to expresses an internal wish of which we are not aware. The miracle brings this into awareness

so our minds can choose between the Holy Spirit's sanity of Atonement and the ego's madness of separation.

(II.5) An empty storehouse, with an open door, holds all your shreds of memories and dreams. Yet if you are the dreamer, you perceive this much at least: that you have caused the dream, and can accept another dream as well. But for this change in content of the dream, it must be realized that it is you who dreamed the dreaming that you do not like. It is but an effect that *you* have caused, and you would not be cause of this effect. In dreams of murder and attack are you the victim in a dying body slain. But in forgiving dreams is no one asked to be the victim and the sufferer. These are the happy dreams the miracle exchanges for your own. It does not ask you make another; only that you see you made the one you would exchange for this.

Again, the *you* that Jesus addresses is the decision maker. The purpose of his course is to return our attention to the mind so we can look at our faulty decision. Once we chose the ego, it closed the door on the right mind with guilt, and then closed the door on the mind with the world, ensuring we would never become mindful and choose again. This is why looking is such a prominent theme in our symphony, and why the miracle lends its name to the Course's title. It opens the closed doors and enables us to look, *and does nothing else*. To repeat this important point, the miracle does not ask us to change dreams or behavior, but merely to watch what we do that we may recognize the mind's power of decision. Non-judgmentally observing our specialness—the need for pleasure and avoidance of pain—exposes the madness in having chosen an insane teacher. This is what enables us to choose another One.

In addition, the miracle helps us realize that if we are angry, in pain, or upset for any reason, it is what our wrong minds wanted. Recall the line from the previous chapter: "The secret of salvation is but this: that you are doing this unto yourself" (T-27.VIII.10:1). Here we read: "[The miracle] does not ask you make another [dream]; only that you see you made the one you would exchange for this." The miracle of forgiveness is a gentle process of looking where we had forgotten to look before, and seeing meaningful choice without judging ourselves (or others) for past mistakes.

(II.6:1) This world is causeless, as is every dream that anyone has dreamed within the world.

The world is causeless because the separation has already been undone, never having happened. Separation cannot be a cause, or even exist if it has no effects—illusions can only breed illusions.

(II.6:2-5) No plans are possible, and no design exists that could be found and understood. What else could be expected from a thing that has no cause? Yet if it has no cause, it has no purpose. You may cause a dream, but never will you give it real effects.

Although within the dream we are free to dream anything we wish, we have no power to turn what we wish into reality. We can believe we are separate and the world is real, but the Atonement teaches that our belief does not make it so. Note the word *design*. By discounting any intelligent (i.e., divine) design for the world, Jesus answers those who profess this theory for the world's creation.

(II.6:6-8) For that would change its cause, and it is this you cannot do. The dreamer of a dream is not awake, but does not know he sleeps. He sees illusions of himself as sick or well, depressed or happy, but without a stable cause with guaranteed effects.

We are not aware we dream because of the veil the ego drew across our minds. We think we are here, no different from when we sleep at night and experience our dreams as reality. The exceptions are those lucid dreamers who know they are dreaming while they sleep, and this is Jesus' interim goal for us: to become aware that life here is a dream, even as we seem to be living here. We do not need to change the world of dreams (the effect), but only the mind that dreams such a world (the cause) (T-21.in.1:7). Now this all-important line:

(II.7:1) The miracle establishes you dream a dream, and that its content is not true.

This is the sum and substance of *A Course in Miracles*. Our symphony can be reduced to this succinct statement, the reason there is *no hierarchy of illusions* and *no order of difficulty in miracles*. The world is a dream, and its foundation in the thought system of separation (sin, guilt, and fear) is unreal, being only a defense against the truth.

(II.7:2-3) This is a crucial step in dealing with illusions. No one is afraid of them when he perceives he made them up.

Although we may have a nightmare and be terrified while we sleep, the fear goes when we awaken because it was based on an illusion. If we think the dream is real we will inevitably be afraid, which is why we need the miracle to teach us that the seeming reality of the ego's world lies in the wrong-minded wish that the separation be so.

(II.7:4-12) The fear was held in place because he did not see that he was author of the dream, and not a figure in the dream. He gives himself the consequences that he dreams he gave his brother. And it is but this the dream has put together and has offered him, to show him that his wishes have been done. Thus does he fear his own attack, but sees it at another's hands. As victim, he is suffering from its effects, but not their cause. He authored not his own attack, and he is innocent of what he caused. The miracle does nothing but to show him that he has done nothing. What he fears is cause without the consequences that would make it cause. And so it never was.

We remain in a fearful state since we are not able to undo its cause. As long as we perceive the objects of our fear to be external, it can never be undone. No sooner would we eliminate the seeming source of fear in the world than the mind's unconscious fear would project out another form, and another, and another. The experience of fear is unending because its true cause has not ended. We do not realize that the cause of all fear lies in the mind's decision for the ego, the belief that our attack on God has had real effects—our punishment. This punishment for sin is seen as coming from outside, not from its simple cause that is the mind's single error. The problem, therefore, never resides in the dreams of sin and punishment, attack and pain, but in the fact that we are dreaming them. Moreover, not only is the dream itself nonexistent, our role as dreamer is as well: perfect Oneness cannot fall asleep, let alone dream of separation; fear and suffering have no cause, meaning that the dreaming mind does not exist.

(II.9:3) The miracle is the first step in giving back to cause the function of causation, not effect.

The cause is the mind, and the miracle restores to it its causal function. Jesus is teaching us how the miracle reverses the reversal of effect and cause, and restores its proper perspective: the world of bodies is the effect, and the mind's separated self is the cause, choosing the dreams its specialness desires and cherishes.

(II.9:4-5) For this confusion has produced the dream, and while it lasts will wakening be feared. Nor will the call to wakening be heard, because it seems to be the call to fear.

As long as we identify with a special self, we will believe that the call of Atonement is the gravest threat to our existence, for in its gentle presence the separated self would disappear. Indeed, our fear of dissolution demands that we do anything not to hear its gentle call, even making a mindless, decaying world of hate to hide in.

(II.10) Like every lesson that the Holy Spirit requests you learn, the miracle is clear. It demonstrates what He would have you learn, and shows you its effects are what you want. In His forgiving dreams are the effects of yours undone, and hated enemies perceived as friends with merciful intent. Their enmity is seen as causeless now, because they did not make it. And you can accept the role of maker of their hate, because you see that it has no effects. Now are you freed from this much of the dream; the world is neutral, and the bodies that still seem to
move about as separate things need not be feared. And so they are not sick.**

The miracle is not the end of the journey, but is necessary for its completion. It releases us from the insane thought that the body is the cause of the mind, the world the determiner of our experience. It undoes the ego's ploy of reversing effect and cause, restoring them to their proper place: the mind is *cause* of the body, which is its *effect*. Choosing the miracle allows us to realize that our feelings of attack and judgment are chosen by the mind, seeking objects—sinners deserving punishment—onto which it can project its hidden judgment of itself. This realization brings the "enemy" back within where it can finally be chosen against, undoing the misperception that another deserves our hate. Having become right-minded, we look out and see no enemies, only "friends with merciful intent." As the workbook says: "And you will see [your brother] suddenly transformed from enemy to savior; from the devil into Christ" (W-pI.161.12:6). With the burden of guilt and fear lifted from its weary shoulders, the world of sickness becomes neutral. Our having corrected the error of separation allows the truth of Christ's Oneness to be reflected in our healed perception of shared interests.

(II.11:1-2) The miracle returns the cause of fear to you who made it. But it also shows that, having no effects, it is not cause, because the function of causation is to have effects.

We are not made fearful by anything external, but only by the mind's decision to be an ego, which would establish fear as causative and real. The Holy Spirit turns the tables on the ego by teaching the Atonement: if there is no cause because the separation is an illusion, there can be no effects; without its seeming cause, there is no world to fear.

(II.11:3-7) And where effects are gone, there is no cause. Thus is the body healed by miracles because they show the mind made sickness, and employed the body to be victim, or effect, of what it made. Yet half the lesson will not teach the whole. The miracle is useless if you learn but that the body can be healed, for this is not the

lesson it was sent to teach. **The lesson is the *mind* was sick that thought the body could be sick; projecting out its guilt caused nothing, and had no effects.**

Since the body cannot be healed as it cannot be sick, Jesus' meaning is that the mind's wrong-minded purpose for the body is healed. Only the mind can be healed for only the mind is sick, and the body's appearances are irrelevant. We are still tempted to look to the body as proof of healing. If someone has physical symptoms, we conclude that the person is not healed. Yet healing depends only on the *purpose* given to the symptoms. Guilt's purpose (the cause) makes the body sick, which has nothing to do with the body itself (the effect). Right-minded purpose sees the body as a means of restoring awareness of the mind's decision-making ability to choose between mindlessness and mindfulness; the former keeps us asleep when we project guilt, the latter awakens us through the miracle.

(II.12:1) This world is full of miracles.

If this line is taken out of context, it can seem to suggest that the world is filled with external miracles, which would give the separated world a reality it does not have (*ideas leave not their source*). The world, however, *is* full of miracles when it reflects the right-minded purpose of ending the dream of separation and specialness.

(II.12:2-7) They stand in shining silence next to every dream of pain and suffering, of sin and guilt. They are the dream's alternative, the choice to be the dreamer, rather than deny the active role in making up the dream. They are the glad effects of taking back the consequence of sickness to its cause. The body is released because the mind acknowledges "this is not done to me, but *I* am doing this." And thus the mind is free to make another choice instead. Beginning here, salvation will proceed to change the course of every step in the descent to separation, until all the steps have been retraced, the ladder gone, and all the dreaming of the world undone.

The world was made to deny the mind's power as the dreamer, leaving us as bodies at the bottom of the ego's ladder where cause and effect have been split off and reversed. We believe we are victims of everything done around us, denying salvation's secret: I am doing this to myself (T-27.VIII.10:1). When we can say to Jesus, "Our ways are not working and there must be another teacher to guide us," he is able to teach us this is our dream. We learn that as long as our minds feel impoverished, unfairly treated, and alone, we fulfill the ego's secret wish of perpetuating our separated existence, but accepting no responsibility for it. Enter the miracle, which does not choose for us but illuminates the right-minded decision we can make. Seeing this helps us ascend the ladder that separation led us down.

(III.1:1-5) What waits in perfect certainty beyond salvation is not our concern. For you have barely started to allow your first, uncertain steps to be directed up the ladder separation led you down. The miracle alone is your concern at present. Here is where we must begin. And having started, will the way be made serene and simple in the rising up to waking and the ending of the dream.

Once again, Jesus urges us not to take on a function that is his and not ours. He asks only that we look at our egos without judgment. This is the choice for the miracle that places our feet firmly on the ladder that reverses projection and leads us home. What extends from the mind's right-minded decision is not our concern, since that inevitably leads to the confusion of cause and effect, content and form, mind and body. We have seen that our task is not to seek for love, but only for the barriers we have placed between ourselves and love (T-16.IV.6:1). As our investment in the ego diminishes, the path becomes easier, for our choice of Jesus as our teacher becomes heavily reinforced.

(III.1:6-8) When you accept a miracle, you do not add your dream of fear to one that is already being dreamed. Without support, the dream will fade away without effects. For it is your support that strengthens it.

We are reminded that the problem is not the ego or its feverish dreams of hate, but our belief in them. When we withdraw this belief, they simply evanesce. The power of dreams lies in the mind's decision maker, not the dream itself. And despite our choice to believe in illusions, we cannot make them real or change God's Mind about His Son.

(III.2) No mind is sick until another mind agrees that they are separate. And thus it is their joint decision to be sick. If you withhold agreement and accept the part you play in making sickness real, the other mind cannot project its guilt without your aid in letting it perceive itself as separate and apart from you. Thus is the body not perceived as sick by both your minds from separate points of view. Uniting with a brother's mind prevents the cause of sickness and perceived effects. Healing is the effect of minds that join, as sickness comes from minds that separate.

This passage makes sense only when we remember that sickness is the belief in separation, a condition of the mind and not the body. This means that it takes *two* to make a sickness: one who chooses it, another who supports it. It is essential, once again, to understand that God did not respond to the separation, let alone recognize it. If He had, He would have made it real (cf. the ego's third law of chaos [T-23.II.6]). To restate this, if God had joined with us in our insanity, the separation would be a fact and there would be no hope of its undoing. His remaining sane in the face of illusion gave birth to the principles of Atonement (the separation never happened) and healing (while it takes two to establish a sickness, it takes one to effect a healing). These are reflected in the dream by our looking beyond the body's appearance to the mind's decision. By so doing, we deliver Jesus' message that choosing the ego is a choice for illusion, with no effect upon the truth of his love.

(III.5) The cause of pain is separation, not the body, which is only its effect. Yet separation is but empty space, enclosing nothing, doing nothing, and as unsubstantial as the empty place between the ripples that a ship has made in passing by. And covered just as fast, as water rushes in to close the gap, and as the waves in joining cover it. Where is the gap between the waves when they have joined, and covered up the space which seemed to keep them separate for a little while? Where are the grounds for sickness when the minds have joined to close the little gap between them, where the seeds of sickness seemed to grow?

If we look to the rear of a ship as it sails on, we see a gap between the waves. As quickly as the boat passes by, however, the waves come together and close the gap, and it is gone. Likewise, in the instant that the separation seemed to happen, the Holy Spirit arose within the mind as the memory we took with us into the dream, dissolving its core: the mind's sickness in choosing the ego. God's undivided Will established the separation's unreality—the Mind of God could not, and did not turn against Itself—that is reflected in our undoing the seeming gap between ourselves and others when we join Jesus' vision of the common need shared by all God's Sons.

(III.6) God builds the bridge, but only in the space left clean and vacant by the miracle. The seeds of sickness and the shame of guilt He cannot bridge, for He can not destroy the alien will that He created not. Let its effects be gone and clutch them not with eager hands, to keep them for yourself. The miracle will brush them all aside, and thus make room for Him Who wills to come and bridge His Son's returning to Himself.

God (or His Holy Spirit) cannot overrule our will, nor impose His truth on a fearful mind. Rather, His Love calls this mind to no longer embrace the thought system of sin and hate, the birthplace of the embodied self that is born, lives a while, and dies. Choosing the miracle reflects our decision to identify with a different self, non-judgmental and kind, and this change of mind invites Jesus to be our teacher and is the prerequisite for the return home.

"The Greater Joining," the next section to be examined, teaches that true joining is only on the level of the mind, having nothing to do with the body at all. Ultimately, the greater joining is our self with the Holy Spirit, behind which is our rejoining the Self we never left.

(IV.1:1) Accepting the Atonement for yourself means not to give support to someone's dream of sickness and of death.

It cannot be stated often enough that Jesus is not speaking of behavior. His message is only that the mind should not make the sickness or death of others real, meaning that our minds are not affected by bodily dreams. This right-minded response to suffering demonstrates the alternate to dreams of pain. By choosing to accept the Atonement, we deny the reality of the separation. Recall the above discussion that the separation is illusory because it takes two to establish it, and God never partook of what never happened. Indeed, the Father does not even know about the illusion for He never shared His Son's insanity. Taking Him as our model, we do not have to share another's delusions of sickness. This frees us to be loving in whatever form can be accepted without fear. We do not proclaim the Course's metaphysics and make the sick guilty because they are not feeling well or need medical attention. Rather, our kindness helps them at the level they can accept at that moment. This gentleness of the holy instant, wherein our minds do not support the illusion of separation and sickness, is possible only when we truly know the world is a dream.

(IV.1:2-5) It means that you share not his wish to separate, and let him turn illusions on himself. Nor do you wish that they be turned, instead, on you. Thus have they no effects. And you are free of dreams of pain because you let him be.

We need always remember that pain is not of the body. It is experienced there, and convincingly so, but since the body is nothing, pain is merely an effect that has never left its source in the mind. We demonstrate this healing truth when we do not give another's dream any power to affect our peace.

(IV.1:6-10) Unless you help him, you will suffer pain with him because that is your wish. And you become a figure in his dream of pain, as he

in yours. So do you and your brother both become illusions, and without identity. You could be anyone or anything, depending on whose evil dream you share. You can be sure of just one thing; that you are evil, for you share in dreams of fear.

Pain is the choice to be separate. Whenever we push love away, or any of its symbols, suffering is inevitable. The purpose of the miracle is to bring pain back to its source in the mind's decision to exclude God and His Son, the source of all perceived evil and suffering. When we separate from another in the special relationship, we are painfully reminded of this original attempt at love's exclusion. Our reinforced guilt rises up as a shared identity of evil and fear, buttressed by pain, all of which conceals our true Identity as Christ, God's innocent Son.

(IV.2) There is a way of finding certainty right here and now. Refuse to be a part of fearful dreams whatever form they take, for you will lose identity in them. You find yourself by not accepting them as causing you, and giving you effects. You stand apart from them, but not apart from him who dreams them. Thus you separate the dreamer from the dream, and join in one, but let the other go. The dream is but illusion in the mind. And with the mind you would unite, but never with the dream. It is the dream you fear, and not the mind. You see them as the same, because you think that *you* are but a dream. And what is real and what is but illusion in yourself you do not know and cannot tell apart.

Recall: "Nothing so blinding as perception of form" (T-22.III.6:7). Nothing in the perceptual world of dreams should be believed because it bespeaks separation, the fundamental illusion. The great seduction of the world is to make its dreams of specialness real, either through attachment, detachment, or attack. The world's sole purpose is to distract us from the dreaming mind that can choose to awaken in an instant and end the dream. Perceiving the sameness of God's separated Sons is impossible if the dream of bodies is given power to affect us, but is inevitable when the mind chooses the Holy Spirit as its Teacher. When we recognize that our decision maker is the cause of all dreams, and our lives as bodies merely effects, our eyes begin to open to the truth of who we are: one split mind, common to all God's Sons in the dream; one Self, the Christ that God created as His unified Son.

(IV.3:1-3) Like you, your brother thinks he is a dream. Share not in his illusion of himself, for your Identity depends on his reality. Think, rather, of him as a mind in which illusions still persist, but as a mind which brother is to you.

Clearly we are the same, sharing one mind: the Holy Spirit's Atonement, and the ego's belief in separation that includes its strategy of mindlessness. If we see ourselves as bodies, separate from each other, we share in illusions and make them real for both of us. On the other hand, with Jesus beside us we look past the shadows of appearance to the mind's light that reminds us of our shared reality shining through the clouds of sin, guilt, and specialness.

(IV.3:4) He is not brother made by what he dreams, nor is his body, "hero" of the dream, your brother.

The dream's "hero" is the body (T-27.VIII). What unites us as God's Son is not the ego's dreams of special bodies that only seem to unite, but the decision-making mind in which we share illusions or truth, madness or reason.

(IV.3:5-7) It is his reality that is your brother, as is yours to him. Your mind and his are joined in brotherhood. His body and his dreams but seem to make a little gap, where yours have joined with his.

The gap is the dance of death in which we pleadingly invite each other to partake: "Join me on the dance floor—love me, argue with me, take advantage of me." Whatever the form, we crave partners in sin to demonstrate that the ego's specialness is real and not our fault. Jesus asks us to see how we encourage others to play this hateful game of bodies that roots us together in the dream from which we must never awaken. Looking through his eyes,

however, the mind is able to choose again and see our brothers as partners in innocence, not guilt.

(IV.4) And yet, between your minds there is no gap. To join his dreams is thus to meet him not, because his dreams would separate from you. Therefore release him, merely by your claim on brotherhood, and not on dreams of fear. Let him acknowledge who he is, by not supporting his illusions by your faith, for if you do, you will have faith in yours. With faith in yours, he will not be released, and you are kept in bondage to his dreams. And dreams of fear will haunt the little gap, inhabited but by illusions which you have supported in your brother's mind.

As innocent Sons we are not separated by the ego's gap, for the mind is one. Yet our egos continually call us to reinforce the dream through the specialness of sickness and hate. At the same time, the Holy Spirit's Voice calls us to see past the dream figures and rejoin the dreamer. Hearing that call, we strengthen it in each other and this frees us both. If we place our faith (the mind's power of decision) in illusions, however, we invite sin and guilt to lurk within, and our lives to be haunted by the fear of punishment we have made real in our shared dream. As minds are joined, we choose not just for ourselves but for the Sonship, remaining in Heaven or hell *together, or not at all*.

(IV.5) Be certain, if you do your part, he will do his, for he will join you where you stand. Call not to him to meet you in the gap between you, or you must believe that it is your reality as well as his. You cannot do his part, but this you *do* when you become a passive figure in his dreams, instead of dreamer of your own. Identity in dreams is meaningless because the dreamer and the dream are one. Who shares a dream must be the dream he shares, because by sharing is a cause produced.

Our brothers cannot fail to do their part, as we did ours, since minds are one. However, the fear of our shared interest as minds causes us to leave the realm of dreamer and take up residence in the dream. We continually seek to participate in each other's nightmares of judgment, suffering, and death, reinforcing the special selves we value above all else. It is essential to see how enthusiastically we keep our promise to stay asleep, joining in the dreams of love and hate that bind us to an existence of mindless bodies and keep the mind hidden and inaccessible to change.

(IV.6) You share confusion and you are confused, for in the gap no stable self exists. What is the same seems different, because what is the same appears to be unlike. His dreams are yours because you let them be. But if you took your own away would he be free of them, and of his own as well. Your dreams are witnesses to his, and his attest the truth of yours. Yet if you see there is no truth in yours, his dreams will go, and he will understand what made the dream.

The theme of sameness is restated. We are not the same in the body's dream, for bodies were made to accentuate differences among God's Sons. Returning to the dream's source in the mind, however, we recognize our inherent sameness. This demonstrates the mind's causal nature and offers others the opportunity of attaining the same recognition. In this way the mind is healed of dreams and can return to its natural state as decision maker. Recall that it takes two to make sickness, but only one healed mind to end it. Illusions have no power over truth.

(IV.7:1-2) The Holy Spirit is in both your minds, and He is One because there is no gap that separates His Oneness from Itself. The gap between your bodies matters not, for what is joined in Him is always one.

Because we fear the Oneness that renders our separated state meaningless, Jesus' loving presence poses a real threat to the ego. It has no choice except to protect itself, which it has done by making him different from the rest of God's Sons. This effectively established the "reality" of the dream of separation, nullifying his message—then and now—of our inherent sameness. With no gap within the Sonship, or between the Son and his Source, there is no *I*, as that self is rooted in the

ego's thought system of separation. Jesus, or any egoless symbol, proclaims the sameness and oneness of God's Son on the levels of illusion and truth, thereby dismissing the perceived gap as nonexistent.

(IV.7:3-7) No one is sick if someone else accepts his union with him. His desire to be a sick and separated mind can not remain without a witness or a cause. And both are gone if someone wills to be united with him. He has dreams that he was separated from his brother who, by sharing not his dream, has left the space between them vacant. And the Father comes to join His Son the Holy Spirit joined.

Once again we see the ego's need for allies. Since without the support of another the thought of separation could not stand, we continually reinforce each other's wrong-minded thought system, either by joining with it (special love) or attacking it (special hate). But let one person decline the invitation and not be affected by the dream, and the decision for the ego will lose its potency because it will have lost its ally in specialness. As the ego's thought system dissolves, a quiet space arises that allows the mind to choose again. In that holy instant of forgiveness, God's memory returns to bless the Son He never left, and with him the Sonship awakens from its dreams of hate and spite.

(IV.8:1) The Holy Spirit's function is to take the broken picture of the Son of God and put the pieces into place again.

The Holy Spirit does not see differences among the separated fragments of the Sonship, with one being more special than another. His true perception looks upon everyone as the same, sharing the one need to awaken from the dream. This shared purpose of forgiveness reunites the broken pieces of the broken dream of separation.

(IV.8:2) This holy picture, healed entirely, does He hold out to every separate piece that thinks it is a picture in itself.

Forgiveness is central to healing. Our special partners, perceived as autonomous and separate from us, are the ones with whom we must practice remembering our common need and goal, even in the face of multitudinous differences of form. As we remember the Holy Spirit's single purpose for all relationships, we learn to generalize His forgiveness until it embraces the entire Sonship.

The following paragraph begins with a prayer that Jesus says to God on our behalf:

(IV.9:1) I thank You, Father, knowing You will come to close each little gap that lies between the broken pieces of Your holy Son.

God, of course, does not come to close the gap. How can He close a gap that does not exist? But because we banished the Creator from our minds, welcoming Him back is experienced as His healing the separation. In truth, of course, we are simply accepting the healing Presence of His Voice as our Teacher.

(IV.9:2-3) Your Holiness, complete and perfect, lies in every one of them. And they are joined because what is in one is in them all.

This extremely important phrase, "every one of them," highlights Jesus' principle of *no exceptions*. The greatest abusers, villains, and criminals, so perceived by the world, are still part of the complete picture of Christ. It is helpful to observe how we pick and choose those whom we will embrace or exclude from His perfect Oneness.

(IV.9:4-7) How holy is the smallest grain of sand, when it is recognized as being part of the completed picture of God's Son! The forms the broken pieces seem to take mean nothing. For the whole is in each one. And every aspect of the Son of God is just the same as every other part.

The Sonship of God does not consist of homo sapiens alone, or so-called living things. Since all form is illusory and there is no hierarchy of illusions, the distinction between animate and inanimate falls away. As "there is no life outside of Heaven" (T-23.II.19:1), nothing here can be alive; a grain of sand is no more or less alive than a person. We are all equally non-living; not dead, which is a state that presupposes prior life. Each and every

form is nothing but a projected fragment of the mind's original and illusory thought of separation. When the thought was projected as a world, it fragmented into billions upon billions of pieces, each one appearing as separated and independent. Though we categorize these forms as living and non-living, such discrimination cannot grant life to what is non-life. Similarly, none of the atomic elements that comprise what we call matter is real. Despite this, form can serve a mighty purpose in the dream by providing opportunities for us to correct the mind's mistake of choosing the wrong teacher, recognizing that materiality expresses the Son's continuing decision to be separate from his Source.

(IV.10:6) The seeds of sickness come from the belief that there is joy in separation, and its giving up would be a sacrifice.

Believing we had destroyed God, we became joyful in the experience of being on our own. How, then, could we not feel it a sacrifice to lose our autonomous existence, with the physical world as the means of preserving our sick and separated self? Bodies that house these insane thoughts of separation inevitably fight with each other to save their special identity, so much so that they kill to protect themselves, sacrificing other bodies that they might live.

(IV.10:7-10) But miracles are the result when you do not insist on seeing in the gap what is not there. Your willingness to let illusions go is all the Healer of God's Son requires. He will place the miracle of healing where the seeds of sickness were. And there will be no loss, but only gain.

Jesus here undoes everything the ego has told us; namely, that by choosing the Holy Spirit we would lose, and only by following the ego would we gain. Needless to say, the truth is exactly the opposite: the separation never occurred as nothing could only give rise to nothing. The miracle heals the mind's sick thought that illusion could replace truth, madness replace reason, and hell take the place of Heaven. And we are glad and thankful it is so.

(V.3) You share no evil dreams if you forgive the dreamer, and perceive that he is not the dream he made. And so he cannot be a part of yours, from which you both are free. Forgiveness separates the dreamer from the evil dream, and thus releases him. Remember if you share an evil dream, you will believe you are the dream you share. And fearing it, you will not want to know your own Identity, because you think that It is fearful. And you will deny your Self, and walk upon an alien ground which your Creator did not make, and where you seem to be a something you are not. You will make war upon your Self, which seems to be your enemy; and will attack your brother, as a part of what you hate. There is no compromise. You are your Self or an illusion. What can be between illusion and the truth? A middle ground, where you can be a thing that is not you, must be a dream and cannot be the truth.

The miracle of forgiveness sets the cause-effect relationship in its proper sequence, so that the dream of a world is seen as never having left its source in the dreaming mind: *ideas* (effect) *leave not their source* (cause). It is when they are reversed and we forget we are minds that fear enters, leading us to believe we are at the mercy of forces beyond our control. The internal war against God and His creation is projected into a world that seeks our punishment and death, "proven" when our bodily selves suffer and die. But "God thinks otherwise" (T-23.I.2:7), and a dream cannot make illusions real, or reality an illusion. If we are as God created us, we cannot be the ego-created self of our dreams. This is the corrected sense of *one or the other*: we are asleep or awake, at home in God or dreaming of exile (T-10.I.2:1). Salvation's simple message is that only one of these is true: Self or self. The choice is easy once the alternatives are clearly seen.

(V.7:1-2) You who believe there is a little gap between you and your brother, do not see that it is here you are as prisoners in a world perceived to be existing here. The world you see does not

exist, because the place where you perceive it is not real.

The problem is not the world, the body that has arisen from the gap, or the gap itself. The problem is the belief in the gap's reality, born of our having taken the *tiny, mad idea* seriously. Notwithstanding our experience, which deceives, we do not see the world through physical eyes, but through the mind's eye that has identified with the ego that is rooted in the thought that the separation actually happened. The Atonement tells us, however, that there is in fact no gap at all. Consequently, it cannot be a cause, and so it has no effects. Where, then, is the world, or the self that perceives it?

(V.7:3) The gap is carefully concealed in fog, and misty pictures rise to cover it with vague uncertain forms and changing shapes, forever unsubstantial and unsure.

The ego causes a fog to fall across the mind so we are no longer aware of its thoughts. We do not really see what is there, just as driving in fog is dangerous because we cannot see what is ahead of us. Note how Jesus describes this world: "vague uncertain forms and changing shapes, forever unsubstantial and unsure." This corrects our perceptual experience that is the exact opposite, our senses telling us that the world is substantial and very sure. Recall, "Nothing so blinding as perception of form" (T-22.III.6:7), meaning that the world, being a projection of a delusional thought system, is an hallucination. Nevertheless, while we sleep, these dreams of a world seem palpably real.

(V.7:4-5) Yet in the gap is nothing. And there are no awesome secrets and no darkened tombs where terror rises from the bones of death.

Jesus is referring to the secret dream from which we flee with a vengeance, leading us to seek the world's dream for protection. His love assures us we are mistaken, that there is no dark, guilty secret in our mind to fear, and that both the wrong-minded thought system of separation and the world of death that arose from it are made up.

(V.7:6) Look at the little gap, and you behold the innocence and emptiness of sin that you will see within yourself, when you have lost the fear of recognizing love.

The important theme of looking returns. "Look at the little gap," Jesus says, which we do by being taught to look at the world as a projection, the "outside picture of an inward condition" (T-21.in.1:5) that houses the belief that the gap is real. Jesus helps us look at our relationships differently, not as real or problematic, nor even as needing to be healed, but as mirrors of the guilt we do not want to see. This motif has returned over and over in our symphony, and in these final movements it becomes ever more powerful.

The specific words in the above passage are important: "when you have lost the fear of recognizing love." We fear love because in its presence we do not exist as separated selves, and as a shield from the incursion of truth we turn love into specialness. How, then, could we not be afraid of Jesus and his course, for we would do anything not to look within and see the Atonement, the ego's fear (see T-21.IV.2-3). Listening to its insane counsel, we remain mindless bodies that we believe protect us from the mind's sin and certain destruction.

We come now to the Holy Spirit's response to the pledge we made with our special partners (VI.4-5):

(VI.6:1-2) Let this be your agreement with each one; that you be one with him and not apart. And he will keep the promise that you make with him, because it is the one that he has made to God, as God has made to him.

These words do not mean literally, on the level of form, that others have to agree with us. We do not need them to be healed, for if that were the case we would be victimized by their ego choices. In making this agreement with our erstwhile special partners, we reinforce the agreement—*in us*—that we first made with God to be His Son. This covenant, which of course is symbolic, exists as a memory within everyone's right mind. When we agree not to participate in another's dream of sin, sickness, anger, and death, we do not give it power to change our mind's love and peace. This enables us

to say to our brothers: "Your sins against me or others have had no effect, and so they are forgiven." Our loving thought will remain in their minds until the time they choose to accept it, being a reminder that they can make the same choice to remember their promise to God that we have made in the holy instant. This is the shift in purpose Jesus helps us achieve, and which alone gives meaning to an otherwise meaningless world.

Very simply, Jesus asks us to allow him in our minds so together we can look at the special relationship differently, freeing the truth that teaches others, not by words or actions, but by the love we have accepted as our reality. As this love naturally extends through our minds, it will be kind, gentle, and compassionate, taking whatever form will be most helpful. This is why we should look only to the mind's content and not judge the behavioral forms.

(VI.6:3-9) God keeps His promises; His Son keeps his. In his creation did his Father say, "You are beloved of Me and I of you forever. Be you perfect as Myself, for you can never be apart from Me." His Son remembers not that he replied "I will," though in that promise he was born. Yet God reminds him of it every time he does not share a promise to be sick, but lets his mind be healed and unified. His secret vows are powerless before the Will of God, Whose promises he shares. And what he substitutes is not his will, who has made promise of himself to God.

This is the right-minded use of promise. Instead of swearing allegiance to the ego, we now pledge fidelity to the Holy Spirit, reflecting our promise to God Who "reminds" us of it each time we forgive. We need to be aware of these promises for that is how we counteract the sick thought system of separation. We first recognize the ego's commitment to the ego of another, the secret vow to join the dance of specialness and death as defense against our agreement to Jesus to remember our inherent sameness. Thus we remember our sacred promise to God: "I will."

(VII.2:1-2) The beautiful relationship you have with all your brothers is a part of you because it

is a part of God Himself. Are you not sick, if you deny yourself your wholeness and your health, the Source of help, the Call to healing and the Call to heal?

Sickness has nothing to do with the body or its symptoms, but only with the mind's decision to be with the ego instead of God: choosing separation over wholeness, illness over health. Forgiveness of our special partners, which means recognizing our shared interests, reflects this sane decision and is the source of all healing.

(VII.2:3-6) Your savior waits for healing, and the world waits with him. Nor are you apart from it. For healing will be one or not at all, its oneness being where the healing is. What could correct for separation but its opposite?

Our saviors are our brothers in specialness, who need to be reminded of the right-minded choice they can make, as we have made in the holy instant. Healing is one because the Sonship is one. We can see how the theme of oneness is always with us on our symphonic journey to the Oneness that is our Self.

(VII.2:7-10) There is no middle ground in any aspect of salvation. You accept it wholly or accept it not. What is unseparated must be joined. And what is joined cannot be separate.

Recall Jesus' words: "This course will be believed entirely or not at all" (T-22.II.7:4). The situation is one or the other, and each choice represents a perfectly integrated thought system: the ego's 100 percent separation and hate, or the Holy Spirit's 100 percent oneness and love. The famous biblical injunction "What therefore God hath joined together, let not man put asunder" (Matthew 19:6) is herewith turned around to mean that what God has joined as one is always one: the Christ Whom He created as His undivided Son.

(VII.3:1-4) Either there is a gap between you and your brother, or you are as one. There is no in between, no other choice, and no allegiance to be split between the two. A split allegiance is but faithlessness to both, and merely

sets you spinning round, to grasp uncertainly at any straw that seems to hold some promise of relief. Yet who can build his home upon a straw, and count on it as shelter from the wind?

We continue with the theme that God's Sons are either different or the same, and obviously cannot be both. The principle of *one or the other* to the contrary, the ego has us maintain a split allegiance between itself and itself (i.e., *its* God), which glorifies its illusory doctrine of differences. This madness is a house of straw, with the body being the embodiment of the ego's nothingness, hence its fragility. Yet the truth is that we are not only one in Heaven but also in the dream, wherein we share the insanity of separation as well as the need to awaken from the nightmare of guilt. Deciding between these two, differences or sameness, is the only meaningful choice we can make here.

(VII.3:5-6) The body can be made a home like this, because it lacks foundation in the truth. And yet, because it does, it can be seen as not your home, but merely as an aid to help you reach the home where God abides.

The body can be seen "as an aid to help you reach the home where God abides" because it can serve a purpose different from making the world real, the illusory effect of an illusory cause. With Jesus as our teacher, we use the body as an instrument to return our awareness to the thought in the mind that made it. This reversal of projection, the miracle's pathway of mindlessness to mindfulness, allows our decision maker to undo its mistaken choice.

(VII.4:1-4) With *this* as purpose is the body healed. It is not used to witness to the dream of separation and disease. Nor is it idly blamed for what it did not do. It serves to help the healing of God's Son, and for this purpose it cannot be sick.

As we well know, Jesus is not speaking of symptoms, but the change in *purpose* for the body. Since the body cannot be sick or well, this passage is about the purpose the mind has projected onto the body. Since the purpose of guilt is the sickness that needs to be healed through forgiveness, the body can become a classroom of learning and salvation from guilt, rather than a prison of suffering, punishment, and death.

(VII.4:5-9) It will not join a purpose not your own, and you have chosen that it not be sick. All miracles are based upon this choice, and given you the instant it is made. No forms of sickness are immune, because the choice cannot be made in terms of form. The choice of sickness seems to be of form, yet it is one, as is its opposite. And you are sick or well, accordingly.

We are sick if our minds choose the ego; we are well if we choose the Holy Spirit. This is so regardless of the presence or absence of physical (or psychological) symptoms. We need always be reminded that *A Course in Miracles* is not about the body but about changing the mind's purpose for it. For this reason it is a mistake to judge others by their sick or healthy appearance, because no one can ever understand purpose from perceiving the body. To say that purpose is everything is to say that purpose is *content*, while the body is a *form* that has not left its source.

(VII.5:1-2) But never you alone. This world is but the dream that you can be alone, and think without affecting those apart from you.

This theme is echoed in the workbook lesson, "When I am healed I am not healed alone" (W-pI.137). If minds are one and my mind is sick because I have chosen the ego, I send a message throughout the Sonship that the ego is right and God is wrong. On the other hand, my choosing the Holy Spirit in the holy instant sends the healing message that the ego is wrong and God is right. Once again, while this makes no sense to us as separated bodies, as minds above the battleground looking down upon the fragmented and insane world, this teaching is eminently sane.

(VII.5:3-6) To be alone must mean you are apart, and if you are, you cannot but be sick. This seems to prove that you must be apart. Yet all it means

is that you tried to keep a promise to be true to faithlessness. Yet faithlessness is sickness.**

This is why the ego emphasizes sickness, for it proves we are separate bodies and that separation is real. Our mind's faith has been placed in the ego, the definition of *faithlessness*, for we have faith in nothing. It is only this "faithless" mind that is ill, while health is certain when we put our faith in the Teacher of healing and forgiveness.

(VII.5:7-11) It is like the house set upon straw. It seems to be quite solid and substantial in itself. Yet its stability cannot be judged apart from its foundation. If it rests on straw, there is no need to bar the door and lock the windows and make fast the bolts. The wind will topple it, and rain will come and carry it into oblivion.

From here to the end of the section, Jesus uses the biblical symbol of the house, the foundation built on straw that represents the ego's thought system of illusion, protected by our experience of the body's seeming solidity. Taking care of the body and obsessing about its health is pointless if we do not do anything about the mind. If our minds are rooted in judgment and attack, no matter how we treat the body, no matter how many decades it may live, there is ultimately no sense in paying attention to what is inherently unreal. To be sure, Jesus is not saying not to take care of the body. Very often, since we have misused this embodied self, taking care of it can reflect a right-minded choice wherein we use it not as an instrument of pain but of health. Still, the body should never be the focus, for it would merely distract us from the mind, which is the ego's perennial purpose for physical existence. When we are right-minded, everything we do with the body will be helpful, regardless of its appearance. But if we have banished love, regardless of the body's "health," we will have gained nothing except illusions of well-being, leading to the smugness of achievement that prevents the real "work" of changing one's mind and being healed.

(VII.6) What is the sense in seeking to be safe in what was made for danger and for fear? Why burden it with further locks and chains and

heavy anchors, when its weakness lies, not in itself, but in the frailty of the little gap of nothingness whereon its stands? What can be safe that rests upon a shadow? Would you build your home upon what will collapse beneath a feather's weight?

The vulnerable body continues as our subject, but only to point out the weakness of the underlying thought system that is based on the illusory gap of separation. Jesus is helping us shift attention from the body to the mind that has chosen mindlessness as its home. Once mindfulness has returned we are able to see the ego for what it is. We remember to laugh at our silliness in ever having believed its feeble lies and placing faith in its feeble home that needed our care, concern, and protection.

Closing

This final paragraph is an excellent summary of the chapter, bringing together its themes of contrasting the ego's promise with the Holy Spirit's purpose of restoring to the mind its proper function of causation.

(VII.7:1-3) Your home is built upon your brother's health, upon his happiness, his sinlessness, and everything his Father promised him. No secret promise you have made instead has shaken the Foundation of his home. The winds will blow upon it and the rain will beat against it, but with no effect.

Whatever happens in the world will have no effect upon us if our minds are healed. Our secret promise to the ego cannot undo our promise to God; in dreams, yes, but dreams cannot establish reality, nor can they make illusions true. Our home in God, expressed in the dream by the right-minded thought system of forgiveness, has not disappeared because we closed our eyes. The thought of Atonement remains the only truth within the world of illusion, and is the solidity of our home away from home.

(VII.7:4-6) The world will wash away and yet this house will stand forever, for its strength lies not within itself alone. It is an ark of safety, resting on God's promise that His Son is safe forever in Himself. What gap can interpose itself between the safety of this shelter and its Source?

The Atonement tells us the separation was a non-event. Even though we are free to believe whatever we wish about the gap and what is needed to protect it, we cannot make it real. The world is still causeless for its cause, the gap of separation in which the mind has placed its faith, never happened. This truth is our ark of safety, sheltering us against the ego's raging winds of sin and hate. Throughout the ego's storms, our beloved Teacher is reminding us that we remain forever an Effect of our Source, the Cause Whose Love we have never left.

(VII.7:7-8) From here the body can be seen as what it is, and neither less nor more in worth than the extent to which it can be used to liberate God's Son unto his home. And with this holy purpose is it made a home of holiness a little while, because it shares your Father's Will with you.

We are asked not to pay attention to the body, only to the mind's foundation on which it is built: fear and attack, or forgiveness and love. From that one choice follows everything we experience in the world. If we choose the ego, our lives will be painful; if we choose love, peace alone will be our experience. The forms of our dreams are irrelevant, for the mind's content is the sole cause of everything. And when we decide to make Jesus our teacher, his lessons become the bricks on which our right-minded home is built—solid, holy, dependable. His love is our ark of safety, the loving arms of forgiveness that carry us to our eternal home.

Chapter 29

THE AWAKENING

Introduction

Just when we thought it was safe to go back in the water, the shark of specialness rears its ugly head again. The main theme of this chapter is idols, a synonym for special relationships that is a term not used here although the word *special* appears once. We will revisit this theme in a slightly different form from what we saw in Chapter 28 when we discussed cause and effect. Our focus now on idols/special relationships is not so much related to what we do with each other (as heretofore was almost always the case), but to how we use the world and the ego itself as substitutes for God. This is the primary meaning of *idols*, and the last time we systematically looked at this term was in Chapter 10, "The Idols of Sickness." There, too, it referred to the false god we made as substitute for our Creator.

Purpose continues as a major theme in these final chapters as well, as does the important theme of change, implicit in everything we discuss. The separation marks the first change, and all our wrong-minded changes are projected fragments of that original mistake. The Holy Spirit's change of Atonement, where we begin this movement of our symphony, is the correction for the original change, not to mention its undoing.

The Atonement Principle

This statement of the Atonement principle comes at the chapter's opening and opens our discussion as well. God is, and there can be nothing else because what appears to exist outside our Source, the only reality, must be illusory.

(I.1:1-5) There is no time, no place, no state where God is absent. There is nothing to be feared. There is no way in which a gap could be conceived of in the Wholeness that is His. The compromise the least and littlest gap would represent in His eternal Love is quite impossible. For it would mean His Love could harbor just a hint of hate, His gentleness turn sometimes to attack, and His eternal patience sometimes fail.

The theme of *the gap* continues from Chapter 28, and Jesus reaffirms the happy fact that the separation could not have happened. Since God and His Love are constant, so too is the wholeness of truth. This means it is impossible for even the tiniest of *tiny, mad ideas* to arise in the Mind of perfect Wholeness and Oneness. One can make no compromise with God, which is why we speak of the Course's perfect non-dualistic thought system. Illusion has no place in the Creator's Mind, and His all-encompassing totality can have nothing to do with a separated and fragmented world. Heaven and the world are mutually exclusive states: perfection cannot be in imperfection; love finds no home in fear; and unity does not exist in a state of separation.

We turn to "The Changeless Dwelling Place," and will return to this beautiful section at the movement's close.

(V.1) There is a place in you where this whole world has been forgotten; where no memory of sin and of illusion lingers still. There is a place in you which time has left, and echoes of eternity are heard. There is a resting place so still no sound except a hymn to Heaven rises up to gladden God the Father and the Son. Where Both abide are They remembered, Both. And where They are is Heaven and is peace.

Jesus speaks of the right mind, once we have chosen it unequivocally. It is the Holy Spirit's dwelling place, home of the memory of God's Love, and doorway to the real world that awaits our decision to awaken from the feverish dreams of guilt and fear, returning to the Heaven we never left.

(V.2:1-2) Think not that you can change Their dwelling place. For your Identity abides in Them, and where They are, forever must you be.

The *tiny, mad idea* is the belief that change is possible, that God's Son can dwell in a mind that is outside the Mind of God and Christ, his true home and Self. How silly to believe in lies when truth brings only happiness and everlasting peace!

(V.2:3-4) The changelessness of Heaven is in you, so deep within that nothing in this world but passes by, unnoticed and unseen. The still infinity of endless peace surrounds you gently in its soft embrace, so strong and quiet, tranquil in the might of its Creator, nothing can intrude upon the sacred Son of God within.

Over and over, Jesus reminds us that God has nothing to do with a nonexistent world that is unnoticed and unseen by Him. As a result, we need to be vigilant for the ego's need to bring our Creator into the world of illusion. The ego's method in its madness is that if God were involved with the illusion, it would mean the illusion were real; so real, in fact, that it had the power to disturb God and motivate Him to respond to it. The above, then, is the Holy Spirit's loving response to the insanity of believing that change is possible, and that God's Son has actually set up residence outside Heaven.

The passages we examine now bring the theme of idols to various expressions of the Atonement principle:

(II.6:1-2) Such is the promise of the living God; His Son have life and every living thing be part of him, and nothing else have life. What you have given "life" is not alive, and symbolizes but your wish to be alive apart from life, alive in

death, with death perceived as life, and living, death.

In our insane dreams we have given life to a body that is non-life; and because it was made as a substitute for our true life in spirit, it is an idol. The body symbolizes our mind's wish to live apart from our Source, magically believing we can find life in a moribund existence. This shabby substitution for reality embodies the ego's thought of death in a separated and corporeal existence that is outside the Mind of the living God.

(VIII.7) Where is an idol? Nowhere! Can there be a gap in what is infinite, a place where time can interrupt eternity? A place of darkness set where all is light, a dismal alcove separated off from what is endless, *has* no place to be. An idol is beyond where God has set all things forever, and has left no room for anything to be except His Will. Nothing and nowhere must an idol be, while God is everything and everywhere.

This statement of the Atonement dismisses everything the ego tells us is true. In the clarification of terms, Jesus says of the ego that it is nothing and nowhere (C-2.6). To conceal its inherent nothingness, the ego made the universe and then the body to perceive and proclaim it good, as the biblical God said when He looked at his creation. And the world is good indeed—*for the ego*! The universe's seeming immensity points to its reality as a *something*, preventing the recognition that it is but a cover of nothingness for the nonexistent ego and its thought system of idols: guilt, fear, and death.

(VIII.9:1-4) God has not many Sons, but only One. Who can have more, and who be given less? In Heaven would the Son of God but laugh, if idols could intrude upon his peace. It is for him the Holy Spirit speaks, and tells you idols have no purpose here.

Idols have a definite purpose within the ego system, but since a thought system made of illusions is nothing, they must be purposeless in the end. Similarly, to put our faith in the ego is to put it in the faithless, for it is faith in what does not exist. Note, too, the theme of laughter that is so prominent in these later chapters. It is the only sane response to the ego's patent insanity, both ontologically as well as in our everyday life.

(VIII.9:5) For more than Heaven can you never have.

The ego wanted us to be more than Heaven, telling God at the beginning: "Your Love is not enough. I want more than everything." And because we wished for the opposite of everything, we believe it was accomplished.

(VIII.9:6-11) If Heaven is within, why would you seek for idols that would make of Heaven less, to give you more than God bestowed upon your brother and on you, as one with Him? God gave you all there is. And to be sure you could not lose it, did He also give the same to every living thing as well. And thus is every living thing a part of you, as of Himself. No idol can establish you as more than God. But you will never be content with being less.

The everything of God is in us, and in every seeming fragment of the Sonship—*without exception*. The ego's rejoinder is: "I'll show You!" It then makes up a world in which we continually strive to be happy at another's expense, finding pleasure in desperate attempts to demonstrate that the specialness we have here is better than the love we had in Heaven. Since this is sheer nonsense, we strive to prove that truth is wrong and authenticate as true what can never be. And so we identify with the body, the ego's instrument of separation and attack.

The "living thing" Jesus refers to is not a form, because he has already told us there is nothing alive here. Rather, he means the seeming fragments of God's Son, whose "life" is present in each part as a memory held within the mind. This is denied by the mindless body, and its inherent nothingness is the next theme we consider.

The Nothingness of the Body

(II.1:1) Why would you not perceive it as release from suffering to learn that you are free?

Jesus asks the same question as in the above passages, saying to us, in effect: "Why would you choose the nothing you think you have, when you already have everything? All you need do to remember this everything of God is follow what I am teaching. Looking at the ego's idols of specialness without judgment allows me to help you forgive them. You will be freed from all suffering as the memory of God's Love rises in your awareness, dissolving the petty nothingness with which you have identified. Come, my children, listen, look, and come home with me."

(II.1:2-4) Why would you not acclaim the truth instead of looking on it as an enemy? Why does an easy path, so clearly marked it is impossible to lose the way, seem thorny, rough and far too difficult for you to follow? Is it not because you see it as the road to hell instead of looking on it

as a simple way, without a sacrifice or any loss, to find yourself in Heaven and in God?

The ego tells us that if we listen to the Holy Spirit and recognize the world is a dream, we would find ourselves in the hell of oblivion and annihilation. It says that Heaven is continuing down the path of judgment, reinforcing our identity as separate and special individuals. We keep this self intact by projecting its concomitant sin onto everyone else, blaming others for our misery. We perceive Jesus, and subsequently his course, as leading us to hell because it is the road (the easy path of forgiveness) that leads beyond individual existence to the Oneness of Heaven, the ego's definition of hell. This is why we need a Teacher Who uses contrasts to point out the difference between joy and pain, freedom and imprisonment, Heaven and hell.

(II.8:1-7) Sickness is a demand the body be a thing that it is not. Its nothingness is guarantee that it can *not* be sick. In your demand that it be

more than this lies the idea of sickness. For it asks that God be less than all He really is. What, then, becomes of you, for it is you of whom the sacrifice is asked? For He is told that part of Him belongs to Him no longer. He must sacrifice your self, and in His sacrifice are you made more and He is lessened by the loss of you.

Since the body is inherently nothing, being a projection of a thought of nothing, using it for attack (e.g., sickness) is insane. True sickness is not found in bodily symptoms but in the mind's insanity that believes that nothing is something. What, then, is sacrificed? Surely not the body, but the Christ that is our Self. This is the basis for the childhood and childish game of seesaw we play with God: one up, the other down. If He wins, we lose and must sacrifice our self and die, the ultimate loss; if we win and get the self we want, God is destroyed. *One or the other* remains the cardinal rule of the ego's game.

(II.8:8) And what is gone from Him becomes your god, protecting you from being part of Him.

What is gone from God is *us*: the self we believe we stole. We saw in the previous chapter that in the separation "the Father was deprived of His Effects" (T-28.II.8:1). When His Son was taken from Him, God was diminished to such an extent that He disappeared, the central tenet in the ego's dream. Without His Son, God cannot exist, for there is no Creator without His extension. The war with God is indeed a life-and-death struggle, the same as we experience every moment of our lives here. This explains why we become so exercised over nothing; even the most trivial thing symbolizes the ontological battle with our Source in which there is a winner and loser. The world attests to the seeming fact that we are the victors, which is the reason we do not want to let go of our individual and worldly existence.

(II.9:1-2) The body that is asked to be a god will be attacked, because its nothingness has not been recognized. And so it seems to be a thing with power in itself.

The body must be attacked because it was made by attack. Indeed, it is the embodiment of the thought of attack: we exist because we killed God. We made other bodies so as to project onto them our "secret sins and hidden hates" (T-31.VIII.9:2). This nightmarish dream is perpetuated by the belief that our enemies must kill because they were made in the image and likeness of our murderous selves: the power that destroyed Heaven and established the separated self as God.

(II.9:3) As something, it can be perceived and thought to feel and act, and hold you in its grasp as prisoner to itself.

It seems as if we are the body's prisoners, subject to its punitive laws of guilt and punishment that lead to the insane thought that if only we could die, we would be free. We do not realize that the body is not the prisoner, or even the jailer. These roles belong to the mind that is both victim and victimizer, the one locked behind bars and the one holding the keys. We are unaware of the true situation because the ego has buried it, leaving our awareness focused only on the mindless and imprisoning world of attack, suffering, and death.

(II.9:4-6) And it can fail to be what you demanded that it be. And you will hate it for its littleness, unmindful that the failure does not lie in that it is not more than it should be, but only in your failure to perceive that it is nothing. Yet its nothingness is your salvation, from which you would flee.

We hate our body for its littleness and vulnerability, and because we think it causes pain, we hate it for the thought system it represents that demands our suffering. Nonetheless, it is not the body we hate, as we saw before (T-28.VI.1-3), but the mind's guilt. The problem is hardly that the body is not healthier, stronger, or better looking than it is, but that we do not realize its nothingness, the effect of a cause that is nothing. This fact is our salvation because the body's lack of value, which comes from the ego's valuelessness, is the defense against the Holy Spirit's value of forgiveness. If we truly saw that the body is nothing, and that choosing it and the ego was a mistake, we would easily correct it by changing our minds and being with the everything that is Heaven's abundance. It is the mind's corrective power of decision that will save us, from which Jesus tells us we are constantly fleeing.

(II.10:1-2) As "something" is the body asked to be God's enemy, replacing what He is with littleness and limit and despair. It is His loss you celebrate when you behold the body as a thing you love, or look upon it as a thing you hate.

It makes no difference whether we love the body or hate it. Either way we have made the body real, for love and hate are heads and tails of the same coin of specialness. As long as we see the body this way we affirm the reality of the thought of separation that gave rise to it. If that were so, it would mean that God is an illusion. This, once again, is why we cling so tenaciously to the world of bodies, and why our resistance to this course is so strong. We do not want to let the body go, for then we would disappear into the Heart of God, which to the ego means death. We struggle with Jesus' teachings and find them difficult because we are literally fighting for the lives of the idols we made as substitute for the glorious Self we truly are. In one way or another, we seek to make compromises with *A Course in Miracles* by attempting to bring a spot of truth into the illusion, a touch of love into our specialness. By so doing we believe we have everything—truth *and* our individuality. However, Jesus is reminding us that this is impossible, for truth cannot be compromised in any way. God's Love is all there is:

(II.10:3) For if He be the sum of everything, then what is not in Him does not exist, and His completion is its nothingness.

What is not in God (i.e., the body) does not exist, and the body's nothingness means God's completion. Either God's perfect Wholeness is everything—the All in All—and the ego and body nothing, or the body is real and God is nothing. We fear this simple truth of *one or the other*, for if God is the sum of everything, what is not in Him is unreal and our special self is an illusion. We are "saved" from this truth if we can involve God with our bodies, as we did with the biblical God Who created them. This explains the Bible's great popularity, for by its teaching the coexistence of truth/spirit and illusion/flesh, the ego's world of opposites is affirmed, in contra-distinction with *A Course in Miracles* where truth and illusion cannot both be real: the separated self does not coexist with God.

(II.10:4-7) Your savior is not dead, nor does he dwell in what was built as temple unto death. He lives in God, and it is this that makes him savior unto you, and only this. His body's nothingness releases yours from sickness and from death. For what is yours cannot be more or less than what is his.

If God is everything, then all He created must share His eternal life. The ones we attack and wish were dead are also part of this life. Their bodies may attack or be sick, but their right minds remain unsullied and pure, holding within them the memory of life that is the Self. As do ours. In that blessed fact, reflecting the Fact of Heaven's perfect Oneness, lies our salvation because it undoes our worshipping at the ego's temple of sickness and death.

Idols: The Ego's Toys

We begin this section on idols with "The Forgiving Dream":

(IX.1:1-2) The slave of idols is a willing slave. For willing he must be to let himself bow down in worship to what has no life, and seek for power in the powerless.

In the ego's dreams we are slaves of the body, our own and others'. Moreover, we are *willing* slaves because the mind has freely chosen this servitude, the body establishing both that we exist and are not responsible for our enslaved existence. Although we do seem helpless before the strength of the ego's secret and worldly dreams, the truth is that our decision-making minds have denied their own power and given it over to the powerless body.

(IX.1:3-4) What happened to the holy Son of God that this could be his wish; to let himself fall lower than the stones upon the ground, and look to idols that they raise him up? Hear, then, your story in the dream you made, and ask yourself if it be not the truth that you believe that it is not a dream.

Our elder brother says to us: "Look at the dream, and because you do not believe you are dreaming it, I will speak to you of your dreams of specialness, the idols you believe will make you whole and happy. This way you will understand how you found yourselves in this sorry state of affairs, and will then allow me to lead you out of it."

(IX.2:1-2) A dream of judgment came into the mind that God created perfect as Himself. And in that dream was Heaven changed to hell, and God made enemy unto His Son.

The dream of judgment is another way of speaking of the original thought of separation. We judged that God's Love was not enough and that His Oneness would not allow us any freedom. In our delusional state we believed we could have a life independent of our Source, and because of projection we perceived that God was judging us. This was the impetus for us to quickly leave the mind and make a world to escape the vengeful wrath of the Enemy.

(IX.2:3-5) How can God's Son awaken from the dream? It is a dream of judgment. So must he judge not, and he will waken.

This accounts for why we are so loathe to give up judgment; it is terribly difficult, for example, to read a paper, hear a news broadcast, or drive to work without making dozens of judgments and not thinking twice about them. The reason is clear: if we cease to judge, we will awaken from the dream. As the ego and its world began with judgment, what we call our life is inextricably woven with this original unforgiveness of the Creator. It is our oxygen and nutritional source, for without judgment, the ego tells us, we would cease to exist.

The importance of this idea is also emphasized in the *Psychotherapy* pamphlet, where Jesus tells therapists that healing is accomplished when they forget to judge their patients (P-3.II.6:1; 7:1). Similarly, to restate this essential thought, if we truly want to be healed and awaken from the dream, we must give up judging others. It is helpful for us to be aware of how much we hold on to our misperceptions, *and why*. Doing so is how we maintain the illusion that the dream of separation is true, as is our separated state. This helps us understand why students have so much resistance to Jesus and the Course, whose clearly-stated purpose is forgiveness, the letting go of judgment.

(IX.2:6-7) For the dream will seem to last while he is part of it. Judge not, for he who judges will have need of idols, which will hold the judgment off from resting on himself.

It is we who made the first judgment, which overwhelmed us with guilt and led to the belief that God would punish us for our sin against Him. To support this gross misperception, we need special hate idols onto whom we can project this guilt so our sin will rest on them in the judgment that demands their punishment instead of our own.

(IX.2:8-9) Nor can he know the Self he has condemned. Judge not, because you make yourself a part of evil dreams, where idols are your "true" identity, and your salvation from the judgment laid in terror and in guilt upon yourself.

Judgment is the purpose of relationships here—the idols we think we love or hate—for we need special objects onto whom we can project our guilt. This not only "protects" us from our evil self, rooting us in dreams of sin and punishment, but even more to the point, keeps the mind's decision maker from choosing to remember its Self.

(IX.3:1-2) All figures in the dream are idols, made to save you from the dream. Yet they are part of what they have been made to save you from.

Idols are part of the dream, made to save us from the dream. Recall our discussion in Chapter 28 about the dreams of death to which we invite our special partners to join. The ego counsels that these idols of specialness will free us from guilt and pain, at their expense. Yet they merely reinforce the dream of fear and retribution, strengthening our identity with the dream. To state it another way: *the dream of guilt leaves not its source in the mind.*

(IX.3:3-4) Thus does an idol keep the dream alive and terrible, for who could wish for one unless he were in terror and despair? And this the idol represents, and so its worship is the worship of despair and terror, and the dream from which they come.

This reflects that important line from "The Two Pictures": "It is essential to realize that all defenses *do* what they would defend" (T-17.IV.7:1). The purpose of defenses is to keep us from the despair and terror we feel within, but all they do is strengthen the thought system of terror and despair that is their cause. They increase our fear because the very fact that we need to project onto others teaches us there is something within that needs the defense of projection. It must follow that the more we use others to escape our terror, the guiltier we will feel: the infamous guilt/attack cycle that maintains the mind's worship of the ego and its gods, the idols of specialness.

(IX.3:5-7) Judgment is an injustice to God's Son, and it *is* justice that who judges him will not escape the penalty he laid upon himself within the dream he made. God knows of justice, not of penalty. But in the dream of judgment you attack and are condemned; and wish to be the slave of idols, which are interposed between your judgment and the penalty it brings.

This pregnant passage exposes the ego's purpose for projection. Finding the ego's just punishment for

our sin intolerable, we dream of seeing it in others, wishing that they suffer the penalty that is the just deserts of our sinful actions against the all-loving God. In this way justice is served as guilt demands there be a sinner, driving us to make a world of idols who become the justified recipients of the sin we have projected.

(IX.4:1-2) There can be no salvation in the dream as you are dreaming it. For idols must be part of it, to save you from what you believe you have accomplished, and have done to make you sinful and put out the light within you.

It is when we finally recognize this truth that we can say and mean: "There must be another way, another dream that will work better than mine. There must be someone within who can help, because what I am doing has not brought me peace." To state it differently, our idols have not succeeded in undoing the guilt over what we believe we accomplished: the murder of God, the secret dream of separation that established a need for the world's dream of hate that would save us from the mind's thoughts of sin and punishment (the chart's wrong-minded box [see Appendix]).

In the rest of this and the following paragraph we find an important analogy Jesus has used before, but never as dramatically. The world is a childish game with toys that are not real and not to be taken seriously, for how can the make-believe be a cause for concern? This is the theme he now develops:

(IX.4:3-5) Little child, the light is there. You do but dream, and idols are the toys you dream you play with. Who has need of toys but children?

Although we dreamt we put out the light of innocence, it remains within our minds. This makes sense to us when we raise ourselves up to look down upon the world's battleground whereon we think we coexist with everyone else, each out to get the other in the spirit of *kill or be killed*. On this battleground life is serious indeed, for when we separate effect (the body) from cause (the mind), worldly events are tragic. Bringing effect to cause, however, we realize the cause is nothing—the separation never happened—and the world can be perceived anew. Jesus is asking us to look with him at our anguished concerns, seeing them transformed into silly toys that have no effect on our holy minds. We have merely played with them a while to make them seem real, granting the toys power to change us, helping us avoid responsibility for the wrong mind's secret dreams of hate. But toys are toys, calling only for the response of a soft smile and gentle laughter.

(IX.4:6-8) They pretend they rule the world, and give their toys the power to move about, and talk and think and feel and speak for them. Yet everything their toys appear to do is in the minds of those who play with them. But they are eager to forget that they made up the dream in which their toys are real, nor recognize their wishes are their own.

Watching children play with toys, we would recognize Jesus' description. He is telling us we are like those little ones, except that our purpose is vicious. We use our toys of specialness to serve the ego's goal of keeping us mindless, forgetting we are dreamers and not the hated dream figures of our projections.

(IX.5:1-5) Nightmares are childish dreams. The toys have turned against the child who thought he made them real. Yet can a dream attack? Or can a toy grow large and dangerous and fierce and wild? This does the child believe, because he fears his thoughts and gives them to the toys instead.

In dreams and the fantasies of a child, toys can certainly "grow large and dangerous and fierce and wild"—but not in reality. This is obvious when we observe children, but not so clear when we think of ourselves. Whatever frightens us in the world, no matter how many millions may agree about the origin of our fear, the fact remains that it lies only in thoughts of sin and punishment, which have never left their source in the mind. A toy is still a toy, and illusions can affect nothing except in childish dreams in which our projected imagination has run away from us.

(IX.5:6) And their reality becomes his own, because they seem to save him from his thoughts.

This reveals the purpose of the world of special idols: we need others to protect us from the guilt we believe is real within our sinful minds and deserves punishment.

(IX.5:7-9) Yet do they keep his thoughts alive and real, but seen outside himself, where they can turn against him for his treachery to them. He thinks he needs them that he may escape his thoughts, because he thinks the thoughts are real. And so he makes of anything a toy, to make his world remain outside himself, and play that he is but a part of it.

These are our thoughts of guilt, judgment, and attack, all within the mind and part of its secret dream. We project them and see separation and blame all around us, and they must be there because we put them there, having first made them real in the mind: *projection makes perception.* Despite the effective strategy of mindlessness, we can recognize the source of the ego's toys by allowing the miracle to turn our attention inward. There we understand that we play the part of victim, besieged by idols that we invented and then forgot we did so. This is the outcome of the ego's dream of judgment that began in the mind, and has never left it to travel into the far country of our specialness.

(I.1:6-9) All this do you believe, when you perceive a gap between your brother and yourself. How could you trust Him, then? For He must be deceptive in His Love. Be wary, then; let Him not come too close, and leave a gap between you and His Love, through which you can escape if there be need for you to flee.

The first part of this paragraph (see above) described the ego's insanity in believing that God behaved as an ego, reflected in the thoughts and actions of the biblical deity. Such belief is inevitable once we see our brother separate from us, for no one can perceive separation in the Sonship without also seeing it in its Creator. This justifies our keeping distance from Him, preserving the individual self the ego would have us believe would be extinguished by His Love. Our idols come to the rescue for they reinforce the specialness that keeps God and His Son at arm's length, a gap of seeming safety that not only keeps our perceived enemies at bay, but also protects us from our guilt.

(I.2) Here is the fear of God most plainly seen. For love *is* treacherous to those who fear, since fear and hate can never be apart. No one who hates but is afraid of love, and therefore must he be afraid of God. Certain it is he knows not what love means. He fears to love and loves to hate, and so he thinks that love is fearful; hate is love. This is the consequence the little gap must bring to those who cherish it, and think that it is their salvation and their hope.

In that cherished gap of separation, believed in the mind and perceived in the body, are found the seeds of our insanity. In madness we believe that love is to be feared while fear and hate are cherished, love marking the end of the ego while hate makes reality of the ego's illusory self, reinforcing the thought system of separate interests that sustains our special identity.

(I.3:1-3) The fear of God! The greatest obstacle that peace must flow across has not yet gone. The rest are past, but this one still remains to block your path, and make the way to light seem dark and fearful, perilous and bleak.

The fear of God, the fourth obstacle to peace (T-19.IV-D), is that in His Presence our special identity would cease to exist. Hence, we continually seek to push Him away, strengthening our already enormous guilt. Since we do not want to give back what we stole from Heaven, we attempt to split the guilt off from our individual self by giving it to someone else. However, since we share the same mind, what we do to others we must also perceive they do to us. This projection reflects the secret oath we take with each other (T-28.VI.4-5), upheld by our shared dance of specialness and death, and preserved by the belief that guilt can leave its source in our minds and exist in another.

(I.3:4-6) You had decided that your brother is your enemy. Sometimes a friend, perhaps, provided that your separate interests made your friendship possible a little while. But not without a gap perceived between you and him, lest he turn again into an enemy.

We always have to be on our guard, because others are as traitorous as we. Indeed, they are the same traitors. We must perceive them this way, people we cannot trust, because *we* are persons we cannot trust, having betrayed God's Love by breaking the promise to be His Son. We therefore made up everyone in our lives in the image of guilt, special love or special hate, as has been done to us by them. Inevitably we all dance to this vicious and dissonant melody of self-preservation, but make others responsible for the sinful gap between us.

(I.3:7) Let him come close to you, and you jumped back; as you approached, did he but instantly withdraw.

We fear intimacy and are repulsed by the thought of getting close to others, but not for the reasons we think. If we truly allowed ourselves to experience our shared needs, interests, and goals, it would be but a short step to the realization that we and God are one, the separation never happened, and the person we experience ourselves to be never happened either.

(I.3:8-10) A cautious friendship, and limited in scope and carefully restricted in amount, became the treaty that you had made with him. Thus you and your brother but shared a qualified entente, in which a clause of separation was a point you both agreed to keep intact. And violating this was thought to be a breach of treaty not to be allowed.

Jesus uses the language of international diplomacy to characterize what we do with each other: negotiating pacts or treaties of specialness. Yet just as nations do not trust one another when they make agreements, neither do we, which is why our special relationships are imbued with such tension and distrust. It goes without saying that we secretly want others to violate our treaties, for their perfidy would justify the hate that protects our mind's secret guilt.

(I.4:1-5) The gap between you and your brother is not one of space between two separate bodies. And this but seems to be dividing off your separate minds. It is the symbol of a promise made to meet when you prefer, and separate till you and he elect to meet again. And then your bodies seem to get in touch, and thereby signify a meeting place to join. But always is it possible for you and him to go your separate ways.

We always have an out in our relationships. Even though we may protest our mutual love, we do not really love others but only what they can do for us. Ultimately, what others give is the gift of perpetuating our existence within the dream as innocent victims. This is best achieved by their infidelity, which enables us to say to the world and to God: "We are not the sinners, for these are the ones who break their promises and betray our trust."

(I.4:6-7) Conditional upon the "right" to separate will you and he agree to meet from time to time, and keep apart in intervals of separation, which do protect you from the "sacrifice" of love. The body saves you, for it gets away from total sacrifice and gives to you the time in which to build again your separate self, which you truly believe diminishes as you and your brother meet.

Our oath to each other is to maintain the separation, thereby sacrificing our shared self that reflects Heaven's one Self. The dynamic Jesus refers to here is the cannibalistic element of special love we have seen before (e.g., T-16.V). Our special self is continually traded for another's, diminishing who we are by seeking to augment our inadequate self with one deemed greater. The ego convinces us that time is needed to replace what we have lost, even while we exult in having stolen the specialness we need. This fruitless plan is secured by our not being able to challenge the ego's premises of separation and attack, which remain buried in the unconscious mind by our identifying with the mindless and

besieged body. Further, we know our "love" is special because it is not total, inclusive, or permanent.

(I.5) The body could not separate your mind from your brother's unless you wanted it to be a cause of separation and of distance seen between you and him. Thus do you endow it with a power that lies not within itself. And herein lies its power over you. For now you think that it determines when your brother and you meet, and limits your ability to make communion with your brother's mind. And now it tells you where to go and how to go there, what is feasible for you to undertake, and what you cannot do. It dictates what its health can tolerate, and what will tire it and make it sick. And its "inherent" weaknesses set up the limitations on what you would do, and keep your purpose limited and weak.

Everything occurs in the mind, which houses the ego's need to maintain separation, but to exclude sin by projecting itself. This dynamic is more than familiar to us by now, and is the culmination of the ego strategy of mindlessness. We transfer power from the mind's decision maker to the body that, being mindless, appropriates this power in our experience. Awareness of the mind's decision-making ability is kept hidden beneath the previously discussed double shield of oblivion (guilt and the world), and our limited lives become governed by the body's seemingly immutable laws. All the while the mind, the unknown power behind the body's throne, directs our lives from birth to death, it alone being responsible for the gaps that keep us separate from each other and from our God.

(I.8:1-2) The body, innocent of goals, is your excuse for variable goals you hold, and force the body to maintain. You do not fear its weakness, but its lack of strength *or* weakness.

These important lines state that we fear the body, not because it is weak but because it is nothing. Whether we think it strong *or* weak, we think it is real. The fact that the body is neither is what truly threatens us, for its inherent nothingness exposes the nothingness of the ego, which means our nonexistence.

(I.8:3-7) Would you know that nothing stands between you and your brother? Would you know there is no gap behind which you can hide? There is a shock that comes to those who learn their savior is their enemy no more. There is a wariness that is aroused by learning that the body is not real. And there are overtones of seeming fear around the happy message, "God is Love."

This makes no sense unless we understand that the individual self is dependent upon the belief that God is fear. To believe He is a punishing Father means our sin is real and the separation an actual event. The gap among God's Sons, forged in anger, is herewith justified, solidifying our separated and bodily existence that is barricaded behind the ego's walls of specialness. Simply stated, God's wrath means we exist, while His Love dissolves the self that never was.

(I.9) Yet all that happens when the gap is gone is peace eternal. Nothing more than that, and nothing less. Without the fear of God, what could induce you to abandon Him? What toys or trinkets in the gap could serve to hold you back an instant from His Love? Would you allow the body to say "no" to Heaven's calling, were you not afraid to find a loss of self in finding God? Yet can your self be lost by being found?

This is our fear: we would "find a loss of self in finding God." Note how often Jesus returns to this central idea in his thought system. We need to read these words over and over because the mind's fear instructs our eyes to gloss over them in self-protection. Consequently, we adhere to everything in the special world of "toys and trinkets," idols of specialness, to keep God away by maintaining our mindless (i.e., corporeal) state. We revel in reinforcing our identity within the dream, blaming others for our misery so that we would never find our Self in God.

The Purpose of Idols

"Seek Not Outside Yourself," the next section to be considered, is built around the theme that is its title. Like a musical leitmotif, "seek not outside yourself" recurs throughout, unifying Jesus' message of mindfulness that corrects our ongoing experience of being a mindless body.

(VII.1:1-6) Seek not outside yourself. For it will fail, and you will weep each time an idol falls. Heaven cannot be found where it is not, and there can be no peace excepting there. Each idol that you worship when God calls will never answer in His place. There is no other answer you can substitute, and find the happiness His answer brings. Seek not outside yourself.

The ego's maxim is "Seek and do not find," and it will have us fail in our seeking for worldly pleasure or happiness. The world is all about this pursuit, which is the reason the ego made the body. Seeking for idols without for the truth that is only

within, we are never able to return to the mind—the locus of the problem *and* the answer.

(VII.1:7-9) For all your pain comes simply from a futile search for what you want, insisting where it must be found. What if it is not there? Do you prefer that you be right or happy?

We of course want to be right, our purpose for coming here. The world obliges by proving we are right about the separation and God is wrong, and we strive to show Him how right we are. The problem, however, is that no one is truly happy here because the world of illusion is not our home. This fact is the cause of all pain, which we seek to remedy through various forms of magic: external remedies for the internal problem of guilt and homelessness.

(VII.1:10–2:5) Be you glad that you are told where happiness abides, and seek no longer

elsewhere. **You will fail. But it is given you to know the truth, and not to seek for it outside yourself.**

No one who comes here but must still have hope, some lingering illusion, or some dream that there is something outside of himself that will bring happiness and peace to him. If everything is in him this cannot be so. And therefore by his coming, he denies the truth about himself, and seeks for something more than everything, as if a part of it were separated off and found where all the rest of it is not. This is the purpose he bestows upon the body; that it seek for what he lacks, and give him what would make himself complete. And thus he wanders aimlessly about, in search of something that he cannot find, believing that he is what he is not.

This is our story, the sad and desperate state of trying to cope with the mind's despair, terror, and self-hate. We cannot deal with them, and in order not to feel the pain of our existence, we continually seek outside for another and another and still another mindless cover under which to hide. Despite these frantic attempts, we never find the peace and comfort we seek, and must content ourselves with the illusory succor that specialness offers in place of love, our true Identity and home. Somewhere inside we know the difference between illusion and truth, and the gnawing thought that exposes the ego's lies will never be denied: how can nothing ever substitute for everything?

(VII.3) The lingering illusion will impel him to seek out a thousand idols, and to seek beyond them for a thousand more. And each will fail him, all excepting one; for he will die, and does not understand the idol that he seeks *is* but his death. Its form appears to be outside himself. Yet does he seek to kill God's Son within, and prove that he is victor over him. This is the purpose every idol has, for this the role that is assigned to it, and this the role that cannot be fulfilled.

Death is a thought that has nothing to do with the body. It is the final proof that the ego is right and God is wrong: if death were real, life is not eternal

and God has lied; if death were real, the body once lived, dreams are reality, and the ego has triumphed over spirit. Yet the true idol, the mind's decision for the ego's illusory thought system of death, remains hidden by barriers of guilt and hate, protected from all incursions of the truth.

(VII.4:1-4) Whenever you attempt to reach a goal in which the body's betterment is cast as major beneficiary, you try to bring about your death. For you believe that you can suffer lack, and lack *is* death. To sacrifice is to give up, and thus to be without and to have suffered loss. And by this giving up is life renounced.

Recall that the ego thought system is logically cohesive and internally consistent, wherein if we subscribe to any of its insane thoughts, we accept all of them. Striving to please the body's appetites in any form, we cannot help but embrace the entirety of the ego's system, of which sacrifice is a key component. Recall that the ego was born through sacrifice of the Self, forever enshrining loss as salvation, with death being the inevitable and cherished conclusion of its plan to triumph over life.

(VII.4:5-6) Seek not outside yourself. The search implies you are not whole within and fear to look upon your devastation, but prefer to seek outside yourself for what you are.

These sentences clearly state our belief that there is something missing inside (the scarcity principle or sense of lack), a hole we try to fill by taking idols from the outside and feeding off them. That way we magically hope our specialness will make us whole so we will not feel the despairing pain of the mind's guilt.

(VII.5) Idols must fall *because* they have no life, and what is lifeless is a sign of death. You came to die, and what would you expect but to perceive the signs of death you seek? No sadness and no suffering proclaim a message other than an idol found that represents a parody of life which, in its lifelessness, is really death, conceived as real and given living form. Yet each must fail and crumble and decay, because a

form of death cannot be life, and what is sacrificed cannot be whole.

The search for idols will always end in futility, for how can the lifeless grant life or augment it? They are merely sick parodies of God's glorious creation, the spirit that is the Christ. Idols come and go, love and hate, suffer and die, and cannot be the true Self that is complete, changeless, and eternal: "what is sacrificed cannot be whole."

(VII.6:1) All idols of this world were made to keep the truth within from being known to you, and to maintain allegiance to the dream that you must find what is outside yourself to be complete and happy.

Here again is our theme of purpose. Idols were made to keep the truth within from being known, which comprises the ego's double shield of oblivion. To review, the first is the secret dream of the murderer, which protects us from the right mind's Atonement principle; the second is the world's dream of our being the murdered. Restating this, we have the mind's idol of guilt over the sin of murder, and then the projected sin-laden idols of the world. We all are bound by the ego's oath to be faithful to the purpose these idols were designed to serve.

(VII.9:6–10:3) The fear of God is but the fear of loss of idols. It is not the fear of loss of your reality. But you have made of your reality an idol, which you must protect against the light of truth. And all the world becomes the means by which this idol can be saved. Salvation thus appears to threaten life and offer death.

It is not so. Salvation seeks to prove there is no death, and only life exists. The sacrifice of death is nothing lost.

We do not really fear God's punishment of death and destruction, as the ego would have us think; rather, we fear the disappearance into His Love that would nullify our individuality and specialness. And so we are afraid of Jesus and resistant to his teachings, not to mention being terrified of releasing our judgments and hate. Salvation threatens our very existence as an angry ego self, and we experience this resistance not only in understanding the

Course's words, but even more importantly in putting them into practice. This application cannot be done by force of will; only a gentle letting go, over time, undoes our fear and heals the belief in illusion. Salvation then can be accepted for what it is: the end of death that opens the doorway to eternal life.

The next section in the text, "The Anti-Christ," offers us one of the clearest statements in *A Course in Miracles* about the nature of the ego thought system and the idol we have made of it. Our worshipped idols of specialness are nothing more than shadowy fragments, projected images of the original idol that is the ego deity of sin and wrath.

(VIII.1:1-5) What is an idol? Do you think you know? For idols are unrecognized as such, and never seen for what they really are. That is the only power that they have. Their purpose is obscure, and they are feared and worshipped, both, *because* you do not know what they are for, and why they have been made.

In truth, idols are distractions of nothing, to distract us from nothingness. We all study idols—the cosmos, bodies, relationships—but never learn what they really are because we do not understand their purpose. Indeed, their only power lies in the capacity the mind gives them to shift our attention from what the ego is truly doing. Once more, we see that purpose explains everything in our world, including this course. When we understand the intention of the ego thought system that we serve, we will be able to change our life's purpose from mindlessness to mindfulness. What distinguishes *A Course in Miracles* from many other spiritual paths is its bypassing the *forms* of idols to their *content* (or purpose). These forms, some aspect of the body's behavior, are never the problem, which is always the mind's denial of its decision-making ability. This leads to our worshipping idols instead of accepting the Self that is God's only creation.

(VIII.1:6-9) An idol is an image of your brother that you would value more than what he is. Idols are made that he may be replaced, no matter what their form. And it is this that never is perceived and recognized. Be it a body or a

thing, a place, a situation or a circumstance, an object owned or wanted, or a right demanded or achieved, it is the same.

Since it is never the idol's form that is the issue, our specific judgments of others and the world are irrelevant. It is the simple fact that we have them at all that should be our focus: the wish to be other than God's perfect creation. This wish, projected out, leads to the perception that our special hate objects are guilty of the sin of separating from love, betraying its promise of oneness and eternal life.

(VIII.2:1-4) Let not their form deceive you. Idols are but substitutes for your reality. In some way, you believe they will complete your little self, for safety in a world perceived as dangerous, with forces massed against your confidence and peace of mind. They have the power to supply your lacks, and add the value that you do not have.

One of the more important sections on special relationships is "The Choice for Completion" (T-16.V). The ego's choice is for special idols—people, objects, substances, and the like—to complete us and supply the lacks that constitute our profound sense of inadequacy and loss. The Holy Spirit's choice is that we realize we are already complete as spirit, as is everyone else. Recognizing the universality of the mind's abundance is our true safety, and remembrance of love's presence within us is the only need we have within the dream of separation, scarcity, and death.

(VIII.2:5-7) No one believes in idols who has not enslaved himself to littleness and loss. And thus must seek beyond his little self for strength to raise his head, and stand apart from all the misery the world reflects. This is the penalty for looking not within for certainty and quiet calm that liberates you from the world, and lets you stand apart, in quiet and in peace.

Jesus lifts the veil of denial to expose the futility of seeking outside ourselves for happiness and joy, safety and peace. He teaches us to see how the world's idols enslave us to the little thought system of guilt and misery, perceived external to our minds; how we have listened to the ego's counsel never to look within to the true source of pain. Now we understand that the decision for the ego's thought system of separation and guilt was itself a defense against the right mind's peaceful certainty that is our strength as God's Son.

(VIII.3:1-2) An idol is a false impression, or a false belief; some form of anti-Christ, that constitutes a gap between the Christ and what you see. An idol is a wish, made tangible and given form, and thus perceived as real and seen outside the mind.

While *anti-Christ* is used by Christians to denote the devil, in *A Course in Miracles* it means the ego that places itself in opposition to our Identity as Christ. We project these idols of anti-Christ so they will appear to be outside us. We have seen, though, how our bodies that are equipped with sensory organs are "senses without sense" (T-28.V.5:6), for they tell us there is a world to be perceived where, in fact, none exists. Jesus, on the other hand, teaches that delusions and hallucinations have no power to change reality from the perfect and undivided oneness that it is.

(VIII.3:3-4) Yet it is still a thought, and cannot leave the mind that is its source. Nor is its form apart from the idea it represents.

Cause and effect, mind and body are one—*ideas leave not their source*. The body, a projection of thought, has never left the mind; "its form [is not] apart from the idea [i.e., separation] it represents." Our special idols but remain as illusory as the *tiny, mad idea* that is their source.

(VIII.3:5-9) All forms of anti-Christ oppose the Christ. And fall before His face like a dark veil that seems to shut you off from Him, alone in darkness. Yet the light is there. A cloud does not put out the sun. No more a veil can banish what it seems to separate, nor darken by one whit the light itself.

This is the Atonement principle. No matter what we believe, no matter how many clouds of guilt (the body's special idols) we put between ourselves and the light, it has not gone away. Yet even though the light is always there, we will not experience its resplendence unless we first go through the ego's clouds with Jesus (or the Holy Spirit), as he comforts us in the workbook: "...think of me holding your hand and leading you [through the clouds]. And I assure you this will be no idle fantasy" (W-pI.70.9:3-4).

(VIII.4:1-3) This world of idols *is* a veil across the face of Christ, because its purpose is to separate your brother from yourself. A dark and fearful purpose, yet a thought without the power to change one blade of grass from something living to a sign of death. Its form is nowhere, for its source abides within your mind where God abideth not.

The purpose of idols is to maintain the separation, and at the same time make it possible for us to eschew responsibility for it; i.e., our unhappiness is not due to wrong-minded choices, but to the failure of our special partners to live up to their bargains with us. However, illusions of separation and attack cannot intrude upon the reality of God's undivided Son. As the idol's source is in the part of the mind where God has been banished, possible only in dreams, it has no power to affect God's living and eternal creation, the memory of which awaits our certain acceptance.

(VIII.4:4-9) Where is this place where what is everywhere has been excluded and been kept apart? What hand could be held up to block God's way? Whose voice could make demand He enter not? The "more-than-everything" is not a thing to make you tremble and to quail in fear. Christ's enemy is nowhere. He can take no form in which he ever will be real.

This variation of the Atonement principle teaches that the ego's idols are nothing. How can nothing affect everything, nowhere replace the everywhere? In dreams the impossible has happened, but let forgiveness gently waken us unto Christ, and fearful illusions will softly fade into the light of truth dawning on our minds.

(VIII.6:1) An idol is established by belief, and when it is withdrawn the idol "dies."

This oft-repeated theme heralds the end of the ego. Being nothing, the ego thought system has no power in itself, for its "power" lies simply in our belief in it. When we withdraw this belief the ego disappears. No matter how powerful it seems to be, the ego owes its very existence to the decision maker's choice to make it real, which is why the ego fears the mind's power and sets upon its strategy to make us mindless.

(VIII.6:2-6) This is the anti-Christ; the strange idea there is a power past omnipotence, a place beyond the infinite, a time transcending the eternal. Here the world of idols has been set by the idea this power and place and time are given form, and shape the world where the impossible has happened. Here the deathless come to die, the all-encompassing to suffer loss, the timeless to be made the slaves of time. Here does the changeless change; the peace of God, forever given to all living things, give way to chaos. And the Son of God, as perfect, sinless and as loving as his Father, come to hate a little while; to suffer pain and finally to die.

This wonderfully evocative passage summarizes the nature of the ego's world. Despite Jesus' kindness, if we identify with our bodily selves we could be tempted to believe he is making fun of us. After all, the above passage is wonderful only when we are learning to detach from this self, realizing how silly life here really is. But believing we are this self, we must also believe there is a power past omnipotence and a place beyond the infinite. Because our individual lives will inevitably witness to this seeming truth, it is helpful when we are tempted to be upset, about something trivial or of great magnitude, to reread this passage. It provides a perspective within which to right-mindedly evaluate our concerns, recognizing they are not what they appear to be. It does not seem as if we are making them up because our idols seem so very real and beyond our control. Nevertheless, their sole purpose is to root our attention in the dream by compelling us to worship at the ego's altar of specialness. This ensures that we will never return to the mind's simple truth that the ego's nightmares are illusory and have no effect on our reality as Christ.

(VIII.8) What purpose has an idol, then? What is it for? This is the only question that has many answers, each depending on the one of whom the question has been asked. The world believes in idols. No one comes unless he worshipped them, and still attempts to seek for one that yet might offer him a gift reality does not contain. Each worshipper of idols harbors hope his special deities will give him more than other men possess. It must be more. It does not really matter more of what; more beauty, more intelligence, more wealth, or even more affliction and more pain. But more of something is an idol for. And when one fails another takes its place, with hope of finding more of something else. Be not deceived by forms the "something" takes. An idol is a means for getting more. And it is this that is against God's Will.

In this world, idols seem to serve many varied purposes, but there is in truth only one: that we have more specialness than others. The form does not matter, for we can get as much ego mileage being more inadequate than another as we can being more brilliant. All that is important is that it be more of the something special. "More" means different, which means separate, which means we are right

and God is wrong. This insanity began when we declared to God, "I want more than everything," and the ego's madness persists in our current society wherein what we have is never enough. It must be like this as *ideas leave not their source*, and we are an idea that has never left its source: the thought of wanting more.

The anti-Christ is not against God's Will in the sense that our Creator opposes the ego. God knows nothing about it, for how can a Will of perfect Oneness know of separation and attack? A non-dualistic truth does not recognize a dualistic illusion. Since we began with a belief that we wanted something more than everything, all happenings in the world of time and space have been nothing but split-off fragments of that original thought. Recall this statement: "The tiny tick of time in which the first mistake was made, and all of them within that one mistake…" (T-26.V.3:5).

In *A Course in Miracles*, Jesus offers us another way of looking at the separation and the world that arose from it as an echo of guilt. It is only when we recognize that there is something inherently wrong with the thought of wanting more than everything that we see another purpose for being here. His teaching enables us to make this shift from the ego's nightmare world of idols to the Holy Spirit's dreams of forgiveness, thus changing the purpose for all relationships. This shift in purpose is one of our symphony's most important and recurring themes, and is the heart of the next section.

The Holy Spirit's Purpose

(II.7:1-3) The body does not change. It represents the larger dream that change is possible. To change is to attain a state unlike the one in which you found yourself before.

The body does not change because not only is it not the problem, but it is nonexistent, never having left its source in the illusory mind. It is the mind's purpose that has to change: from guilt to forgiveness; from dreaming nightmares to awakening through the Holy Spirit's happy dreams. This undoes the original change from unity to separation. Once the mind's

error is corrected and we are restored to our natural state of oneness, external change is irrelevant.

(II.7:4-8) There is no change in immortality, and Heaven knows it not. Yet here on earth it has a double purpose, for it can be made to teach opposing things. And they reflect the teacher who is teaching them. The body can appear to change with time, with sickness or with health, and with events that seem to alter it. Yet this but means the mind remains unchanged in its belief of what the purpose of the body is.

As we have seen many times, Heaven does not and cannot know about the original change, for if God knew, it would have actually happened. It is the memory of Heaven's knowledge, the Holy Spirit, that makes possible our utilizing change for a right-minded purpose. Turned over to our Teacher, the body's purpose shifts from prison to classroom as we learn the lessons of forgiveness that set us free from the guilt that had bound us in chains.

These next passages come at the end of "Dream Roles," where Jesus told us that dreams are based on fear, wherein we allot roles to others and then proceed to get angry when they do not fulfill the functions we gave them. Now we hear about *his* role for us in our dreams:

(IV.5:1-2) How happy would your dreams become if you were not the one who gave the "proper" role to every figure which the dream contains. No one can fail but your idea of him, and there is no betrayal but of this.

This last line means no one can truly betray or fail us. People do so only when we *believe* they are betraying us, which means the problem is never what they have done, but only our perceptions of them. Underlying this is the real problem of our needing to have them fail us. We draw imaginary lines in the sand, waiting for, if not encouraging others to cross the made-up boundary so we can attack them. We want people to be unfaithful and unkind, for this justifies our pointing an accusing finger at them, magically hoping to avoid punishment for our sin. While this does not justify ego behavior, our judgmental reactions to these wrong-minded choices remain our responsibility.

(IV.5:3-4) The core of dreams the Holy Spirit gives is never one of fear. The coverings may not appear to change, but what they mean has changed because they cover something else.

We understand that the forms of our lives may not necessarily change just because we invite Jesus to be our teacher. However, the meaning we have given them will most definitely change. It is not that we study this course and bring Jesus our ego

concerns, and then suddenly we get the right job, find a mate, win the lottery, or are healed of cancer. What does change is that regardless of what happens in our world of bodies, we will be peaceful. Realizing that peace comes from the mind's decision and not anything external is our only real hope, because the world offers none. Any hope it seems to offer can be snatched away in an instant. Yet when we choose a different teacher, our dreams change from conflict to peace, hate to forgiveness, fear to love—*content*, not *form*.

(IV.5:5-7) Perceptions are determined by their purpose, in that they seem to be what they are for. A shadow figure who attacks becomes a brother giving you a chance to help, if this becomes the function of the dream. And dreams of sadness thus are turned to joy.

Remember, perceptions are interpretations, independent of the input of our sensory organs. The meaning we give these sensory data is determined solely by the mind's purpose—the ego's or the Holy Spirit's—which is why Jesus never asks us to focus on changing externals, but only on looking within to the source of real change: "...seek not to change the world, but choose to change your mind about the world" (T-21.in.1:7). Free will means that we can choose a Teacher to instruct us how to perceive the world differently, shifting the purpose we have given to situations. Instead of perceiving them as bringing pleasure and avoiding pain, giving us what we want and escaping what we do not want, vision sees relationships as affording us opportunities in which to learn that "All real pleasure comes from doing God's Will" (T-1.VII.1:4).

(IV.6:1-3) What is your brother for? You do not know, because your function is obscure to you. Do not ascribe a role to him that you imagine would bring happiness to you.

Jesus describes what we all do. We need these special people because they provide the material and immaterial things that make us feel good about ourselves. We substitute the specialness we crave for the miracle that reflects the Source that will never disappoint, deteriorate, or die. How, then, could we know our brothers or ourselves?

(IV.6:4) And do not try to hurt him when he fails to take the part that you assigned to him, in what you dream your life was meant to be.

When others fail us by not fulfilling the roles we assigned in our dreams, we feel justified in attacking them. For example, the role we give to our parents is that they always be there for us from the moment we were born—nourishing and nurturing, loving and supportive, kind and understanding—and this generalizes to other authority figures as well. Interestingly enough, our egos cannot wait for them to fail us. We may scream, for example, when our parents do not feed us on time or change us, but the ego loves it because their "sins" set the tone for the rest of our lives. This fulfills the ego's purpose of proving our innocent existence, justifying our self-concept of victim. When our needs are not met, we are right in hating these special people because of what they have done to us or failed to do.

(IV.6:5) He asks for help in every dream he has, and you have help to give him if you see the function of the dream as He perceives its function, Who can utilize all dreams as means to serve the function given Him.

We are all asking for the same help, pleading: "Please show me I am wrong, and do not join me in my dream of death. I may threaten to hurt or kill you if you do not join me, but I still implore you not to get on my ego's dance floor." We need others to demonstrate there is another Teacher from Whom we can learn, another way to perceive relationships: forgiveness and not judgment, the kindness of shared interests in place of attack and separation.

(IV.6:6-7) Because He loves the dreamer, not the dream, each dream becomes an offering of love. For at its center is His Love for you, which lights whatever form it takes with love.

We need always keep in mind that the dreamer is not the body. The Holy Spirit does not love *us*, who are projected figures in the mind's illusory dream, for He knows that everything here is a shadowy image of the deluded dreamer who is terrified of his Identity as God's Son. The Holy Spirit's Love is in the mind, not anywhere else. He would be insane to want to help a dream figure, yet that is what we all beg him to do: "Help this poor, long-suffering body." And He lovingly asks in return: "What body? You whom I love are the dreamer. How could I love what does not exist?" As we have seen many times, the incredible popularity of the Bible is due to its making the dream figures real, even having God share in the ego's mindless madness of miscreation.

(VI.3:1-3) Nothing survives its purpose. If it be conceived to die, then die it must unless it does not take this purpose as its own. Change is the only thing that can be made a blessing here, where purpose is not fixed, however changeless it appears to be.

If the mind has death as its purpose, the body will die. It does not die because of natural laws; the body *has* no natural laws, since what does not exist cannot be natural. The body dies only because it reflects the thought of death, and when we change that thought to life, the body is no longer needed. Its only purpose is as a learning instrument for the split mind, which is the reason it is unnecessary when learning is complete. However, if the right mind elects to remain to teach, the body may remain as its instrument. Nonetheless, the healed mind would know it is not a body because the self is seen only as a decision maker. This is what allows the Son's power to choose, which made the original change from love to attack, to correct its mistake through forgiveness and healing.

(VI.3:4-6) Think not that you can set a goal unlike God's purpose for you, and establish it as changeless and eternal. You can give yourself a purpose that you do not have. But you can not remove the power to change your mind, and see another purpose there.

God's purpose for us is to create and extend love, as He does. Yet in dreams we give ourselves a purpose that is not truly ours, miscreating the ego and its world. The ego, the part of the mind that cherishes separation, fears the mind's power to change its decision and find its purpose of forgiveness. The strategy of our descending into mindlessness is well known to us by now, and this ensures that we never exercise this power and choose against the ego.

(VI.4:1-2) Change is the greatest gift God gave to all that you would make eternal, to ensure that only Heaven would not pass away. You were not born to die.

To the ego we were born to die, which proves the truth of the separation; to the Holy Spirit we were born to learn the lessons of eternal life as taught by the Atonement. Our minds, therefore, have the power to change their purpose from death to life, hell to Heaven, fear to love.

(VI.4:3-11) You cannot change, because your function has been fixed by God. All other goals are set in time and change that time might be preserved, excepting one. Forgiveness does not aim at keeping time, but at its ending, when it has no use. Its purpose ended, it is gone. And where it once held seeming sway is now restored the function God established for His Son in full awareness. Time can set no end to its fulfillment nor its changelessness. There is no death because the living share the function their Creator gave to them. Life's function cannot be to die. It must be life's extension, that it be as one forever and forever, without end.

We need remember that Jesus does not speak of the body's life, but life in the spirit. Its eternal life is reflected by our forgiveness, the ultimate change that undoes all other change and leads to the Changeless. In this way our earthly function of forgiveness gently gives way to our Heavenly function of creation, held for us by the Creator's Will against the time we return from the insane wanderings in the ego's dying world of guilt and punishment.

(VI.5) This world will bind your feet and tie your hands and kill your body only if you think that it was made to crucify God's Son. For even though it was a dream of death, you need not let it stand for this to you. Let *this* be changed, and nothing in the world but must be changed as well. For nothing here but is defined as what you see it for.

To understand this world, we must first understand its purpose, of which there are two: the ego's wish to imprison us in the body's dream of death, or the Holy Spirit's Will of awakening us from the ego's hellish nightmare. Choosing His purpose of forgiveness undoes the world's thinking that we are helpless in the face of the ego's world of sin and suffering, the "natural" laws of its thought system. Its place is joyously taken by our reclaiming the mind's power to choose the change that forevermore cancels out the original change, returning us to our home in God.

(VI.6) How lovely is the world whose purpose is forgiveness of God's Son! How free from fear, how filled with blessing and with happiness! And what a joyous thing it is to dwell a little while in such a happy place! Nor can it be forgot, in such a world, it *is* a little while till timelessness comes quietly to take the place of time.

This is what it means to be a happy learner (T-14.II). Our lives will be filled with an incredible happiness because our shifted purpose is learning that joy is in the mind that has chosen the Teacher of joy, regardless of Hamlet's "slings and arrows of outrageous fortune" (III,i). We gratefully recognize the illusory nature of the world, even with its sufferings, perceiving that meaningful purpose lies in choosing the miracle of forgiveness that leads beyond all dreams to eternal life.

The Miracle

(II.2) You have accepted healing's cause, and so it must be you are healed. And being healed, the power to heal must also now be yours. The miracle is not a separate thing that happens suddenly, as an effect without a cause. Nor is it, in itself, a cause. But where its cause is must it be. Now is it caused, though not as yet perceived. And its effects are there, though not yet seen. Look inward now, and you will not behold a reason for regret, but cause indeed for glad rejoicing and for hope of peace.

The miracle's cause is the mind's decision for it, as is healing. As we were the ones who chose the ego, only we can reverse our decision and choose again: miracles instead of murder, healing in place of sickness. Needless to say at this point in our symphony, all this—the problem of guilt and its solution of forgiveness—is in the mind, since there is nothing outside: *ideas leave not their source*; cause and effect are forever one and indivisible.

(II.3) It has been hopeless to attempt to find the hope of peace upon a battleground. It has been futile to demand escape from sin and pain of what was made to serve the function of retaining sin and pain. For pain and sin are one illusion, as are hate and fear, attack and guilt but one. Where they are causeless their effects are gone, and love must come wherever they are not. Why are you not rejoicing? You are free of pain and sickness, misery and loss, and all effects of hatred and attack. No more is pain your friend and guilt your god, and you should welcome the effects of love.

Why delay our choice for the miracle when pain is the inevitable result of the mind's decision for guilt and judgment? Focusing on the body's pleasure and pain is the cause of all suffering, while returning to the mind its function of causation (T-28.II.9:3) allows us to choose again and escape the miserable effects of hate. Why, Jesus implores, wait for Heaven when it is here for the asking (W-pI.188.1:1)? Choose again remains his only message.

(IV.1:1-3) Do you believe that truth can be but some illusions? They are dreams *because* they are not true. Their equal lack of truth becomes the basis for the miracle, which means that you have understood that dreams are dreams; and that escape depends, not on the dream, but only on awaking.

This is a reference to the first principle of miracles: *there is no order of difficulty* among them. Dreams are dreams, and a dream by any other name, to paraphrase Shakespeare, is still a dream: happiness *and* sadness, peace *and* conflict, life *and* death—all are dreams. It is a fact that we can never find freedom from illusions within the world of duality, but only by awakening from it, a process of healing that begins with our choosing the Holy Spirit's happy dreams of forgiveness that are the means of our return.

(IV.1:4-8) Could it be some dreams are kept, and others wakened from? The choice is not between which dreams to keep, but only if you want to live in dreams or to awaken from them. Thus it is the miracle does not select some dreams to leave untouched by its beneficence. You cannot dream some dreams and wake from some, for you are either sleeping or awake. And dreaming goes with only one of these.

A strong ego temptation is to let go of bad dreams, but keep intact those special dreams in which we think we are happy. This is not healing. There is the truth of God and His Oneness, and nothing else, for everything in duality is illusion, reflecting the either-or principle that is the metaphysical underpinning of *A Course in Miracles*. We are either in Heaven or hell, awake or asleep. In this world we forgive or attack, as we read earlier in our symphony: "Vision or judgment is your choice, but never both of these" (T-20.V.4:7). The mutually exclusive nature of the Holy Spirit's true perceptions and the ego's misperceptions forms the basis of forgiveness and the holy relationship.

Forgiveness and the Holy Relationship

(III.3:1-7) Within the dream of bodies and of death is yet one theme of truth; no more, perhaps, than just a tiny spark, a space of light created in the dark, where God still shines. You cannot wake yourself. Yet you can let yourself be wakened. You can overlook your brother's dreams. So perfectly can you forgive him his illusions he becomes your savior from your dreams. And as you see him shining in the space of light where God abides within the darkness, you will see that God Himself is where his body is. Before this light the body disappears, as heavy shadows must give way to light.

Jesus of course is not speaking literally of seeing another's body disappear. What changes is our perception of the body, which is no longer seen as repository of the guilt that had enshrouded the body in shadows. Instead, the body is seen as a light-filled vessel of guiltlessness. This shift occurs when we withdraw our projections, no longer seeing another's interests as separate from our own (*one or the other*), for we recognize that we share a common need to remember the light and awaken from the dream of darkness (*together, or not at all*).

We cannot do this without help. Since we are the ones who put ourselves to sleep, we need a teacher to instruct us that the way to awaken is through overlooking, looking beyond the guilt we placed on others to our shared innocence. In the special relationship we express our "secret sins and hidden hates" (T-31.VIII.9:2), the mind's dream we do not want to see, which is why it is kept secret. Jesus helps us understand that the darkness we condemn in another is an outward picture of the mind's condition of darkness we try to conceal, and then avoid via projection.

(III.3:8-11) The darkness cannot choose that it remain. The coming of the light means it is gone. In glory will you see your brother then, and understand what really fills the gap so long perceived as keeping you apart. There, in its place, God's witness has set forth the gentle way of kindness to God's Son.

Because the ego's darkness of guilt has no power to do anything, it is not the problem. Attention needs to be focused on the mind's decision maker: the problem *and* the answer. When we choose to listen to the voice of madness, we give darkness power, banishing light from our awareness. But when we forgive, the darkened veils of attack are removed that had shrouded our brothers in hate and blocked true perception of God's Son. The light of Christ's face is revealed, and kindness replaces cruelty as vision restores the sight that judgment had claimed for its own.

(III.3:12-13) Whom you forgive is given power to forgive you your illusions. By your gift of freedom is it given unto you.

This is not the first time we have seen this idea. It appears at least eighteen times in the Course, and is a reference to the gospel where Jesus gives his apostles the power to forgive sins (Matthew 16:19b; John 20:23). Here, he tells us that we all have this power of forgiveness. Appearances to the contrary, this is not the magic of *forgiveness-to-destroy* (S-2.II) where we make sin real and then overlook it, or atone for sin by a life of suffering. We forgive others their illusions by not joining them on the dance floor to share dreams of attack, sickness, and death. If illusions of judgment and hate are not shared, they cannot exist; if we do not agree on the ego's dreams of darkness, because at least one of us holds the light, the dream is unshared and remains the wrong mind's idle illusion. It is only when we agree that sin and guilt are real that they become substantive and demand action. We need recall that the separation is unreal (the Atonement principle) because God did not recognize its existence. By not seeing ourselves as separate from each other, we realize that the same light we have identified within shines equally as bright in others, despite the seeming power of the darkness. This realization constitutes the true power of forgiveness, in which the Sonship is healed and set free as one.

(III.4:1-2) Make way for love, which you did not create, but which you can extend. On earth this means forgive your brother, that the darkness may be lifted from your mind.

We do not extend love; it extends through us: "Make way for love…." Our task is only to remove the ego's blocks of guilt by asking Jesus for help to forgive. When they are gone, love is free to flow, which is why we need never ask him what to do. He is not interested in what happens in the world's dream, but only in releasing the mind's dreams of specialness and death. When we bring these dark thoughts to his light they are gently dissolved, freeing up the love we had heretofore imprisoned. At that point we will automatically know the kind and loving thing to say or do, regardless of the situation. This is the *content* behind the *form* of our "hearing" Jesus tell us specifics, of "hearing" an inner Voice. To repeat, he does not literally tell us how to behave; his abstract love in the right mind is what guides us. The Voice itself is an illusion, as we are told in the clarification of terms (C-6.1:5), it being a specific form of the abstract love we have made way for when we look at our dreams of judgment through Jesus' healing vision.

(III.4:3-4) When light has come to him through your forgiveness, he will not forget his savior, leaving him unsaved. For it was in your face he saw the light that he would keep beside him, as he walks through darkness to the everlasting light.

This is so as light is shared. It does not mean we have saved others because they have saved us. Salvation is immediate and all-inclusive: *When I am healed I am not healed alone* (W-pI.137). All of us, then, become shining reminders of the right-minded thought system that is present in all of us. Our gift to each other is to stand for the Alternative (M-5.III.2:6), the Light that abolishes the darkness when we forgive and see innocence instead of sin.

(III.5:1) How holy are you, that the Son of God can be your savior in the midst of dreams of desolation and disaster.

This same idea opened the section "For They Have Come" in Chapter 26: "Think but how holy you must be from whom the Voice for God calls lovingly…" (T-26.IX.1:1). We are holy because we share the holiness of Christ with our saviors from the dark, belying the ego's appearances of special love and hate.

(III.5:2) See how eagerly he comes, and steps aside from heavy shadows that have hidden him, and shines on you in gratitude and love.

We lift the shadows from our brother's mind by not choosing to make his guilt real, nor giving his ego power to affect us. In this gift of light to him we remember its presence in ourselves, he then becoming the shining witness that strengthens the love we have reinforced in our minds that had been darkened by thoughts of sin and guilt.

(III.5:3-7) He is himself, but not himself alone. And as his Father lost not part of him in your creation, so the light in him is brighter still because you gave your light to him, to save him from the dark. And now the light in you must be as bright as shines in him. This is the spark that shines within the dream; that you can help him waken, and be sure his waking eyes will rest on you. And in his glad salvation you are saved.

God's Son is one, not many. The light that shines in one seemingly separated fragment shines in all. When we withhold it from even one aspect of the Sonship, the whole is plunged in darkness, at least in our mind's awareness: one Christ, one ego; one forgiveness, one guilt. Because we fell asleep as one Son, we shall awaken as one Son. As separation is the effect of a single mistaken choice for sin, salvation awaits our single correction of the miracle.

(VI.1:1-3) How willing are you to forgive your brother? How much do you desire peace instead of endless strife and misery and pain? These questions are the same, in different form.

We cannot forgive others if at the same time we are attracted to a life of strife, misery, and pain. Jesus' questions are the same because our willingness to forgive someone else is our willingness to release the source of suffering in ourselves. Grievances held against another are projections of the mind's guilt that is the cause of all conflict and pain. This is why it is so difficult to forgive and let go of judgments; if we do not experience pain, whom can we blame for making us who we are? As long as we are wedded to the idea of individuality and specialness, we need to make someone responsible. The way to accuse, *par excellence*, is to suffer, making others believe they are the cause of our distress, deserving punishment for our sinful decision to separate from love.

(VI.1:4-5) Forgiveness is your peace, for herein lies the end of separation and the dream of danger and destruction, sin and death; of madness and of murder, grief and loss. This is the "sacrifice" salvation asks, and gladly offers peace instead of this.

The problem is that we do not want to lose our special self, which is bonded to death and destruction, madness and murder, guilt and grief. This makes us who we are, and we all choose to suffer so we may point an accusing finger at some evildoer, whose sinful thoughts and actions are judged to be the cause of our dis-ease. We are loath to sacrifice our painful experience because it would mean sacrificing our separated identity. In this perverse insanity, we gladly eschew salvation's peace for the "joys" of sacrifice, specialness, and self.

(VI.2:1-2) Swear not to die, you holy Son of God! You make a bargain that you cannot keep.

This interesting first line can be read in two ways; one changing the meaning of the other. It does not mean *swear* not to die, i.e., swearing to be eternal. Its proper reading is to swear *not* to die. This refers back to the discussion in the previous chapter of our promises to each other that we would always die; a mutual oath to make the ego thought system real, pledging to uphold it even to our death. Indeed, we uphold it *by* our death. Thus, when Jesus exhorts us to "Swear not to die," he is asking us not to preserve this strange alliance with the ego. Besides its never making us happy, it is a bargain we cannot truly keep, as he tells us:

(VI.2:3-6) The Son of Life cannot be killed. He is immortal as his Father. What he is cannot be changed. He is the only thing in all the universe that must be one.

Life here is a dream, its seeming reality disavowed by the Atonement principle that says nothing happened to change the oneness of God and His Son. We did not kill God in order to live, and He will not kill us as punishment for our sin against Him. Eternity forever remains a state of perfect creation, by definition. Recall: "It is a joke to think that time [or the ego] can come to circumvent eternity, which *means* there is no time" (T-27.VIII.6:5).

This next passage echoes the opening chapter of *Ecclesiastes*, the darkest book in the Bible. It is strange that it even found its way into the canon. Its poetic, if not pessimistic expression of life in the world is almost the exact opposite of everything else in the biblical writings. Here, however, the context is the opposite:

(VI.2:7-10) What *seems* eternal all will have an end. The stars will disappear, and night and day will be no more. All things that come and go, the tides, the seasons and the lives of men; all things that change with time and bloom and fade will not return. Where time has set an end is not where the eternal is.

Jesus is describing how this physical universe is not eternal, for everything here will ultimately cease to exist. This is among the clearest passages in *A Course in Miracles* that teach the illusory nature of the material world. The only thing lasting here is God's Son *because* he is not here. His eternalness is not found in the body or individual identity, but in his Self: God's one Son, at one with his Creator (W-pI.95).

(VI.2:11-14) God's Son can never change by what men made of him. He will be as he was and as he is, for time appointed not his destiny, nor set the hour of his birth and death. Forgiveness will not change him. Yet time waits upon forgiveness that the things of time may disappear because they have no use.

Our true reality as spirit is unaffected by what happens to the body, though the ego made it to be born, deteriorate, and die. This proves we are not changeless and eternal, meaning that our Creator lied and so cannot be God. Time, though made by the ego to establish its dream of separation, can be used by the Holy Spirit as a vehicle for having us learn—over time—that it is not real. This is the same as saying that while the ego made the world for the insidious purpose of excluding God (W-pII.3.2:4), protecting us from the guilt that protects the mind from choosing Him, it can serve another purpose: a classroom of forgiveness in which we learn there is no world, for nothing exists outside ourselves. This is the theme of the next section to be examined, "Seek Not Outside Yourself":

(VII.6:2-6) It is vain to worship idols in the hope of peace. God dwells within, and your completion lies in Him. No idol takes His place. Look not to idols. Do not seek outside yourself.

Without being aware of it, we worship idols in the hope we can attain peace through specialness. Nevertheless, Jesus reminds us that peace comes only from recognizing that our "completion lies in Him," our God Who dwells in the mind as a memory to be recalled when we decide that His Love is all we want. It cannot come from the body or its world. Intrinsic to this process is realizing why we do not want to look within, and continually seek outside ourselves for the special something that will make us whole. It is important as we study this course that we recognize our resistance to it. In fact, we know we are resistant because we still identify with the body. We have discussed before how, when we read *A Course in Miracles* and hear its words, we actually think our brains are thinking about what our eyes see and ears hear. This illustrates the extent to which we maintain our identification with the external.

In addition, we think the Course is outside us because we have a book our bodies tell us is there to hold and read. What makes this course truly helpful, however, is learning it is in our *minds*. God's Love, which Jesus symbolizes, is also in the mind, and *A Course in Miracles* is an expression of this

Presence. But because we think we are here, we take his love into the body, leading to the belief there is an external book that will help us. This, again, demonstrates our bodily identification and why we are compelled to seek outside ourselves for the idols of specialness we think would complete us, bringing happiness and peace. Despite this madness, we remain within the mind, guiltily dreaming of the bodies of others and our own. This establishes the need to approach a section like this as an ideal into which we grow, even though we may still be at the bottom of the ladder (T-28.III.1:2). What helps us ascend is our familiar friend *purpose*:

(VII.7) Let us forget the purpose of the world the past has given it. For otherwise, the future will be like the past, and but a series of depressing dreams, in which all idols fail you, one by one, and you see death and disappointment everywhere.

The idealism of youth often collapses with the understanding that nothing here works. While one cannot effect meaningful world change, we can effect internal change. With this recognition, the love in the mind affects the Sonship as a whole, the right mind not being invested in external change. The world's purpose shifts from a place of idols where we seek happiness, peace, and freedom from pain, to a classroom where we learn that the world offers us nothing. It is the forgiving mind alone that is the source of true happiness and release from suffering.

(VII.8) To change all this, and open up a road of hope and of release in what appeared to be an endless circle of despair, you need but to decide you do not know the purpose of the world. You give it goals it does not have, and thus do you decide what it is for. You try to see in it a place of idols found outside yourself, with power to make complete what is within by splitting what you are between the two. You choose your dreams, for they are what you wish, perceived as if it had been given you. Your idols do what you would have them do, and have the power you ascribe to them. And you pursue them

vainly in the dream, because you want their power as your own.

We try to find salvation outside by splitting off what is inside. We deny the mind's power to choose the ego's weakness over Christ's strength—the opposite of what Jesus later asks of us (T-31.VIII.2)—thereby seeing ourselves as weak and vulnerable. Next, we try to extract strength from everyone and everything around us, whether it is through food, sex, substances, or money, or through control and domination. We seek to wrest power from the bodies of the world to conceal the wrong mind's inherent weakness, and hide the mind's strength to choose otherwise in a decision that would expose the inherent nothingness of the ego and its idols.

(VII.9:1-5) Yet where are dreams but in a mind asleep? And can a dream succeed in making real the picture it projects outside itself? Save time, my brother; learn what time is for. And speed the end of idols in a world made sad and sick by seeing idols there. Your holy mind is altar unto God, and where He is no idols can abide.

Everything we see is a projection, an insane dream that has never left the mind that thought it. Since it is almost inconceivable that we made the world, we need to keep in awareness how real our dreams seem at night. This provides an entrée into our experience of living in a temporal/spatial universe while we still sleep. When we ask for help from the mind's true Teacher, we learn of another purpose for the world of idols; that it be a place of learning in which time is used to exchange the purpose of specialness for forgiveness, guilt giving way to innocence.

(VII.10:4-7) An idol cannot take the place of God. Let Him remind you of His Love for you, and do not seek to drown His Voice in chants of deep despair to idols of yourself. Seek not outside your Father for your hope. For hope of happiness is *not* despair.

Hope of happiness will inevitably end in despair if we seek for it outside ourselves. Genuine hope

lies only within the mind: the locus of the question and its answer; the source of pain and its undoing. Jesus has taught us to see the ego's implicit purpose in our seeking "to drown His Voice in chants of deep despair to idols of [ourselves]." This vast universe is in fact one raucous shriek, a paean to the ego whose goal is to silence the still, small Voice of the Holy Spirit and bury His principle of Atonement, rendering it forever inaccessible to God's Son.

(VIII.5:1-3) What is an idol? Nothing! It must be believed before it seems to come to life, and given power that it may be feared.

The idol, as we have learned, has power because of the mind's belief in it, not because of anything intrinsic to the special object: "It must be believed before it seems to come to life." Note the word *seems*. In truth, the body has no life let alone power, which comes solely from our decision maker having chosen it; that power being the source of our choosing the earth of the ego's thought system of separation, or the Heaven of the Holy Spirit's Atonement. When we give up that power by making a mindless self, we become weak, having placed ourselves at the mercy of forces beyond our control. To restate this important point, as compensation for this weakness, we seek strength from special people, substances, things, or concepts. All these idols will inevitably fail because true strength abides only in the right mind we chose to leave and can return to whenever we decide for the Holy Spirit and His miracle:

(VIII.5:4-6) Its life and power are its believer's gift, and this is what the miracle restores to what *has* life and power worthy of the gift of Heaven and eternal peace. The miracle does not restore the truth, the light the veil between has not put out. It merely lifts the veil, and lets the truth shine unencumbered, being what it is.

We saw this description of the miracle in the opening sentences of Chapter 28: "The miracle does nothing. All it does is to undo" (T-28.I.1:1-2). The miracle does not restore truth, but simply lifts the veil of forgetfulness that keeps awareness of the mind hidden by separating body from mind, holding effect apart from cause. The miracle (the arc on the right-hand side of the chart) returns us to the decision-making part of the mind, penetrating the veil and allowing us to expose the dynamic of projection, understanding that the world is the mere outpicturing of the mind's secret dream. Following the all-important principle *ideas leave not their source,* we recognize that the world has never left the mind, meaning there is no external world except our belief in it. Idea and source, effect and cause, world and mind are one. Finally:

(VIII.5:7) It does not need belief to be itself, for it has been created; so it *is*.

In other words, truth *is*. It does not need belief to be itself. Illusion, on the other hand, needs the mind's belief to exist. Withdrawing our belief in illusion automatically lets truth's memory arise in our minds to heal us.

We return now to the end of "The Forgiving Dream," the final section of Chapter 29.

(IX.6:1-3) There is a time when childhood should be passed and gone forever. Seek not to retain the toys of children. Put them all away, for you have need of them no more.

Jesus refers to the toys of judgment, along with a nod to St. Paul's famous passage in 1 Corinthians (13:11). To this we could certainly add the toys of sin, guilt, and fear, all aspects of the belief that specialness and sacrifice will save us. Our elder brother tells us we have already begun our way up the ladder and are no longer totally identified as children. His encouragement supports our readiness to begin the process of letting go of the ego's childish toys, for they have not delivered on their promises.

(IX.6:4-7) The dream of judgment is a children's game, in which the child becomes the father, powerful, but with the little wisdom of a child. What hurts him is destroyed; what helps him, blessed. Except he judges this as does a child, who does not know what hurts and what will heal. And bad things seem to happen, and he is afraid of all the chaos in a world he thinks is governed by the laws he made.

Jesus is obviously not impressed with children. There is an illusory idea, usually associated with Rousseau, that these little ones are innocent lights of the world, if not beacons of wisdom, to whom the world does horrid things. This is not the Course's understanding at all. To the contrary, children are seen as symbols for demanding mouths that want only to cannibalize their special objects. Jesus is asking us to grow out of this. He is not chastising or challenging us, but simply saying: "I am helping you learn that what you are doing with your life is meaningless. It is a game of judgment that children play, and one that goes nowhere and is far, far beneath Who you really are."

Children do not understand the adult world, which is why Jesus likens us to them. We do not understand his world of forgiveness, believing ours of attack and loss is reality. Take a toy away from a child and it will cry, because in its lack of wisdom it thinks something dreadful has happened. We are no different as adults. People take away our toys of specialness, or interfere with our pursuit of them, and we yell and scream, sometimes threatening retaliative action. We love when we get what we want, and hate when we do not. We special ones, then, are no different from little children who play games of make-believe and think them real.

(IX.6:8-9) Yet is the real world unaffected by the world he thinks is real. Nor have its laws been changed because he does not understand.

Since everything has already happened—the ego's nightmare dreams and the Holy Spirit's happy dreams of correction—there is a place within where we have accepted the Atonement for ourselves, our minds are healed, and the separation already over. Recall: "This world was over long ago. The thoughts that made it are no longer in the mind that thought of them and loved them for a little while" (T-28.I.1:6-7). The real world represents our decision to forgive totally and know that truth is outside the dream. This place of peace has not gone because we dream of idols, wherein we merely play-act that something is happening. In fact, nothing is going on because the mind's thought of separation is nonexistent. It is only the belief in it that seems to give our idols reality, which in turn seems to give their world reality, not to mention making what happens here of vital importance. The world *is* important, but only to children; it has no value to the sane mind other than its potential to help us awaken from the dream to our Self.

(IX.7) The real world still is but a dream. Except the figures have been changed. They are not seen as idols which betray. It is a dream in which no one is used to substitute for something else, nor interposed between the thoughts the mind conceives and what it sees. No one is used for something he is not, for childish things have all been put away. And what was once a dream of judgment now has changed into a dream where all is joy, because that is the purpose that it has. Only forgiving dreams can enter here, for time is almost over. And the forms that enter in the dream are now perceived as brothers, not in judgment, but in love.

When we have attained the real world, we stand outside the dream knowing that its figures are projections of an illusory and impossible thought. Dream actions have no effect upon our peace, nor can they change the recognition of universal sameness when we are confronted with the ego's differentiated perceptions it would have us think are reality. Judgment has given way to vision, and all within the dream are lovingly seen with the common need to escape from hell and return home. No exceptions are possible, for the real world directly reflects Heaven's perfect Oneness. It is the final stage of forgiveness before God completes the journey to where we never left.

(IX.8:1-3) Forgiving dreams have little need to last. They are not made to separate the mind from what it thinks. They do not seek to prove the dream is being dreamed by someone else.

The ego's dreams are designed to make us mindless: we have a mind that we deny, becoming aware only of a body and brain. In the world's dreams, we believe people do things to us, which is why salvation's secret is that we do this to ourselves

(T-27.VIII.10:1). In truth we are dreamers of the dream, not dream figures, and the miracle helps us understand our need to forgive others and ourselves, the core of the Holy Spirit's happy dreams.

(IX.8:4-7) And in these dreams a melody is heard that everyone remembers, though he has not heard it since before all time began. Forgiveness, once complete, brings timelessness so close the song of Heaven can be heard, not with the ears, but with the holiness that never left the altar that abides forever deep within the Son of God. And when he hears this song again, he knows he never heard it not. And where is time, when dreams of judgment have been put away?

Jesus refers to "The Forgotten Song" (T-21.I). It is not something we hear with our ears, for its sweet sounds are internal. When forgiving dreams end the dreams of judgment, we will hear only Heaven's melody of love; the forgotten song that poetically expresses the holiness that has remained with us, even midst the terror of being our Self.

(IX.9) Whenever you feel fear in any form,— and you *are* fearful if you do not feel a deep content, a certainty of help, a calm assurance Heaven goes with you,—be sure you made an idol, and believe it will betray you. For beneath your hope that it will save you lie the guilt and pain of self-betrayal and uncertainty, so deep and bitter that the dream cannot conceal completely all your sense of doom. Your self-betrayal must result in fear, for fear *is* judgment, leading surely to the frantic search for idols and for death.

Here is a rule of thumb to guide us through our day. Jesus asks us to be vigilant for any signs of dis-ease, any indication we are even slightly disquieted. Because the forms are irrelevant—all types of upset stem from the mind's single content of fear—Jesus tells us twice that mild twinges of annoyance are no different from raging fury (W-pI.21.2:5; M-17.4:3-5). As there is one content with many forms, *all* disturbances to our peace are effects of the cause that is the mind's decision for guilt. This projected experience of self-betrayal results in the perception that the world's dream is the cause of our unrest. Yet these flimsy defenses can scarcely contain our doom-filled fear of punishment that continually drives us on a "frantic search for idols" to protect us. Yet each idol will fail since bodies eventually die, the ultimate proof that God's insatiable need for vengeance has been fulfilled.

(IX.10:1-2) Forgiving dreams remind you that you live in safety and have not attacked yourself. So do your childish terrors melt away, and dreams become a sign that you have made a new beginning, not another try to worship idols and to keep attack.

The new beginning, looking forward to "The New Beginning" in Chapter 30, occurs when we recognize that the direction we were heading in was wrong; we desire now to go up the ladder, not remain on its lower rungs. We begin anew when we can say and mean, "There must be another way." This includes letting go of judgment, which enables us to look at the world's idols and acknowledge that they no longer attract us. In such acknowledgment our true safety lies, for forgiveness nullifies fear and God's Son remembers his home in the love that is beyond all dreams.

(IX.10:3) Forgiving dreams are kind to everyone who figures in the dream.

Not some, but *everyone*. Since love is all-inclusive, genuine forgiveness embraces all people, all the time, with no exceptions.

(IX.10:4-6) And so they bring the dreamer full release from dreams of fear. He does not fear his judgment for he has judged no one, nor has sought to be released through judgment from what judgment must impose. And all the while he is remembering what he forgot, when judgment seemed to be the way to save him from its penalty.

Judgment's ultimate penalty is death, a fact the world attempts to hide. Judging others has obviously failed as a strategy because we come here as bodies to escape the mind's fate of certain death, and end up in the grave, regardless of who is to blame. In forgiving dreams, on the other hand, we do not fear the judgment of others because we ourselves have not judged anyone. When we are afraid of what a person might say or do to us, or are concerned with how others think, it is only because we have projected the sin-laden judgment of ourselves. Feeling wretched within, we need people's approval to feel relief. The insanity of that specialness disappears, however, when we recognize that the dream began with us and will end there when we change our minds. The Love of God, which we forgot when we chose to remember the ego, dawns gently in awareness as the long and painful journey ends. Having recognized that death is no longer our desire, we gain release from our former friends: sin, guilt, and judgment.

Closing

We end with "The Changeless Dwelling Place," picking up with paragraph 3. As in other sections with which we have concluded different movements of our symphony, we find here a lovely summary of our preceding discussion:

(V.3) Here is the role the Holy Spirit gives to you who wait upon the Son of God, and would behold him waken and be glad. He is a part of you and you of him, because he is his Father's Son, and not for any purpose you may see in him. Nothing is asked of you but to accept the changeless and eternal that abide in him, for your Identity is there. The peace in you can but be found in him. And every thought of love you offer him but brings you nearer to your wakening to peace eternal and to endless joy.

Our role, implied earlier when we discussed the first two paragraphs of this section, is to accept the

Holy Spirit's loving response to the insane belief that we could change Heaven. God's one Son is protected by the Atonement, which teaches that the oneness of love has never been compromised: "…not one note in Heaven's song was missed." We draw closer to this acceptance each time we offer forgiveness to others, relieving them of the burden of believing they were responsible for our loss of peace. Removing that ill-fated function from their perturbed minds removes the guilt from ours. No longer condemned by the ego, we are saved together as we joyfully awaken from the dream of death, our imprisoned thoughts now freed to return to our eternal life in God.

(V.4:1) This sacred Son of God is like yourself; the mirror of his Father's Love for you, the soft reminder of his Father's Love by which he was created and which still abides in him as it abides in you.

The "sacred Son of God" is any of our partners in special love or hate. No dream of judgment can ever change the love that joins us together. Forever one, love so remains throughout eternity, banishing any ego thought of separation that would take us from our abiding place in God.

(V.4:2-3) Be very still and hear God's Voice in him, and let It tell you what his function is. He was created that you might be whole, for only the complete can be a part of God's completion, which created you.

God's Son is perfectly one. There is no division in his wholeness; no separation or differentiation. When the fragmentation process seemed to occur, our oneness appeared to shatter into billions and billions of pieces, causing us to believe that each of us is distinct from everyone else. We need these separate persons in order to recognize that the separation is an illusion, a projection of an inner thought that we now can change. Our special relationships, looked at with the Holy Spirit, become opportunities for seeing that what was inside was placed outside. He helps us reverse these projections through the miracle, so we may look at the mind's mistaken thoughts and correct them.

(V.5) There is no gift the Father asks of you but that you see in all creation but the shining glory of His gift to you. Behold His Son, His perfect gift, in whom his Father shines forever, and to whom is all creation given as his own. Because he has it is it given you, and where it lies in him behold your peace. The quiet that surrounds you dwells in him, and from this quiet come the happy dreams in which your hands are joined in innocence. These are not hands that grasp in dreams of pain. They hold no sword, for they have left their hold on every vain illusion of the world. And being empty they receive, instead, a brother's hand in which completion lies.

Once again, this vision has nothing to do with external appearances or behavior, but only with our inner sight and thoughts. We no longer see others with interests apart from our own, for reason tells us we share one need, one purpose, one goal. Any perception that fragments the Sonship must then be of the ego, whether the fragmentation is seen in ourselves or another. Regardless of their bodily objects, attack and pain are one because the idea of separation has not left its source in the mind. And where it is, there it can be healed. The happy dreams of forgiveness quietly undo the judgments that seemed to shatter and render incomplete the Son whom God created whole.

(V.6) If you but knew the glorious goal that lies beyond forgiveness, you would not keep hold on any thought, however light the touch of evil on it may appear to be. For you would understand how great the cost of holding anything God did not give in minds that can direct the hand to bless, and lead God's Son unto his Father's house. Would you not want to be a friend to him, created by his Father as His home? If God esteems him worthy of Himself, would you attack him with the hands of hate? Who would lay bloody hands on Heaven itself, and hope to find its peace? Your brother thinks he holds the hand of death. Believe him not. But learn, instead, how blessed are you who can release him, just by offering him yours.

It is necessary to understand that because the Sonship is one, a crucial theme in this course, attacking another means we are attacking ourselves ("It can be but myself I crucify." [W-pI.196]). Constant practice enables us to translate intellectual awareness of this fact into an everyday experience, wherein we truly know that pushing others away through judgment is to join them in the dance of death that condemns no one but ourselves. Jesus repeatedly asks each of us: "Is this hatred really what you want?" If we answer "yes," we must realize the heavy price we pay for valuing our individual identity. It is the cost of sacrificing the peace of everlasting unity for the ephemeral joys of triumph. Who except the insane would make this choice? And are we really that insane?

(V.7:1–8:2) A dream is given you in which he is your savior, not your enemy in hate. A dream is given you in which you have forgiven him for all his dreams of death; a dream of hope you share with him, instead of dreaming evil separate dreams of hate. Why does it seem so hard to share this dream? Because unless the Holy Spirit gives the dream its function, it was made for hate, and will continue in death's services. Each form it takes in some way calls for death. And those who serve the lord of death have come to worship in a separated world, each with his tiny spear and rusted sword, to keep his ancient promises to die.

Such is the core of fear in every dream that has been kept apart from use by Him Who sees a different function for a dream. When dreams are shared they lose the function of attack and separation, even though it was for this that every dream was made.

We saw this in our previous movement as well, where Jesus asked us not to join our brother's dreams of sickness and pain (T-28.IV.1-6). Despite the fact that the world's dreams were made to attack God's Son and keep him separate

from himself, these fearful dreams can be transformed in purpose from anger to forgiveness, death to life. We have come to realize that all attack conceals the right-minded need to awaken from the dream that everyone shares, the common purpose of healing that reflects our unity in Heaven, even as we believe we are bodies living in a separated world of suffering and desire.

(V.8:3) Yet nothing in the world of dreams remains without the hope of change and betterment, for here is not where changelessness is found.

The hope of betterment does not lie in the dream (the body) but in the dream's dreamer (the mind), a theme we understand very well by now. Jesus wants us to recognize the valuelessness of change, unless it is the change from the ego's nightmares to the Holy Spirit's happy dreams of forgiveness.

(V.8:4-6) Let us be glad indeed that this is so, and seek not the eternal in this world. Forgiving dreams are means to step aside from dreaming of a world outside yourself. And leading finally beyond all dreams, unto the peace of everlasting life.

Everlasting life has nothing to do with the body, for immortality comes from realizing that the body is only the projection of the mind's thought of death. All we need do is look carefully at our relationships, being vigilant for thoughts of judgment, hate, and attack: the specialness that breeds separation, even as it is caused by it. Through this mind searching we come to learn that our lives are nothing more than displacements of the wish to keep separate, and understand that this wish held us in misery, being the source of all unhappiness. This is why we are urged not to seek outside ourselves for happiness, but to look only within the mind. There we find the peace that passeth understanding, leading us to the Self that will never die, the eternal life we share with Life Itself.

Chapter 30

THE NEW BEGINNING

Introduction

Chapter 30 is the penultimate movement in our grand symphony. The title of the chapter, "A New Beginning," relates to a comment Jesus made in the last paragraph of Chapter 29 where he referred to the undoing of the ego's first beginning. The ego thought system had its inception in the instant we chose to listen to it instead of the Holy Spirit. Descending the ladder of separation to its inevitable end in the material world of bodies, we filled our minds with idols of specialness, and we continue our discussion of these idols in the current chapter. Changing our minds through the miracle enables us to ascend the ladder the ego led us down. This shift is the new beginning and, as Jesus told us earlier (T-16.VI.8:5), it takes less time to undo the ego (the ascent) than it did to establish it (the descent).

We also find in this chapter, as well as the final one, increased emphasis on the mind's power of decision. Indeed, one of the most important sections of this chapter is its opening, "Rules for Decision." There, Jesus maintains his focus on the need to return to the decision-making point in our minds, represented on the chart by the black dot at the head of the split mind (see Appendix): the site of the old beginning when we chose to hear the ego, and the new beginning when we recognize our mistake and choose differently. Finally, we discuss the theme of purpose, which goes hand in hand with our decision-making ability.

As is our custom, we open with a statement of the Atonement principle. We do this because the thought system of sin, guilt, and punishment derives its meaning from the ego's reaction to the Holy Spirit's Presence in the right mind, which undoes the belief in our individual self. The ego's defense of mindless specialness constitutes its attempt to keep us from ever making the decision for Atonement over separation.

The Atonement Principle

We begin with the Holy Spirit's response when we are tempted to turn away from His Atonement, choosing instead to put our faith in the ego and its thought system of separation and specialness. This is Jesus' message to us:

(II.1:1-3) Do you not understand that to oppose the Holy Spirit is to fight *yourself*? He tells you but your will; He speaks for you. In His Divinity is but your own.

Borrowing the title of Chapter 23, "The War Against Yourself," we see that we fight against Who we truly are by choosing idolatry, worshipping a self that is a shabby substitute for the Self that God created. When we listen to the Holy Spirit's Voice, we choose to remember the Creator's Love that is our Identity as Christ.

(II.1:4-12) And all He knows is but your knowledge, saved for you that you may do your will through Him. God *asks* you do your will. He joins with *you*. He did not set His Kingdom up alone. And Heaven itself but represents your will, where everything created is for you. No spark of life but was created with your glad consent, as you would have it be. And not one Thought that God has ever had but waited for your blessing to be born. God is no enemy to you. He asks no more than that He hear you call Him "Friend."

Succumbing to the ego's temptation to listen to its voice, we choose against God's Will. It is, of course, impossible to truly go against perfect One-ness, which is why the ego will always fail. From this ontological mistake of desiring to be separate and alone comes our pain and misery. Although our suffering is experienced in the body, it remains in the decision-making mind: *ideas leave not their source.* However, as an Idea that has not left Its Source, we are one with our Creator's Will, which is our own. God's Love and Its function of creation are ours as well: Life extends Itself, the blessing of Heaven that embraces Creator and creation as Friend—one God, one Son, one Self.

(II.2:1-5) How wonderful it is to do your will! For that is freedom. There is nothing else that ever should be called by freedom's name. Unless you do your will you are not free. And would God leave His Son without what he has chosen for himself?

The ego's proclamation of freedom is valid only in the world's dualistic dreaming, for who is there to be free, and from what? True freedom is of our will (this section's title is "Freedom of Will"), which means that Cause and Effect, Father and Son, are forever united as one Will, free from all illusions of separation. As Oneness can only extend to oneness, nothing exists apart from this perfect unity of wills.

(II.2:6-10) God but ensured that you would never lose your will when He gave you His perfect Answer. Hear It now, that you may be reminded of His Love and learn your will. God would not have His Son made prisoner to what he does not want. He joins with you in willing you be free. And to oppose Him is to make a choice against yourself, and choose that you be bound.

This is the warning that the Holy Spirit, God's Answer to the separation, gave us in the original instant when we listened to both His Voice and the ego's, tempted to deny the truth of Atonement. Jesus comforts us by saying that when we gave in to the lure of individuality and chose the ego, nothing

terrible happened because illusion had no effect on reality, nor our Identity. Nevertheless, our wrong-minded decision has affected our experience. From that insane moment on we perceived ourselves as we were not, feeling the loss of freedom and power that inevitably followed the choice against our Self. Jesus continues his argument in the next section, "Beyond All Idols":

(III.6:1-2) Nothing that God knows not exists. And what He knows exists forever, changelessly.

Since God does not know about the separation, He does not know about the individual self that is so conflicted: are we real or illusory? We struggle in accepting not only a self that is not who we are, but a self that does not exist. An illusion remains an illusion, regardless of its form, and God knows only the Christ that is our eternal and changeless Self.

(III.6:3-4) For thoughts endure as long as does the mind that thought of them. And in the Mind of God there is no ending, nor a time in which His Thoughts were absent or could suffer change.

By our attempts to change the reality of the Self, we seek to deny our Identity. Such insanity is the source of all our difficulties and dis-ease that, albeit illusory, is real to us within the dream as long as our minds choose to remain asleep. Jesus' good news is that Heaven's changeless reality is totally unaffected by these mad thoughts of change, suffering, and death.

(III.6:5-7) Thoughts are not born and cannot die. They share the attributes of their creator, nor have they a separate life apart from his. The thoughts you think are in your mind, as you are in the Mind which thought of you.

This restates one of our symphony's central themes: *ideas leave not their source.* This works in reality and illusion. As spirit, we remain within the Mind of God and have never left our Source; within the projected dream, the separated world and body with which we identify have never left their source that is the mind's insane thought of separation. Because the principle of projection (ideas *do* leave their source) is a lie, the world does not exist because the separation never happened—nothing resulting in nothing. In truth we are a Thought, an Idea in the Mind of God, and the Atonement teaches that though we can dream of inhabiting a world apart from reality, it has no effect on the happy fact that we forever remain as God created us: *a Oneness joined as One.*

(III.6:8-9) And so there are no separate parts in what exists within God's Mind. It is forever One, eternally united and at peace.

God's Mind is perfect Oneness, and "there are no separate parts" in His Mind. This theme of our oneness as the Child of Oneness recurs now with increasing emphasis, in this movement and in our symphony's stirring conclusion.

(III.7) Thoughts seem to come and go. Yet all this means is that you are sometimes aware of them, and sometimes not. An unremembered thought is born again to you when it returns to your awareness. Yet it did not die when you forgot it. It was always there, but you were unaware of it. The Thought God holds of you is perfectly unchanged by your forgetting. It will always be exactly as it was before the time when you forgot, and will be just the same when you remember. And it is the same within the interval when you forgot.

As we drift toward the ego, and even when we clearly choose its insanity, the Holy Spirit gently speaks to us: "Do not be upset. When things are particularly difficult and painful, recall these words: Although you are free within the dream to believe you changed reality and your Self, your true Identity as Christ is unchanged, unchanging, and unchangeable. It simply waits for you to awaken from the dream and return to It." In spite of our wrong-minded choice, we retain the memory that we are an eternal Thought of God. What we forgot has not left our holy minds, and the Holy Spirit's Voice softly reminds us that at any given instant we can be reborn to the Life we never left. Only in dreams could we abandon our love and our Self.

In other words, "not one note in Heaven's song was missed," the principle of Atonement that is the only truth within the illusory dream. It is to keep this truth from awareness that the ego implements its strategy of drowning out the Holy Spirit's Thought, hardly an unfamiliar theme in our symphony. The ego's secret dream of sin, guilt, and fear comes from the belief we destroyed Heaven and obliterated its Love, while the world's dream arose to "protect" us from the terror caused by the mind's madness. The seeming grandeur and quasi-infinite nature of the universe notwithstanding, the fact remains that it is all unreal. The reality of God and His Son is unchanged.

We turn now to the ego's fear of the mind's power to choose Atonement, and continue with "Beyond All Idols."

The Ego's Fear of the Atonement

Our discussion begins by looking at the ego's attempts to drown out the Voice that tells us nothing happened, for what God does not know cannot exist outside His Wholeness: perfection cannot see imperfection; love does not recognize fear; oneness is unknowing of separation. This Atonement truth threatens our very existence as special and autonomous selves, and our belief in idols keeps the defense going, a theme we explored in Chapter 29 and will see again here. Recall that *idols* is another term for special relationships, the attempt to deny the incompletion we experienced when we believed we threw away our completion by separating from Completion Itself. We sought to make ourselves whole by joining with externals, magically hoping they would supply our lack and bring us peace.

(III.1:1-2) Idols are quite specific. But your will is universal, being limitless.

We know the world is an illusion because it is a place of specifics, while the workbook tells us that the natural state of the mind is abstraction, by which Jesus means non-specificity (W-pI.161.2:1). All this is a way of saying that *A Course in Miracles* is a non-dualistic thought system. Non-specific oneness is the only reality, meaning that God and Christ are not persons or beings Who are distinct from Each Other. In contrast, everything here is specific and distinct, the opposite of our will that is a synonym for our true and limitless Self.

(III.1:3-4) And so it has no form, nor is content for its expression in the terms of form. Idols are limits.

The limitless cannot be expressed in form, because form is a limitation. Recall Jesus' earlier words (T-8.VII.7) when he corrects the famous opening of John's gospel, "In the beginning was the Word…. And the Word was made flesh." Jesus tells us this is impossible because, being spirit, the Word of God cannot be made flesh: the two exist in mutually exclusive dimensions of truth and falsity. Recognizing that spirit cannot be expressed in form shows us how very different this course is from most other spiritualities, contemporary and ancient. Yet although spirit cannot be directly expressed in the world, its loving oneness is reflected through forgiveness and the miracle.

(III.1:5-10) They are the belief that there are forms that will bring happiness, and that, by limiting, is all attained. It is as if you said, "I have no need of everything. This little thing I want, and it will be as everything to me." And this must fail to satisfy, because it is your will that everything be yours. Decide for idols and you ask for loss. Decide for truth and everything is yours.

This is the story of our everyday lives, settling for the little, unsatisfying things of the world. And behind the pursuit of the special somethings that will make us whole is the ontological snubbing our noses at God, saying: "Your everything is not enough. We want more than Your Kingdom of Oneness in which our special selves cannot exist.

We are establishing our own kingdom: *Heaven's Opposite!*" This declaration of independence became enshrined in the body, attracting other bodies to it—as individuals, and as like-minded social, political, racial, and religious groups. When we finally realize that these special idols of nothingness will fail, a price too painful to pay, we will change our minds and choose Jesus' truth of forgiveness instead of the ego's lies of attack.

(III.2) It is not form you seek. What form can be a substitute for God the Father's Love? What form can take the place of all the love in the Divinity of God the Son? What idol can make two of what is one? And can the limitless be limited? You do not want an idol. It is not your will to have one. It will not bestow on you the gift you seek. When you decide upon the form of what you want, you lose the understanding of its purpose. So you see your will within the idol, thus reducing it to a specific form. Yet this could never be your will, because what shares in all creation cannot be content with small ideas and little things.

Recall our theme of *form and content*. It is never the form that attracts us, either through pain or pleasure, but its underlying content: the purpose of maintaining the thought system of littleness and limitation. Changing forms perpetuates the ego's content, and often under the illusion that this shift has been significant. However, the only truly significant shift is from the bodily forms of specialness to the wrong mind's content of guilt, and on to the right mind's content of forgiveness. In this way we reflect Heaven's loving Will by choosing to awaken from the nightmare that substituted the limited for the limitless, conflict for peace, hate for love.

(III.3:1) Behind the search for every idol lies the yearning for completion.

This reminds us of the ego's "Seek and do not find," the theme that will return in our symphony's final movement. We continually seek for the completion to correct the emptiness and lack we feel within, but will never find. The only thing that truly completes us is choosing the Teacher Who reminds us, through His Atonement, of the joyful fact of our completion as Christ that illusions of incompletion and specialness have never changed.

(III.3:2) Wholeness has no form because it is unlimited.

Here again is a clear articulation of the cardinal principle of the Course's non-dualistic metaphysics that so terrifies the limited ego, being the statement of its inherent nonexistence: God is, and there is nothing else. Spirit and form have nothing to do with each other, for how can truth be involved in the illusory world, regardless of its seemingly holy forms? To restate the obvious, God cannot know about the separation because it never happened. Although we may experience our right-minded thoughts as coming from Him (or His Voice), He does not interact with us in the dream. True help comes only from the mind's remembering, through the decision to forgive, that our reality and our Creator's are forever outside the ego's dreams of specialness and sin.

(III.3:3) To seek a special person or a thing to add to you to make yourself complete, can only mean that you believe some form is missing.

This is exactly the behavior the ego fosters. We reinforce belief in the scarcity principle (something is missing in us) by seeking externals to make us whole or happy, whether that entails taking a breath because our lungs require oxygen, snuggling up to another body because we feel alone, or seeking any of the world's idols to make us feel special, peaceful, and secure.

(III.3:4-5) And by finding this, you will achieve completion in a form you like. This is the purpose of an idol; that you will not look beyond it, to the source of the belief that you are incomplete.

Once more we see the Course's emphasis on *purpose*, the subject of our next section. It is imperative that we see how the ego has us seek idols to prove that the separation happened. This makes God wrong and the ego right, and shows that we can get what we need from something external to us, not from His Wholeness and Love.

The true purpose of the world's idols is to keep us from looking within our minds, the only source of meaningful change. Therefore, becoming aware of our decision-making self is vital to Jesus' teachings. The ego's strategy of mindlessness militates against this awareness, since we cannot choose again by changing a mind we do not know we have.

(III.3:6-7) Only if you had sinned could this be so. For sin is the idea you are alone and separated off from what is whole.

The ego tells us that the separation is reality and our incompletion is truth: God's Wholeness has been compromised and the special self is the sinful effect. Our identifying with the mindless body ensures that this belief will go unchallenged and uncorrected.

Jesus continues his discussion of idols, reintroducing another theme from Chapter 29: no matter how real and powerful our idols appear to be, the special ones crucial for our salvation, they never cease being toys of children.

(IV.1:1) You will attack what does not satisfy, and thus you will not see you made it up.

We walk around angrily attacking because the world and its contents do not give us what we need, want, and demand. We do not realize that we, the decision-making part of the mind, made up the world to fail us. Life is our dream, though we have conveniently forgotten we are its dreamer.

(IV.1:2) You always fight illusions.

Like Don Quixote tilting at windmills, we fight against something that does not exist. We do battle with nations, people, our bodies, and microorganisms—all of which do not exist outside the dream. Yet within these insane dreams we clearly are defeated. We continue to seek and not find, desperately trying to cannibalize what we believe we need to complete us and make us happy, not remembering that our Source is the only thing that will end the war and bring the peace that will never die.

(IV.1:3) For the truth behind them is so lovely and so still in loving gentleness, were you aware

of it you would forget defensiveness entirely, and rush to its embrace.

We saw this idea before (T-13.III). If we really knew it was not crucifixion but redemption we feared, and this fear was based on illusions, we would leap into our Father's Arms and the world would disappear. To ensure this never happens, as we have repeatedly seen, the ego made the world to keep us mindless and protected from the mind's power to choose. Here again we see an implicit statement of *purpose*, the motivation behind our having miscreated the world. The ego's fear is that if we recognized the mind as the locus of salvation and the home of our completion, we would rush to embrace it. Its fear, of course, is well-founded. The world *would* fade into its nothingness, and our now defenseless self would fade as well, ending the separation that never truly began.

To restate this, to guard against the inevitability of our return to the mind, we continually choose to be mindless, abetted by the idols of specialness that prove we have accomplished the impossible, establishing a home outside Heaven. Though deep within we know this is a lie, we still strive to preserve the illusion. The fact that nothing here survives itself is proof positive we have failed in our attempts to erect a truth outside of truth. Our attempts to maintain the illusion of immortality through making up myths of after-lives, souls surviving bodies, merely witness to the insanity of trying to create a world of individuality that is opposite to Heaven's eternal and undivided Oneness.

(IV.1:4-6) The truth could never be attacked. And this you knew when you made idols. They were made that this might be forgotten.

We made the world of idols for the purpose of forgetting our source in the mind and Source in spirit, choosing not to remember the Atonement that says truth cannot be separated from or attacked. We cannot help fearing the uncompromising nature of reality, which belies the ego's assertions of separation and self.

(IV.1:7-8) You attack but false ideas, and never truthful ones. All idols are the false ideas you made to fill the gap you think arose between yourself and what is true.

The gap is the home of the *tiny, mad idea*. We quickly fill it with thoughts of sin and fear, and then just as quickly cover them with the idolatrous world of special love and hate. The ego tells us that inside the gap is our guilt, in back of which stands a vengeful deity hellbent on destroying us. Never questioning the patent insanity of this thinking, we fail to recognize that in this gap is found only the mind's wrong decision, easily corrected by our choosing a different teacher. The mind's amnesia allows us to obey the ego's dictates that sound an ominous warning: "Do not go within, for doing so means certain death."

(IV.1:9-10) And you attack them for the things you think they represent. What lies beyond them cannot be attacked.

Idols represent our hidden guilt, the reason for our need to attack everyone and everything around us, seeing them as repositories of the sin we do not want to see in ourselves. The title of this section, "The Truth Behind Illusions," uncovers our fear of letting these idols go, for we would remember the truth of our invulnerable and innocent Self, forgetting the self we made as Its shabby substitute.

(IV.2:1) The wearying, dissatisfying gods you made are blown-up children's toys.

Again, this reverts to our discussion of the image of children's toys (T-29.IX.4-6), the objects of specialness that seem so real and powerful to us. Indeed, even though it is nothing, the world contains such seeming power that we can scarcely fail to be attracted to it, along with our lives of suffering and pain. We note Jesus' perception of us as little boys and girls who believe that everything here is essential to their happiness, although the pursuit of the body's survival is a depleting and disappointing game that only delusional children would play.

(IV.2:2-7) A child is frightened when a wooden head springs up as a closed box is opened

suddenly, or when a soft and silent woolly bear begins to squeak as he takes hold of it. The rules he made for boxes and for bears have failed him, and have broken his "control" of what surrounds him. And he is afraid, because he thought the rules protected him. Now must he learn the boxes and the bears did not deceive him, broke no rules, nor mean his world is made chaotic and unsafe. He was mistaken. He misunderstood what made him safe, and thought that it had left.

Children are frightened by the unexpected. This is not surprising, for the mind programmed the world to engender fear. Since we believe that anxiety has external causes, we must learn that what is outside are mere toys: projected fragments of the secret toys of guilt that are the mind's make-believe thoughts telling us we have done the impossible. The correction of Atonement—the principle of nothing happened—belies the ego's rules for the mindless world that controls our behavior and determines our thoughts and feelings. Jesus teaches us that the "controlling" world is not the problem, nor do its rules restrict or protect us. The mind alone determines our fate, as decisions for the ego or Holy Spirit are the cause of all we think, feel, and do. In this fact lies our only hope and protection.

(IV.3:1) The gap that is not there is filled with toys in countless forms.

There is no gap between ourselves and God, a frequently occurring motif in these final chapters. Having listened to the voice of madness, we believe the gap of separation is real and is the birthplace of sin. Overwhelmed with the guilt of thinking we destroyed Heaven, we conceal this thought behind the ego's toys of specialness. It should be clear by now that the world's purpose is to keep the gap that is not there filled with countless forms of nothingness. These root our attention in the body and safely hide the mind behind the cherished barricades of hate.

(IV.3:2-10) And each one seems to break the rules you set for it. It never was the thing you thought. It must appear to break your rules for

safety, since the rules were wrong. But *you* are not endangered. You can laugh at popping heads and squeaking toys, as does the child who learns they are no threat to him. Yet while he likes to play with them, he still perceives them as obeying rules he made for his enjoyment. So there still are rules that they can seem to break and frighten him. Yet *is* he at the mercy of his toys? And *can* they represent a threat to him?

Each idol of specialness is the ego's slave, and as long as we remain asleep we believe these toys have the power to bring us pleasure or pain. The ego's childish games can become quite serious in the dream, powerful enough to cause real effects and threaten our happiness and very existence. But let forgiving eyes rest on the truth, and we joyously realize that the toys of guilt have no effect on God's holy Son, our Self. It was only the mind's decision to dream that gave toys the power to hurt or heal. With Jesus happily beside us, our level confusion—mind and body—is undone for we see him alone as the answer to pain, and the choice for the ego as the sole cause of suffering. The miracle is Jesus' means of correcting our investment in the idols of specialness, as we now read:

(VIII.2) The miracle is means to demonstrate that all appearances can change because they *are* appearances, and cannot have the changelessness reality entails. The miracle attests salvation from appearances by showing they can change. Your brother has a changelessness in him beyond appearance and deception, both. It is obscured by changing views of him that you perceive as his reality. The happy dream about him takes the form of the appearance of his perfect health, his perfect freedom from all forms of lack, and safety from disaster of all kinds. The miracle is proof he is not bound by loss or suffering in any form, because it can so easily be changed. This demonstrates that it was never real, and could not stem from his reality. For that is changeless, and has no effects that anything in Heaven or on earth could ever alter. But appearances are shown to be unreal *because* they change.

Plato is the first known philosopher to have stressed the importance of knowing the difference between appearance and reality, and we can see his influence in the Course's Neoplatonic teaching. Miracles return the mind's attention to its ability to choose between truth and illusion, the changeless in God's Son and the forever changing ego. More specifically, the miracle enables us to recognize the distinction between the right-minded illusion of change (forgiveness) and the wrong-minded illusion (the separation). Both give way to the truly changeless: God's perfect Son, the Christ He created one with Him. Given this truth, how can he suffer or be vulnerable to perceived threat? Though his body may be in pain and fear attack, a dream figure does not feel. In dreams, yes, but the healed mind dismisses all such thoughts with the simple truth that dreams are untrue, and so have no effects.

(VIII.1) Appearances deceive, but can be changed. Reality is changeless. It does not deceive at all, and if you fail to see beyond appearances you *are* deceived. For everything you see will change, and yet you thought it real before, and now you think it real again. Reality is thus reduced to form, and capable of change. Reality is changeless. It is this that makes it real, and keeps it separate from all appearances. It must transcend all form to be itself. It cannot change.

"Changeless Reality," the title of this section, is the Atonement thought that runs throughout this symphonic movement as a comforting motif. Because the reality of God and Christ cannot be changed, the body that changes must be an empty figure in an idle dream, a part of a causeless world that has never been. Reality can never deceive or be deceived, but the mind that dreams of fantasies is indeed mistaken in its belief, having put its faith in the ephemeral and changeable.

Temptation is a word that has appeared on and off in our symphony, but is increasingly referred to in this and the following chapter. As used in the Course, the term does not refer to what we usually think of as being tempted by the world's special toys. Our real temptation, to which we fell prey at

the beginning, is believing in the ego's lies of individuality rather than the reality of God's perfect Oneness: guilt and hate becoming preferable to love; conflict to the peace of God. Because of the temptation to listen to the ego's illusions instead of his truth, Jesus says to us:

(VIII.3:1-3) What is temptation but a wish to make illusions real? It does not seem to be the wish that no reality be so. Yet it is an assertion that some forms of idols have a powerful appeal that makes them harder to resist than those you would not want to have reality.

As we go through our lives, we establish many idols in maladaptive attempts to find a haven of peace within the storms of hate and fear. In doing so, it does not seem as if we are stating that we want reality to be an illusion and God to be dead, but are merely expressing the desire for a warm, comforting body next to us, enough money to live without care, and a healthy body. Yet behind our saying "I want, I want, I want" is the wish to prove that God is wrong, the Holy Spirit is misleading us, and the ego is our only and trusted friend.

(VIII.3:4) Temptation, then, is nothing more than this; a prayer the miracle touch not some dreams, but keep their unreality obscure and give to them reality instead.

Our wish is that the miracle not be all-inclusive, that we not generalize its healing to all situations. The world's definition of miracles, of course, has only served to make real the illusion of differentiation, for we prefer to think of external miracles that make the material world a reality. This explains why students of *A Course in Miracles* can still be tempted to see miracles as involving the world. But how can things change externally when there is no external? This is an example of the confusion of form and content, body and mind, that Jesus cautions us against, because we want there to be real needs and worldly concerns that involve God and His Holy Spirit. If that were the case, though, we would have successfully demonstrated that reality is illusion, and illusion reality.

We have again seen the ego's purpose for the gap: making real the separation, and then the world as the defense against the pain the ego tells us is justified because of the sinful, murderous gap between ourselves and God. We ascend the ego's ladder of separation by learning a different purpose for the world of idols that guilt had wrought, the focus of this next part of our symphony.

Purpose

The theme of purpose is the focus of the section "The New Interpretation." The emphasis is not about giving up the world of idols—our special attachments to the body—but of learning to recognize the ego's purpose so we can see how idols do not serve us well. Only then can our minds be open to another purpose for their existence.

(VII.1:1-5) Would God have left the meaning of the world to your interpretation? If He had, it *has* no meaning. For it cannot be that meaning changes constantly, and yet is true. The Holy Spirit looks upon the world as with one purpose, changelessly established. And no situation can affect its aim, but must be in accord with it.

We are the ones who choose the world's purpose and meaning, not the other way around. Jesus' point is that while we share the same purpose in content, choosing murder as the means to achieve our special goals, this is not the case in form. As the mind's purpose for the body is to win at the expense of another body, what gives this world meaning is whatever allows us to triumph over another. In addition, some are excited by one thing, and others by something else; e.g., some believe their purpose is to be poor, which will bring them closer to God, while others believe that wealth and success are Heaven's goals for them. We each have different preferences, and our purpose is to achieve whatever we think will meet our needs. These individual purposes give our projected world all the meaning it has.

Despite these specific differences, we hold in common the mind's underlying purpose of proving God wrong and the ego right. Jesus helps us see that true meaning and purpose must be one (forgiveness) because truth is one (love). When we see more than one meaning here, we know the ego is at work. Every encounter becomes holy (T-8.III.4:1) because all situations can serve the single purpose of having us remember our holy Self. Perceiving the world as a screen onto which we project our "secret sins and hidden hates" (T-31.VIII.9:2), we give ourselves a chance to re-evaluate them, recognizing that these thoughts come from the mind's decision that we can now happily change.

(VII.1:6-8) For only if its aim could change with every situation could each one be open to interpretation which is different every time you think of it. You add an element into the script you write for every minute in the day, and all that happens now means something else. You take away another element, and every meaning shifts accordingly.

This passage illustrates the insanity of the ego's thought system of differentiation and change. There is no dependability in the ego's world, which depends on instability for its existence, having begun with the unstable thought of separation. This impermanence of meaning vanishes as our minds shift teachers, enabling the light of forgiveness to supply the meaning that lasts until we remember our Meaning in Heaven.

(VII.2) What do your scripts reflect except your plans for what the day *should* be? And thus you judge disaster and success, advance, retreat, and gain and loss. These judgments all are made according to the roles the script assigns. The fact they have no meaning in themselves is demonstrated by the ease with which these labels change with other judgments, made on different aspects of experience. And then, in looking back, you think you see another meaning in what went before. What have you really done, except to show there was no meaning

there? But you assigned a meaning in the light of goals that change, with every meaning shifting as they change.

As we shall see presently, we first decide on the day we want—peace or conflict—and then perceive events as either facilitating or hindering achievement of that goal. The meaning, therefore, does not lie in the specific forms themselves, but in the purpose the mind assigns to them. This is why our perceptions of people, objects, and situations, not to mention our reactions to them, are so variable. The fact that our needs are always in flux demonstrates the inherent lack of meaning we have given the world. The unchanging purpose of forgiveness alone reflects Heaven's single meaning of love, granting stability and consistency to our experience here:

(VII.3) Only a constant purpose can endow events with stable meaning. But it must accord *one* meaning to them all. If they are given different meanings, it must be that they reflect but different purposes. And this is all the meaning that they have. Can this be meaning? Can confusion be what meaning means? Perception cannot be in constant flux, and make allowance for stability of meaning anywhere. Fear is a judgment never justified. Its presence has no meaning but to show you wrote a fearful script, and are afraid accordingly. But not because the thing you fear has fearful meaning in itself.

There is only one meaning in the world from the perspective of the wrong and right minds. The different purposes our egos perceive belie their underlying purpose of proving the separation is real. The early workbook lessons help us realize that the world in and of itself is meaningless, for what meaning can illusions have? We are the ones who project meaning onto the world, and this will always be some expression of fear, the origin and core of dreams. Without exception, the ego's dreams rest upon the lie that God will punish us. This justifies our fear, with judgment being the ego's defense against our sin-laden projections onto the bodily world, the source of the meaning we give to our experiences here. Notwithstanding these

meaningless perceptions, the world does become meaningful when we allow the Holy Spirit to transform it into a classroom in which we learn His lessons of forgiveness.

(VII.4) A common purpose is the only means whereby perception can be stabilized, and one interpretation given to the world and all experiences here. In this shared purpose is one judgment shared by everyone and everything you see. You do not have to judge, for you have learned one meaning has been given everything, and you are glad to see it everywhere. It cannot change *because* you would perceive it everywhere, unchanged by circumstance. And so you offer it to all events, and let them offer you stability.

Even midst the ego's world of multiplicity, we can see the Holy Spirit's single purpose of forgiveness in all things, reducing illusion's multitudinous forms to its single content of fear. Hence the highly unstable world of our personal experience is changed into the solid guarantor of salvation's promise. The first principle of miracles ensures that our lives become simple: many forms, one content; many problems, one solution. The miracle judges all situations as providing the same opportunity to recall our projections, allowing the decision-making mind to choose again.

(VII.5:1) Escape from judgment simply lies in this; all things have but one purpose, which you share with all the world.

We have just seen that every meaning we give to the world comes from a judgment of what is good and bad for us, which may not be the same for others. Since we have differing perceptions of what we need, we hold different perceptions of what is around us. Nevertheless, the right-minded purpose of forgiveness—letting go of judgment—is the only meaning for the world that will release us from the ego's prison of hate and fear.

(VII.5:2-6) And nothing in the world can be opposed to it, for it belongs to everything, as it belongs to you. In single purpose is the end of all ideas of sacrifice, which must assume a different

purpose for the one who gains and him who loses. There could be no thought of sacrifice apart from this idea. And it is this idea of different goals that makes perception shift and meaning change. In one united goal does this become impossible, for your agreement makes interpretation stabilize and last.

Here again we see this important theme of sacrifice, so clearly articulated in Chapters 25 and 26. Jesus teaches us that "no one can lose for anyone to gain," which is "the rock on which salvation rests" (T-25.VII.12:1,7). The world's view of justice is that someone must lose for another to win; our happiness is best served at another's expense. As we have discussed, even though we share the common purpose of death we have different purposes, and these differ as to whom we want to die (and when and how) and whom to live. Yet forgiveness undoes this insanity of differences by realigning perception into the one meaning of shared rather than separate interests.

(VII.6:1-3) How can communication really be established while the symbols that are used mean different things? The Holy Spirit's goal gives one interpretation, meaningful to you and to your brother. Thus can you communicate with him, and he with you.

Even within the dream communication is possible because we speak the same language of the Holy Spirit's forgiveness. This does not necessarily mean we communicate with another person externally, for Jesus speaks only of the mind where we have mistakenly believed that others have to be sacrificed in the service of our specialness. Our teacher accentuates for us the ego's thought system of differences, its insanity corrected by the Holy Spirit's uniting the world's differing symbols into His single interpretation of the miracle.

(VII.6:4) In symbols that you both can understand the sacrifice of meaning is undone.

The symbols we understand are those of forgiveness: no one loses and everyone gains. You and I are brothers walking the same path. Consequently, it is not the case that I return home by climbing on

your shoulders, pushing you into the mud of guilt. The ego says this is so, because its birth was attended by the belief we have done this to God. However, lies do not establish reality, nor can they change the truth of our shared innocence.

(VII.6:5-18) All sacrifice entails the loss of your ability to see relationships among events. And looked at separately they have no meaning. For there is no light by which they can be seen and understood. They have no purpose. And what they are for cannot be seen. In any thought of loss there is no meaning. No one has agreed with you on what it means. It is a part of a distorted script, which cannot be interpreted with meaning. It must be forever unintelligible. This is not communication. Your dark dreams are but the senseless, isolated scripts you write in sleep. Look not to separate dreams for meaning. Only dreams of pardon can be shared. They mean the same to both of you.

The only dream we truly share is forgiveness (the meaning here of *pardon*), as its heart is the recognition of the inherent oneness of God's Son. In our healed minds we must bring everyone with us, for we cannot awaken from the dream at another's expense. To repeat this vital point, vision has nothing to do with form or behavior, but only with the mind's decision. Our healed perception undoes the ego's thought system that began with the insane notion that God had to be sacrificed so we could have the specialness we craved, believing it was necessary for our survival. Over and over our special relationships relive the ontological thought of sacrifice and attack. People are important insofar as they give us what we want, and this establishes meaning as the ego judges it. Consider infants once again, who perceive their parents as existing solely to feed and clothe them, keep them clean, loved, and happy. They are, in a phrase, gaping mouths demanding to be fed—physically and emotionally. Unfortunately we never outgrow this infantile way of interacting with the world, the reason Jesus continually refers to us as children.

In summary, the ego's purpose for the world is to have our specialness needs met. The Holy Spirit's shift in meaning helps us recognize that people's value does not lie in their special characteristics. His true perception looks past the ego's misperceptions of differences, seeing all relationships as offering the same opportunity to heal the mind's belief in separate interests. Our choosing vision instead of judgment marks the new beginning of deciding with the Holy Spirit instead of the ego, pain giving way to the joy of awakening to our reality as Christ.

The Process of Decision Making

We begin with the chapter's Introduction, and then continue on to its opening section, "Rules for Decision." Unlike other sections in our symphony's closing movements that are written in increasingly beautiful blank verse, this has a different tonality. While also in iambic pentameter, the language does not approximate the lofty poetry of its neighbors. Since its form and content are more akin to the workbook, it would seem that Jesus was providing Helen and Bill with a hint of the next book to be scribed.

The subject of "Rules for Decision" is our learning we have a mind with the power to choose and, needless to say, we would be happier choosing the Holy Spirit as our decision-making Partner. Afterward, Jesus returns to the beautiful language that carries us along to the glorious end to our journey, traversing the upper reaches of the ladder of Atonement. This section, then, may be seen as an interlude wherein Jesus tells us specifically what we need do to herald the "new beginning" of changing teachers, learning how joyful our days will become when we listen to his gentle guidance and instruction.

(In.1:1-5) The new beginning now becomes the focus of the curriculum. The goal is clear, but now you need specific methods for attaining it. The speed by which it can be reached depends on this one thing alone; your willingness to practice every step. Each one will help a little, every time it is attempted. And together will these steps lead you from dreams of judgment to forgiving dreams and out of pain and fear.

The clear goal is to learn the lesson of shared interests, no longer to pursue separate interests in having our needs met at the expense of God and His Son. The workbook, especially Part I, is geared toward our practicing the lesson for the day, each in its own way reflecting the theme of listening to the Holy Spirit's Voice instead of the ego's. Our new Teacher needs only our willingness to walk with Him through dreams of judgment, which He transforms into happy or forgiving dreams, the stepping-stones toward the ultimate goal of leaving dreams entirely.

(In.1:6) They are not new to you, but they are more ideas than rules of thought to you as yet.

Jesus is telling us that while we may have an intellectual understanding of these rules and principles, we need to put them into practice. He encourages us, when our thoughts have retreated to the ego's specialness, to be as diligent as we can to join with his lamp of forgiveness that shines away all judgment. Our daily practice facilitates this integration of intellect and experience that lifts us above the world and takes us home.

(In.1:7-8) So now we need to practice them awhile, until they are the rules by which you live. We seek to make them habits now, so you will have them ready for whatever need.

Jesus refers to *overlearning*, a psychological concept that appears later (T-31.I,III). It means learning something over and over until it becomes second nature. In this sense we have overlearned the ego's lessons, necessitating the mindful practice each day that will undo belief in the ego's lies. Jesus is asking us to be vigilant for the ego's temptations to choose separation and judgment instead of unity and forgiveness. To this end he provides seven rules for decision as aids in our practice, though there is but one; the other rules are there to help us when we forget the first.

(I.1:1-2) Decisions are continuous. You do not always know when you are making them.

Each instant our minds are deciding for the ego or Holy Spirit, decisions that take place outside time, although they are reflected in the temporal world we believe we inhabit. The purpose of this section, not to mention the Course itself, is to have us become increasingly aware of the mind that makes these decisions—not the body's brain—for the ego has kept this out of awareness. Exposing the veils of specialness so we may pass beyond them, *A Course in Miracles* helps us understand the world's purpose in keeping this decision-making part of ourselves hidden.

(I.1:3) But with a little practice with the ones you recognize, a set begins to form which sees you through the rest.

Restating this, we begin to realize we are not happy when we decide to see others as enemies, or when we make issues of nonexistent problems. A *set* is a psychological term (also used in mathematics) that here means *mindset*. The Course's goal, specifically in the workbook, is to help establish a mindset that sees all situations as opportunities to look within, our asking Jesus to help us recognize that what we perceived in the world is the illusory effect of the mind's decision. Therefore, our older brother has us begin the journey in the mindless body, where we think we are, bringing us via his miracle to the mind where we truly are.

(I.1:4) It is not wise to let yourself become preoccupied with every step you take.

In this practical and gentle guidance, Jesus is telling us not to be silly about our daily practice. It is not necessary to look at our every thought. For example, we need not ponder how we are buttering our breakfast toast. We butter the toast and move on with the day. Otherwise, we will unconsciously use this seeming diligence as a distraction, defending against the attack thoughts we should really be vigilant for, in order to see them

as the cause of the deleterious effects that daily plague our lives and bring pain to us and others.

(I.1:5) The proper set, adopted consciously each time you wake, will put you well ahead.

We open our eyes every morning with this happy thought: "This is another day I can attend Jesus' school of forgiveness." His school consists of the classroom that is our life, in which our newly hired teacher instructs us. He utilizes the curriculum of our special relationships to serve as the framework within which he shows us that what we experience outside is a projection of what we first made real inside. Without the outer forms of these lessons, we would have no possibility of recognizing the mind that has chosen wrongly. We become happy learners (T-14.II) because we now awake joyfully, awaiting the day's events that will teach us how to be genuinely happy. However, when our eyes open with the thought, "Damn, another dreary day dawns," it is because we do not want to learn Jesus' lessons, choosing misery instead. Yet even this can be a positive experience if we see it as focusing attention on our resistance to learning, which in turn shines a light on our need for help, as we continue to read:

(I.1:6-7) And if you find resistance strong and dedication weak, you are not ready. *Do not fight yourself.*

This last statement is in italics to highlight its extreme importance. Jesus is telling us not to struggle against the ego, but simply to acknowledge our fear: "My ego is with me and I will have a miserable day, which in my insanity I still cherish." If we can look at this wrong-minded choice without judgment, we will have done well.

Do not fight yourself: We do not force ourselves to take a step we are too fearful to take, a step we do not believe will help us. It follows, then, that we should not try to do something because we think it is spiritual, like meditating or doing a workbook lesson. Exerting gentle pressure can be helpful, but fighting against the ego merely makes it stronger, the meaning behind the famous scriptural injunction, "resist not evil" (Matthew 5:39). When we resist evil, we give reality to its illusory nature. If this lesson were truly learned there would be no wars, for resisting the ego reinforces its weak thought system of external power we magically think we can undo through opposition and force.

(I.1:8-9) But think about the kind of day you want, and tell yourself there is a way in which this very day can happen just like that. Then try again to have the day you want.

Jesus is not talking about the day we win the lottery or the object of our love smiles invitingly. Rather, he refers to the day in which we learn the happy lessons of what it means to be forgiven—the source of true joy.

Now the first rule:

(I.2) (1) The outlook starts with this:

Today I will make no decisions by myself.

This means that you are choosing not to be the judge of what to do. But it must also mean you will not judge the situations where you will be called upon to make response. For if you judge them, you have set the rules for how you should react to them. And then another answer cannot but produce confusion and uncertainty and fear.

Jesus cautions us about making decisions with the ego, an idea to which we will return at the end of the section. We think we know what is best for us, and then ask Jesus to help us get what we want. This is so even when our request seems altruistic, such as when we ask him to heal a loved one. Yet how can we truly judge what is in another's best interest, let alone our own? Such knowledge presupposes awareness of the Atonement path of everyone involved—past, present, and future (see, e.g., M-10). We arrogantly seek help *after* we have judged what the answer should be. And this must clash with the true answer of forgiveness that is contained in our right minds. Confusion, uncertainty, and fear are the inevitable result of such conflict and blatant insanity.

(I.3) This is your major problem now. You still make up your mind, and *then* decide to ask what you should do. And what you hear may

not resolve the problem as you saw it first. This leads to fear, because it contradicts what you perceive and so you feel attacked. And therefore angry. There are rules by which this will not happen. But it does occur at first, while you are learning how to hear.

We are all experts at this ego ploy. It is for this reason that Jesus tells us not to ask for the specific help that would keep us at the bottom of the ladder. At the beginning of one's journey it is certainly a good thing to experience Jesus being there to help on any specific level we believe requires his help. Still, this will not take us very far, for when we ask for specifics we arrogantly tell him that we know the problem, and thus demand that he solve the problem we have defined for him. Given this, we can never recognize that the real problem is that *we believe we have a problem.* Since this is not the answer the ego wants to hear, it attacks us for betraying our promise to it. Unaware of our fear of choosing against the ego, we project this perceived betrayal onto others whom we condemn for our secret sin, and whom we then fear for their presumed attacks on us.

The second rule:

(I.4) (2) Throughout the day, at any time you think of it and have a quiet moment for reflection, tell yourself again the kind of day you want; the feelings you would have, the things you want to happen to you, and the things you would experience, and say:

If I make no decisions by myself, this is the day that will be given me.

These two procedures, practiced well, will serve to let you be directed without fear, for opposition will not first arise and then become a problem in itself.

It cannot be said too often that Jesus is not talking about form, like wanting to gain a promotion at work or have a relationship evolve as we wish. His focus is always on our state of mind, since that is all there is. Even midst a raucous ego attack we can remember that if we are feeling angry, anxious, or hurt, it must be what we have chosen to feel because it is our dream. This awareness comes from the place of sanity in our minds that realizes this was not a good decision. In this way, the cause of fear—our belief in separation—is undone through our choice for Jesus and his peace in place of the ego's thought system of conflict and death.

(I.5:1-3) But there will still be times when you have judged already. Now the answer will provoke attack, unless you quickly straighten out your mind to want an answer that will work. Be certain this has happened if you feel yourself unwilling to sit by and ask to have the answer given you.

We need to be aware of how much we do not want Jesus' answer, but sneakily want *our* answers to *our* questions under the guise of asking for his help. We can say that for our egos Jesus is the puppet and we the ventriloquist, throwing his voice so that the dummy will mouth the special answer that was secretly dictated and hidden from view. The more conscious we can be of this subtle ego dynamic, the easier it will be to drop our defenses against love, accepting that our specialness does not work and that his answer alone is what we truly want.

(I.5:4-5) This means you have decided by yourself, and can not see the question. Now you need a quick restorative before you ask again.

We can see how the rules that follow the first are attempts to return us to the original rule of making a decision with the Holy Spirit rather than the ego. It is important that the discomfort of our wrong-minded choice not be rationalized, but looked at for the mistake it was. Only then can our minds be restored to sanity and reason.

(I.6:1-2) (3) Remember once again the day you want, and recognize that something has occurred that is not part of it. Then realize that you have asked a question by yourself, and must have set an answer in your terms.

This is a reference to asking the Holy Spirit for specific help: *our* question that demands *our*

answer. As this important point was overlooked by so many students, Jesus dictated *The Song of Prayer* to Helen a year after *A Course in Miracles* was published. He made the same point we find here, that his course was not about asking for specifics; i.e., asking that we be given parts of the song—our special idols—for the alleged purpose of remembering the non-specific song of love itself (S-1.I). This is the question we need ask ourselves: "Do I want a day in which my idols give me what I think I need, or a day that will help lead me beyond them? The third rule follows:

(I.6:3-6) Then say:

> *I have no question. I forgot what to decide.*

This cancels out the terms that you have set, and lets the answer show you what the question must have really been.

We come to recognize that if we are upset, it is because we chose the ego instead of the Holy Spirit. Recall the much earlier discussion of the steps Jesus provides when we find ourselves unpeaceful, beginning with "*I must have decided wrongly, because I am not at peace*" (T-5.VII.6:7-11). This enables us to shift attention from the specialness we thought we needed to be happy to our need to forgive, which helps us attain the peace we truly want.

(I.7) Try to observe this rule without delay, despite your opposition. For you have already gotten angry. And your fear of being answered in a different way from what your version of the question asks will gain momentum, until you believe the day you want is one in which you get *your* answer to *your* question. And you will not get it, for it would destroy the day by robbing you of what you really want. This can be very hard to realize, when once you have decided by yourself the rules that promise you a happy day. Yet this decision still can be undone, by simple methods that you can accept.

Anger arises because *our* day is not going right, even if we thought we did the right thing by asking Jesus' help. Because we believe our unhappiness is his fault, we must realize how we have set ourselves up. Entrapped by the ego, regardless of the answer we "hear," we will believe our guilt is real and punishment justified. Once again we have usurped the role of truth by adopting our own answer to our own question, slyly obliterating the true answer of forgiveness to the problem of separation. Experiencing the causal connection between our unhappiness and the mind's mistaken decision allows us to undo it, and leads to the fourth rule:

(I.8:1-2) (4) If you are so unwilling to receive you cannot even let your question go, you can begin to change your mind with this:

> *At least I can decide I do not like what I feel now.*

If we cannot really change our minds, we can at least realize we are not at peace. We may not be ready to go back to the decision maker where the mistake was made, but we can at least recognize we no longer wish to tolerate being depressed, angry, and fearful. This takes us to rule five:

(I.8:3–9:2) This much is obvious, and paves the way for the next easy step.

(5) Having decided that you do not like the way you feel, what could be easier than to continue with:

> *And so I hope I have been wrong.*

This is a key step. Remember Jesus' question to us: "Do you prefer that you be right or happy?" (T-29.VII.1:9). We all want to be right; otherwise we would not only admit being mistaken about a specific subject, but also about the original decision to separate. Being wrong makes our very existence a mistake, which is why we need to prove other people wrong, insisting we are right. This insanity provides seeming witness to the truth of our innocent and special self.

(I.9:3-4) This works against the sense of opposition, and reminds you that help is not being thrust upon you but is something that you want and that you need, because you do not like the way you feel. This tiny opening will be enough

to let you go ahead with just a few more steps you need to let yourself be helped.

This reverts to an early theme in our symphony where Jesus spoke of the conflict that develops when what we do conflicts with what we want (T-2.VI.5-6). For instance, even though we do the right and loving thing for another, we hate the one we are assisting; or we help someone out of a difficult situation, but resent the imposition we believe Jesus has placed on us. In other words, we really do not want to behave altruistically, but do so because it is the spiritual thing to do. Another illustration of this dynamic would be not wanting to do the workbook lessons, thinking they are silly and impractical, but since Jesus thinks we should, we do them. Nonetheless, our resistance breaks through, for example, when we forget the lessons throughout the day. It is obvious that healing can never work as long as we feel such conflict. We need to realize that what *we* are doing is silly and impractical, and accept that we would much rather be wrong so that we can be happy. This allows us to proceed to the sixth rule, on our way back to the first one that will heal us:

(I.10:1–11:4) Now you have reached the turning point, because it has occurred to you that you will gain if what you have decided is not so. Until this point is reached, you will believe your happiness depends on being right. But this much reason have you now attained; you would be better off if you were wrong.

(6) This tiny grain of wisdom will suffice to take you further. You are not coerced, but merely hope to get a thing you want. And you can say in perfect honesty:

> *I want another way to look at this.*

Having accepted the happy fact that our way does not work, we are open at last to the other way, even if we are not sure what it is. This motivates us to admit our mistaken decision and make the right one, deciding for the right teacher and his thought system of forgiveness. We are ready for the seventh and final step:

(I.11:5–12:4) Now you have changed your mind about the day, and have remembered what you really want. Its purpose has no longer been obscured by the insane belief you want it for the goal of being right when you are wrong. Thus is the readiness for asking brought to your awareness, for you cannot be in conflict when you ask for what you want, and see that it is this for which you ask.

(7) This final step is but acknowledgment of lack of opposition to be helped. It is a statement of an open mind, not certain yet, but willing to be shown:

> *Perhaps there is another way to look at this.*
> *What can I lose by asking?*

We are beginning to recognize where we have gone off course (pardon the pun), not only in wanting God to be wrong, but everyone else too. We sacrificed others so we would get what we wanted (*one or the other*), and now finally see how this has brought nothing except misery and pain. The willingness to be corrected has allowed us to reflect Helen and Bill's holy instant of agreeing to find another way. How, then, can we lose, for we realize at the very least that this other way cannot be any worse than our own? The peace we desire above all else can be achieved only through genuinely asking Jesus for help, the "single unequivocal call" he has long waited for (T-4.III.7:10).

(I.12:5-6) Thus you now can ask a question that makes sense, and so the answer will make sense as well. Nor will you fight against it, for you see that it is you who will be helped by it.

What else makes sense than to ask sincerely for help of the Teacher Who offers us only what we truly want? Having recognized the total insanity of seeking for the peace we could never find, we now ask for help in removing the judgments that stand in the way of our true seeking and true finding.

(I.13:1-4) It must be clear that it is easier to have a happy day if you prevent unhappiness from entering at all. But this takes practice in the rules that will protect you from the ravages

of fear. **When this has been achieved, the sorry dream of judgment has forever been undone. But meanwhile, you have need for practicing the rules for its undoing.**

Jesus is urging us to practice his teachings, which cannot be learned only on an intellectual level. The principle of forgiveness, or letting go of judgment, must be applied day in and day out, morning to night. This returns us to the first rule: we can make no decisions by ourselves and be happy. Deciding for the ego is the choice for judgment and fear, while taking Jesus' guiding hand liberates us from sorrow and pain.

(I.13:5–14:9) Let us, then, consider once again the very first of the decisions which are offered here.

We said you can begin a happy day with the determination not to make decisions by yourself. This seems to be a real decision in itself. And yet, you *cannot* make decisions by yourself. The only question really is with what you choose to make them. That is really all. The first rule, then, is not coercion, but a simple statement of a simple fact. You will not make decisions by yourself whatever you decide. For they are made with idols or with God. And you ask help of anti-Christ or Christ, and which you choose will join with you and tell you what to do.

Jesus here summarizes his discussion, returning us to the beginning. We cannot make decisions by ourselves because they must be made with God or the ego. This is an irrevocable rule of the split mind, for once we entertain the thought of separation, our split minds must choose between truth and illusion, a decision that determines all subsequent thoughts and actions. Incidentally, the motif of *a simple statement of a simple fact* is a favorite of Jesus' because it is used two other times (T-26.III.4:5; W-pI.77.6:7).

(I.15) Your day is not at random. It is set by what you choose to live it with, and how the friend whose counsel you have sought perceives your happiness. You always ask advice before you can decide on anything. Let this be understood, and you can see there cannot be coercion here, nor

grounds for opposition that you may be free. There is no freedom from what must occur. And if you think there is, you must be wrong.

Jesus explodes the world's myth that events occur beyond our control, that we are victims of forces outside our minds. The truth is that we alone are the dreamers of our world of dreams, and we can be free only of the decision for the adviser who brought us here and ensured that we would never awaken. To accomplish this happy fact of liberation, we need only return to the decision-making mind and choose a different Teacher. "How simple is salvation!" (T-31.I.1:1) We are ready to return to the second rule:

(I.16:1-3) The second rule as well is but a fact. For you and your adviser must agree on what you want before it can occur. It is but this agreement that permits all things to happen.

The mind first chooses the ego or the Holy Spirit as its adviser. From that decision everything follows, for it is our dream. Nothing can occur in our lives without our first having chosen a teacher. Do we choose dreams of attack and fear that reinforce the dream of separation, or happy dreams of forgiveness that will awaken us from these nightmares? No other choice is possible.

(I.16:4-7) Nothing can be caused without some form of union, be it with a dream of judgment or the Voice for God. Decisions cause results *because* they are not made in isolation. They are made by you and your adviser, for yourself and for the world as well. The day you want you offer to the world, for it will be what you have asked for, and will reinforce the rule of your adviser in the world.

Decisions are made "for the world as well" because minds are joined. Any decision we make strengthens those of others: either reinforcing their ego or helping them recognize that the wrong-minded decision was mistaken, our choosing the holy instant having made us a symbol of right-minded thinking. We cannot choose for others, but since we are one, our presence in the mind supports their decision making: God or the ego.

(I.16:8-9) Whose kingdom is the world for you today? What kind of day will you decide to have?

Here again we have returned to the original choice point where we decided for the wrong king and served in the wrong kingdom. The world of time and space is the effect of that decision, made not only once but every moment of every day, for time is not linear. By continually choosing the ego, we re-enact the unholy instant when "terror took the place of love" (T-26.V.13:1). However, when we realize that everything negative that happens in our lives is because our minds chose guilt, we can correct that cause by choosing forgiveness instead of judgment. Jesus is asking us to question ourselves: are we happy or upset, peaceful or conflicted? Very simply, he wants us to recognize that our experience of the day is the direct result of its source, the mind's decision for the Holy Spirit or the ego.

An interesting thing occurs between paragraphs 16 and 17: the step of deciding for the Holy Spirit is not articulated, though it is clearly implied. The happiness of forgiveness that was set into motion by this right-minded decision for the miracle is now our subject.

Forgiveness – The Miracle – The Holy Relationship

(I.17:1) It needs but two who would have happiness this day to promise it to all the world.

True happiness cannot be of the ego, because its illusory forms are fleeting and depend upon the excluding laws of specialness. What Jesus means by our having decided for the Holy Spirit is that we chose to undo the ego's thought system of separation that says our happiness depends on another's loss, that peace, happiness, and love come at another's expense—*one or the other*. Yet we learn from our teacher that happiness comes only from the principle of one *and* the other: "The ark of peace is entered two by two…" (T-20.IV.6:5); we lift the veil "together, or not at all" (T-19.IV-D.12:8); "Salvation is a collaborative venture" (T-4.VI.8:2). Incidentally, this characteristic of the holy relationship does not necessarily mean joining with another in form; for example, the object of our forgiveness may have died or no longer be physically present in our lives.

(I.17:2) It needs but two to understand that they cannot decide alone, to guarantee the joy they asked for will be wholly shared.

Recall that these words were originally meant for Helen and Bill, who were doing the Course together. It is rare to have a partner in such specific form, and this is irrelevant for our salvation. True joining is between the decision-making mind and the Holy Spirit, and in that holy instant we experience everyone as sharing the common purpose of awakening from the dream of separation and aloneness. Having joined with the Teacher of sanity, our minds can no longer justify the grievances that allowed us to be innocent victims of what the world seemed to do to us.

(I.17:3-5) For they have understood the basic law that makes decision powerful, and gives it all effects that it will ever have. It needs but two. These two are joined before there can be a decision.

The ego's system only needs *me*: When I join with the ego I join with myself, thereby excluding the Sonship and driving myself further into hell. On the other hand, to join truly with the Holy Spirit means that in my mind I have already joined with others. This is not contingent upon their joining with me, because if it were, I would merely be continuing the ego's dependence on special people. And so our joining with the Holy Spirit is reflected in the experience of sharing His purpose of forgiveness with the world.

(I.17:6-8) Let this be the one reminder that you keep in mind, and you will have the day you want, and give it to the world by having it

yourself. Your judgment has been lifted from the world by your decision for a happy day. And as you have received, so must you give.

The judgment we placed upon ourselves by choosing against God, projected outside us, is lifted by reversing our mistaken choice. We join with the world because *ideas leave not their source*: a united mind means a united world. Having made the decision to listen to Jesus, we are helped to look at our special relationships, all those people we made into enemies even though we may have cloaked them in the raiments of love. They were our enemies because we perceived them as having something we lacked, which our delusional thinking told us they took from us.

(II.3:1-4) Look once again upon your enemy, the one you chose to hate instead of love. For thus was hatred born into the world, and thus the rule of fear established there. Now hear God speak to you, through Him Who is His Voice and yours as well, reminding you that it is not your will to hate and be a prisoner to fear, a slave to death, a little creature with a little life. Your will is boundless; it is not your will that it be bound.

This is the happy result when we decide with the Holy Spirit rather than the ego. When we choose the latter, our hatred of others is made stronger, reinforcing the hatred of ourselves and binding us still further to the ego and its thought system of fear and death. Yet when we listen to Jesus, we embark on a new beginning, journeying up the ladder that takes us home instead of maintaining the inexorable descent to hell. Our elder brother helps us realize that by shifting perceptions of others we strengthen the same shift of ourselves. This frees us, along with the Sonship, to remember our limitless life as Christ, sharing in the eternal grandeur that is God's glorious creation.

(II.3:5-8) What lies in you has joined with God Himself in all creation's birth. Remember Him Who has created you, and through your will created everything. Not one created thing but gives you thanks, for it is by your will that it was

born. No light of Heaven shines except for you, for it was set in Heaven by your will.

These poetic words express the unity of creation that is unbroken by idle fantasies of separation and hate. Beyond them all is the unchanging Will that created one life, one light, one love.

(II.4) What cause have you for anger in a world that merely waits your blessing to be free? If you be prisoner, then God Himself could not be free. For what is done to him whom God so loves is done to God Himself. Think not He wills to bind you, Who has made you co-creator of the universe along with Him. He would but keep your will forever and forever limitless. This world awaits the freedom you will give when you have recognized that you are free. But you will not forgive the world until you have forgiven Him Who gave your will to you. For it is by your will the world is given freedom. Nor can you be free apart from Him Whose holy Will you share.

Jesus continues his joyous song of life and freedom, singing of the gifts forgiveness brings our thankful hearts that join in Heaven's unending hymn of oneness. Gone are grievances, softly washed away by the will that is liberated from the shackles of guilt and hate. Its chains unbound, God's healing blessing is freed to extend throughout the Sonship in its clarion call of release from the world of limits and pain.

(III.4:1) It never is the idol that you want.

When we listen to the right Voice and join with the One Who represents true joining, we recognize that we cannot join with idols of illusion. Furthermore, the peace and happiness we want above all else are unattainable when we indulge in the silly games of specialness.

(III.4:2-4) But what you think it offers you, you want indeed and have the right to ask for. Nor could it be possible it be denied. Your will to be complete is but God's Will, and this is given you by being His.

The idol offers us the completion we seek, but it is not as our erstwhile teacher (the ego) told us it would be. When we looked at "The Choice for Completion" in Chapter 16, we saw that this choice can be wrong- or right-minded. The ego tells us we choose to complete ourselves by joining with something outside that supplies our lack. Jesus, however, instructs us that we complete ourselves by joining with his love, the reflection of Heaven's Will.

(III.4:5-6) God knows not form. He cannot answer you in terms that have no meaning.

Once again we read, as we have frequently done in our symphony, the theme that God does not know about form or separation. Any attempt to bring Him into the dream is nothing more than the ego's insane attempt to make illusions real. This is totally antithetical to the purpose of the Course, which teaches us to recognize the illusory nature of the world and body, using them as the springboard for our return to the decision-making mind.

(III.4:7) And your will could not be satisfied with empty forms, made but to fill a gap that is not there.

The world's purpose is to fill the gap of separation with idols, the objects of specialness. They seek to cushion the pain of our guilt but merely solidify the belief the gap is real, all the while we magically hope it will disappear.

(III.4:8-10) It is not this you want. Creation gives no separate person and no separate thing the power to complete the Son of God. What idol can be called upon to give the Son of God what he already has?

This idol worship includes Jesus. As we make our way up the ladder, we must realize that Jesus too is not a separate person. At the beginning of the journey, as previously discussed, it is clearly important to experience him as a comforting brother whose love helps us move up the rungs, but we will never make it to the top as long as we see him as separate from us, having something we lack. This is why we are reminded that everything we see in Jesus is in ourselves: the love of God's Son is one, complete, and whole within itself—there *is* no hierarchy within the Sonship of God.

(III.5:1-2) Completion is the *function* of God's Son. He has no need to seek for it at all.

We simply accept our completion, another important symphonic theme. The ego counters this simplicity by having us seek and never find what we want, for the seeking itself reinforces our sense of lack and incompletion.

(III.5:3-4) Beyond all idols stands his holy will to be but what he is. For more than whole is meaningless.

As we saw before (T-29.VIII.8), we desired more than everything and told our Creator: "The everything of Your Love is not enough. I want more than perfect wholeness." The guilt over this perceived blasphemy is what we strive to deny, making a world in which we seek to find the completion that is beyond all idols, the title of this section.

We return now to "The Truth behind Illusions" and its treatment of idols as toys:

(IV.4:1-2) Reality observes the laws of God, and not the rules you set. It is His laws that guarantee your safety.

We set the rules of separation and specialness, demanding that God and the Holy Spirit follow them rather than our abandoning these insane laws to follow Theirs, which alone ensure true safety.

(IV.4:3-11) All illusions that you believe about yourself obey no laws. They seem to dance a little while, according to the rules you set for them. But then they fall and cannot rise again. They are but toys, my child, so do not grieve for them. Their dancing never brought you joy. But neither were they things to frighten you, nor make you safe if they obeyed your rules. They must be neither cherished nor attacked, but merely looked upon as children's toys without a single meaning of their own. See one in them and you will see them all. See none in them and they will touch you not.

Illusions obey the laws of chaos but, as Chapter 23 told us, these are not lawful at all and contradict

Jesus' laws of not fighting ourselves, not resisting evil, and above all, not making the error real. He urges us never to cherish or attack our special idols, or judge ourselves for having them. We need only look with his love beside us, seeing them as the children's toys they are. While idols may look real and seem compellingly attractive in their dances of hate, they are lifeless, their gifts of life and death illusory. To accord even a single meaning to an idolized object of our specialness validates all illusions, invalidating the truth that there is in fact no hierarchy of illusions. The theme of looking, central to the process of forgiveness, is repeated in the next paragraph:

(IV.5:1-8) Appearances deceive *because* they are appearances and not reality. Dwell not on them in any form. They but obscure reality, and they bring fear *because* they hide the truth. Do not attack what you have made to let you be deceived, for thus you prove that you have been deceived. Attack has power to make illusions real. Yet what it makes is nothing. Who could be made fearful by a power that can have no real effects at all? What could it be but an illusion, making things appear like to itself?

We return to the theme of appearance and reality, illusion and truth. The *forms* of the world engender fear only because our minds have chosen the *content* of fear. It is the mind's decision alone that makes us afraid, for illusions have no effect unless we believe in them. All power in the dream rests with the dreamer and not the dream figures; change the dreamer's mind and the perceived dream changes accordingly.

(IV.5:9-11) Look calmly at its toys, and understand that they are idols which but dance to vain desires. Give them not your worship, for they are not there. Yet this is equally forgotten in attack.

Recall one of the principal statements of the motif of looking at the ego with Jesus:

We are ready to look more closely at the ego's thought system because together we have the lamp that will dispel it.... Let us be very calm in doing this ... (T-11.V.1:3-4).

Jesus asks us not to fight against the ego or feel guilty, because when we "look calmly at its toys" they are seen to have no power. Once more, it is only belief in their reality that accords idols whatever strength we perceive in them. Consequently we should refrain from idol worship, but not because idols are evil. Their inherent nothingness can hurt no one, and it is only the need to worship them that is the threat. By our adoration we reinforce an illusion of nothingness: the insane belief we destroyed truth, substituting specialness in its place.

(IV.5:12-15) God's Son needs no defense against his dreams. His idols do not threaten him at all. His one mistake is that he thinks them real. What can the power of illusions do?

Jesus continues with this theme: deciding with the Holy Spirit means looking at the ego and its nothingness. Realizing we look at something that is only a toy brings gentle smiles to our faces, wherein we laugh at the madness in thinking that a nonexistent idol was real and important, hurtful or wonderful. In the end, an illusion remains an illusion and requires no defense or protection.

(IV.6:1) Appearances can but deceive the mind that wants to be deceived.

This important thought underlies the message of Jesus' course. The ego works because we want it to. We deceive ourselves because we do not wish reality to be true, and this nourishes the illusion that we live.

(IV.6:2-3) And you can make a simple choice that will forever place you far beyond deception. You need not concern yourself with how this will be done, for this you cannot understand.

This, too, is a recurring theme in our symphony. We cannot understand salvation because the mechanism for its attainment is beyond our comprehension. Indeed, the mindless body and brain were made so we would not understand the mind, let alone what heals it. We need simply accept that if we fulfill our function of forgive-

ness, looking without judgment, the ego's undoing will naturally follow.

(IV.6:4-6) But you will understand that mighty changes have been quickly brought about, when you decide one very simple thing; you do not want whatever you believe an idol gives. For thus the Son of God declares that he is free of idols. And thus *is* he free.

All we need do is look at the special relationship with our right minds, realizing it has not brought us lasting happiness or peace, which the ego's allies of guilt, fear, and sickness could never achieve. Until we accept this happy fact we will not realize the truth of Jesus' teachings, remaining imprisoned by the mind's decision to believe in lies. Yet at any instant we can choose again and enjoy our freedom from the ego's idolatry.

(IV.7) Salvation is a paradox indeed! What could it be except a happy dream? It asks you but that you forgive all things that no one ever did; to overlook what is not there, and not to look upon the unreal as reality. You are but asked to let your will be done, and seek no longer for the things you do not want. And you are asked to let yourself be free of all the dreams of what you never were, and seek no more to substitute the strength of idle wishes for the Will of God.

Salvation is not real, the reason it is a paradox; it reflects reality, but is not reality. When we look at the ego with Jesus we realize that illusions are not there to see. We begin by accepting that our interpretations were wrong, and those we perceived as enemies were our friends. At the journey's end we come to understand that the world itself is a dream, and we forgive what literally never happened. Jesus' smile will be our own as we watch the ego's grandiose wishes gently disappear into the Will that alone is grandeur, being the strength of God Himself.

(IV.8:1-2) Here does the dream of separation start to fade and disappear. For here the gap that is not there begins to be perceived without the toys of terror that you made.

The "here" is the holy instant when our minds decide against the "toys of terror," the special things that attract or repulse us. These special relationships are designed to cover the gap of separation so we will not look at it, for the ego tells us our fear is justified because God will destroy our sinful selves. When, however, we finally look within we see there is nothing there. To be sure, not only is there nothing in the gap, there is no gap: the separation was only an idle fantasy with no effect upon reality.

(IV.8:3-13) No more than this is asked. Be glad indeed salvation asks so little, not so much. It asks for nothing in reality. And even in illusions it but asks forgiveness be the substitute for fear. Such is the only rule for happy dreams. The gap is emptied of the toys of fear, and then its unreality is plain. Dreams are for nothing. And the Son of God can have no need of them. They offer him no single thing that he could ever want. He is delivered from illusions by his will, and but restored to what he is. What could God's plan for his salvation be, except a means to give him to Himself?

Forgiveness, the only rule for happy dreams, "quietly does nothing.... It merely looks, and waits, and judges not" (W-pII.1.4:1,3). We are asked to do no more. This gentle looking, which is the meaning of our asking help of the Holy Spirit, is how the gap ends along with its bitter dreams. We do not try to make dreams better, or attack and avoid them. They offer us nothing that we need, nor contain anything to oppose. To repeat, we do nothing except look at the substanceless ego without judgment, for this alone reveals the unreality of dreams and heals them. And as we are healed, the love in our right mind may or may not guide us to worldly action, but that is not our concern.

The beginning of "The Justification for Forgiveness" is the second place in the text where Jesus speaks of what he describes in *The Song of Prayer* as "forgiveness-to-destroy" (S-2.II). As seen earlier, He also discusses it in the workbook (W-pI.126.1-7; W-pI.134.1-5). The section opens with an echo of the discussion in Chapter 6 (T-6.in.1).

(VI.1:1) Anger is *never* justified.

Jesus does not say "Do not get angry," but "Do not justify it when you do." Anger asserts that someone is responsible for our lack of peace and sense of dis-ease. This is not the truth. Another might have done something reprehensible, but what does that have to do with us, a mind? If we believe a hateful deed can affect us, it is only because we gave it that power. The cause of our unhappiness can lie only in the mind, not in the body of another. How, then, can anger be justified?

(VI.1:2) Attack has *no* foundation.

Attack would have a foundation only if others did something to hurt us. Clearly we can be attacked within the dream, but attack is not ours unless we choose to join with the ego's dance of hate. Anger is our choice, not anyone else's, for we are not dream figures (bodies) but dreamers (minds), choosing between happy dreams and nightmares.

(VI.1:3-5) It is here escape from fear begins, and will be made complete. Here is the real world given in exchange for dreams of terror. For it is on this forgiveness rests, and is but natural.

We let go of fear by recognizing that everything we perceive outside is a projection of the mind's guilt-inducing attack thoughts. By returning us within, the miracle frees us to choose the right mind's Teacher, Who gently guides us from the ego's world of terror to the lawns of Heaven that constitute the real world. This state of total forgiveness is all that is natural in a world of illusion, reflecting Heaven's loving Oneness that is the only reality.

(VI.1:6-8) You are not asked to offer pardon where attack is due, and would be justified. For that would mean that you forgive a sin by overlooking what is really there. This is not pardon.

Here again, Jesus uses *pardon* as a synonym for *forgiveness*. When a two-syllable word is needed for the line's meter, the three-syllable *forgiveness* is sometimes set aside, though the meaning of the two is identical. Jesus speaks here of *forgiveness-to-*

destroy, wherein we say to another: "Even though you did something terrible, I forgive you." This makes the error real, and a truer statement would be: "I have projected the unforgiveness of myself onto you, and it is this I would forgive." The issue is never what others have done, but how we perceive what they have done. Perception is always interpretation, never a fact.

(VI.1:9-10) For it would assume that, by responding in a way which is not justified, your pardon will become the answer to attack that has been made. And thus is pardon inappropriate, by being granted where it is not due.

For example, if I already judged you as having committed a sin, how could I possibly let that perception go? Such a response would never be justified because at the same time I forgave you, believing I was following spiritual principles, I secretly established the reality of sin by perceiving you as attacking me. This can only be an interpretation born of my hidden belief that *I* have sinned. This passage from the workbook also speaks of forgiveness-to-destroy:

> When you feel that you are tempted to accuse someone of sin in any form, do not allow your mind to dwell on what you think he did, for that is self-deception. Ask instead, "Would I accuse myself of doing this?" (W-pI.134.9:2-3).

Incidentally, what we accuse ourselves of may not be the same on the bodily level of form, but will always be the same content of the mind's guilt over separating from love, which is the source of all judgment and attack.

(VI.2) Pardon is *always* justified. It has a sure foundation. You do not forgive the unforgivable, nor overlook a real attack that calls for punishment. Salvation does not lie in being asked to make unnatural responses which are inappropriate to what is real. Instead, it merely asks that you respond appropriately to what is not real by not perceiving what has not occurred. If pardon were unjustified, you would be asked to sacrifice your rights when you return forgiveness for attack. But you are merely asked to see forgiveness as the natural reaction to distress that rests on error, and thus calls for help. Forgiveness is the only sane response. It *keeps* your rights from being sacrificed.

The only natural thought in the ego's most unnatural world is forgiveness, wherein we recognize the inherent worthlessness of all things that move, change, and die. This vision is the basis for letting go of guilt and grievance, illusion and projection—the meaning of salvation. We never forgive what happened, for what could ever happen in God's perfect world? We merely forgive the Son of God's exchange of madness for truth in which he sacrificed his oneness. Thus the miracle gives equal response to all calls for help, as madness brought to sanity can only disappear in God's single answer: *what is false is false, and what is true has never changed* (W-pII.10.1:1; italics added).

(VI.3) This understanding is the only change that lets the real world rise to take the place of dreams of terror. Fear cannot arise unless attack is justified, and if it had a real foundation pardon would have none. The real world is achieved when you perceive the basis of forgiveness is quite real and fully justified. While you regard it as a gift unwarranted, it must uphold the guilt you would "forgive." Unjustified forgiveness is attack. And this is all the world can ever give. It pardons "sinners" sometimes, but remains aware that they have sinned. And so they do not merit the forgiveness that it gives.

Accepting the happy truth that only truth is true allows our dreams of spite to give way to the gentle light of the real world, which arises in our healed vision. When attack is no longer needed to defend against illusion, recognized as illusion, it disappears, and Jesus' gift of forgiveness dawns on the mind now desirous of nothing except his love. Could any grievance still hold sway, or false forgiveness cross our sinless minds? Christ's vision sees God's Sons as one, first in illusion and then in truth. Their sins were harmless illusory thoughts that lasted an instant, and then were gone in the blazing light of forgiveness that embraces the sinless reality of Heaven's one creation.

(VI.4:1) This is the false forgiveness which the world employs to keep the sense of sin alive.

If we accuse others of having done something to hurt us or those with whom we identify, we have made the sin of separation real. Any attempt at forgiveness, therefore, is only forgiveness-to-destroy. As a reflection of the Oneness of Heaven, however, true forgiveness recognizes that nothing has been done because nothing *can* be done. Illusions remain illusions, and the Love of God is unchanged by thoughts of specialness, separation, and sin. Most importantly, since His Love remains perfectly whole within our minds, It is perfectly whole within everyone.

(VI.4:2-9) And recognizing God is just, it seems impossible His pardon could be real. Thus is the fear of God the sure result of seeing pardon as unmerited. No one who sees himself as guilty can avoid the fear of God. But he is saved from this dilemma if he can forgive. The mind must think of its Creator as it looks upon itself. If you can see your brother merits pardon, you have learned forgiveness is your right as much as his. Nor will you think that God intends for you a fearful judgment that your brother does not merit. For it is the truth that you can merit neither more nor less than he.

Implicit in the above are the ego's faithful allies: sin, guilt, and fear. We accuse ourselves of unforgivable sin, so intolerable that we project it onto others. This merely reinforces the guilt that demands punishment from God, the ultimate avenger whom we can only fear. Yet this fearful thought of God's "justice" is made up because the real terror is that God knows nothing about us, knowing nothing about sin. Stated simply, He knows nothing about nothing because it is nothing, and it is the very nothingness of our self that we cannot accept. To defend this nothingness, the ego concocts its tale of sin and guilt that justifies our fear of God's wrath. To protect ourselves from our "Enemy," we flee into the world and believe we are safe. Still, we are pursued by the demons of projected guilt, and will believe they are there until we recognize that such perceptions are totally unjustified. We forever remain as God created

us, at one with creation, our Self, and our Creator. We all, without exception, deserve the pardon that reflects the love that is our natural inheritance as God's true Son.

(VI.5:1-3) Forgiveness recognized as merited will heal. It gives the miracle its strength to overlook illusions. This is how you learn that you must be forgiven too.

Forgiveness-to-destroy means that forgiveness is not merited: "You do not deserve it, but in my goodness I bestow it upon you anyway." This reinforces sin in both of us. Nevertheless, the Holy Spirit's kind forgiveness undoes your perception of sin because illusions have no effect. Further, since whatever I accuse you of is a projection of my perceived sin, recognizing the illusory nature of your sin generalizes to my own as well, happily forgiving us both.

(VI.5:4-8) There can be no appearance that can not be overlooked. For if there were, it would be necessary first there be some sin that stands beyond forgiveness. There would be an error that is more than a mistake; a special form of error that remains unchangeable, eternal, and beyond correction or escape. There would be one mistake that had the power to undo creation, and to make a world that could replace it and destroy the Will of God. Only if this were possible could there be some appearances that could withstand the miracle, and not be healed by it.

We are back to the theme that opened our symphony: *There is no order of difficulty among miracles.* Since every problem is the same, every correction must be the same as well. Indeed, this is why we hold on to grievances, able to forgive almost everyone for almost everything, but not *everyone* for *everything*. As long as one grievance remains outstanding—one spot of darkness to mar the light, one sin to change the changeless—we have affirmed the ego's power to undo creation's perfect Oneness.

(VI.6) There is no surer proof idolatry is what you wish than a belief there are some forms of

sickness and of joylessness forgiveness cannot heal. This means that you prefer to keep some idols, and are not prepared, as yet, to let all idols go. And thus you think that some appearances are real and not appearances at all. Be not deceived about the meaning of a fixed belief that some appearances are harder to look past than others are. It always means you think forgiveness must be limited. And you have set a goal of partial pardon and a limited escape from guilt for you. What can this be except a false forgiveness of yourself, and everyone who seems apart from you?

This central motif of healing continually returns now in our symphony: all illusions are equally unreal, and so there is no order of difficulty in their undoing. This holds not only for specific problems we believe are more impervious to the miracle, but for specific people we believe are beyond forgiveness' limitless healing. Either all illusions are illusions, or all illusions are real and efficacious. There can be no middle ground in salvation's promise: oneness *or* separation, truth *or* illusion, vision *or* judgment. It is never both. Every appearance of loss and pain disappears before the reality of truth's perfection, for God's Son remains the perfect creation of his Father's perfect Will.

(VI.7:1) It must be true the miracle can heal all forms of sickness, or it cannot heal.

If the miracle did not heal sickness in all its forms, there would be a hierarchy of illusions, the first law of chaos (T-23.II.2). Since there are no problems on the level of form, it does not matter whether the problem is large or small, an AIDS epidemic or a splinter in one's finger. All forms are illusory because they come from the thought of separation that is *the* illusion. Our teacher needs us to go through the day watching the temptation to give the world power to make us sick or well, to feel happy or sad, angry or fulfilled. Fragmenting the world into sources of pleasure or pain affirms the ego's laws, granting them powers past omnipotence, beginning with the power to destroy Heaven.

(VI.7:2-5) Its purpose cannot be to judge which forms are real, and which appearances are true. If one appearance must remain apart from healing, one illusion must be part of truth. And you could not escape all guilt, but only some of it. You must forgive God's Son entirely.

Forgiving all God's Sons, excluding no one, is what the ego defends against most vigorously, for it does mean the end of the ego's reign. To preserve its kingdom, the ego splits and fragments the unity of God's Son, forging compromises at every turn between truth and illusion: some people or situations are wonderful, some hateful, and some are wonderful sometimes and hateful at others. Though differentiation and distinction are powerful weapons in the ego's war of separation, they are easily passed by when we are "armed" with the miracle and its first principle.

(VI.7:6) Or you will keep an image of yourself that is not whole, and will remain afraid to look within and find escape from every idol there.

The ego's fear is that if we were to look within we would escape the ego's pantheon of idols, no longer needing specialness to protect us from the guilt that vanishes from the healed and forgiven mind. Hence the ego strategy to keep us forever mindless in a mindless world of separated bodies, our "permanent" home.

(VI.7:7-8) Salvation rests on faith there cannot be some forms of guilt that you cannot forgive. And so there cannot be appearances that have replaced the truth about God's Son.

Over and over Jesus returns to salvation's simple message: illusions have no power over truth. And since God's Son cannot be changed by guilt-driven dreams of death, the all-inclusive nature of forgiveness for what never happened is always justified.

(VI.8:1-4) Look on your brother with the willingness to see him as he is. And do not keep a part of him outside your willingness that he be healed. To heal is to make whole. And what is whole can have no missing parts that have been kept outside.

The great temptation is to keep some part of others outside our willingness that they be healed. Their being healed, through forgiveness, weakens the ego belief that we truly made a self that excluded God, and a world that ensures He would never enter our kingdom of specialness. We re-enact this insanity every time we exclude someone from our private space, and by failing to see the Sonship as whole we sustain the illusion that our special self exists.

(VI.8:5) Forgiveness rests on recognizing this, and being glad there cannot be some forms of sickness which the miracle must lack the power to heal.

Forgiveness is total because love, which it reflects, is total. The miracle's all-inclusive nature heals the thought that we could separate from perfect Oneness and fragment the wholeness of God's Son. The multitudinous forms of sickness that the sick thought of separation manifests are irrelevant, and therein lies the healing power of the miracle.

(VI.9:1) God's Son is perfect, or he cannot be God's Son.

This does not mean that part of God's Son is perfect. It means he is perfect *as one Son*. The world is simply a dream of fragmentation in which God's apparently imperfect Sons are separated. Although this makes no sense for it is not our experience, we reflect this perfection by no longer seeing others' interests as separate from our own. Our healed perception (vision) undoes the ego's belief of *one or the other*, as we learn that happiness cannot come at another's expense, any more than a country's peace can be secured at the price of another country's pain. We are being taught that the Sonship of God is one, and we grow into that awareness by practicing the idea that our interests are shared, for they are the same. This perfect idea opens the mind to remembering the perfection of God's Son.

(VI.9:2) Nor will you know him, if you think he does not merit the escape from guilt in all its consequences and its forms.

Our brother merits escape from guilt because we do. If we choose not to believe he deserves to be free, it is because we want to retain our guilt and renew the mind's vow to be faithful to the ego's dreams of separation and hate.

(VI.9:3-4) There is no way to think of him but this, if you would know the truth about yourself.

I thank You, Father, for Your perfect Son, and in his glory will I see my own.

This is what Jesus means by the workbook lesson, "Love is the way I walk in gratitude" (W-pI.195). We are grateful for every person and circumstance because of their capacity to be the screen onto which we project the guilt that is unknown to us. Having the Holy Spirit reinterpret our misperceptions of others, we recognize in what is outside us the mirror of what is inside, gaining access to the unconscious mind. Having returned from the far country of a mindless world, we are free to identify with the grandeur of God's Son instead of the ego's grandiosity.

(VI.9:5-6) Here is the joyful statement that there are no forms of evil that can overcome the Will of God; the glad acknowledgment that guilt has not succeeded by your wish to make illusions real. And what is this except a simple statement of the truth?

The theme of salvation's simplicity returns. We need to understand, with a gentleness and patience that respect the mind's fear, how relevant the above words are for our daily living. Though we have striven to fragment the Sonship, giving certain parts power to affect us, the Atonement corrects our insanity by quietly reminding us that illusions have no power over truth, separation cannot interrupt the eternal flow of Heaven's Oneness.

(VI.10) Look on your brother with this hope in you, and you will understand he could not make an error that could change the truth in him. It is not difficult to overlook mistakes that have been given no effects. But what you see as having power to make an idol of the Son of God you will not pardon. For he has become to you a graven image and a sign of death. Is this

your savior? Is his Father wrong about His Son? Or have you been deceived in him who has been given you to heal, for your salvation and deliverance?

All this comes down to the simple practice of looking at our brothers without the distorted sight the ego imposes on us. The complex veils of specialness, the ego's "laws" that govern these insane relationships, are all based on sin, ours and another's. Our special partners are idols of death the ego has substituted for the eternal Self we share with God's separated Sons. Becoming sane, we are no longer deceived in God's one creation, nor its one Creator. Truth has returned to our deluded minds through the forgiveness that saved us from illusion.

We now look more specifically at the miracle, as we turn back to "Changeless Reality":

(VIII.4:1-2) Reality is changeless. Miracles but show what you have interposed between reality and your awareness is unreal, and does not interfere at all.

The miracle does not do or change anything, but merely shows that we are the dreamer of the world of dreams, and what we dream is not true (T-28.I.1:1; T-28.II.4:2; 7:1). The Atonement teaches that our dreams had no effect upon the truth, nor did the changes we seemed to introduce into the mind affect our changeless reality as Christ.

(VIII.5:1-6) *Because* reality is changeless is a miracle already there to heal all things that change, and offer them to you to see in happy form, devoid of fear. It will be given you to look upon your brother thus. But not while you would have it otherwise in some respects. For this but means you would not have him healed and whole. The Christ in him is perfect. Is it this that you would look upon?

Again, the miracle does nothing except show us the healing truth, which is present in God's Son as his inherent sameness. Its vision allows us to no longer see our brothers through the fragmenting eyes of specialness. However, we cannot know we are the

same as long as we see others as having power to affect us. We answer "yes" to Jesus' question—"Do you wish to see our brothers as I do?"—if we choose to see ourselves as healed together, and "no" if we prefer to reinforce the ego thought system of separation, judgment, and attack.

(VIII.5:7) Then let there be no dreams about him that you would prefer to seeing this.

These are the dreams of specialness in which we cast another as the villain. This "other," be it a person, object, or microorganism, now has the power to affect us, meaning our bodies. Even when we seem to get what we want, this is hardly a permanent arrangement. Moreover, we retain our hatred of others because we believe that what we finally got from them was ours to begin with, and we needed it only because they first took it from us. This insanity reflects the ego's fourth and fifth laws of chaos (T-23.II.9-12), and acts as a seemingly successful countermeasure to the Holy Spirit's happy dreams of forgiveness.

(VIII.5:8-9) And you will see the Christ in him because you let Him come to you. And when He has appeared to you, you will be certain you are like Him, for He is the changeless in your brother and in you.

These words echo a beautiful passage from John's first letter, one of Helen's favorite scriptural quotations:

> Beloved, now are we the sons of God, and it doth not yet appear what we shall be: but we know that, when he shall appear, we shall be like him; for we shall see him as he is. And every man that hath this hope in him purifieth himself, even as he is pure (1 John 3:2-3).

John's reference of course is to Jesus, that when he appears we will realize we are like him. The passage here, and in the following lines, is adapted to mean that the way we see others is the way we choose to see ourselves, through the eyes of vision or judgment: the changeless, eternal Christ or the inconstant, ephemeral ego.

(VIII.6:1-3) This will you look upon when you decide there is not one appearance you would hold in place of what your brother really is. Let no temptation to prefer a dream allow uncertainty to enter here. Be not made guilty and afraid when you are tempted by a dream of what he is.

Recall Jesus' temporal ancestor Plato, who emphasized the difference between appearance and reality, and whose wisdom is echoed in this course. Jesus asks us to decide against letting the appearance of our brothers deceive us as to the reality of their Self, and in listening to his truth we turn against the temptation to listen to the ego's lies. This need to make others part of our illusory dreams expresses the wish to see the dream as real, and then hold them responsible for it. Such temptation is not a sin deserving death but a mistake that Jesus lovingly corrects for us.

(VIII.6:4-6) But do not give it power to replace the changeless in him in your sight of him. There is no false appearance but will fade, if you request a miracle instead. There is no pain from which he is not free, if you would have him be but what he is.

This freedom from pain exists only in the mind's perception. Although it does not necessarily mean that others will consciously accept the healing and experience this release, it does mean that the forms we attacked by seeing them as real, positively or negatively, will be gone from the mind because they came only from that mind's faulty self-perception. When we are right-minded, our defenseless presence tells others they can make the same healing choice we did. This allows them the freedom to choose to accept this healing at any point on their Atonement path.

(VIII.6:7-9) Why should you fear to see the Christ in him? You but behold yourself in what you see. As he is healed are you made free of guilt, for his appearance is your own to you.

We fear to see the Christ in others because this would absolve them of our projected sins, at the same time forgiving our own. This would cause our

special self to disappear, and rather than lose this specialness by letting it metamorphose into the sinless Self, we choose to maintain our sin by putting it in others and blaming them for our unhappiness and misery.

We return now to the theme of purpose with the section "The Only Purpose":

(V.1:1) The real world is the state of mind in which the only purpose of the world is seen to be forgiveness.

The real world is not a place. It is the state of the healed mind in which we have chosen, once and for all, to let the Holy Spirit be our Teacher. As our Adviser, He helps us look through His eyes so we no longer perceive the world's different purposes, the numerous ways in which we satisfy our special needs at the expense of others, concurrently trying to stop them from doing the same to us. Having come this far, we realize that our only purpose in being here is learning to forgive. Since forgiveness is an earthly reflection of the undifferentiated oneness of Heaven's love (W-pI.186.14:2), the ego and its specialness must disappear when our healing is complete.

(V.1:2-3) Fear is not its goal, for the escape from guilt becomes its aim. The value of forgiveness is perceived and takes the place of idols, which are sought no longer, for their "gifts" are not held dear.

One of Jesus' purposes for his course is to convince us that our idols of love and hate are of no value. He accomplishes this by showing how our special relationships reinforce guilt, which inevitably leads to pain. These idols of specialness, incidentally, include not only people and objects, but the worshipping of problems. It makes no difference to the ego if we idolize our own damaged body or another's, as long as we remain mindlessly certain that problems come from the world. This recognition of the valuelessness of the thought system of guilt and hate changes our perceptions, and is the happy result when we choose our beloved brother as our teacher instead of the ego.

We turn back to the real world as Jesus describes its characteristics for us:

(V.1:4) No rules are idly set, and no demands are made of anyone or anything to twist and fit into the dream of fear.

This succinctly describes our lives in the ego's dream of fear. We manipulate others so they will alleviate our guilt, yet we secretly hope they will not succeed in meeting our demands so we can be justified in hating them, blaming them for our discomfort. Such specialness reinforces the ego's thought system, leaving us trapped in its very vicious circle of guilt and projection. In addition, the same game we play with our special partners they play with us. This is the reason relationships never truly work here. Designed to bring genuine happiness to no one, they support the ego's goal of destroying love by strengthening the belief that guilt, sacrifice, and pain are salvific.

(V.1:5-6) Instead, there is a wish to understand all things created as they really are. And it is recognized that all things must be first forgiven, and *then* understood.

There is no way we can know anything until we release the blocks that prevent us from true understanding. These barriers are the thoughts of guilt that demand the body be made real as a defense, including the brain that was specifically made not to understand that all problems stem from the mind's faulty decision making. As long as the decision for the ego remains intact we can never achieve true understanding. Only forgiveness can release us from this "fool-proof" (though not "God-proof") prison of guilt and judgment (T-5.VI.10:6).

(V.2:1-7) Here, it is thought that understanding is acquired by attack. There, it is clear that by attack is understanding lost. The folly of pursuing guilt as goal is fully recognized. And idols are not wanted there, for guilt is understood as the sole cause of pain in any form. No one is tempted by its vain appeal, for suffering and death have been perceived as things not wanted and not striven for. The possibility of freedom has been grasped and welcomed, and the means

by which it can be gained can now be understood. The world becomes a place of hope, because its only purpose is to be a place where hope of happiness can be fulfilled.

There is no hope in the world, despite what the ego tells us. The world's only hope lies in there not being any hope here because the world is the projection of the ego's hopelessness. There is genuine hope in our minds, however, when we decide against this despair and choose the Holy Spirit as our Teacher. In that single decision for salvation we pass beyond the futile dreams of guilt and attack, recognizing they hold nothing that we want. Who except the insane would choose the pain of death when the joyful promise of eternal life is held out to them? No longer mad with guilt, we choose reason over madness and identify with the only hope possible. Happiness is now free to return to God's Son who once believed he suffered, liberating him from the thought that pain was a just desert for his sins.

(V.2:8) And no one stands outside this hope, because the world has been united in belief the purpose of the world is one which all must share, if hope be more than just a dream.

No one stands outside the Atonement principle, which says that the oneness of God's Son has never been fragmented. For our minds to be healed, all that is needed is that we share the purpose of healing with everyone and everything, undoing the ego's myth of separation and differentiation. Recall that only one teacher of God is needed to save the world: *us*. Whoever is reading those words in the manual (M-12.1) learns that the only teacher of God needed for salvation is the one reading them. When our minds are healed, we understand that this one teacher embraces the Sonship as a whole, with no one excluded from sharing in the certain hope of the Atonement.

(V.3) Not yet is Heaven quite remembered, for the purpose of forgiveness still remains. Yet everyone is certain he will go beyond forgiveness, and he but remains until it is made perfect in himself. He has no wish for anything but this. And fear has dropped away, because he is

united in his purpose with himself. There is a hope of happiness in him so sure and constant he can barely stay and wait a little longer, with his feet still touching earth. Yet is he glad to wait till every hand is joined, and every heart made ready to arise and go with him. For thus is he made ready for the step in which is all forgiveness left behind.

Although forgiveness is outside Heaven, it is needed as long as we believe in guilt, which keeps God's memory hidden behind its veil. We gladly wait for oneness to return to the Son's holy mind, for having attained the real world we are free of the chains of the ego's temporal world of dreams, for what is time but a device to imprison us in guilt? When we have accepted Atonement's truth, forgiveness having cleansed the mind of its illusions, the thought of healing is freed to bless all creation that still believes in separation. Joyfully, we prepare for God's last step:

(V.4:1-2) The final step is God's, because it is but God Who could create a perfect Son and share His Fatherhood with him. No one outside of Heaven knows how this can be, for understanding this is Heaven itself.

Forgiveness does not take us home, but simply reverses the ego's ladder the separation led us down. By helping us choose against the ego, like the miracle and salvation, it cancels out the interference our specialness put between us and the truth. Jesus is instructing us that we cannot understand reality or how forgiveness works, but we can understand that we will be happier when we forgive. Nothing else is required for our return to the Heaven we never left.

(V.4:3-5) Even the real world has a purpose still beneath creation and eternity. But fear is gone because its purpose is forgiveness, not idolatry. And so is Heaven's Son prepared to be himself, and to remember that the Son of God knows everything his Father understands, and understands it perfectly with Him.

The real world is the state in which our minds are permanently healed of the insane belief in separation. We know there is a dream, but know, too, that our reality is outside it; the state attained by Jesus and all enlightened beings. Their forms may appear to be here, but they understand that their reality is beyond the dream, totally unaffected by the world of illusions. However, unlike God, Who knows nothing of the dream at all, those in the real world need one more step—*God's last step*—to complete the journey. This "step" is a metaphor that marks the dream's end in which everything disappears, for there is no longer an individual self that is aware of unreality.

(V.5) The real world still falls short of this, for this is God's Own purpose; only His, and yet completely shared and perfectly fulfilled. The real world is a state in which the mind has learned how easily do idols go when they are still perceived but wanted not. How willingly the mind can let them go when it has understood that idols are nothing and nowhere, and are purposeless. For only then can guilt and sin be seen without a purpose, and as meaningless.

When we understand the world is nothing more than an idle dream, the mind lets its idols go. We realize that the purpose of sin and guilt is to reinforce the dream of separation in which the hero is our individual self. Yet without a belief in the dream's reality and a desire to remain in it, sin and guilt are meaningless and fall away. God's purpose of creation becomes the Son's only truth, and joy reigns supreme in the Kingdom for its prodigal son is home.

(V.6:1-2) Thus is the real world's purpose gently brought into awareness, to replace the goal of sin and guilt. And all that stood between your image of yourself and what you are, forgiveness washes joyfully away.

We see again that forgiveness does nothing except look at the illusion without judgment. In its gentle perception the world of illusion evanesces, and the mind is washed clean of guilt in the gladness of healing.

(V.6:3-5) Yet God need not create His Son again, that what is his be given back to him. The gap

between your brother and yourself was never there. And what the Son of God knew in creation he must know again.

All that happens is that we accept Jesus' Atonement message that the separation was an aberrant and illusory thought. Nothing has to be done because the knowledge God's Son had in creation never left him. Yet while he slept, the Holy Spirit held the Atonement in safekeeping and extended its healing throughout the Sonship, patiently awaiting its sure acceptance.

(V.7:1-2) When brothers join in purpose in the world of fear, they stand already at the edge of the real world. Perhaps they still look back, and think they see an idol that they want.

The theme of "looking back" has important biblical and mythological antecedents. For example, Lot's wife looked back and turned into a pillar of salt (Genesis 19:26; see also Jesus' words in Luke 9:62); Orpheus was told not to look back at Eurydice, and when he did, she died; those who looked at Medusa's face and did not turn away became stone. This motif runs through the rest of the section, in which Jesus tells us not to look back to the ego as we ascend his ladder of forgiveness: "Do not be tempted by the idols of guilt, fear, and hate. Do not try to analyze where you have come from, or think about where you are heading. Simply hold my hand and follow my daily instructions to choose the miracle and forgive." To end the dream of suffering, our older brother is asking us to seek his help in perceiving that relationships are mirrors of the mind's decision and not a means to complete ourselves; to recognize shared instead of separate interests as our only purpose for being in this illusory world of sin and fear.

(V.7:3-5) Yet has their path been surely set away from idols toward reality. For when they joined their hands it was Christ's hand they took, and they will look on Him Whose hand they hold. The face of Christ is looked upon before the Father is remembered.

This is our formula: We look upon the face of Christ in our brothers and remember God. We remember our Father and our Self by learning there are no barriers of separate interests to keep God's Son divided. Christ's face symbolizes the innocence that is restored to our awareness when we forgive. We thus forgive our partners in specialness not for what they have done, but for what they have *not* done. They have not taken away our innocence, nor have we, for nothing has come between us and the Love of Christ, God's sinless Son.

(V.7:6-8) For He must be unremembered till His Son has reached beyond forgiveness to the Love of God. Yet is the Love of Christ accepted first. And then will come the knowledge They are one.

The coming of knowledge is God's last step, which is beyond our concern. Earlier we were told that peace is the goal of this course, not knowledge (T-8.I.1:1-2), and peace inevitably comes when we forgive God's Son. This is immediately followed by the remembrance that God and Christ are one, eternally united in Their Love.

(V.8) How light and easy is the step across the narrow boundaries of the world of fear when you have recognized Whose hand you hold! Within your hand is everything you need to walk with perfect confidence away from fear forever, and to go straight on, and quickly reach the gate of Heaven itself. For He Whose hand you hold was waiting but for you to join Him. Now that you have come, would He delay in showing you the way that He must walk with you? His blessing lies on you as surely as His Father's Love rests upon Him. His gratitude to you is past your understanding, for you have enabled Him to rise from chains and go with you, together, to His Father's house.

One can well imagine Jesus' joy in singing to us of the end of pain. The choice was always ours, and taking his hand we are happily led through dreams of terror to the blessing of Heaven's love, which is our own. And with us go all who shared these dreams that seemed to imprison us in chains of despair and pain. Now they are gone, their place taken by the joined and grateful hands that take us home together as one Son.

(V.9:1) An ancient hate is passing from the world.

In "For They Have Come" (T-26.IX) Jesus speaks of the "ancient hate." The word *ancient* as it appears here and there does not refer to the world's dream, but to the mind's hate that existed in the ontological instant, outside time, when God's Son chose separation over oneness. Hate was then born into the world, a hate that is now coming to an end through our forgiveness, strengthening us as we journey up the ladder with Jesus as our teacher, guide, and friend.

(V.9:2-3) And with it goes all hatred and all fear. Look back no longer, for what lies ahead is all you ever wanted in your heart.

The idea of not looking back means not looking through the eyes of the ego, Jesus saying to us: "Do not be tempted by the lies the ego will tell you to root you in the dream. All of them reflect some aspect of specialness and pain that keeps the Sonship divided within itself and separate from its Source. Yet all your heart ever truly wished for was to be at peace in its home in God."

(V.9:4-12) Give up the world! But not to sacrifice. You never wanted it. What happiness have you sought here that did not bring you pain? What moment of content has not been bought at fearful price in coins of suffering? Joy has no cost. It is your sacred right, and what you pay for is not happiness. Be speeded on your way by honesty, and let not your experiences here deceive in retrospect. They were not free from bitter cost and joyless consequence.

We are not told to give up the world because it is evil, but because we recognize its inherent nothingness. Ultimately we understand it offers nothing because it is nothing, and so the concept of sacrifice is meaningless. What can be sacrificed if it is not wanted, let alone does not exist? What has been lost when only the deceptive world of pain and suffering was our reality, its place gratefully taken by the truth of Heaven's joy?

(V.10:1-4) Do not look back except in honesty. And when an idol tempts you, think of this:

> *There never was a time an idol brought you anything except the "gift" of guilt. Not one was bought except at cost of pain, nor was it ever paid by you alone.*

The cost of guilt is not only in us but in everyone, for we share the same pain and reinforce it in each other when we embrace it in ourselves. The honesty Jesus asks of us is admitting our desire for the pain that specialness brings because it allows us to point an accusing finger at another, thereby escaping punishment for our sin. Fulfilling this need is the underlying attraction of the special relationship, whose "gifts" of guilt and pain we no longer want.

(V.10:5-8) Be merciful unto your brother, then. And do not choose an idol thoughtlessly, remembering that he will pay the cost as well as you. For he will be delayed when you look back, and you will not perceive Whose loving hand you hold. Look forward, then; in confidence walk with a happy heart that beats in hope and does not pound in fear.

We want to be merciful to others because we want to be merciful to ourselves. If they pay the cost, we must as well because we are one in hate and in mercy. Recall that looking back means rushing to our "friends"—guilt, fear, attack, and pain—and looking forward is expressed by taking Jesus' hand and climbing the hope-filled ladder of forgiveness. We have already seen that while we cannot choose the ego for others, we can reinforce their wrong-minded choice that costs all of us the peace that is our natural inheritance and only joy.

(V.11:1-2) The Will of God forever lies in those whose hands are joined. Until they joined, they thought He was their enemy.

This symbolizes the shift in our thought system that comes when we choose the Teacher that says we cannot awaken from the dream by ourselves, at another's expense, for the rock on which salvation rests is that no one loses and everyone gains

(T-25.VII.12). When we hold ourselves apart from others, we make the separation real and this reminds us of the ontological sin that demanded we be punished by God, our mortal enemy.

(V.11:3-5) But when they joined and shared a purpose, they were free to learn their will is one. And thus the Will of God must reach to their awareness. Nor can they forget for long that it is but their own.

We remember the unity of our will with God's by not seeing another's interests as separate from our own. Even though we cannot know God's Will while in the world, we can indeed know Its reflection, understanding how it is the means of our return home. We recall that we feel better when we give up seeing others as enemies, recognizing that neither happiness nor pain comes from outside the mind. Learning that we all ascend together the ladder of awakening, as we together descended into hell, we gladly accept the steps of forgiveness we take with Jesus. At the ladder's end we remember we are not separate thoughts, having shared not only a common purpose but a common self. This remembrance leads us beyond the world of idols entirely to the one Self we both share and are.

Closing

As we close this movement we return to "Beyond All Idols," which beautifully adumbrates what we can expect when we recognize we are one Thought in the Mind of God, a Thought that has never left its Source:

(III.8) The Thoughts of God are far beyond all change, and shine forever. They await not birth. They wait for welcome and remembering. The Thought God holds of you is like a star, unchangeable in an eternal sky. So high in Heaven is it set that those outside of Heaven know not it is there. Yet still and white and lovely will it shine through all eternity. There was no time it was not there; no instant when its light grew dimmer or less perfect ever was.

This alone is our truth: the eternal spirit of God's Son is forever changeless. Its shining reality in God waits patiently upon our decision to awaken from the transient dreams of mortality. As the text says: "Love waits on welcome, not on time..." (T-13.VII.9:7).

(III.9) Who knows the Father knows this light, for He is the eternal sky that holds it safe, forever lifted up and anchored sure. Its perfect purity does not depend on whether it is seen on earth or not. The sky embraces it and softly holds it in its perfect place, which is as far from earth as earth from Heaven. It is not the distance nor the time that keeps this star invisible to earth. But those who seek for idols cannot know the star is there.

Jesus reminds us that the experience of separation from our Source is only an idle dream that our insanity chose to believe in. Yet this madness had no effect on our reality as God's perfect Thought of Love, held secure in the resplendent light of our Creator's Self, the Heavenly sky that holds God's singular star forever in His Heart.

(III.10) Beyond all idols is the Thought God holds of you. Completely unaffected by the turmoil and the terror of the world, the dreams of birth and death that here are dreamed, the myriad of forms that fear can take; quite undisturbed, the Thought God holds of you remains exactly as it always was. Surrounded by a stillness so complete no sound of battle comes remotely near, it rests in certainty and perfect peace. Here is your one reality kept safe, completely unaware of all the world that worships idols, and that knows not God. In perfect sureness of its changelessness and of its rest in its eternal home, the Thought God holds of you has never left the Mind of its Creator Whom it knows, as its Creator knows that it is there.

The changeless reality of Heaven's star is forever safe from the ego's insane dreams of despair and death. As the Thought that is our Self has never left its Source, how could a nonexistent world that never left its nonexistent source affect our perfect peace? Incidentally, this paragraph served as the inspiration for "Awake in Stillness," one of Helen's lovelier poems (*The Gifts of God*, p. 73).

(III.11) Where could the Thought God holds of you exist but where you are? Is your reality a thing apart from you, and in a world which your reality knows nothing of? Outside you there is no eternal sky, no changeless star and no reality. The mind of Heaven's Son in Heaven is, for there the Mind of Father and of Son joined in creation which can have no end. You have not two realities, but one. Nor can you be aware of more than one. An idol *or* the Thought God holds of you is your reality. Forget not, then, that idols must keep hidden what you are, not from the Mind of God, but from your own. The **star shines still; the sky has never changed. But you, the holy Son of God Himself, are unaware of your reality.**

We have long been preparing for the consummation of the journey, Chapter 31, when we at last remember Who we are, forgetting the ego's dualistic world of separation, loss, and death. Looking one more time at the idols of specialness, we say and mean: "This is madness." Our illusions softly fade into nothingness, leaving only the Thought God holds of us as truth—"The mind of Heaven's Son in Heaven is." We are almost home, wherein the radiant star of God's Love has quietly abided until our eyes could open to its eternal Self. We are ready for our symphony's concluding movement, the ultimate vision that passes us through the final veils of illusion to the truth of our reality.

Chapter 31

THE FINAL VISION

Introduction

We come now to the final movement of our symphony, appropriately entitled "The Final Vision." The last movement of a great symphony (Beethoven, of course, immediately comes to mind) is often a grand culmination of the preceding music, if not always in form, certainly in content. In Chapter 31 we find a confluence of the text's major themes in one glorious whole—a fitting conclusion indeed to this magnificent work.

We read at the chapter's end, "The journey closes, ending at the place where it began" (T-31.VIII.12:3), referring to the journey that began in madness when we believed we could be separate from our Source. We took this idea seriously, joined with the ego, and it was downhill from there. In Chapter 30 we were ready for a new beginning, to ascend the ladder the ego led us down: from the mind to the world, and then returning to the mind to choose again (recall that on the chart [see Appendix], the dot atop the split mind represents our decision-making self). The ego's thought system began when we turned away from the Holy Spirit, and culminated in making the world. Following the Holy Spirit's miracle we return to the choice point we had left, and make another decision. This is the predominant theme of this final movement, its closing section being "Choose Once Again." In addition to the chapter's review of our familiar symphonic themes, with sublime variation, we find ourselves back at the beginning: the decision maker, now filled with the wisdom that allows for the ultimate and irrevocable choice to end the dream and return home, where God "would have us be" (T-31.VIII.12:8).

The Atonement Principle

The Atonement principle begins this last stage of the journey. It is the Holy Spirit's response to the *tiny, mad idea,* telling us how the separation from God was an illusion, that what is an impossibility never happened. This simple statement of a simple fact caused the ego to develop its strategy to keep us from hearing God's Voice. We examine one statement that describes the insanity of the ego's belief that it could accomplish its goal:

(I.6) Is this a little Voice, so small and still It cannot rise above the senseless noise of sounds that have no meaning? God willed not His Son forget Him. And the power of His Will is in the Voice that speaks for Him. Which lesson will you learn? What outcome is inevitable, sure as God, and far beyond all doubt and question? Can it be your little learning, strange in outcome and incredible in difficulty will withstand the simple lessons being taught to you in every moment of each day, since time began and learning had been made?

The still, small Voice of the Holy Spirit carried with It the end of the dream, even as it seemed to begin. His Presence, the memory of Who we are as Christ, heralds the end of the self we have striven to uphold and sustain. As we saw at the beginning of our symphony, when presented with the voices of the ego and Holy Spirit, we preferred the ego's lies about the separation and chose it as our teacher. The ego's one fear, then, great enough to inspire a cosmos, was that we would recognize our mistaken decision to listen to the wrong voice. Coming to our senses at last, we would inevitably choose to correct the error.

Jesus is asking us to weigh carefully the outcomes of these two choices. He is teaching us to see how the ego's lessons bring only pain, while the choice for the Holy Spirit and His Atonement ensures our eternal peace, causing the ego to disappear back into the nothingness from which it came. This means that the individual self, which never existed in the first place, would "merely cease to seem to be" (M-14.2:12). The ego's need for self-preservation motivated its strategy of seeing to it that we never changed our mind by causing us to forget we even had one. Once we were mindless, changing the mind became impossible, for how can you change what you do not know you have? Consequently, the ego told us that remaining in the mind was extremely dangerous. Accepting its tale of sin, guilt, and fear, we believed that mindlessness was protection against certain destruction at the hands of an avenging God seeking to take back the life we imagined we stole from Him. This delusional thought that left our Creator for dead is what *A Course in Miracles* refers to as *sin*.

We have seen many, many times how *purpose* is everything, and we need to consider the insanity of this world and how the Holy Spirit is its correction. As we never paused to consider the total madness of the ego's lies, we blindly followed its pathways to hell. We never heard the deception in the ego's tale that we could protect ourselves from annihilation by leaving the mind and making a world in which to hide. The body, therefore, convinces us that the world we experience is true, the ego's strategy (its purpose), again, being to render us mindless with no memory of our source (the mind) and our Source (the Mind). A central metaphor in the Course is the dream, and Jesus wants us to remember we are the dreamer, not the dream figure, a mind, not a body. Yet in this world, having forgotten the dream's origin, we believe that what happens here is reality, and that the figures who come and go are real.

The Ego's Fear of the Atonement

We turn now to some statements, equally as powerful as others, of the role the body plays in the ego's strategy. Remember that the ego tells us we are sinful and if we remain in our minds, God will destroy us as punishment for what we did to Him. Giving its counsel how to be saved from this sin, the ego has us make a world, fragmenting the Sonship into trillions of bodies and projecting its secret sin and hidden hate (T-31.VIII.9:2) onto another. As the core of the ego system is the principle of *one or the other*, if I get rid of my sin, thereby making myself sinless, someone else will have it: it cannot be we are both innocent or guilty. Thus if I am innocent, you must be guilty; and if I can demonstrate your guilt because of sin, I will have proven my innocence and escaped God's wrath. While this madness seems to take place in bodies that hold grievances against other bodies, in truth it takes place solely in the insane mind; the world's dream being nothing more than a fragmented shadow of the mind's original and secret dream.

(III.1:5-6) You never hate your brother for his sins, but only for your own. Whatever form his sins appear to take, it but obscures the fact that you believe them to be yours, and therefore meriting a "just" attack.

This is another statement of projection. What we hate in another mirrors what we hate in ourselves, perhaps not on the level of form, but always on the level of content. The ego helps us escape Atonement by making sin real in the mind, and then seeing it in another's body that deserves the punishment we secretly believe should be ours.

(III.2:1) Why should his sins be sins, if you did not believe they could not be forgiven in you?

While the ego tells us our sins are unforgivable and beyond redemption, we can escape them by making believe, like the proverbial ostrich, they are no longer there because we do not see them. Having fallen for the ego's story, we fail to recognize that we do not see our sins because they have been repressed and projected. To be sure, we do see sin—*in everyone but ourselves*. This is why we are invested in attack and judgment, and resist letting them go.

(III.2:2-11) Why are they real in him, if you did not believe that they are your reality? And why do you attack them everywhere except you hate yourself? Are *you* a sin? You answer "yes" whenever you attack, for by attack do you assert that you are guilty, and must give as you deserve. And what can you deserve but what you are? If you did not believe that you deserved attack, it never would occur to you to give attack to anyone at all. Why should you? What would be the gain to you? What could the outcome be that you would want? And how could murder bring you benefit?

We need a teacher, his course, and ongoing instruction in order to learn that sin and evil are never outside us, despite what our sensory organs report. If we do see wickedness, meaning we made it real by giving it power over us, it is because we first made it real in ourselves. Rather than see it in the mind, we perforce see it everywhere else. How could we not when *projection makes perception*, one of the key themes in our symphony, is a fact of the split mind? Guilt demands punishment, and having decided for guilt, we must also believe our attack on truth deserves attack on us, justifying our counterattacks. Given our madness, Jesus asks us to reconsider the original decision that set off this cascade of aggression: "Is this really what you want, when the peace of God is yours for the choosing?"

We turn now to a specific description of the body. This closing movement in our symphony returns to the important theme of what the body is and the purpose it serves. It is not the seat of the problem, nor the answer; it is a simple projection of what we do not want to see and accept in our minds.

(III.3:1-2) Sins are in bodies. They are not perceived in minds.

Jesus does not mean this as truth, because as a thought sin is only in the mind. His words here reflect the ego's perspective as it carries forth its strategy of mindlessness, having us perceive sin as external (i.e., in the body).

(III.3:3) They are not seen as purposes, but actions.

Here, again, is the theme of *purpose*. As the foundation of the ego thought system, sin proves that the separation is real. It serves the even more insidious purpose of compelling us to flee the mind voluntarily. By learning from the ego of our sinfulness, we did not feel coerced into leaving for we believed that remaining in the mind meant clear destruction. Sin mobilized us into the action of becoming mindless and sinful bodies, ensuring that we would never change our minds and accept the Atonement.

(III.3:4-7) Bodies act, and minds do not. And therefore must the body be at fault for what it does. It is not seen to be a passive thing, obeying your commands, and doing nothing of itself at all. If you are sin you *are* a body, for the mind acts not.

This is the case when we follow the ego's strategy: we believe we have sinned and, denying this "fact," project our sinfulness onto others, denying there is a mind. We end up hating the body for what it supposedly has done to make us suffer. Needless to say, the *your* in "your commands" refers to the decision-making mind, the body's commander and source of the problem.

(III.3:8-11) And purpose must be in the body, not the mind. The body must act on its own, and motivate itself. If you are sin you lock the mind within the body, and you give its purpose to its prison house, which acts instead of it. A jailer does not follow orders, but enforces orders on the prisoner.

The ego arranges things so that the body is the jailer *and* the jail, the determiner of what we are and will always be. Recall our earlier discussions of Chapters 27 and 28, especially "Reversing Effect and Cause" (T-28.II). The body is the effect of the mind, which is its cause (as seen on the chart), but the ego reverses the order so it seems as if the body affects us: others are the cause of who we are, physically and psychologically, not to mention that our own body determines how we feel. This, of course, expresses the ego's strategy of convincing us that the body is autonomous and real, and we are mindless creatures enslaved by a cruel master we cannot control.

(III.4:1-5) Yet is the *body* prisoner, and not the mind. The body thinks no thoughts. It has no power to learn, to pardon, nor enslave. It gives no orders that the mind need serve, nor sets conditions that it must obey. It holds in prison but the willing mind that would abide in it.

Jesus presents the right-minded view of the body: everything is done on the level of the mind, and nothing on the bodily level. For example, if we do not like what a puppet does on stage, we do not assail, criticize, or fire it; we instead complain to the puppeteer who makes the puppet act and speak for it. Analogously, the body cannot be the problem, for it literally does nothing because it is nothing. Bodies simply do not exist—they do not live, they do not die, they are nothing. The mind alone is the cause of all the body thinks, feels, says, and does.

(III.4:6-7) It sickens at the bidding of the mind that would become its prisoner. And it grows old and dies, because that mind is sick within itself.

Our minds chose the body and made up the laws that govern it—the laws of birth and life, pleasure and pain, aging and death. How can the body cause our experiences when it simply follows the mind's program for it? Because this reality is not our belief, we need a voice of wisdom that comes from outside the body (the right mind) to explain its true nature. This theme has been discussed quite often in our symphony, and we see it enunciated again here in the final movement.

(III.4:8-10) Learning is all that causes change. And so the body, where no learning can occur, could never change unless the mind preferred the body change in its appearances, to suit the purpose given by the mind. For mind can learn, and there is all change made.

The learning that takes place in the mind is the sole agent of change. The body cannot learn because there is nothing there that *can* learn, it never having left its source in the mind. Being nothing more than an epiphenomenon of the mind's illusory thought system, the body is truly nothing. This central motif of our symphony goes hand in hand with the Course's emphasis on the decision-making mind and the body's inherent nothingness.

(III.5:1) The mind that thinks it is a sin has but one purpose; that the body be the source of sin, to keep it in the prison house it chose and guards and holds itself at bay, a sleeping prisoner to the snarling dogs of hate and evil, sickness and attack; of pain and age, of grief and suffering.

Our wrong minds program the body to be the source of attack, grief, and pain, as well as pleasure. When the mind places itself under the body's laws, we seem to follow them, though in truth we are under no laws but God's (W-pI.76). While this is clearly not the case in the world, where the body's laws hold sway, it is the all-powerful mind that gave its power to the body and became its slave. This makes it imperative that we remember that we are still the decision-making mind, which is the problem *and* the answer. Attaining this awareness, the prerequisite for awakening from the dream of hate and death, is the single goal of *A Course in Miracles*.

(III.5:2-4) Here are the thoughts of sacrifice preserved, for here guilt rules, and orders that the world be like itself; a place where nothing can find mercy, nor survive the ravages of fear except in murder and in death. For here are you made sin, and sin cannot abide the joyous and the free, for they are enemies which sin must kill. In death is sin preserved, and those who think that they are sin must die for what they think they are.

This is another succinct statement of the relationship between mind and body, subsumed under the larger theme of the ego's strategy to keep us from accepting the Atonement. By making us mindless bodies the ego ensures we can never change our minds and choose against it. Understanding this underlying purpose for everything, we need to see how it is applied in our daily lives wherein we continually search for bodily problems that need to be solved—seeking solutions for problems that do not truly exist. The mind's guilt rules the body that knows nothing of it, and we fear being joyous and free because in that experience there is no ego, specialness, or *I*. Death to the ego becomes our escape from pain, the ultimate sacrifice we insanely think of as joy. Yet true freedom and joy come only when we accept the Atonement and realize our sins never happened, meaning there is nothing to forgive or atone for.

Bringing forward this theme of seeking and not finding we proceed to "The Real Alternative." To repeat, once the ego made the world and body it drove us to find external solutions for external problems, seeing to it that we would never find them. This, of course, is why there has never been, and never will be peace in the world. Since the world's solutions entail winners and losers, and as egos we identify with the world, we cannot recognize that the only true solution is that no one loses and everyone wins.

(IV.1:1-4) There is a tendency to think the world can offer consolation and escape from problems that its purpose is to keep. Why should this be? Because it is a place where choice among illusions seems to be the only choice. And you are in control of outcomes of your choosing.

Once again we see the all-important theme of purpose. Because the world's purpose is to keep the real problem of guilt hidden and unsolved, it makes no sense to look to the world to solve problems that were made to distract us and keep us mindless. Here it seems that choices consist of one or the other: we will reside in place *a* or *b*, live with person *c* or *d*, take job *e* or *f*. We think happiness lies within these decisions, and conclude that when we are not happy it is because we decided incorrectly and need to choose again. However, no worldly choice will ever satisfy when we refuse to do the

one thing that will bring us peace: returning to the mind to choose a different teacher.

(IV.1:5) Thus you think, within the narrow band from birth to death, a little time is given you to use for you alone; a time when everyone conflicts with you, but you can choose which road will lead you out of conflict, and away from difficulties that concern you not.

We attempt to solve our problems through specialness, which takes many forms including eliminating the problem of unconscious guilt by killing another psychologically, or even physically. In our delusional thinking we believe we act in our best interests by getting rid of a problem perceived to be external. It naturally does not work that way, and we can see Jesus poking gentle fun at the importance we give to our very little lives.

(IV.1:6-8) Yet they *are* your concern. How, then, can you escape from them by leaving them behind? What must go with you, you will take with you whatever road you choose to walk along.

As long as we believe we are guilty egos, our fate as bodies *is* our concern. Denying this does not dissolve the concern but merely dismisses it from awareness. The ego and its strategy of mindless, endless, and insoluble problems remain with us until our minds choose against them. Salvation from all this conflict *is* very simple.

(IV.2:1-6) Real choice is no illusion. But the world has none to offer. All its roads but lead to disappointment, nothingness and death. There is no choice in its alternatives. Seek not escape from problems here. The world was made that problems could not *be* escaped.

The point of this section is that the world offers us endless possibilities for choice, but none of them truly works because their purpose is to keep us in the body, in life *and* death. Indeed, everything here exists for the purpose of preventing our return to the mind where, as the workbook tells us (W-pI.79, 80), there is only one problem (the belief in separation) and one solution (accepting the Atonement). This is the one alternative the ego never lets us consider.

It should be clear by now that the world conveniently provides us with enough subterfuges and camouflages so we would never go within—its fundamental purpose. The ego makes up one illusory problem after another, all of which stem from guilt we can never be free from; we can hardly escape a problem we unknowingly cling to. We think the problem is the guilt of others, impelling us to focus on their bodies in the magical hope we would escape from the mind's guilt we do not even know exists. Truly, nothing can ever work here because we are looking in the wrong place for the problem and its solution. A brilliant and most effective defense, to be sure!

(IV.2:7-9) Be not deceived by all the different names its roads are given. They have but one end. And each is but the means to gain that end, for it is here that all its roads will lead, however differently they seem to start; however differently they seem to go.

All worldly roads lead to death because nothing here lasts, another way of understanding why the world offers nothing. Then, too, by looking to the world for help, we reinforce the mind's guilt over having turned away from our inner Help, reminiscent of the original turning away from God, love, and eternal life.

"Self-Concept versus Self" is our next section, one of the most important in *A Course in Miracles*. Jesus saves some of his hardest-hitting passages for the end, and here we see depicted in no uncertain terms the ego's murderous strategy. The ego begins by telling us we are guilty for having committed the unpardonable sin of destroying Heaven, selfishly telling God His Love was not enough. We did not care that what we wanted had to be purchased at His expense, for we preferred our specialness to His perfect Oneness and Love. These thoughts constitute the secret dream, which we find intolerable because our guilt is so overwhelming. The ego advises us that we can be saved only by projecting our guilt, thereby keeping the separate identity we stole from God and giving away the sin. Others

now have it, establishing their guilt and our innocence, the insane hope being that God will see them as sinners and not us. By so doing we have our cake of separation and enjoy digesting the specialness it brings, while others are punished for our sinfulness. In fact, we live our lives compiling long lists of names, replete with details of the terrible things people have done to us and others, all with the purpose of convincing God to destroy them. No one born into the world escapes the guilt-driven burden of this vicious game of avoiding the punishment demanded by our sin.

The first part of this section is structured around the two faces of the ego's strategy, opening with the "face of innocence" that covers the sinful face of guilt.

(V.1) The learning of the world is built upon a concept of the self adjusted to the world's reality. It fits it well. For this an image is that suits a world of shadows and illusions. Here it walks at home, where what it sees is one with it. The building of a concept of the self is what the learning of the world is for. This is its purpose; that you come without a self, and make one as you go along. And by the time you reach "maturity" you have perfected it, to meet the world on equal terms, at one with its demands.

We claim we are who we are because of what the world has done to us, beginning with our birth. We did not choose to be born, for example, as our parents are clearly responsible for this; nor are genetic inheritance and environment our doing. The developing self is something the world has given us, and the meaning of our existence consists of mastering a life of defense and attack to preserve a fragile and vulnerable identity.

(V.2:1-3) A concept of the self is made by you. It bears no likeness to yourself at all. It is an idol, made to take the place of your reality as Son of God.

Though the words are not used here, Jesus refers to the ego's "parody" or "travesty" of God's glorious creation of Christ, God's one Son (T-24.VII.1:11; 10:9). The ego's substitute self is the idol we worship, a shabby illusion we claim is filled with the grandeur of the divine; a substitution for which we assert our total lack of responsibility.

(V.2:4-5) The concept of the self the world would teach is not the thing that it appears to be. For it is made to serve two purposes, but one of which the mind can recognize.

This is similar to what we read near the end of Chapter 27 where Jesus spoke of two levels of dreams: the mind's secret dream and the world's dream of the body (T-27.VII.11,12). The fearful world of murderous and sinful stalkers—abusing and betraying us—mimics the mind's thought system of sin, guilt, and fear. Most obligingly the world allows us to put on the "face of innocence," the culmination of the ego's strategy wherein our sinfulness is found in others and perceived by God Who will exact His vengeance on their sinful selves.

Here is the first of the two purposes served by our self-concept. As innocent victims have no recourse except to fight back because of what the cruel world has done to them, they cannot be held accountable for their acts of aggression:

(V.2:6-9) The first presents the face of innocence, the aspect acted on. It is this face that smiles and charms and even seems to love. It searches for companions and it looks, at times with pity, on the suffering, and sometimes offers solace. It believes that it is good within an evil world.

These "innocent" ones do not make the first attack, and when they do, it is justified because they were attacked first. This defenseless "face of innocence" justifies war and pre-emptive strikes against the wicked, personally and collectively, reinforcing its position by forging special alliances that defend good against evil, truth against its enemies.

(V.3:1–4:2) This aspect can grow angry, for the world is wicked and unable to provide the love and shelter innocence deserves. And so this face is often wet with tears at the injustices the world accords to those who would be generous and good. This aspect never makes the first attack.

But every day a hundred little things make small assaults upon its innocence, provoking it to irritation, and at last to open insult and abuse.

The face of innocence the concept of the self so proudly wears can tolerate attack in self-defense, for is it not a well-known fact the world deals harshly with defenseless innocence? No one who makes a picture of himself omits this face, for he has need of it.

What the ego never tells us is that we *want* to be treated badly—"Beware of the temptation to perceive yourself unfairly treated" (T-26.X.4:1)—so we can claim our innocence in the face of another's sin. Our attacks are just and re-direct God's wrath to the ones we made into sinners, attested to by the injustices perpetrated on our sinless heads. This insane defense is mandatory if the ego thought system is to survive. How else could our sin be preserved if not seen elsewhere? What better defense than to have God Himself share in our misperception? Cunningly we adopt the face of God's innocent Son, firmly establishing its reality by juxtaposing it with His guilty Son, perceived in an evil victimizer by a vengeful Father hellbent on his punishment.

(V.4:3–5:2) The other side he does not want to see. Yet it is here the learning of the world has set its sights, for it is here the world's "reality" is set, to see to it the idol lasts.

Beneath the face of innocence there is a lesson that the concept of the self was made to teach. It is a lesson in a terrible displacement, and a fear so devastating that the face that smiles above it must forever look away, lest it perceive the treachery it hides.

This underlying face is what the ego strives to keep hidden, the reason for its "face of innocence." The section will make perfect sense if we understand that these two faces pertain to *purpose*. We put on the "face of innocence"—making a world into which we are born as victims, innocent effects of what others have done to us—so others become the sinners that God will destroy. This truly makes us accomplices to murder. In fact, it is really we who are the murderers because our hidden face has set up the scenario of guilt, blame, and punishment that ensures our separated self is forever preserved as reality, while others pay the price for our immortality with their deaths.

(V.5:3) The lesson teaches this: "I am the thing you made of me, and as you look on me, you stand condemned because of what I am."

Note that this is the same theme, with different notes, that we saw at the beginning of Chapter 27: "'Behold me, brother, at your hand I die'" (T-27.I.4:6). We say to our special partners: "I am the abused, rejected, and suffering person you made. I am what you see, and as you look on my pain, know that your sin has damned you for eternity."

The following passage, which comes later in the section, incisively explains the purpose behind our suffering:

(V.15:8-10) If you can be hurt by anything, you see a picture of your secret wishes. Nothing more than this. And in your suffering of any kind you see your own concealed desire to kill.

This is the underlying face immortalized by Oscar Wilde in *The Picture of Dorian Gray*, the British writer's only novel. It tells the tale of a dissolute man who presents a beautiful and innocent face to the world, while his evil nature makes its way into the hideously ugly portrait of himself that he tries to hide in a closet. We are all Dorian Gray, for underlying our "face of innocence" is the face that says to our special love/hate partners: "I want you, who are insensitive to my pain, to be unfaithful, to abandon me, and to make me ill. In this way God will discover your sins (not mine!) and lead you to hell." This is our "concealed desire to kill."

One can readily understand why no one really likes this course, once it is understood, for who wants to scratch beneath the surface to look upon the hidden face of hate and murder? While this theme has appeared before, we see how Jesus saves his most forceful statements for the symphony's final movement. We return now to paragraph 5:

(V.5:4) On this conception of the self the world smiles with approval, for it guarantees the pathways of the world are safely kept, and those who walk on them will not escape.

"The [unforgiving] thought protects projection ..." (W-pII.1.2:3). Our guilt-driven face is protected by our attacks, which continue unabated as long as their cause remains concealed in the mind. This clever subterfuge preserves the ego thought system through denial and projection, as does the world that is its effect.

(V.6:1-5) Here is the central lesson that ensures your brother is condemned eternally. For what you are has now become his sin. For this is no forgiveness possible. No longer does it matter what he does, for your accusing finger points to him, unwavering and deadly in its aim. It points to you as well, but this is kept still deeper in the mists below the face of innocence.

These two self-concepts (sin and sinless), neither of which is learned in the world, are the essence of the ego's dream of separation. They are learned in the mind before we are born. The ego has us escape from the terrifying burden of our guilt through projection, so that others have our sin and will be killed instead of us, even if they did nothing wrong. We revel in world catastrophes and tragedies, and are even disappointed if the number of deaths from them are low. In our perversely vicious insanity, we like others to suffer because that proves God is punishing them instead of us. Though the dream is a total lie, within the illusion of separation and sin it hangs heavy on our hearts.

(V.6:6-8) And in these shrouded vaults are all his sins and yours preserved and kept in darkness, where they cannot be perceived as errors, which the light would surely show. You can be neither blamed for what you are, nor can you change the things it makes you do. Your brother then is symbol of your sins to you who are but silently, and yet with ceaseless urgency, condemning still your brother for the hated thing you are.

How ingenious! The ego escapes sin's hook forever, or so it seems, for its secret sin remains shrouded in the darkness beneath the "face of innocence," loudly proclaiming the sins of others as an unchanging and unredeeming reality. A villainous world cannot but arise from this hate, from which there is no apparent escape.

(V.7:1-5) Concepts are learned. They are not natural. Apart from learning they do not exist. They are not given, so they must be made. Not one of them is true, and many come from feverish imaginations, hot with hatred and distortions born of fear.

Yet there is escape, for concepts are not learned in a world over which we have no control, but in the mind that chose the ego as its teacher. Our decision makers made these concepts of innocence and guilt, preserving them through projection with the ego's world of hate protecting the concepts' unreality from ever being recognized.

(V.7:6-10) What is a concept but a thought to which its maker gives a meaning of his own? Concepts maintain the world. But they can not be used to demonstrate the world is real. For all of them are made within the world, born in its shadow, growing in its ways and finally "maturing" in its thought. They are ideas of idols, painted with the brushes of the world, which cannot make a single picture representing truth.

The maker of concepts is, again, our decision-making mind. "Concepts maintain the world," and the fundamental ego concept is the "face of innocence" purchased at another's expense. Although concepts do sustain the world of specialness, they cannot establish its reality (the Atonement principle). Idols remain idols, shabby substitutes for the truth with no more substance than a tiny wisp of smoke. The nothingness of the ego gives rise only to the nothingness of its images, regardless of their lure of palpable pleasure and pain. .

(V.8:1) A concept of the self is meaningless, for no one here can see what it is for, and therefore cannot picture what it is.

Once more Jesus reminds us that we do not understand purpose. The world's dream has taken its shape to convince us we are born innocent and

defenseless, and it is the cruel insensitivity of others that made us the killers we are. This justifies our hateful and defensive actions because evil was first done to us. Until we understand the purpose of seeing sin without and innocence within, we will never get beyond them to the Innocence of Christ that is our true inheritance as God's Son.

(V.8:2) Yet is all learning that the world directs begun and ended with the single aim of teaching you this concept of yourself, that you will choose to follow this world's laws, and never seek to go beyond its roads nor realize the way you see yourself.

The world is an obstacle because we made it to prevent us from returning to the mind, the origin of the self-concept. Moreover, our true reality, which is beyond the split mind entirely, has no concept as the non-dualistic Self cannot be conceptualized. To paraphrase the workbook: "Christ is, and then we cease to speak" (W-pl.169.5:4).

(VII.6:1-2) The concept of yourself that now you hold would guarantee your function here remain forever unaccomplished and undone. And thus it dooms you to a bitter sense of deep depression and futility.

Depression and futility develop because the self-concept we hold does not bring us happiness or peace. After a while we become tired of being the innocent victim who is always unfairly treated. The other shoe drops and we go on the attack. That becomes wearisome, too, because we are always on the defensive, vigilant that the world not do to us what we believe we did to it. Nothing happens here except the ego's projections of guilt, and the only thing that truly works is guilt's undoing through fulfilling our special function of forgiveness.

(VII.7:1) The concept of the self stands like a shield, a silent barricade before the truth, and hides it from your sight.

The purpose for making a "face of innocence" is to hide the face of the murderer, both designed to shield us from the mind's decision maker that would choose the Atonement. The world serves the purpose of being a huge distraction, and all that pertains to the body—its pains and pleasures—keep us in a perpetual state of mindlessness.

(VII.7:2-6) All things you see are images, because you look on them as through a barrier that dims your sight and warps your vision, so that you behold nothing with clarity. The light is kept from everything you see. At most, you glimpse a shadow of what lies beyond. At least, you merely look on darkness, and perceive the terrified imaginings that come from guilty thoughts and concepts born of fear. And what you see is hell, for fear *is* hell.

Everything here is hell because the world is seen through the eyes of fear, the defense against our mind's choosing love. *Projection makes perception*: having looked within and seen the darkness of guilt and fear, we see only the darkness of pain, suffering, and death in the world around us. If we do see some light and hope, it is often distorted by the veils of specialness that dash our hopes into the darkness of despair and disillusionment.

The theme of temptation is now prominent as we move slowly toward the symphony's consummation:

(VII.12:1-3) Whatever form temptation seems to take, it always but reflects a wish to be a self that you are not. And from that wish a concept rises, teaching that you are the thing you wish to be. It will remain your concept of yourself until the wish that fathered it no longer is held dear.

It is the wish to remain separated that gives rise to the concept of a guilty, sinful self, which is covered by the concept of an innocent self. This, then, is the great temptation: to listen to the ego's lies instead of the Holy Spirit's truth, the mind's mistaken decision that remains in force until we choose again.

(VII.12:4) But while you cherish it, you will behold your brother in the likeness of the self whose image has the wish begot of you.

Listening to the ego we choose to be sinful, which keeps our individual identity intact and the separation alive and well. To protect this concept of a sinful self we project it onto another, part of the ego's clever strategy of preserving its existence by keeping us away from the decision-making mind. This need for self(ego)-preservation is the root cause of everything in the ego system, in the mind and in the world.

(VII.12:5) For seeing can but represent a wish, because it has no power to create.

Remember the distinction Jesus makes between willing and wishing (e.g., T-7.X.4; also W-pI.73). *Willing* is equated with creating, while *wishing* is the ego's miscreating, a defense against our true function of creation. The Atonement teaches that the illusion of miscreation has no effect on the truth of our holy Self, for what we think we see with our eyes are merely shadowy fragments of the mind's illusory wish that God's Son be other than what he is.

The Mind – Learning

We shift gears and look at the heart of this chapter, if not *A Course in Miracles* itself: the power of our minds to learn. The ego made learning to keep us from truly learning, which means to remember the nature of the problem *and* its solution. Learning was used by the ego to establish a thought system that would drive us out of our minds, literally and figuratively. Leaving the mind, insane with guilt, we became mindless creatures that continued the insanity of separation and specialness. Learning to

undo this madness is the theme that opens "The Savior's Vision":

(VII.1:1-2) Learning is change. Salvation does not seek to use a means as yet too alien to your thinking to be helpful, nor to make the kinds of change you could not recognize.

Process is another major theme of our symphony. Forgiveness is not something we do quickly, leaping from a self of innocence and its underlying guilt into the arms of the Self, for which there is no concept. We need first to change our self-concept to a right-minded one that benignly reflects true innocence instead of the ego's false face of sin. Recall the end of Chapter 27 where Jesus comforts us that we do not directly awaken to reality from nightmares (T-27.VII.13). Rather, we go gently from nightmares to happy dreams, and only then to awakening. We learn at our own pace, not allowing fear to raise insurmountable obstacles to the inevitable change that is our salvation.

(VII.1:3-4) Concepts are needed while perception lasts, and changing concepts is salvation's task. For it must deal in contrasts, not in truth, which has no opposite and cannot change.

We again see Jesus explaining why *A Course in Miracles* is written as it is, replete with concepts of the ego as well as their undoing through forgiveness. All are illusory, for this course comes within the ego framework (C-in.3:1), using the world's dualistic language and concepts but with a new meaning. We are not asked to give up the false self. We are simply asked to change the self-concept we have. In lieu of seeing our self as built on the principle of *one or the other*, we begin to develop a self-concept that sees everyone sharing the same interest and need: to choose the Holy Spirit's sanity of the miracle as the means of undoing the ego's insanity of attack. While a forgiving self is an illusory concept, it is one that softly leads us on the journey that takes us beyond concepts entirely. Thus we learn to see all things as opportunities for unlearning the ego's lessons of guilt and judgment. Though not Heaven, these right-minded concepts are the quintessential stepping-stones that lead us there.

(VII.1:5-9) In this world's concepts are the guilty "bad"; the "good" are innocent. And no one here but holds a concept of himself in which he counts the "good" to pardon him the "bad." Nor does he trust the "good" in anyone, believing that the "bad" must lurk behind. This concept emphasizes treachery, and trust becomes impossible. Nor could it change while you perceive the "bad" in you.

We build up a concept of a "good" self at the expense of another's "bad" one, and our innocence is defined by the sins of others. We search out evildoers, bringing them to justice so *we* are not found wanting by God. We walk the earth with beady eyes, like starving dogs of fear sent out to find morsels of guilt (T-19.IV-A.12:5-7; 15:6). Successful in our search, we pounce on the sinners and triumphantly devour them, once again demonstrating our innocence for all to see. Yet the treacherous world we have made, forged by the mind's unconscious guilt, ensures that this innocence will be stolen again and again, necessitating further excusable attacks in self-defense.

(VII.2:1-2) You could not recognize your "evil" thoughts as long as you see value in attack. You will perceive them sometimes, but will not see them as meaningless.

It is because of this that we attack: we do not want to see what we believe to be our own evil, needing to attack it elsewhere. Occasionally we see our evil thoughts and think them real, overwhelming ourselves with doubt and hate. However, it does not matter whether we attack another or ourselves, for we must realize that all negative thoughts—inadequacy, failure, despair—are made-up defenses, as are our judgments of others. They are part of the same ego scheme to have our guilt be so real that we need something external—i.e., magic—to remedy the bad feelings we harbor within our minds. When we judge or attack, we cannot return to their source: the decision to see ourselves as guilty in order to keep God's Love away. Indeed, there is no better way to exclude Jesus than to attack. Again, the ego does not care whether we judge another or ourselves. Love and hate, in any form, can never coexist.

(VII.2:4-5) You cannot give yourself your innocence, for you are too confused about yourself. But should *one* brother dawn upon your sight as wholly worthy of forgiveness, then your concept of yourself is wholly changed.

This explains why forgiveness is the Course's basic teaching. We cannot change our minds because we do not know we have them. Still, we can be taught to change our thinking about others. By learning to see innocence in them and not evil, we correspondingly see the same right-minded goodness in ourselves.

We return now to "The Simplicity of Salvation," this chapter's opening section. Here at the very end of the text Jesus is gently remonstrating us, as he originally did with Helen, for complaining his course is too difficult. This is his answer to her and to all of us:

(I.1:1-5) How simple is salvation! All it says is what was never true is not true now, and never will be. The impossible has not occurred, and can have no effects. And that is all. Can this be hard to learn by anyone who wants it to be true?

Who could ask for anything simpler? What is true is true; what is false is false. Additionally, Jesus has shown us how to distinguish one from the other. Surely this cannot be difficult if we really want to learn, which is his whole point. Without specifically using the term, Jesus speaks of *resistance* as he points out why we have such trouble with his simple principle of salvation. Our discomfort is not because of him or his "difficult" course. It comes from the simple fact that our egos do not want us to learn the Course's easy lessons. He continues:

(I.1:6-10) Only unwillingness to learn it could make such an easy lesson difficult. How hard is it to see that what is false can not be true, and what is true can not be false? You can no longer say that you perceive no differences in false and true. You have been told exactly how to tell one from the other, and just what to do if you become confused. Why, then, do you persist in learning not such simple things?

These words can be infuriating if we delude ourselves into thinking we are faithful and diligent students of *A Course in Miracles*. We need to get in touch with the part of our minds that does not want to learn its simple lessons of salvation: reality is true, illusion false; forgiveness heals, attack is pain.

(I.2:1-6) There is a reason. But confuse it not with difficulty in the simple things salvation asks you learn. It teaches but the very obvious. It merely goes from one apparent lesson to the next, in easy steps that lead you gently from one to another, with no strain at all. This cannot be confusing, yet you are confused. For somehow you believe that what is totally confused is easier to learn and understand.

In effect, Jesus says to us: "There is a reason you do not learn my course, but do not blame me for your difficulty in accepting salvation. What I am teaching is simple and clear. The reason for your confusion is that you have identified with a thought system of confusion, which you learned from the ego. You cling to this identity and do not want to give it up, preferring specialness to forgiveness, judgment to salvation."

(I.2:7-8) What you have taught yourself is such a giant learning feat it is indeed incredible. But you accomplished it because you wanted to, and did not pause in diligence to judge it hard to learn or too complex to grasp.

Jesus is telling us we need look at the ego insanity we have learned, a complex thought system in which we turned our Creator upside down, turning Him from a loving Father into a hateful god. Furthermore, we took the glorious Self He created as spirit and distorted its purity, placing our deformed self in a body. Not only did we learn all this, we taught our self to make a world in which it could exist and survive, even deluding ourselves into thinking we could attain happiness and peace in this barren wasteland that is devoid of life. A giant learning feat indeed!

(I.3:1) No one who understands what you have learned, how carefully you learned it, and the pains to which you went to practice and repeat the lessons endlessly, in every form you could conceive of them, could ever doubt the power of your learning skill.

This, then, is Jesus' answer to Helen and to all of us. "Do not tell me you cannot learn this course. Look at what your incredibly powerful mind *has* learned." How can we argue? Navigating through this world is difficult, living in the body is a complicated achievement, and coping with our specialness needs is a daunting task. The principles of existence require incredible amounts of time and effort to master. "Of course," Jesus would continue, "you can learn what is so simple, especially when the last thirty chapters have explained that what is true is true, what is false is false, and how forgiveness corrects your mistaken learning." Jesus is not rebuking us, but helping us realize that our arguments to him are specious and unworthy of our powerful minds.

(I.3:2-3) There is no greater power in the world. The world was made by it, and even now depends on nothing else.

Here again we see how God had nothing to do with this world. Our decision-making minds made it, not just the world we perceive but the very world itself. When, accepting the Atonement for ourselves, we awaken from the ego's dream, the universe will disappear, just as when we open our eyes in the morning our sleeping dreams are gone.

(I.3:4) The lessons you have taught yourself have been so overlearned and fixed they rise like heavy curtains to obscure the simple and the obvious.

We discussed *overlearning* when we considered Chapter 30 (see p. 182). Again, it is a psychological/ educational term that describes having learned something over and over until it becomes habitual. We so overlearned the ego's thought system of sin, guilt, and fear that the obvious and simple truth became hidden from our awareness.

(I.3:5-6) Say not you cannot learn them. For your power to learn is strong enough to teach you that your will is not your own, your thoughts do not belong to you, and even you are someone else.

Since none of this is meaningful to a brain, conditioned to believe in time and space, we need to open ourselves to the fact that we indeed have a mind that has learned the incredible. This mind made the body, learned how to live in it and, even

more impressively, how to live with other bodies. Jesus is therefore more than justified in asking us why we cannot learn the simple truth that the thought system of separation is not real.

(I.4:1-3) Who could maintain that lessons such as these are easy? Yet you have learned more than this. You have continued, taking every step, however difficult, without complaint, until a world was built that suited you.

This is true on the macrocosmic level of the one Son who made the world, as well as the personal level. We dreamed a dream, writing a script of a life that suits us, the perfect form in which to demonstrate we are sinless victims of a victimizing world made up of bodies, families, countries, cultures, etc. All these are dreamt by the mind to root us in the "innocent" world of mindlessness.

(I.4:4) And every lesson that makes up the world arises from the first accomplishment of learning; an enormity so great the Holy Spirit's Voice seems small and still before its magnitude.

Think back to Jesus' earlier explanation of the making of the universe, how we projected the first error and made the world, whose purpose was to hide the mind that thought it. We again see how our master symphonist brings together the themes of his magnificent symphony, a glorious whole that is greater than the sum of its parts:

> You who believe that God is fear made but one substitution. It has taken many forms, because it was the substitution of illusion for truth; of fragmentation for wholeness. It has become so splintered and subdivided and divided again, over and over, that it is now almost impossible to perceive it once was one, and still is what it was. That one error, which brought truth to illusion, infinity to time, and life to death, was all you ever made. Your whole world rests upon it. Everything you see reflects it, and every special relationship that you have ever made is part of it.
>
> You may be surprised to hear how very different is reality from what you see. You do not realize the magnitude of that one error. It was so vast and so completely incredible that from it

a world of total unreality *had* to emerge. What else could come of it? Its fragmented aspects are fearful enough, as you begin to look at them. But nothing you have seen begins to show you the enormity of the original error, which seemed to cast you out of Heaven, to shatter knowledge into meaningless bits of disunited perceptions, and to force you to make further substitutions.

That was the first projection of error outward. The world arose to hide it, and became the screen on which it was projected and drawn between you and the truth (T-18.I.4:1–6:2).

(I.4:5-6) The world began with one strange lesson, powerful enough to render God forgotten, and His Son an alien to himself, in exile from the home where God Himself established him. You who have taught yourself the Son of God is guilty, say not that you cannot learn the simple things salvation teaches you!

This is the original dream of God's one Son: the secret dream that we sinned against God and then forgot Him and His wrath, establishing a separated self in exile to protect us from annihilation. Think again of the Adam and Eve myth that ends with God being the great Exiler Who punishes His children for their sin. The cosmic tale of sin, guilt, punishment, and death has had an extraordinary hold on the consciousness of Western man, for it contains the origins of his individual self. This very tall tale began with one simple lesson, and it is almost impossible to recognize in the complex nature of the universe the single mistake at its root, the one error that demanded a massive defensive system to protect God's Son from ever recognizing the illusion for what it is.

(I.5) Learning is an ability you made and gave yourself. It was not made to do the Will of God,

but to uphold a wish that it could be opposed, and that a will apart from it was yet more real than it. And this has learning sought to demonstrate, and you have learned what it was made to teach. Now does your ancient overlearning stand implacable before the Voice of truth, and teach you that Its lessons are not true; too hard to learn, too difficult to see, and too opposed to what is really true. Yet you will learn them, for their learning is the only purpose for your learning skill the Holy Spirit sees in all the world. His simple lessons in forgiveness have a power mightier than yours, because they call from God and from your Self to you.

Jesus is appealing to us now—as he has done throughout the text, but nowhere as cogently as here—to recognize the power of the mind. He is asking that we turn our minds over to him to be their teacher instead of the ego, instructing us in the proper use of learning. Though still an illusion, right-minded thinking will free us from the fantasies of rebellion, hate, and death that we have labored under from the beginning. Our teacher says to us: "I understand your fear, but do not try to justify it. Do not say your difficulty in learning this course is caused by its language, the "all-powerful" ego, or the sinful people who make forgiveness impossible. You are not learning my course for the simple reason that it frightens you, and you use the power of your mind to oppose its teaching." To say this one more time, Jesus does not shake a rebuking finger at us. He gently lifts the veil so we can see guilt and resistance for the illusions they are, and then see beyond them to the light of Atonement that dissolves the ego. The key to this process is the mind's power to decide, the overriding theme of *A Course in Miracles*.

The Decision Maker

Attention is focused now on what our learning skill is directed toward: the decision maker, represented on the chart by the familiar black dot at the head of the split mind. In the middle of the section

"Self-Concept versus Self," paragraphs 9 through 13, Jesus provides us with the clearest statement of the fact there is a decision-making agent in our minds. Even though he never uses the term *decision maker*, here or anywhere in the Course (except in the manual in a slightly different context [M-5.II.1:7]), he is referring to the part of the mind that decides between the ego and the Holy Spirit. This is the "someone" or "something" that comes before the concept of the self, and chooses to adopt the sinless "face of innocence" as defense against the sinful face of the murderer. Before we consider Jesus' argument that the decision maker precedes any concept (or face), we look at some specific statements to that effect:

(V.10:4) Who is, then, the "you" who made it?

(V.12:6) Yet who was it that did the choosing first?

(V.12:7) …someone must have first decided on the one to choose, and let the other go.

(V.13:2-3) Something must have gone before these concepts of the self. And something must have done the learning which gave rise to them.

"You," "someone," and "something" all refer to the decision maker, the architect of our self-concept; the part of the mind that chose the ego over the Holy Spirit, made the face of the murderer, and then the covering "face of innocence." These, then, are the most pointed statements in the text of the decision-making mind that chooses and learns, or better, follows the Holy Spirit and *un*learns the ego's lessons of separation and specialness. When Jesus says at the end of the text "choose again," he is addressing our decision maker. Which concept of the self will we adopt? Will we choose Jesus as our teacher, or continue to listen to the ego's voice of illusion? These are the only meaningful questions to think about as we turn to a more in-depth discussion of this core theme of *A Course in Miracles*:

(V.9:2-7) Let us consider, then, what proof there is that you are what your brother made of you. For even though you do not yet perceive that this is what you think, you surely learned by now that you behave as if it were. Does he react for you? And does he know exactly what would happen? Can he see your future and ordain, before it comes, what you should do in

every circumstance? He must have made the world as well as you to have such prescience in the things to come.

Jesus begins by having us examine the ego's underlying premise that projection works: *ideas do leave their source.* Can others really make us feel what they want us to feel? Are they god-like, omnipotent and omniscient, with the ability to know everything about us, including our actions and reactions? Are we truly innocent victims of the decisions of others, powerless to effect meaningful change in our lives?

(V.10:1-5) That you are what your brother made of you seems most unlikely. Even if he did, who gave the face of innocence to you? Is this your contribution? Who is, then, the "you" who made it? And who is deceived by all your goodness, and attacks it so?

Again, Jesus refers to the mind's decision maker that established the plan for demonstrating our innocence at the expense of another's sin. Jesus asks again: Can this be the case? And what, then, of our guilt, which continually denies the goodness we like to think is ours? To quote the workbook, "Peace to such foolishness!" (W-pI.190.4:1).

(V.10:6-11) Let us forget the concept's foolishness, and merely think of this; there are two parts to what you think yourself to be. If one were generated by your brother, who was there to make the other? And from whom must something be kept hidden? If the world be evil, there is still no need to hide what you are made of. Who is there to see? And what but is attacked could need defense?

This can be a difficult passage to follow, so I shall go through it carefully to clarify its meaning. The concept of the "face of innocence" is foolish because there are really *two* faces: the victim and the victimizer; the innocent effect of another's sin and the sinner who is the cause of our distress. And yet these two faces are already split off parts of a larger sinful self that our decision-making minds have chosen. In other words, there is the decision maker that identifies as a sinful self, and then fragments that self into sinless ("face of inno-cence") and sinful selves (our brother, the cause of what we have become).

Once again, Jesus asks us to consider that if our sinful brother "made us," it must be the decision-making self that made him, splitting off the sin it first made real. This self must continually strive to keep its guilty secret hidden from the innocent one it strives to be, not to mention the guilty person onto whom the sin has been projected. The above fact of the split mind belies the ego's conclusion that the world is evil. If that were so, there would be no need to protect the mind's belief that *it* is evil. Nevertheless, our secret sin and hidden hate, made real by the decision maker's identification with the ego, demands that we see evil all around us, but never in our innocent self that establishes that sin and evil are real *outside the mind*.

(V.11) Perhaps the reason why this concept must be kept in darkness is that, in the light, the one who would not think it true is you. And what would happen to the world you see, if all its underpinnings were removed? Your concept of the world depends upon this concept of the self. And both would go, if either one were ever raised to doubt. The Holy Spirit does not seek to throw you into panic. So He merely asks if just a little question might be raised.

The ego's strategy is again articulated, for it is the key to understanding our "face of innocence," let alone the purpose of the world. The mind must be kept in the darkness of guilt and attack in order to prevent it from realizing that the darkness is an illusion, with no power to extinguish Christ's holy light. In reality, though, all that would be extin-guished are the pseudo self-concepts with which we have identified, as well as the universe that arose to protect them. Despite this simple truth, we are not asked to do more than question the reality of the darkness, for that "little willingness" is enough to ensure the eventual dissolution of what never was.

(V.12) There are alternatives about the thing that you must be. You might, for instance, be the thing you chose to have your brother be. This shifts the concept of the self from what is wholly passive, and at least makes way for active choice, and some acknowledgment that interaction must have entered in. There is some understanding that you chose for both of you, and what he rep-resents has meaning that was given it by you. It also shows some glimmering of sight into percep-tion's law that what you see reflects the state of the perceiver's mind. Yet who was it that did the choosing first? If you are what you chose your brother be, alternatives were there to choose among, and someone must have first decided on the one to choose, and let the other go.**

As part of his gentle approach, Jesus encourages us to take small steps before the ultimate one of rec-ognizing that our decision makers chose an illusion, behind which stands the truth of our Identity as Christ. He guides us in the process that gradually leads us from seeing ourselves as the innocent vic-tim to the guilty victimizer. This opens the mind to understand there were indeed alternatives, inno-cence or guilt, and therefore there was something in us that chose between them. This is the decision maker, the "someone [who] must have first decided on the one to choose." And what it chose is what it perceives: *projection makes perception*.

(V.13) Although this step has gains, it does not yet approach a basic question. Something must have gone before these concepts of the self. And something must have done the learning which gave rise to them. Nor can this be explained by either view. The main advantage of the shifting to the second from the first is that you somehow entered in the choice by your decision. But this gain is paid in almost equal loss, for now you stand accused of guilt for what your brother is. And you must share his guilt, because you chose it for him in the image of your own. While only he was treacherous before, now must you be condemned along with him.

Again, "Something must have gone before." This "something" is the decision-making self that precedes the faces of sin and innocence, and it is imperative that we journey beyond both if we are to return to the Self. If not, we are condemned to the ego's imprisoning hell of guilt, in which everyone pays the price of suffering and death.

Revisiting the middle part of "The Simplicity of Salvation," we explore the two choices open to us and the effects of our decision. The decision maker chooses between the ego's guilt and the Holy Spirit's guiltlessness, from which two worlds arise. This refers only to the *perception* of these worlds, for what we see externally is a projection of what the mind has chosen.

(I.7:1-3) The lessons to be learned are only two. Each has its outcome in a different world. And each world follows surely from its source.

Remember, *ideas leave not their source* and *projection makes perception*. If we choose guilt, we will look out on a guilty world; if we choose guiltlessness, we will see only a guiltless world. It must be this way because there is nothing outside the mind, and the thought system we have made real within is what the world without shows us.

(I.7:4-8) The certain outcome of the lesson that God's Son is guilty is the world you see. It is a world of terror and despair. Nor is there hope of happiness in it. There is no plan for safety you can make that ever will succeed. There is no joy that you can seek for here and hope to find.

This is our familiar theme of seeking and not finding, since this "dry and dusty world" (W-pII.13.5:1) was made to thwart our desire for true success and lasting happiness. Jesus gives a similar albeit more elaborate description at the beginning of Chapter 13, when he describes the world as "the delusional system of those made mad by guilt" (T-13.in.2:2). It is essential that we look at the world through open eyes, recognizing it as a place of despair, loss, and death. If we deny its reality by seeing it through rose-colored glasses, thinking "all is as it should be," peace is just around the corner, and love is fluttering its wings as it hovers over us in blessing, we deny the mind's guilt that is the world's source. This is why it is essential to look with Jesus' non-judgmental vision as we interpret the world we see. If we truly believed things here were wonderful, we would believe things were wonderful inside. If that were the

case, we would not be here. The fact that we experience ourselves as bodies tells us things are not at all wonderful in our minds. Realizing this is the miracle that opens the door within so we can ultimately make another choice.

(I.7:9–8:1) Yet this is not the only outcome which your learning can produce. However much you may have overlearned your chosen task, the lesson that reflects the Love of God is stronger still. And you will learn God's Son is innocent, and see another world.

The outcome of the lesson that God's Son is guiltless is a world in which there is no fear, and everything is lit with hope and sparkles with a gentle friendliness.

We understand by now that Jesus does not mean this externally. We could have this right-minded shift while in a death camp in Auschwitz or Bosnia, or while dying of cancer. We would be looking out on a guiltless world because we would be seeing through the mind's guiltless vision. This makes the physical world irrelevant to vision since perception is interpretation, not fact (e.g., M-17.4:1-2). What alone matters is following the pathway of the miracle from the mindless to the mindful so we may choose the Son's true innocence over his presumed guilt. Once seen clearly the right choice is certain, for what can be stronger than the truth?

(I.8:2-3) Nothing but calls to you in soft appeal to be your friend, and let it join with you. And never does a call remain unheard, misunderstood, nor left unanswered in the selfsame tongue in which the call was made.

Although our eyes may see the same cruelty, suffering, and death as before, the healed mind, via our Teacher, reinterprets attacks as expressions of fear—calls for the love that has been denied and is believed will never return. This soft appeal is heard, even when in the form of a crazed killer, maniacal dictator, or a little child in terror.

(I.8:4-5) And you will understand it was this call that everyone and everything within the world has always made, but you had not perceived it as it was. And now you see you were mistaken.

Nothing outside has changed. The mind has merely chosen again. It is our learning that is different, and we cannot recognize this even as a possibility if we do not know we have a mind. And so we need a Teacher to reinterpret the world for us, through the miracle's "royal road" that leads us within so we may see the external as a projection of the mind's decision. We then walk the same world as before, "where starved and thirsty creatures come to die" (W-pII.13.5:1), but hear the desperate calls for help in everything we look upon. Everyone here is saddened by the hopelessness of existence, without possibility of returning home nor believing there is one to return to. Very simply, then, our right-minded purpose is learning to hear that call in *all* people, with no one excluded.

(I.8:6-8) You had been deceived by forms the call was hidden in. And so you did not hear it, and had lost a friend who always wanted to be part of you. The soft eternal calling of each part of God's creation to the whole is heard throughout the world this second lesson brings.

This is the essence of living in the real world wherein we know the world is a dream, understanding that its content is not hate but the fear of losing our special self. We cling to this identity, believing it is who we are, at the same time terrified it will be snatched from us as we snatched it from God. While some express this fear in socially acceptable ways, others in manifestly unacceptable ones, the call remains the same in spite of its disparate and deceptive forms. Our healed answer is always one: love saying to love that it simply be itself.

(I.9) There is no living thing that does not share the universal Will that it be whole, and that you do not leave its call unheard. Without your answer is it left to die, as it is saved from death when you have heard its calling as the ancient call to life, and understood that it is but your own. The Christ in you remembers God with all the certainty with which He knows His Love. But only if His Son is innocent can He be Love. For God were fear indeed if he whom He created innocent could be a slave to guilt. God's

perfect Son remembers his creation. But in guilt he has forgotten what he really is.

Who, knowing its consequences, would ever choose anything other than the memory of God's guiltless Son? Being one, the Sonship cannot be fragmented into guilty and innocent parts: if one member of the Sonship is guilty, we all are guilty; if we truly see Christ's innocence in one, we all must share His innocence. Guilt and fear are the ego's sick attraction to littleness, as forgiveness is the call that attracts us to our home in perfect love.

(I.10) The fear of God results as surely from the lesson that His Son is guilty as God's Love must be remembered when he learns his innocence. For hate must father fear, and look upon its father as itself. How wrong are you who fail to hear the call that echoes past each seeming call to death, that sings behind each murderous attack and pleads that love restore the dying world. You do not understand Who calls to you beyond each form of hate; each call to war. Yet you will recognize Him as you give Him answer in the language that He calls. He will appear when you have answered Him, and you will know in Him that God is Love.

This is our choice: the ego's thought system of guilt, fear, and hate; or the Holy Spirit's Atonement that heralds the end of death and our return to eternal life. Deciding for the latter means we see through Christ's vision, recognizing in each expression of hate the fervent call to be proven wrong: "Please show me there is another choice my mind can make to free me from the hateful hell I have made." Being right-minded, we respond with a gentle defenselessness that reflects the choice available to all God's Sons to remember the love that God created as Himself.

(I.11:1) What is temptation but a wish to make the wrong decision on what you would learn, and have an outcome that you do not want?

Here again is the theme of being tempted to hear the wrong voice, with the horrendous and painful consequences that eventually compel us to choose again: a different Teacher with a different outcome.

(I.11:2-10) It is the recognition that it is a state of mind unwanted that becomes the means whereby the choice is reassessed; another outcome seen to be preferred. You are deceived if you believe you want disaster and disunity and pain. Hear not the call for this within yourself. But listen, rather, to the deeper call beyond it that appeals for peace and joy. And all the world will give you joy and peace. For as you hear, you answer. And behold! Your answer is the proof of what you learned. Its outcome is the world you look upon.

As always, Jesus relies on our feeling miserable, having decided for the ego, as motivation for us to choose again. Recall: "You who are steadfastly devoted to misery must first recognize that you are miserable and not happy. The Holy Spirit cannot teach without this contrast, for you believe that misery *is* happiness" (T-14.II.1:2-3). Our Teacher lovingly contrasts our pain with His joy, appealing to us to recognize what our mistaken decision has wrought, asking: "My brothers, is this what you really want? Beyond your insane wish for separation is the eternal call of your Father, willing only that His Son return to where he never left. How much longer are you willing to endure the pain of being separate from your only happiness?" We need listen to our own call, for it is the Call of our Self to remember that we are our Self. What we hear and see within is what we will hear and see without: *projection* [or extension] *makes perception*, and Christ sees only Himself in all He looks upon.

We return to another section we examined earlier, "The Real Alternative." Jesus is teaching that the world offers no viable alternatives, for its choices are always among illusions. Real choice lies in the mind between two thought systems, only one of which is true:

(IV.3:1-3) There is no choice where every end is sure. Perhaps you would prefer to try them all, before you really learn they are but one. The roads this world can offer seem to be quite large in number, but the time must come when everyone begins to see how like they are to one another.

Most of us try one road after another after another, at least in our formative years. We strive mightily to make sense out of our world, seeing what works for us and what does not. In the midst of this insanity, Jesus gently informs us there is no hope here at all, for every road leads to death. On our hearing this, the ego not unexpectedly tempts us with despair:

(IV.3:4-7) Men have died on seeing this, because they saw no way except the pathways offered by the world. And learning they led nowhere, lost their hope. And yet this was the time they could have learned their greatest lesson. All must reach this point, and go beyond it.

We all must arrive at the point when we recognize that the world offers nothing ("The world I see holds nothing that I want" [W-pI.128]). This is the key that opens our heretofore closed mind to the next step. Recognizing that the world gives us nothing provides the opportunity to realize there must be something else. Instead of looking to the world, we look beyond it to the decision-making mind. This has been Jesus' purpose for us from the beginning, his using a different perception of our relationships to lead us within, the *sine qua non* for returning home.

(IV.3:8-10) It is true indeed there is no choice at all within the world. But this is not the lesson in itself. The lesson has a purpose, and in this you come to understand what it is for.

The purpose of learning that the world offers nothing is to return decision to its proper source in the mind. Otherwise we will become hopelessly depressed, having correctly recognized there is no hope here. If we do not realize there is hope elsewhere, suicide is the only sensible response to the absurd situation of our existence, the conclusion drawn by Camus in his brilliant essay *The Myth of Sisyphus*. There *is* hope, and our beloved brother leads us from the meaningless world to the decision-making mind that is the home of meaningful choice and the way out of hell.

(IV.4:1-2) Why would you seek to try another road, another person or another place, when

you have learned the way the lesson starts, but do not yet perceive what it is for? Its purpose is the answer to the search that all must undertake who still believe there is another answer to be found.

The purpose of the world is to learn there is no world; the purpose of searching and never finding meaningful answers is to understand why that is not possible in a hope-deprived world. This recognition leads us to understand that hope does not lie here, but only in the mind that can truly decide for change, and will.

(IV.4:3-8) Learn now, without despair, there is no hope of answer in the world. But do not judge the lesson that is but begun with this. Seek not another signpost in the world that seems to point to still another road. No longer look for hope where there is none. Make fast your learning now, and understand you but waste time unless you go beyond what you have learned to what is yet to learn. For from this lowest point will learning lead to heights of happiness, in which you see the purpose of the lesson shining clear, and perfectly within your learning grasp.

We waste time if we do not move on and learn there is indeed a mind, for that is where learning occurs. Brains do not learn as they merely carry out the program the mind has given them, which contains two alternatives: God's Son is guilty or guiltless. That is all. This simple lesson of the mind's power to choose and the body's inherent impotence suffices to lead us beyond the shadowy world of guilt's darkness to the blazing light of Heaven's truth.

(IV.5:1-3) Who would be willing to be turned away from all the roadways of the world, unless he understood their real futility? Is it not needful that he should begin with this, to seek another way instead? For while he sees a choice where there is none, what power of decision can he use?

Simply stated, the ego does not want us to remember the mind's power of decision. To ensure that we never will, it miscreates a mindless body

that finds itself stranded in a world, with our having no recourse except to accommodate to its shadow reality of sin, guilt, and fear in order to survive. We cannot know our true hope until we recognize the futility of the mind's mistaken choice for the ego and its world, which will never bring us happiness. Without such recognition, giving up on the world would feel like a sacrifice we would resent for the rest of our life.

(IV.5:4) The great release of power must begin with learning where it really has a use.

The mind's power of decision is of no use in the world because nothing is there to decide between: hell or hell, murder or murder. This is no choice. The only meaningful decision is between life and death, and life is found only in the mind through acceptance of the Atonement.

(IV.5:5) And what decision has power if it be applied in situations without choice?

We see once again the ego's purpose for the world, for we all go through years of meaningless searching for peace, happiness, and hope—all for nought. At this point, as we observed just above, contemplation of suicide is more than understandable. There *is* nothing here, and when we delude ourselves into thinking otherwise, we invite in disappointment and despair. The more quickly we learn that the world holds nothing for us, the more quickly we will be motivated to seek elsewhere, saying: "There must be another way." We need to watch our resistance to learning what is so very simple. Although we know deep within ourselves that the world does not work, we continue to pretend it does in the hope that despite the world having failed us before, tomorrow is another day. But how can the world not fail since it was programmed by the wrong mind to fail, and *ideas leave not their source*?

(IV.6:1–7:2) The learning that the world can offer but one choice, no matter what its form may be, is the beginning of acceptance that there is a real alternative instead. To fight against this step is to defeat your purpose here. You did not come to learn to find a road the

world does not contain. **The search for different pathways in the world is but the search for different forms of truth. And this would *keep* the truth from being reached.**

Think not that happiness is ever found by following a road away from it. This makes no sense, and cannot be the way.

The only meaningful purpose for the world is to learn there is only fear, suffering, and death to be found here. Regardless of the deceptive frames of specialness, Christ's vision enables us to see beyond the world's illusory alternatives to the true one of right-minded thinking. Although the ego made the moribund world to attack God and our Self, it can still serve the purpose of teaching us the truth: God's Son can never die, "for what has life has immortality" (W-pII.13.5:4).

(IV.7:3) To you who seem to find this course to be too difficult to learn, let me repeat that to achieve a goal you must proceed in its direction, not away from it.

Jesus is again saying that the reason we have trouble with his course is that we do not want to learn it. He is not judging us for our fear. He merely asks us to look at the resistance to becoming mindful instead of mindless. Acknowledging this we will not feel guilty, and hence will have no need to be defensive. This frees us to look at why we are afraid of his lessons. The first step in our healing, therefore, is accepting that we do not wish to be healed.

(IV.7:4-7) And every road that leads the other way will not advance the purpose to be found. If this be difficult to understand, then is this course impossible to learn. But only then. For otherwise, it is a simple teaching in the obvious.

We must never forget the Course's metaphysics that everything occurs on the mind level. *Everything.* Nothing happens here because there is no *here.* In fact, what is in the split mind is not here either. However, before we undo the illusion there is an ego, we must first move beyond the illusion of hope in the world, believing the Holy Spirit helps our bodily selves, or even that God is present in

materiality. Such belief has taken us in a direction opposite to Jesus' teaching. Following the arc of projection on the chart's left-hand side, which leads from the mind to the world, has prevented our learning his course that would have us follow the miracle's arc on the right-hand side, returning us to the mind and our salvation.

(IV.8:1-2) There *is* a choice that you have power to make when you have seen the real alternatives. Until that point is reached you have no choice, and you can but decide how you would choose the better to deceive yourself again.

Many times people engage in self-deception by attempting to use *A Course in Miracles* to make themselves happier in the dream, thinking this is Jesus' purpose. We need to remember that his unequivocal focus is on teaching the two alternatives our minds can choose between: the ego's separation and the Holy Spirit's Atonement.

(IV.8:3-4) This course attempts to teach no more than that the power of decision cannot lie in choosing different forms of what is still the same illusion and the same mistake. All choices in the world depend on this; you choose between your brother and yourself, and you will gain as much as he will lose, and what you lose is what is given him.

The theme of sacrifice returns: I win, you lose. Our choices here—in relationships, business, politics, etc.—have to do with maximizing gain and minimizing loss, always at another's expense. This zero-sum game of the ego virtually destroys the world's only true meaning, which is learning that we all win or we all lose: *together, or not at all.*

(IV.8:5) How utterly opposed to truth is this, when all the lesson's purpose is to teach that what your brother loses *you* have lost, and what he gains is what is given *you*.

This is the rock on which salvation rests (T-25.VII.12). Since we are the same, not different, we share the two thought systems of separation and Atonement. Further, since *projection makes perception*, if we see others as guilty we must have seen ourselves that way; but if we see their innocence this must be our self-concept as well. Throughout the final movement of his symphony, our composer crystallizes the focus of his curriculum: learning occurs only in the mind, with one of two teachers; and of the two, only one is sane.

These next three paragraphs are based on the theme "He has not left his Thoughts." They close the text's section and beautifully express the heart of the Atonement: the separation from God is an illusion because *Ideas leave not their Source* and, its corollary, *Their Source has not left Them.* This holy idea undoes the ego's thought that led us into a world of futility and death. Its inspiring beauty accompanies us as we gently walk with Jesus the only road, the pathway of forgiveness, that leads us home. This extended passage is a moving summary of all we have been considering, and needs no additional words from me:

(IV.9-11) He has not left His Thoughts! But you forgot His Presence and remembered not His Love. No pathway in the world can lead to Him, nor any worldly goal be one with His. What road in all the world will lead within, when every road was made to separate the journey from the purpose it must have unless it be but futile wandering? All roads that lead away from what you are will lead you to confusion and despair. Yet has He never left His Thoughts to die, without their Source forever in themselves.

He has not left His Thoughts! He could no more depart from them than they could keep Him out. In unity with Him do they abide, and in Their Oneness Both are kept complete. There is no road that leads away from Him. A journey from yourself does not exist. How foolish and insane it is to think that there could be a road with such an aim! Where could it go? And how could you be made to travel on it, walking there without your own reality at one with you?

Forgive yourself your madness, and forget all senseless journeys and all goal-less aims. They have no meaning. You can not escape from what you are. For God is merciful, and did not let His Son abandon Him. For what He is be thankful,

for in that is your escape from madness and from death. Nowhere but where He is can you be found. There *is* no path that does not lead to Him.

We turn now to the theme of our only real choice. This is not even a true choice since it is the decision between truth and illusion:

(VI.1) You see the flesh or recognize the spirit. There is no compromise between the two. If one is real the other must be false, for what is real denies its opposite. There is no choice in vision but this one. What you decide in this determines all you see and think is real and hold as true. On this one choice does all your world depend, for here have you established what you are, as flesh or spirit in your own belief. If you choose flesh, you never will escape the body as your own reality, for you have chosen that you want it so. But choose the spirit, and all Heaven bends to touch your eyes and bless your holy sight, that you may see the world of flesh no more except to heal and comfort and to bless.

Because spirit and flesh cannot coexist, the Word cannot be made flesh (T-8.VII.7:1-3). Their mutually exclusive states means there can be no interface between spirit and ego, Heaven and the world. Despite the ego's blatant lies, the separation we make real in our minds becomes the separated world we make real for our bodies. Yet the simplicity of choice remains: the healing comfort of Heaven or the futility of existence in a rotting body, doomed to die.

(VI.2:1-3) Salvation is undoing. If you choose to see the body, you behold a world of separation, unrelated things, and happenings that make no sense at all. This one appears and disappears in death; that one is doomed to suffering and loss.

If we make the ego real, the above is what we will see: the seemingly endless cycle of birth, life, and death. However, the ego's hopeless world of pain and despair is easily undone by salvation's miracle, which awaits our choice.

(VI.2:4-7) And no one is exactly as he was an instant previous, nor will he be the same as he is now an instant hence. Who could have trust where so much change is seen, for who is worthy if he be but dust? Salvation is undoing of all this. For constancy arises in the sight of those whose eyes salvation has released from looking at the cost of keeping guilt, because they chose to let it go instead.

Restating this, salvation does nothing except undo the ego thought system we chose, shining away its darkness with the unchanging truth of Atonement: God's Son remains as He created him. Our perceptions of each other must then remain constant, for they are based on the Holy Spirit's vision of a common goal that reflects Heaven's unchanging and perfect Oneness.

(VI.3:1) Salvation does not ask that you behold the spirit and perceive the body not.

This important statement highlights the little steps God asks us to take to Him (W-pI.193.13:7). We do not go from nightmares to reality, hatred to love. We are asked only to have the willingness to take the intermediate steps of forgiveness. Salvation asks us to understand that the body is not our reality, and though this perception is our only meaningful choice, it is not one we need make right away. Recall that the miracle does not awaken us from the dream, but only establishes that we are dreaming (T-28.II.7:1). It brings to mind the happy dreams of correction we can choose, shared rather than separate interests, without having to open our eyes before we are ready.

(VI.3:3-7) For you can see the body without help, but do not understand how to behold a world apart from it. It is your world salvation will undo, and let you see another world your eyes could never find. Be not concerned how this could ever be. You do not understand how what you see arose to meet your sight. For if you did, it would be gone.

Here again we hear Jesus telling us: "You cannot understand how salvation works because you do not know spirit, let alone the mind. However, I can teach you how and why to forgive your brother, and that what you see outside is a projection of what you have first made real within. In addition, I am teaching you to see that everyone shares the same need and purpose." If we would choose to learn Jesus' simple lessons of forgiveness, salvation would come easily to our minds and we would enter the real world of peace and joy.

(VI.3:8) The veil of ignorance is drawn across the evil and the good, and must be passed that both may disappear, so that perception finds no hiding place.

The ego thought system is dualistic, consisting of good and evil. We hide our decision-making self in evil and then project it onto others, leaving ourselves with the illusion we are good. *A Course in Miracles* presents us with the means of journeying past these misperceptions to knowledge, beyond both good and evil to rest in God.

(VI.3:9-11) How is this done? It is not done at all. What could there be within the universe that God created that must still be done?

All that is done is unlearning the ego's lies, thereby accepting the truth of our Self. Since nothing was ever done to need correction, what can there be to do? God, His Holy Spirit, and Jesus do nothing, but Their loving Presence in our minds stands for the Alternative, reminding us we can choose again.

(VI.4) Only in arrogance could you conceive that you must make the way to Heaven plain. The means are given you by which to see the world that will replace the one you made. Your will be done! In Heaven as on earth this is forever true. It matters not where you believe you are, nor what you think the truth about yourself must really be. It makes no difference what you look upon, nor what you choose to feel or think or wish. For God Himself has said, "Your will be done." And it is done to you accordingly.

The above paragraph prefigures Lesson 189, which restates this theme and ends in a lovely prayer to God (W-pI.189.8-10). While the ego's arrogance would think it knew the problem and the answer, our humility simply asks to be told what they are. This allows the ego's wishes to transmute into the right-mind's will of forgiveness, which in turn dissolves into the Will of God. Until that time love merely waits, unaffected by the whims of illusion that cannot change the reality of our Self, the Son Heaven established as the Christ of God.

(VI.5) You who believe that you can choose to see the Son of God as you would have him be, forget not that no concept of yourself will stand against the truth of what you are. Undoing truth would be impossible. But concepts are not difficult to change. One vision, clearly seen, that does not fit the picture as it was perceived before will change the world for eyes that learn to see, because the concept of the self has changed.

This is the Atonement theme once again. Regardless of the concepts we hold about ourselves or others—alternately sinful and "innocent"—the truth about us cannot be changed. Because illusions are so unstable it cannot be difficult to change concepts from guilt to true innocence, separate to shared interests. The right-minded illusion of a forgiving self then gives way to the memory of our Self, and vision disappears into the knowledge of God.

(VI.6) Are you invulnerable? Then the world is harmless in your sight. Do you forgive? Then is the world forgiving, for you have forgiven it its trespasses, and so it looks on you with eyes that see as yours. Are you a body? So is all the world perceived as treacherous, and out to kill. Are you a spirit, deathless, and without the promise of corruption and the stain of sin upon you? So the world is seen as stable, fully worthy of your trust; a happy place to rest in for a while, where nothing need be feared, but only loved. Who is unwelcome to the kind in heart? And what could hurt the truly innocent?

Salvation rests upon our decision: do we choose to see a forgiven world in which God's Sons are blessed as one, or a world of separate bodies in which the only decision is who is to be killed—ourselves or others—and when. The guilt-driven vulnerability we see within gives rise to a world of danger and death, while accepting the invulnerability of God's innocent Son engenders a world of learning in which our grateful minds joyously embrace the Holy Spirit's lessons of love, for they will happily lead us home.

(VI.7) Your will be done, you holy child of God. It does not matter if you think you are in earth or Heaven. What your Father wills of you can never change. The truth in you remains as radiant as a star, as pure as light, as innocent as love itself. And you *are* worthy that your will be done!

This lovely expression of the Atonement reinforces the end of guilt and remembrance of our Self: innocent, radiant with Heaven's light, and impervious to the delusional thoughts of sin and death.

(VII.14:1) Be vigilant against temptation, then, remembering that it is but a wish, insane and meaningless, to make yourself a thing that you are not.

Temptation has nothing to do with what the body does, for it occurs only in the mind: the temptation to listen to the ego instead of Jesus, self instead of Self, and to make a body to house this shabby self-concept of sin.

(VII.14:2-3) And think as well upon the thing that you would be instead. It is a thing of madness, pain and death; a thing of treachery and black despair, of failing dreams and no remaining hope except to die, and end the dream of fear.

This is what we are tempted to believe about ourselves. The insane symbol of nothingness is the self we think is so grand and glorious—a travesty of the truly grand and glorious Self that God created, our eternal Identity as Christ.

(VII.14:4-5) *This* is temptation; nothing more than this. Can this be difficult to choose *against*?

Jesus is asking us once again to consider what is so difficult about his requests. While we fear losing our special self, the terror we feel is not that God would swoop down and destroy us. Rather, it is that we would "swoop up" and embrace Him, disappearing forever into His Heart (W-pII.14.5:5) and leaving our cherished self nowhere. Jesus is not teaching this. His comforting love patiently leads us from nightmares to happy dreams, wherein we do not go from self to selflessness. Instead, we take his gentle steps of exchanging a wrong-minded self for a right-minded one. This is the process, to which we shall return presently, that guides us through the various self-concepts of the ego's thought system to the Holy Spirit's Correction. In His self-concepts, we for a while retain an individual self, but one that becomes less angry, judgmental, and depressed, and correspondingly more joyful, peaceful, and content.

(VII.14:6-9) Consider what temptation is, and see the real alternatives you choose between. There are but two. Be not deceived by what appears as many choices. There is hell or Heaven, and of these you choose but one.

In painstaking detail Jesus has repeatedly explained the difference between hell and Heaven: the former is separation, specialness, and exclusion (*one or the other*); the latter is reflected in the inherent sameness of our split minds, sharing the common interest of walking the pathway of forgiveness that will take us home (*together, or not at all*).

We conclude this section with the first part of "Choose Once Again":

(VIII.1:1-3) Temptation has one lesson it would teach, in all its forms, wherever it occurs. It would persuade the holy Son of God he is a body, born in what must die, unable to escape its frailty, and bound by what it orders him to feel. It sets the limits on what he can do; its power is the only strength he has; his grasp cannot exceed its tiny reach.

Jesus constantly returns to the important theme of the body's inherent nothingness. Despite our experience, the body is not a prison of limitation even though we have dreamt it so. Since the decision-making mind is the true jailer, the temptation to see ourselves as bodies (the ego's embodiment) causes us to forget we are children of Eternal Life, Whose strength is our own. Jesus continues by asking us this vital question:

(VIII.1:4-6) Would you be this, if Christ appeared to you in all His glory, asking you but this:

> ***Choose once again if you would take your place among the saviors of the world, or would remain in hell, and hold your brothers there.***

For He *has* come, and He *is* asking this.

This is a reference to "For They Have Come" (T-26.IX) and is the only meaningful question to ask. It has been posed from the beginning, but we made a world of time and space ("a giant learning feat") to drown it out. It is Jesus' expectation that as we have come this far on the journey with his course, devoting much time and effort to learning it, we would open our minds in welcome to his healing voice of correction and share it with our brothers. Thus we undo the Sonship's belief in hell, gently replacing it with Heaven's Love.

(VIII.2) How do you make the choice? How easily is this explained! You always choose between your weakness and the strength of Christ in you. And what you choose is what you think is real. Simply by never using weakness to direct your actions, you have given it no power. And the light of Christ in you is given charge of everything you do. For you have brought your weakness unto Him, and He has given you His strength instead.

This is another variation of the theme of choosing the right teacher. The decision for the Holy Spirit is the decision for the strength of innocence, while deciding for the ego embraces the weakness of having separated from love, preferring guilt instead. Yet the only power in weakness is what our minds give it. Bringing the mistaken choice to our true strength undoes the error, releasing the mind to the love that is our natural state and source of true power.

(VIII.3:1-2) Trials are but lessons that you failed to learn presented once again, so where you made a faulty choice before you now can make a better one, and thus escape all pain that what you chose before has brought to you. In every difficulty, all distress, and each perplexity Christ calls to you and gently says, "My brother, choose again."

This is the one purpose we should have on our minds from the moment we wake up to the time we go to sleep, day in and day out, for we now understand that everything that happens in our lives presents us with the possibility of choosing again. It does not matter whether we judge something as good or bad—a relationship, job, business investment, lab report, or world event—for no worldly outcome can affect our inner peace. If we are rightminded we will hear in all situations the soft and gentle Voice calling to us: "My brother, choose again." This is what Jesus is asking we take with us when we complete his course, spending the rest of our days learning what his wisdom has taught. Acquiring his vision, accordingly, should be our only purpose for remaining here.

This means that nothing in the world has any meaning in itself. Whatever purpose we think something has is merely what our minds have given it, the central message of the early workbook lessons. The ego's meaning for the world is this: "Who has to be sacrificed to meet my needs?" In response, Jesus has offered a very practical course as correction. But it means nothing if we do not apply its teachings of forgiveness. Again, regardless of what occurs, there is his loving tap on our shoulder, saying: "My brother, choose again. Let us together look at the situation differently."

(VIII.3:3-7) He would not leave one source of pain unhealed, nor any image left to veil the truth. He would remove all misery from you whom God created altar unto joy. He would not leave you comfortless, alone in dreams of hell, but would release your mind from everything that hides His face from you. His Holiness is

yours because He is the only power that is real in you. His strength is yours because He is the Self that God created as His only Son.

Christ's strength, as reflected in this world, is based upon the first principle of miracles. His vision sees all problems as one, the mind's mistaken choice for the ego, and His innocence is the single answer to all forms of suffering. Illusions cannot stand when truth's light shines upon them, and every concept of God's Son disappears into the radiance of Christ's joyous face, beyond which is the Holiness that God created as His holy Son.

(VIII.4:1-3) The images you make cannot prevail against what God Himself would have you be. Be never fearful of temptation, then, but see it as it is; another chance to choose again, and let Christ's strength prevail in every circumstance and every place you raised an image of yourself before. For what appears to hide the face of Christ is powerless before His majesty, and disappears before His holy sight.

No matter what the cruelties of the world do to us or our loved ones, they could not affect us unless we chose the ego's weakness over Christ's strength. Jesus' words help us to remember that the world of dreams is powerless in itself: "Let them [the figures in the dream] be as hateful and as vicious as they may, they could have no effect on you unless you failed to recognize it is your dream" (T-27.VIII.10:6). As in so many places, Jesus is telling us not to feel guilty if we choose the ego's shabby images of specialness over our Self. Instead, we should simply see our mistake as another chance to choose differently. This is what he meant in urging us, *"Do not fight yourself"* (T-30.I.1:7), and earlier: "...trust implicitly your willingness, whatever else may enter. Concentrate only on this, and be not disturbed that shadows surround it. That is why you came" (T-18.IV.2:3-5).

We hear our elder brother lovingly say to us: "You came here because you embraced a thought system that haunts you and controls everything you do. Do not let this upset you, nor think that you are not learning this course quickly enough. See your perceived failures as calls for help that allow you to choose again, forgiveness over judgment, and know that my love is supporting your learning." His kind and authoritative voice is a wonderful example of the strength of Christ's Love, so strong that the world's power dissolves in the soft gentleness of Its Presence.

(VIII.4:4-5) The saviors of the world, who see like Him, are merely those who choose His strength instead of their own weakness, seen apart from Him. They will redeem the world, for they are joined in all the power of the Will of God.

Our having chosen Christ's strength for ourselves, it must extend to all the world for the reflected Oneness of God's Will is the unity of the fragmented Sonship: one need, one purpose; one healing, one self.

(VIII.5:1-4) Learn, then, the happy habit of response to all temptation to perceive yourself as weak and miserable with these words:

> *I am as God created me. His Son can suffer nothing. And I am His Son.*

Jesus wants us to contrast this statement with the paltry image we have made of ourselves. These words assume a central importance in the workbook's one-year training program, helping us replace a self-concept of weakness and vulnerability with the concept of a strong and joyous self that remembers the mind's power of decision.

(VIII.5:5-7) Thus is Christ's strength invited to prevail, replacing all your weakness with the strength that comes from God and that can never fail. And thus are miracles as natural as fear and agony appeared to be before the choice for holiness was made. For in that choice are false distinctions gone, illusory alternatives laid by, and nothing left to interfere with truth.

Armed by the strength of Christ we watch our problems disappear, although not necessarily in form. It is our negative experience of these external problems that goes, for we see them now as learning opportunities: "Trials are but lessons that we failed to learn…." While we all learned the lesson

that the world exists to fulfill our special needs, we recognize at last that suffering was caused by our failure to *un*learn that lesson, having learned it all too well. Changing our teacher has allowed us to be taught the meaning of the miracle, within which the world becomes a classroom in which the Holy Spirit teaches us we are the same, having one split mind. And so we all walk together the path from weakness to strength, out of hell to the Heaven that is our Self.

(VIII.6:1) You *are* as God created you, and so is every living thing you look upon, regardless of the images you see.

The phrase "living thing" has appeared many times in the text, and in the workbook as well, and requires a brief comment on two levels. The first is that since nothing here is living, Jesus is speaking to us on the level of our experience, which is that things here are alive. He tells us that we must include everything we perceive here through the eyes of forgiveness and exclude no one. On a deeper level the phrase is an oxymoron, because all things here are non-living. Jesus explains the real world in a similar way for the world is not real. Still, the state of mind known as the real world reflects the reality of Heaven in which no distinctions can be made, for separation and specialness cannot exist in perfect oneness. As a result, since everything here is a "thing"—animate or inanimate—all matter is a split-off, projected fragment of the one Son of God who believed he separated, and then chose to deny the life that is reflected in the right mind's Atonement principle. We have seen earlier that Jesus refers to even the smallest grain of sand as part of God's Son (T-28.IV.9:4). In that sense a grain of sand is a "living thing" as well. As there is no life in the world, distinctions between life and non-life are spurious, the only meaningful distinction being between the mind's thoughts of death and life, separation and Atonement. This is why Jesus emphasizes that we are to include *all* in our vision. To exclude one object of our projections from the Sonship means we have excluded every one, "living" and "non-living" alike, which includes ourselves and even those in the real world, like Jesus.

(VIII.6:2) What you behold as sickness and as pain, as weakness and as suffering and loss, is but temptation to perceive yourself defenseless and in hell.

We are "defenseless and in hell" because we made the error of separation real, affirming that there is a hierarchy of illusions: for example, sick and well bodies. The problem is never the form the ego's hell takes, but our having chosen the ego in the first place. Problem *and* solution rest together within the decision-making mind, kept apart by the ego.

(VIII.6:3) Yield not to this, and you will see all pain, in every form, wherever it occurs, but disappear as mists before the sun.

The sun shines its light and warmth, and the morning mist disappears. We shine the warm light of God's Love onto our perceptions, and the ego's world is gone. All that is required for this happy fact to dawn on our minds is for us to recognize the temptation to choose against it. We then share in Jesus' gentle smile at the silliness of believing there could ever be anything we would want other than God's Love.

(VIII.6:4-5) A miracle has come to heal God's Son, and close the door upon his dreams of weakness, opening the way to his salvation and release. Choose once again what you would have him be, remembering that every choice you make establishes your own identity as you will see it and believe it is.

The way we perceive others is the way we perceive ourselves. The choice is ours. Since time is over, never having been, the miracle of forgiveness has already happened and patiently awaits our acceptance. How long, Jesus asks, will we delay our release from guilt by being tempted by the ego's weakness? The next section addresses the temporal process within which we learn to make the final choice for Atonement.

Process

We have already discussed how we do not go from a world of concepts directly to the world in which concepts do not exist; we proceed step by step. This gradual process of unlearning is made explicit in the following passages:

(V.8:3-5) Now must the Holy Spirit find a way to help you see this concept of the self must be undone, if any peace of mind is to be given you. Nor can it be unlearned except by lessons aimed to teach that you are something else. For otherwise, you would be asked to make exchange of what you now believe for total loss of self, and greater terror would arise in you.

The concepts of the self we must undo are the "face of innocence" and the killer's face it masks. Again, it is a gradual undoing, and we need not fear that we will be "abruptly lifted up and hurled into reality" (T-16.VI.8:1). The journey we take with Jesus lifts us from the nightmares of the wrong-minded self to the happy dreams of the right-minded self, from which we joyfully awaken to Christ, our true Self.

(V.9:1) Thus are the Holy Spirit's lesson plans arranged in easy steps, that though there be some lack of ease at times and some distress, there is no shattering of what was learned, but just a re-translation of what seems to be the evidence on its behalf.

We are speaking of a step-by-step process. As we do not awake in the morning to a non-self, we need not fear learning this course. Nonetheless, over time and as we practice daily, we develop a self that smiles more frequently (W-pI.155.1:2). No longer finding mornings to be fearful and conflicted, we are grateful as another day dawns to herald our learning the miracle's valuable lessons that will end our misery. What changes is the decision maker's identification, from the wrong-minded self to the right-minded one. The timing of this shift rests solely with us.

(V.14:1-4) The concept of the self has always been the great preoccupation of the world. And everyone believes that he must find the answer to the riddle of himself. Salvation can be seen as nothing more than the escape from concepts. It does not concern itself with content of the mind, but with the simple statement that it thinks.

The decision to think is the problem, not what we think (the meaning of *content* in sentence 4). This is not to be confused with the "thinking" of God that is simply creation. Jesus refers to the thinking of the split mind, telling us that salvation's goal is the end of concepts (i.e., thinking), including the cerebral activity of the world's greatest brains. We need recognize that the ego's purpose is to attack, kill, and get away with it. Choosing it as our teacher means that murder is our choice as well, an insane decision we now happily undo. Form itself is irrelevant to such a shift, for it is only the mind's content of choosing the ego that needs to be addressed. This undoing, once more, is a gradual process in which we correct faulty self-concepts by understanding that their purpose is to keep us in hell.

(V.14:5) And what can think has choice, and can be shown that different thoughts have different consequence.

This refers back to the middle part of "Self-Concept versus Self," which dealt with the decision-making part of the mind that can learn, choosing to identify with the thought system of the ego or Holy Spirit.

(V.14:6) So it can learn that everything it thinks reflects the deep confusion that it feels about how it was made and what it is.

We actually think we were born, an event that gave us life. Yet dream figures do not live, regardless of their form. By asking our Teacher for help in returning to the mind where learning occurs, we learn to understand the ego's strategy and its charade of life. This enables us to choose again: the Thought of Life over thoughts of death.

(V.14:7) And vaguely does the concept of the self appear to answer what it does not know.

Our self-concepts appear to answer the question of who we are, but they cannot know because the brain was specifically made to keep our identity as minds hidden; the body being the second line of the ego's defensive system, with the mind's guilt as the first.

(V.15:1-3) Seek not your Self in symbols. There can be no concept that can stand for what you are. What matters it which concept you accept while you perceive a self that interacts with evil, and reacts to wicked things?

The Self is not only beyond idols (T-30.III) but beyond concepts, since non-dualistic reality cannot be conceptualized. It makes no difference, for example, if we perceive evil in ourselves or in another, whose guilt establishes our goodness. Either way we establish the separation as real, with parts of the Sonship at war with other parts, insanely "uniting" in the coexistence of the delusional concepts of good and evil that are the core of specialness.

(V.15:4-5) Your concept of yourself will still remain quite meaningless. And you will not perceive that you can interact but with yourself.

Everyone in the dream we call our life, including our experienced self, is a split-off part of the decision-making self, as in our dreams at night where every figure is a split-off fragment of the mind/brain. Experience lies, and Jesus teaches us not to trust our perceptions that speak of an outside world that affects us. Our minds alone determine how we think, feel, and act, and the mind alone is the focus of the Course's curriculum. It is our only hope.

(V.15:6-7) To see a guilty world is but the sign your learning has been guided by the world, and you behold it as you see yourself. The concept of the self embraces all you look upon, and nothing is outside of this perception.

Projection makes perception: when we choose our self-concepts over Self, separation in place of oneness, we look out on a fragmented world that is riddled with guilt and attack, the cosmic lie that is the ego's hell on earth.

(V.16:1-2) You will make many concepts of the self as learning goes along. Each one will show the changes in your own relationships, as your perception of yourself is changed.

The focus now is on the *process* by which we change our concepts. These changes will mirror the changes in our minds. As we shift our identification from the ego's guilt to the Holy Spirit's forgiveness, the concepts we hold of others will shift correspondingly. It cannot *not* be that way because *projection makes perception*. What we decide within determines what we perceive and experience without—guilt or forgiveness, attack or kindness.

(V.16:3-7) There will be some confusion every time there is a shift, but be you thankful that the learning of the world is loosening its grasp upon your mind. And be you sure and happy in the confidence that it will go at last, and leave your mind at peace. The role of the accuser will appear in many places and in many forms. And each will seem to be accusing you. Yet have no fear it will not be undone.

We are beginning to detach ourselves from what the world had seemingly taught us, recognizing that it was the mind that taught the world. Our decision maker is becoming increasingly at home in the right-minded thought system of forgiveness and healing, an inevitable result of choosing Jesus as its teacher. Since healing remains a process, there will still be temptations to see others as guilt-driven accusers, the projections of our own secret sins and hidden hates. However, when these ego thoughts surface we look at them with Christ's vision, seeing them as meaningless defenses against the happy truth of our reality.

(V.17:1) The world can teach no images of you unless you want to learn them.

Another important theme returns, which we have seen in many variations in our symphony. We can learn nothing from the world unless we first wanted to learn it. The world cannot teach us to be hateful; it is we who seek to hold the world responsible for the hatred in our minds. Similarly, the world cannot teach us we are forgiven; only our decision-making minds can do that by accepting the Atonement.

(V.17:2) There will come a time when images have all gone by, and you will see you know not what you are.

This is the end of the journey, heralded by the end of concepts. The journey began at the bottom of the ladder with our "face of innocence." As we slowly ascended, we began to understand that this face was the cover for the face of the murderer. Our journey continued as we increasingly recognized that the concepts of guilt and innocence, victim and victimizer, were made-up perceptions that were projections of the mind's belief in sin. Through this recognition we learned the meaning of forgiveness that leads past all concepts and judgments, allowing us to accept the final concept of shared interests that takes us to the Oneness of Christ, our true Self.

(V.17:3-4) It is to this unsealed and open mind that truth returns, unhindered and unbound. Where concepts of the self have been laid by is truth revealed exactly as it is.

When we chose to follow the ego we taught ourselves its concepts. Gradually, we free our minds to unlearn the lies we put there and established as true. Once again, the process of unlearning begins when we realize that what we perceive without emanates from what we have made real within. This clears the mind to accept the truth that has awaited our return to the Mind we never left.

(V.17:5) When every concept has been raised to doubt and question, and been recognized as made on no assumptions that would stand the light, then is the truth left free to enter in its sanctuary, clean and free of guilt.

Recall Jesus' words: "To learn this course requires willingness to question every value that you hold" (T-24.in.2:1). When we journey past concepts, the final one that needs undoing and is the basis for the rest is that we exist at all. Gone then would be sin and guilt, their place taken by the glorious truth of God's Son as He created Him.

(V.17:6-9) There is no statement that the world is more afraid to hear than this:

> *I do not know the thing I am, and therefore do not know what I am doing, where I am, or how to look upon the world or on myself.*

Yet in this learning is salvation born. And What you are will tell you of Itself.

This is the source of our terror, for the world was made so we never unlearn the lies we received from the ego. Since this learning occurs in the mind, it can only be unlearned there. If we are mindless we can unlearn nothing, allowing the ego's lessons of separation, guilt, and death to remain within. Identifying with the false self, we stand in terror of moving beyond its thought system of *one or the other* because we believe it leads nowhere. To protect us from disappearing into the abyss of nothingness, the ego roots our attention in the world that covers the mind so it cannot choose again. Our only meaningful function, then, is to make room for love's truth by embracing Jesus' teachings of forgiveness. This unlearns the thought system of guilt and attack, freeing us to remember the Everything beyond the nothing, which waits patiently for us to correct our mistaken decision about reality and return home.

The Holy Relationship – The Miracle – Vision

Before we reach the Everything that is beyond even the upper reaches of the ladder, we must attain Christ's vision. This we do by learning to silence the ego's raucous shrieks, its world of meaningless concepts. We begin, therefore, with the lovely motif of stillness:

(I.12) Let us be still an instant, and forget all things we ever learned, all thoughts we had, and every preconception that we hold of what things mean and what their purpose is. Let us remember not our own ideas of what the world is for. We do not know. Let every image held of everyone be loosened from our minds and swept away.

We are strongly identified with these concepts, as well as with our belief that we know the world's purpose: minimizing pain and maximizing joy so that our lives and those of our loved ones will be happy. Jesus is asking us to be quiet and let these thoughts go, reminiscent of the prayer in Lesson 189 where he asks us to empty our mind of all concepts, closing with the words: "Forget this world, forget this course, and come with wholly empty hands unto your God" (W-pI.189.7:5). By clearing our minds of illusions we are able to learn the Holy Spirit's lessons of forgiveness, the world's only purpose and means *par excellence* of attaining true and lasting happiness.

(I.13) Be innocent of judgment, unaware of any thoughts of evil or of good that ever crossed your mind of anyone. Now do you know him not. But you are free to learn of him, and learn of him anew. Now is he born again to you, and you are born again to him, without the past that sentenced him to die, and you with him. Now is he free to live as you are free, because an ancient learning passed away, and left a place for truth to be reborn.

As mentioned before, the word *ancient* in *A Course in Miracles* can almost always be understood as a return to the ontological moment when we chose the ego instead of the Holy Spirit, and then corrected our mistake. It refers here to our ancient learning of the ego, which is ongoing since time is not linear. It passes away when we choose to be born again in the holy instant—releasing all concepts of good and evil, innocence and guilt—leaving an unoccupied space in the mind on which God's Word of Atonement can be written (e.g., W-pI.12.5), for us and all the Sonship.

(II.1) An ancient lesson is not overcome by the opposing of the new and old. It is not vanquished that the truth be known, nor fought against to lose to truth's appeal. There is no battle that must be prepared; no time to be expended, and no plans that need be laid for bringing in the new. There *is* an ancient battle being waged against the truth, but truth does not respond. Who could be hurt in such a war, unless he hurts himself? He has no enemy in truth. And can he be assailed by dreams?

We have heard Jesus emphatically say to us, responding to our fear-driven resistance, *"Do not fight yourself"* (T-30.I.1:7). Opposing an illusion makes it real in our experience, as it does the suffering born of conflict. Nevertheless, an illusion cannot escape its source in madness, and truth remains unassailed and awaiting our return to sanity. For this reason Jesus encourages us to be defenseless—in attitude, not necessarily in behavior—in the face of attack. This brings peace where there had been anger, and healing where there had been the ravages of war. Just as Jesus has asked us to take him as our model for learning (e.g., T-6.in.2:1), we can see God's silent response to the separation as our ultimate model: truth does not respond to illusion; it simply shines away the dream shadows of the unreal.

(II.2) Let us review again what seems to stand between you and the truth of what you are. For there are steps in its relinquishment. The first is a decision that you make. But afterwards, the truth is given you. You would establish truth. And by your wish you set two choices to be made, each time you think you must decide on anything. Neither is true. Nor are they different. Yet must we see them both, before you can look past them to the one alternative that *is* a different choice. But not in dreams you made, that this might be obscured to you.

Jesus, of course, refers to the mind's power of decision. The mistaken choice for the ego is what stands between us and the remembrance of our Self. Because the inner world of guilt and outer world of bodies arose to keep us from ever correcting the

mind's mistake, we have perceived ourselves as unwilling victims of a world in which the only meaningful decision is between *kill* and *be killed*. This has left murder as the only alternative in the world of dreams, meaning there are no alternatives other than death and death. Imploringly, Jesus asks us to look with him at the reality of our world, that we may return to the inner world of decision and choose meaningfully: life *or* death. In this way illusion is passed by and truth allowed to ascend in our awareness.

(II.3-4) What you would choose between is not a choice and gives but the illusion it is free, for it will have one outcome either way. Thus is it really not a choice at all. The leader and the follower emerge as separate roles, each seeming to possess advantages you would not want to lose. So in their fusion there appears to be the hope of satisfaction and of peace. You see yourself divided into both these roles, forever split between the two. And every friend or enemy becomes a means to help you save yourself from this.

Perhaps you call it love. Perhaps you think that it is murder justified at last. You hate the one you gave the leader's role when you would have it, and you hate as well his not assuming it at times you want to let the follower in you arise, and give away the role of leadership. And this is what you made your brother for, and learned to think that this his purpose is. Unless he serves it, he has not fulfilled the function that was given him by you. And thus he merits death, because he has no purpose and no usefulness to you.

Once again Jesus refers to our special relationships, where the alternating states of love and hate are really the same, with no meaningful choice between them. Once we see separate needs and interests as real, everything is equally unreal. Whether we win or lose, lead or follow, love or hate, we are seeking respite from the mind's wars of guilt and attack in which we will surely suffer death. We seek and find justified punishment in others, whose ultimate purpose in our dream is met when we suffer at their sinful hands. Having projected our hidden sins onto them, seeing there what we have striven to avoid in ourselves, their death is the only justice that can be served. All the while we never realize it is our own death we have called for and will receive:

(II.5:1-10) And what of him? What does he want of you? What could he want, but what you want of him? Herein is life as easily as death, for what you choose you choose as well for him. Two calls you make to him, as he to you. Between these two *is* choice, because from them there is a different outcome. If he be the leader or the follower to you it matters not, for you have chosen death. But if he calls for death or calls for life, for hate or for forgiveness and for help, is not the same in outcome. Hear the one, and you are separate from him and are lost. But hear the other, and you join with him and in your answer is salvation found.

There is indeed a difference between hearing a brother call for death or life. While they are both illusory, one reinforces the dream of separation and fear, and the other leads us beyond it to salvation. What we want for another can only be what we want for ourselves. Jesus, as always, appeals to our self-interest—what will make *us* feel better—for only forgiveness of others and ourselves will bring the happiness and peace we seek and truly deserve.

(II.5:11) The voice you hear in him is but your own.

If we wish to know which teacher we have chosen to listen to, we need pay attention only to how we perceive others. If we are angry, impatient, or dependent, these differing forms of specialness tell us we are hearing the wrong voice, reinforcing the specialness in others. Yet we have learned that we reinforce it in ourselves as well. Asking Jesus for help means looking through his eyes at our relationships. This frees us from the pain they seemed to engender, for vision sees the world as mirroring a decision the mind has made, which we can now correct and change.

(II.5:12-14) What does he ask you for? And listen well! For he is asking what will come to you, **because you see an image of yourself and hear your voice requesting what you want.**

Our perception has nothing to do with others as such, but only with *how* we perceive them—*projection makes perception*. It cannot be stated too often that what we perceive in our brother reveals what we have first perceived in ourselves and then projected—*projection makes perception*.

(II.6:1-3) Before you answer, pause to think of this:

The answer that I give my brother is what I am asking for. And what I learn of him is what I learn about myself.

It is essential that we pay attention to how we react to others. Are we kind or mean, caring or cruel? This shows us what our minds have decided. If we perceive ourselves as kind, we need to discern whether this kindness is because we want something back, or because we recognize that another's pain is a call for help as well as our own. The latter demonstrates non-exclusivity, while the former reflects the exclusivity of specialness.

Even though it may well be that our response is exclusive in form, right-minded content is all-inclusive because it is based on the recognition that one person's suffering is another's. In the world of form no one can answer everyone's call for help or respond to all expressions of pain; yet Jesus, our loving guide, does not exclude anyone from his compassionate concern. Moreover, if someone suffers, we do not get angry at the ones who seemingly caused it, for that would entrap us still further in the ego's world of *one or the other*. Rather, our elder brother has been teaching us to perceive any call as universal, the healing vision that includes all living things in his comforting love.

The beautiful motif of stillness makes a brief return, recalling us from the strident sounds of ignorance and pain:

(II.6:4) Then let us wait an instant and be still, forgetting everything we thought we heard; remembering how much we do not know.

Our humility leads us to remember that our brother is ourselves, thereby dismissing the ego's arrogance of separation and its insane belief that the special relationship is the key to happiness:

(II.6:5–7:1) This brother neither leads nor follows us, but walks beside us on the selfsame road. He is like us, as near or far away from what we want as we will let him be. We make no gains he does not make with us, and we fall back if he does not advance. Take not his hand in anger but in love, for in his progress do you count your own. And we go separately along the way unless you keep him safely by your side.

Because he is your equal in God's Love, you will be saved from all appearances and answer to the Christ Who calls to you.

The fragmentation of the Sonship into special love and hate objects, a world of winners and losers, preserves the existence of the ego's thought system of separation. When on the other hand we listen to Jesus speak of the shared interests of all, conflict becomes peace while anger turns to love. The call of Christ to Christ can now be heard, and as we return to Heaven we remember we are all God's Son—*a Oneness joined as One.*

And again, we return to stillness as the way to remember the truth we had forgotten:

(II.7:2-4) Be still and listen. Think not ancient thoughts. Forget the dismal lessons that you learned about this Son of God who calls to you.

We need first get in touch with what we have heard from the ego before we can meaningfully make another choice. Further, these ancient thoughts hark back to the original lie: the ego's archetypal belief in sin, the experience of guilt, and the fear of God's wrath. All unforgivenesses of God's innocent Son stem from this ontological insanity.

(II.7:5-6) Christ calls to all with equal tenderness, seeing no leaders and no followers, and hearing but one answer to them all. Because He hears one Voice, He cannot hear a different answer from the one He gave when God appointed Him His only Son.

Being the perfect Son of Perfect Oneness, Christ can see only His one Self, reflected in the shared interests of the separated Sonship. No one is seen as different or apart from anyone, for God's Son remains himself, even in illusion. Only in frenzied dreams of specialness can oneness be shattered into disunited and warring fragments.

(II.8) Be very still an instant. Come without all thought of what you ever learned before, and put aside all images you made. The old will fall away before the new without your opposition or intent. There will be no attack upon the things you thought were precious and in need of care. There will be no assault upon your wish to hear a call that never has been made. Nothing will hurt you in this holy place, to which you come to listen silently and learn the truth of what you really want. No more than this will you be asked to learn. But as you hear it, you will understand you need but come away without the thoughts you did not want, and that were never true.

Again and again this Heavenly music reminds us to set aside the past that never was, and accept what has always been. This is the state of no opposition or conflict, a simple release of the ancient thought system of guilt and hate. Without our self-concepts of sin, there can be no attack or suffering, and who with this understanding could ever again cherish the ego's foolish illusions? The attraction of love for love (T-12.VIII) remains the strongest force within the dream, and in its kindly presence the old attraction of guilt falls easily away.

(II.9:1) Forgive your brother all appearances, that are but ancient lessons you have taught yourself about the sinfulness in you.

The use of the word *ancient* returns us to the ontological instant when the original learning of sin seemed to happen. In fact, there has been no learning since, for the ego sent God's Son into the world to be unaware of the mind, the one place where we can unlearn ancient lessons, and where forgiveness of what never happened can occur.

(II.9:2-7) Hear but his call for mercy and release from all the fearful images he holds of what he is

and of what you must be. He is afraid to walk with you, and thinks perhaps a bit behind, a bit ahead would be a safer place for him to be. Can you make progress if you think the same, advancing only when he would step back, and falling back when he would go ahead? For so do you forget the journey's goal, which is but to decide to walk with him, so neither leads nor follows. Thus it is a way you go together, not alone. And in this choice is learning's outcome changed, for Christ has been reborn to both of you.

The change is that we no longer see ourselves walking alone, for our erstwhile special partners are perceived to be the same as we—different in form, perhaps, but with the same content of the split mind. We see the ego thought system common to us all, at the same time hearing the shared call for release that we choose to answer together. Christ cannot be reborn in one without the other; salvation can never be attained at the expense of someone else. Yet one should not infer from the above discussion that both people have to consciously accept this healing. Jesus' message is that for healing to occur, only one of us must shift the mind's orientation from *one or the other* to *together, or not at all*.

(II.10:1-2) An instant spent without your old ideas of who your great companion is and what he should be asking for, will be enough to let this happen. And you will perceive his purpose is the same as yours.

Our brother's true purpose is not *kill or be killed*—his purpose being to kill us, ours to kill him—but to awaken from the dream through forgiveness. He cannot do so by making us accountable for his dream, nor can we by holding him responsible for ours. We awaken only in the holy instant when we choose against the insane belief that our gain comes when another loses. Knowing we are *both* innocent or guilty helps us make the sane choice for salvation.

(II.10:3-6) He asks for what you want, and needs the same as you. It takes, perhaps, a different form in him, but it is not the form you answer to. He asks and you receive, for you have come with but one purpose; that you learn you love your brother with a brother's love. And as a brother, must his Father be the same as yours, as he is like yourself in truth.

Jesus is expressing the idea of oneness, reflected in the world of our everyday relationships wherein we walk together with *all* living things, without exception. This is what makes *A Course in Miracles* so difficult, because the principle of *together, or not at all* undermines the very foundation on which our special existence rests. There is no individual self in the one Self, and no belief that one wins by another losing, the shadowy fragment of the thought that God lost and the ego triumphed. The Course has taught us that our brother's interests are our own, and this reflected unity prefigures our return to the Oneness of Perfect Love.

(II.11) Together is your joint inheritance remembered and accepted by you both. Alone it is denied to both of you. Is it not clear that while you still insist on leading or on following, you think you walk alone, with no one by your side? This is the road to nowhere, for the light cannot be given while you walk alone, and so you cannot see which way you go. And thus there is confusion, and a sense of endless doubting as you stagger back and forward in the darkness and alone. Yet these are but appearances of what the journey is, and how it must be made. For next to you is One Who holds the light before you, so that every step is made in certainty and sureness of the road. A blindfold can indeed obscure your sight, but cannot make the way itself grow dark. And He Who travels with you *has* the light.

We cannot know this light unless we allow it to illuminate everyone. The importance of this theme in our symphony cannot be overestimated. It is the heart of Jesus' message to us, the prerequisite for salvation. The ego's perception of separate interests is the road to hell, while Christ's vision of shared interests is the pathway leading us home. Which will we choose, Jesus asks: light or darkness, certainty or doubt, salvation or damnation? Our Teacher Who has the light shines it on the answer, in which is found nothing less than the choice for Heaven and our Self.

Now, near the end of "The Savior's Vision," we build to the beautiful climax of our symphony of symphonies:

(VII.8:1) Behold your role within the universe!

This statement is reminiscent of the final section of "The Obstacles to Peace" where Jesus says: "Behold your Friend, the Christ Who stands beside you" (T-19.IV-D.14:1). One can imagine the orchestra's trumpets standing to announce the final peroration.

(VII.8:2-4) To every part of true creation has the Lord of Love and life entrusted all salvation from the misery of hell. And to each one has He allowed the grace to be a savior to the holy ones especially entrusted to his care. And this he learns when first he looks upon one brother as he looks upon himself, and sees the mirror of himself in him.

We learn we are one with everyone by undoing the guilt that caused us to perceive others as enemies. Looking non-judgmentally with Jesus at our special relationships, which once seemed so important, grants us the "savior's vision" that helps us realize we are the same. Behind each special person stand thousands, and behind each of them a thousand more (T-27.V.10:4). In that experience of forgiveness we share the Holy Spirit's true perception and understand the oneness of the Sonship, which is why *every* part of true creation is entrusted with salvation's message.

(VII.8:5-7) Thus is the concept of himself laid by, for nothing stands between his sight and what he looks upon, to judge what he beholds. And in this single vision does he see the face of Christ, and understands he looks on everyone as he beholds this one. For there is light where darkness was before, and now the veil is lifted from his sight.

Generalization is the heart of Jesus' pedagogy, as we saw at the beginning of the workbook (W-in.4-5). We practice with specific relationships

and situations, and generalize to all of them. Thus we climb salvation's ladder and grow to realize that everyone is part of God's glorious Sonship. The darkness of separation and guilt has gradually given way to the light of Heaven's simple truth: God's Son is one, and as he was created so he is throughout eternity.

Here comes an explicit reference to "The Obstacles to Peace":

(VII.9:1) The veil across the face of Christ, the fear of God and of salvation, and the love of guilt and death, they all are different names for just one error; that there is a space between you and your brother, kept apart by an illusion of yourself that holds him off from you, and you away from him.

We find here in the closing pages of our symphony something similar to what Jesus did at the end of "The Obstacles to Peace" (T-19.IV-D). He does not make grand metaphysical statements. He focuses instead on our forgiving the special person against whom we hold the grievances we feel are salvific. In this way we undo the dream's basis of attack and judgment—the guilty thought of separation—and awaken from it. To bring this about we practice specifically with the very people who are the most difficult and problematic. This includes those we think we love, special hate and special love being the same, that we may learn that the gap between us rests on nothing. The ego's lies of sin and guilt to the contrary, we remain forever joined in the Everything of God's Love.

(VII.10:1-4) What is temptation but the wish to stay in hell and misery? And what could this give rise to but an image of yourself that can be miserable, and remain in hell and torment? Who has learned to see his brother not as this has saved himself, and thus is he a savior to the rest. To everyone has God entrusted all, because a partial savior would be one who is but partly saved.

We are all one, a fact we learn by the daily practice of our special function of forgiveness. Not one Son can be excluded from our vision, because God has entrusted His total Love to everyone. Who in his right mind could ever exchange the joy of this Heaven on earth for the unspeakable hell of the ego's allies of attack and judgment?

(VII.10:5) The holy ones whom God has given you to save are but everyone you meet or look upon, not knowing who they are…

This is a reference to the gospel parable (Matthew 25:35) and Jesus' earlier line: "I was a stranger and you took me in, not knowing who I was" (T-20.I.4:3).

(VII.10:5-6) …all those you saw an instant and forgot, and those you knew a long while since, and those you will yet meet; the unremembered and the not yet born. For God has given you His Son to save from every concept that he ever held.

Over and over we have been taught that we experience the joy and love of Christ's vision by practicing it with everyone we meet or even think about—past, present, and future. Not one spot of guilt can remain if we are to be healed, as all concepts disappear when we remember we are the concept-less Son that God created one with Him.

(VII.11:1-4) Yet while you wish to stay in hell, how could you be the savior of the Son of God? How would you know his holiness while you see him apart from yours? For holiness is seen through holy eyes that look upon the innocence within, and thus expect to see it everywhere. And so they call it forth in everyone they look upon, that he may be what they expect of him.

Hell is the ego's world of separation and specialness, and Jesus repeatedly asks us to choose between remaining imprisoned in the darkness of the body, surrounded by the fetid scent of death, and freeing ourselves and our brothers by looking beyond the flesh to the split mind we share together. In this healed perception is found both sin and holiness, and the power to choose correctly—the savior's vision:

(VII.11:5-7) This is the savior's vision; that he see his innocence in all he looks upon, and see his own salvation everywhere. He holds no concept of himself between his calm and open eyes and what he sees. He brings the light to what he looks upon, that he may see it as it really is.

It is not stated but implied, as in so many other parts of this chapter, that before we acquire the savior's vision that sees innocence in all, we first must see their guilt. The positive in *A Course in Miracles* is the undoing of the ego's negative. In dreams we share the same problems, rooted in the concept of sin, and share the same need to escape through forgiveness. Only then comes the vision of God's innocent Son, behind which dawns the memory of God's one Son, the Christ Who is our Self.

(VII.13:1-5) The savior's vision is as innocent of what your brother is as it is free of any judgment made upon yourself. It sees no past in anyone at all. And thus it serves a wholly open mind, unclouded by old concepts, and prepared to look on only what the present holds. It cannot judge because it does not know. And recognizing this, it merely asks, "What is the meaning of what I behold?"

In other words, we do not give the world its meaning; nor do we tell Jesus the "meaning" of a situation and then have his response echo its meaninglessness. Instead, we say we do not understand, undoing past perceptions we thought were real. This invites him to supply his healing concept of forgiveness, meaning we accept the vision in which we see the illusory world's only reality, the shining face of Christ's innocence:

(VII.13:6-7) Then is the answer given. And the door held open for the face of Christ to shine upon the one who asks, in innocence, to see beyond the veil of old ideas and ancient concepts held so long and dear against the vision of the Christ in you.

This joyous experience is the inevitable result of shifting inner teachers. We have at last let Jesus help us see the world as he does, shining through the holy instant that frees us from the past and its tyranny of specialness and guilt.

(VII.15:1-4) Let not the world's light, given unto you, be hidden from the world. It needs the

light, for it is dark indeed, and men despair because the savior's vision is withheld and what they see is death. Their savior stands, unknowing and unknown, beholding them with eyes unopened. And they cannot see until he looks on them with seeing eyes, and offers them forgiveness with his own.

The temporal-spatial world "winds on wearily, and…is very tired now. It is old and worn and without hope" (M-1.4:4-5). It needs the light to relieve its dark suffering and grant release. To whom except God's Son can it look for hope? And who except God's Son is our decision-making mind, poised now to choose again: to forgive whom it had slain, to free whom it had chained? Salvation is here, and would we delay its gentle advent an instant longer?

(VII.15:5-7) Can you to whom God says, "Release My Son!" be tempted not to listen, when you learn that it is you for whom He asks release? And what but this is what this course would teach? And what but this is there for you to learn?

This is the sum and substance of *A Course in Miracles*, the essence of forgiveness that corrects all misperceptions of differences. Since we are the same, if I forgive you, I am forgiving myself. Still further, the only way I can forgive myself is to forgive you. At our request, Jesus has substituted his principle of *together, or not at all* for the ego's *one or the other*, undoing the nucleus of the ego thought system that says God and His Son are different, our interests are separate from His, and we need be concerned only for what satisfies our special needs. This ontological selfishness has carried through every aspect of our world, leaving the answer to all problems as the simple understanding of how alike we truly are. As Harry Stack Sullivan, the founder of interpersonal psychiatry, repeatedly told his students: "We are all far more human than otherwise." In this happy realization we are healed; in this healing is God's Son released; and in his release are we returned to the Heaven we never truly left.

Coda I

We have come to the end of the symphony: a double coda. I have previously mentioned this musical form that comes from the Latin *cauda*, meaning "tail," denoting the end of a relatively large composition. The coda typically uses different material, all of which, however, is thematically related to what preceded it. Beginning with paragraph 7 to the end of the text's final section, "Choose Once Again," we find the equivalent of the Course's coda, somewhat different from what came before, although with the same themes. It is essentially in two parts, which I present separately with very little commentary.

One additional point before we proceed. From Chapter 21 on there are very few first person references in the text. The editorial "we" and "us" occur several times, but the prominence of the "I"—referring specifically to Jesus—is largely gone. Suddenly now the first person returns, and the contrast with its absence for several chapters makes its appearance all the more dramatic. In Coda I we find Jesus' final plea that we choose again and accept his vision of forgiveness, which recapitulates the theme of not perceiving separate interests in the Sonship. If we truly wish to experience the love and joy of this glorious vision, we must share it with everyone, for only then can we leave the world of suffering and death to walk together into the real world, the penultimate step of our journey:

(VIII.7-9) Deny me not the little gift I ask, when in exchange I lay before your feet the peace of God, and power to bring this peace to everyone who wanders in the world uncertain, lonely, and in constant fear. For it is given you to join with him, and through the Christ in you unveil his eyes, and let him look upon the Christ in him.

My brothers in salvation, do not fail to hear my voice and listen to my words. I ask for

nothing but your own release. There is no place for hell within a world whose loveliness can yet be so intense and so inclusive it is but a step from there to Heaven. To your tired eyes I bring a vision of a different world, so new and clean and fresh you will forget the pain and sorrow that you saw before. Yet this a vision is which you must share with everyone you see, for otherwise you will behold it not. To give this gift is how to make it yours. And God ordained, in loving kindness, that it be for you.

Let us be glad that we can walk the world, and find so many chances to perceive another situation where God's gift can once again be recognized as ours! And thus will all the vestiges of hell, the secret sins and hidden hates be gone. And all the loveliness which they concealed appear like lawns of Heaven to our sight, to lift us high above the thorny roads we travelled on before the Christ appeared. Hear me, my brothers, hear and join with me. God has ordained I cannot call in vain, and in His certainty I rest content. For you *will* hear, and you *will* choose again. And in this choice is everyone made free.

Coda II

Although in Coda II the final three paragraphs still come in the first person, Jesus addresses God to Whom he prays on our behalf. In terms of its general form this coda is taken from what is known in Catholic circles as the priestly prayer of Jesus (John 17). If you read that prayer carefully, especially in the context of the gospel itself, it is clear that the biblical savior does not pray for all people but only for "his own." While the scriptural words are beautiful, beneath them is nothing more than the ego's hymn to specialness. Here we see Jesus taking the same form, shifting to the all-inclusive content of his love in a consummate expression of the Course's message:

(VIII.10-11) I thank You, Father, for these holy ones who are my brothers as they are Your Sons. My faith in them is Yours. I am as sure that they will come to me as You are sure of what they are, and will forever be. They will accept the gift I offer them, because You gave it me on their behalf. And as I would but do Your holy Will, so will they choose. And I give thanks for them. Salvation's song will echo through the world with every choice they make. For we are one in purpose, and the end of hell is near.

In joyous welcome is my hand outstretched to every brother who would join with me in reaching past temptation, and who looks with fixed determination toward the light that shines beyond in perfect constancy. Give me my own, for they belong to You. And can You fail in what is but Your Will? I give You thanks for what my brothers are. And as each one elects to join with me, the song of thanks from earth to Heaven grows from tiny scattered threads of melody to one inclusive chorus from a world redeemed from hell, and giving thanks to You.

And now the conductor lowers his baton as he guides the symphony to its majestic close, returning us and all God's Sons to the living Oneness that never ceased to be our home. The final words belong to our loving brother, who has faithfully led us through the world's darkness to the resplendent light of Heaven's eternal love:

(VIII.12) And now we say "Amen." For Christ has come to dwell in the abode You set for Him before time was, in calm eternity. The journey closes, ending at the place where it began. No trace of it remains. Not one illusion is accorded faith, and not one spot of darkness still remains to hide the face of Christ from anyone. Thy Will is done, complete and perfectly, and all creation recognizes You, and knows You as the only Source it has. Clear in Your likeness does the Light shine forth from everything that lives and moves in You. For we have reached where all of us are one, and we are home, where You would have us be.

APPENDIX

HEAVEN – KNOWLEDGE

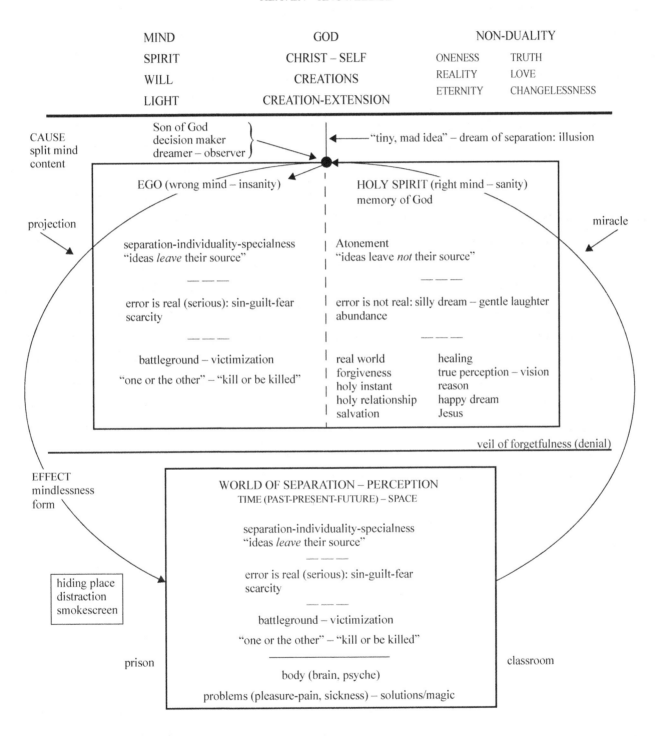

MIND	GOD	NON-DUALITY	
SPIRIT	CHRIST – SELF	ONENESS	TRUTH
WILL	CREATIONS	REALITY	LOVE
LIGHT	CREATION-EXTENSION	ETERNITY	CHANGELESSNESS

CAUSE
split mind
content

Son of God
decision maker
dreamer – observer

"tiny, mad idea" – dream of separation: illusion

EGO (wrong mind – insanity)

HOLY SPIRIT (right mind – sanity)
memory of God

projection

miracle

separation-individuality-specialness
"ideas *leave* their source"

Atonement
"ideas leave *not* their source"

error is real (serious): sin-guilt-fear
scarcity

error is not real: silly dream – gentle laughter
abundance

battleground – victimization

"one or the other" – "kill or be killed"

real world
forgiveness
holy instant
holy relationship
salvation

healing
true perception – vision
reason
happy dream
Jesus

veil of forgetfulness (denial)

EFFECT
mindlessness
form

WORLD OF SEPARATION – PERCEPTION
TIME (PAST-PRESENT-FUTURE) – SPACE

separation-individuality-specialness
"ideas *leave* their source"

error is real (serious): sin-guilt-fear
scarcity

battleground – victimization

"one or the other" – "kill or be killed"

body (brain, psyche)

problems (pleasure-pain, sickness) – solutions/magic

hiding place
distraction
smokescreen

prison

classroom

Frequently Quoted Phrases and Terms

References for frequently quoted principles and phrases:

"Ideas leave not their source": T-26.VII.4:7; 13:2; W-pI.132.5:3; 10:3; W-pI.156.1:3; W-pI.167.3:6

"little willingness": T-18.IV

"…no order of difficulty in miracles": T-1.I.1:1

"…not one note in Heaven's song was missed": T-26.V.5:4

"…a Oneness joined as One": T-25.I.7:1

"Projection makes perception": T-13.V.3:5; T-21.in.1:1

"…tiny, mad idea": T-27.VIII.6:2

"…together, or not at all": T-19.IV-D.12:8

Phrases and terms italicized even though not italicized in *A Course in Miracles*:

ideas leave not their source (variations used, uppercase for God & Christ)

no order of difficulty in miracles (no italics when direct quote with quotation marks; not extended to include "healing," "problems," "illusions")

a Oneness joined as One (some with quotes plus reference; some in italics plus reference)

one or the other (ego principle only; not a quote)

Projection makes perception

tiny, mad idea

together, or not at all

Complete Index of References to *A Course in Miracles*

TEXT

WORKBOOK FOR STUDENTS

MANUAL FOR TEACHERS

CLARIFICATION OF TERMS

PSYCHOTHERAPY: PURPOSE, PROCESS AND PRACTICE

THE SONG OF PRAYER

* * * * * * * * * * *

THE GIFTS OF GOD

ABSENCE FROM FELICITY (2nd Edition)

Please see our Web site, www.facim.org, for a complete listing of publications and available translations. You may also write, or call our office for information:

Foundation for A Course in Miracles®
41397 Buecking Drive
Temecula, CA 92590
(951) 296-6261 • fax (951) 296-5455

Made in the USA
Monee, IL
22 January 2022

89180511R00157